Migration, Mobility
and Modernization

Liverpool Studies in European Population
General Editor DAVID SIDDLE

1. *Urban Population Development in Western Europe from the Late-Eighteenth to the Early-Twentieth Century* edited by RICHARD LAWTON AND ROBERT LEE

2. *The Population Dynamics and Development of Western European Port-Cities, c. 1710–1939* edited by RICHARD LAWTON AND ROBERT LEE

3. *Improving the Public Health: Essays in Medical History* edited by G. KEARNS et al.

4. *The European Peasant Family and Society: Historical Studies* edited by RICHARD L. RUDOLPH

5. *Urban Mortality Change in England and Germany, 1870–1913* by JÖRG VÖGELE

6. *The Demography of Early Modern Towns* by CHRIS GALLEY

7. *Migration, Mobility and Modernization* edited by DAVID J. SIDDLE

Migration, Mobility
and Modernization

edited by
DAVID J. SIDDLE

LIVERPOOL UNIVERSITY PRESS

First published 2000 by
LIVERPOOL UNIVERSITY PRESS
4 Cambridge Street,
Liverpool, L69 7ZU

Copyright © Liverpool University Press 2000

All rights reserved. No part of this book may be reproduced, stored in a
retrieval system, or transmitted, in any form or by any means, electronic,
mechanical, photocopying, recording or otherwise without the prior written
permission of the publishers.

British Library Cataloguing-in-Publication Data
A British Library CIP record is available

ISBN 0–85323–883–9 *cased*
0–85323–963–0 *paper*

Set in Times New Roman by
Northern Phototypesetting Co. Ltd, Bolton
Printed and bound in the European Union by
Alden Press, Oxford

CONTENTS

List of Figures		vii
List of Tables		ix
1	Introduction DAVID SIDDLE, *Liverpool University*	1
2	Nephews, Dowries, Sons and Mothers: the Geography of Farm and Marital Transactions in Eastern Ireland, c. 1820–c.1970 WILLIAM J. SMYTH, *University College, Cork*	9
3	Mobility, Kinship and Commerce in the Alps, 1500–1800 LAURENCE FONTAINE, *CNRS, Paris* and DAVID SIDDLE	47
4	People from the Pits: the Origins of Colliers in Eighteenth-Century South-West Lancashire JOHN LANGTON, *St John's College, Oxford*	70
5	Motives to Move: Reconstructing Individual Migration Histories in early Eighteenth-Century Liverpool DIANA E. ASCOTT and FIONA LEWIS, *Liverpool University*	90
6	Urban Population and Female Labour: the Fortunes of Women Workers in Rheims before the Industrial Revolution ANTOINETTE FAUVE-CHAMOUX, *Ecole des Hauts Etudes en Sciences Sociales, Paris*	119
7	Mobility Among Women in Nineteenth-Century Dublin JACINTA PRUNTY, *National University of Ireland, Maynooth*	131
8	Tramping Artisans in Nineteenth-Century Vienna JOSEF EHMER, *Universität Salzburg*	164
9	Migration and Urbanization in North-West England: a Reassessment of the Role of Towns in the Migration Process COLIN G. POOLEY and JEAN TURNBULL, *Lancaster University*	186
Index		*215*

FIGURES

1	(a) Destination of migrants from the parish of Clogheen-Burncourt *within* Ireland, 1900–68; (b) Clogheen-Burncourt's global migration field, 1900–68	12
2	Distribution of farm-holdings, c.1841	14
3	Distribution of farm-holdings, 1851	17
4	Distribution of farm-holdings, c.1970	18
5	Number of changes in the *names* of families occupying each holding since 1857	20
6	Recipients of land transfers (a) 1851–1900 and (b) 1901–74	22
7	Movement of brides (a) marrying *into* farms *within* the parish, and (b) marrying into farms *outside* the parish of Clogheen-Burncourt	33
8	Movement of male farm occupiers into non-paternal farms 1900–68	34
9	(a) Movement of brides into and within the parish of Clogheen-Burncourt, c.1910–40; (b) Comparisons of activity fields of males and females, c.1940–70 *and* 'bridesheds', 1865–75/c. 1910–40	42
10	Wheat prices for Annecy and Faverges, Savoy, 1740–1800	50
11	Marriages and dowries in Faverges, Savoy, 1700–92	53
12	Marriages and dowries in Faverges, Savoy, 1700–92	54
13	Dowry distributions, Faverges, 1700–87	55
14	The south-west Lancashire coalfield, showing sub-regions and Prescot and Wigan parishes and their constituent townships	71
15	Numbers of colliers' children registered in coalfield sub-regions, 1720–99	72
16	Colliers' mobility in eighteenth-century south-west Lancashire	85
17	Sources	93
18	Jugler Street	96–97
19	William Holme	98
20	Anne Tarleton	100

21	John Clieveland	103
22	Matthew Nicholson – multiple record linkage	106
23	Matthew Nicholson – genealogy from family history	107
24	Birthplaces of persons enumerated in the city and county of Dublin, 1881	134
25a–d	Individual migration patterns of women whose children were admitted to St Brigid's Orphanage, Dublin, 1868–75	140–3
26	Migration patterns of women whose children were admitted to St Brigid's Orphanage, Dublin, 1868–75	144
27	Routes travelled by Christoph Lang and Franz Seeling	177
28	Suggested links between population migration and structural, spatial and individual processes of change in past economy and society	188
29	All moves with an origin in Lancashire or Cheshire and a destination elsewhere in Britain: (a) all migrants born 1750–1830; (b) all migrants born 1831–90; (c) all migrants born 1891–1930	194
30	All moves with a destination in Lancashire or Cheshire and an origin elsewhere in Britain: (a) all migrants born 1750–1830; (b) all migrants born 1831–90; (c) all migrants born 1891–1930	195
31	All moves from Liverpool and Manchester to destinations elsewhere in Lancashire or Cheshire	199
32	The migration paths of (a) Charles W. (1808–72) and (b) John A. (1814–85)	204
33	The migration paths of (a) Thomas B. (1844–90) and (b) Mary W. (1875–1962)	206
34	The migration paths of (a) Olivia S. (1884–1940 and (b) Ada B. (1896–1976)	208
35	The migration path of Joseph Shaw (1748–1823)	210

TABLES

1	Number and size of farms, parish of Clogheen-Burncourt, 1835–1974	16
2	Patterns of succession on existing farm-holdings, 1967	23
3	Structure of farm households, 1901 and 1974	27
4	Estimated annual outputs of the sub-regions of the south-west Lancashire coalfield, 1720–99	70
5	Estimated manpower requirements of south-west Lancashire collieries, 1720–99	73
6	Emigration from the county and city of Dublin, 1 May 1851–21 March 1871	133
7	Season rhythm of migration of journeyman tailors	168
8	Percentage of immigrants among Viennese journeymen in particular suburbs and crafts, 1827–80	169
9	Percentage of married journeymen, Vienna/Schottenfeld, 1857	171
10	Household position of journeymen, Vienna/Schottenfeld, 1857	171
11	Geographic origins of Viennese journeymen	172
12	Geographic origins of Viennese master tailors, 1825–59	173
13	Duration of the first job taken in Vienna: journeyman tailors who arrived in Vienna from 10 to 17 October 1836	175
14	Job histories of Viennese journeyman bakers, 1830–63	176
15	Comparison of sample populations with census populations by gender, marital status and age, 1851 and 1891	190
16	Comparison of sample populations with census population by region of birth, 1851 and 1891	191
17	Distribution of origins and destinations by settlement size and birth cohort	192
18	Settlements accounting for 5 per cent or more of all destinations by birth cohort	193
19	Intra-settlement moves by birth cohort and settlement size	193
20	Mean distance moved by type of move and cohort	196
21	Moves between settlements of different size by birth cohort	197
22	Sequential within-region moves by settlement size and birth cohort of migrant	200
23	Reason for migration by birth cohort, gender and type of move	202

Chapter 1

INTRODUCTION

DAVID SIDDLE

For over a century, scholars who studied migration concentrated on the identification of laws to explain the processes by which towns and cities attracted people to them. In the main they successfully demonstrated how the movement of people in the mass reflected a set of scientific principles concerning gravitation and distance. But since the 1950s, demographic historians and geographers have increasingly remembered that the experience of population mobility is also one which involves decision making and that a proper understanding of migration must involve the behaviour of individuals as well as aggregates. This scholarly rite of passage was probably necessary and may have been unavoidable. Indeed, the introduction to this book is centred on the proposition that early students of migration were not only driven by a common urge to find underlying scientific principles to explain human activity but were also reflecting a culture which was traumatized by the whole experience of urban industrialization which set the main tide of migrants in motion. It can be confidently claimed that, until quite recently, the ethos of the study of migration has been deeply conditioned by this whole raft of experiences. In other words, it was itself the product of the traumatic experience of urbanization and economic expansion.

Migration was not, of course, a new phenomenon. Among traders and craftsmen it was a well-established feature of medieval and Renaissance Europe. But as societies moved towards the modern period, these movements gathered momentum. The alteration in the mode of production, which historians have termed 'modernization', had its roots deep in the seventeenth century, when European traders began to operate in international and colonial markets. This early modern period saw an extending network of trade, commercial and workshop activity both in towns and in smaller centres. At the same time the emerging metropolitan centres attracted ever more migrants. During this period, for example, a sixth of the adult population of England spent some time living in London (Wrigley, 1967). But it was the rise of factories and industries in the eighteenth and nineteenth centuries and a concomitant surge of migrants to the towns which truly transformed Europe and created a new spirit for our age. Changing patterns of movement on this scale left societies extremely vulnerable. It is therefore not surprising that the forces at work through this period of modernization inevitably conditioned the approach of scholars to the study of migration. The argument for such a view can be presented quite briefly. During the modernizing period (1500–1950), much of Europe transformed itself from a basically rural society to one which was predominantly urban. As trade expanded, the emergent bourgeois elite was both small and conservative and easily made alliances with the old ruling autocracies. But the rapid rise in urban populations produced new classes of workers and servants who were not bound by the restrictions and deferences of a previously feudal, essentially rural society. The ruling castes became increasingly apprehensive of such large-scale movements of people. What is more, they found themselves unable to control their intellectuals, who were capable of seeing the shape of things to come. Enlightened philosophers in France and Germany encouraged the belief in values that were to lead eventually to more democratic government. The rising tide of literacy took these ideas beyond the salons to a widening provincial circle. Urban populations could organize themselves much more easily than peasants whose earlier revolutions, although sometimes protracted, were always bound to wilt before well-armed soldiery. The pitchfork was replaced by the barricade. The Revolution in France and the challenge to the older bureaucratic order provided by Napoleon were followed by threats elsewhere. The new political philosophies set themselves against the older orthodoxies of church and kingship, first in terms of a challenge to deference in France, and then as a threat to ownership of the means of production in Germany and England. Men and women, once free of 'chains', began to organize to demand control of their own productive powers. At the same time, the growing poverty of opportunity in the increasingly congested and smoke-filled towns was juxtaposed with the promise of other, newer worlds over the oceans to the west and south. From the beginning of the nineteenth century to the middle of the twentieth, this expansion took over 60 million people to the Americas, Southern Africa and the Antipodes. Few families in the new societies, dominated by the towns, escaped an experience of such a destabilizing upheaval.

The response to all these changes by those who held power was to increase the bureaucratic control of their populations, making use of modernizing systems of communication, organization and information gathering. As the nineteenth century progressed, this systematic collection of information led to well-developed policing structures, passports and border controls and also to the improved collection of information to improve the efficiency of taxation. Increasingly, governments began to have at their disposal sophisticated information on which to base their social and economic policies. It also made it easier to monitor their increasingly unpredictable populations. The nineteenth-century censuses, which form the basis of the first studies of migration, could only have been produced by complex statist bureaucracies. So until very recently, most writers on European migration were in some sense reflecting the general fear of those in authority regarding the potential of ever enlarging conurbations to draw people from surrounding areas into the vortex of industrial urbanization. Their evidence came from precisely those sources which were a direct product of the transformation: the censuses and household listings of increasingly statist political systems that were desperate to understand, manage and control the new and potentially dangerous urban populations. Like the bureaucrats who devised the information-gathering machinery, the approaches of scholars who set themselves the task of understanding the new sources of information were dominated by a determination to categorize and derive principles of process rather than to explain individual behaviour.

Ravenstein (1885; 1889) was the first to model these developments and it is characteristic of the period in which he wrote that he saw things in purely mechanistic terms. According to Ravenstein, migration was the product of the interplay of the forces of expulsion and impulsion released by industrialization: the factors which both pushed people to move from areas of deprivation and then pulled them in particular directions from their rural areas and small towns towards the ever-increasing urban and metropolitan centres. The tendencies of such movements seemed to reflect the inevitability of the processes of modernization, a progression which seemed to have some of the character of hard science. Ravenstein's 'laws' of migration[1] proposed in the 1880s were so successful in establishing the general principles of this phenomenon that in a period when the study of population looked for scientific credibility, they defined most subsequent approaches (Grigg, 1977). Indeed, throughout the period when methodologies were driven by scientific determinism, the persistent explanatory success of Ravenstein's 'laws' was enhanced by the way in which these guidelines seemed capable of further formulation into mathematical models reflecting Newtonian principles of gravity. Increasing analysis of national censuses added fresh definition to this view. They revealed that, as Ravenstein had predicted, the majority of urban migrants came from the immediate hinterland, filling in the gaps left by higher urban death rates, and that the average distance of movement rose with the skill of the migrant (de Vries, 1984). Migration in these terms was no more than the flow of labour responding to the crude laws of supply and demand. Migrants moved through towns in a series of steps up the urban hierarchy and gravity models added apparent refinement to such calculations.

Many studies went on to test such propositions and to find that, in the main, populations did indeed tend to respond to such stimuli in the ways prescribed. Eventually Stouffer (1940) was able to further define this behaviour by the concept of 'intervening opportunities', a mathematical proposition which stated that 'the number of migrants over a certain distance and time is proportional to the number of opportunities in the centre and inversely proportional to the development of intervening opportunities which are produced by economic expansion in the hinterland of larger conurbations'. The 'essential predictability' of such movements was given further definition by Zelinsky (1970). Reflecting also some of the misplaced confidence in development reflected in Rostow's model of economic progress, Zelinsky followed the track of what he termed the 'mobility transition' through *traditional, early transitional, late transitional, advanced* and *super advanced* phases. Within such phases, rural to urban and 'frontier' movements were gradually superseded by urban to urban movements, and then, in the later phases of development, by 'circulation' within and between centres. Others went on to isolate classes of factors which might influence the decision to migrate in terms of the push factors (features of repulsion from the place of origin) and the less tangible pull factors from the place of intended destination (the 'bright lights' syndrome of perceived higher wages and

1 'Most migrants, and especially women, move only short distances. They tend to fill the spaces left by previous migrants. The longer distance (mainly male adults) migrants tend to go to towns. Most out migration areas are agricultural. Towns grow by immigration rather than by natural increase. Migration increases in volume as the economy and its transport networks expand.'

more opportunities). In the mid-1960s, Wolpert (1965) drew attention to the ambivalence of migrant decision making, using field theory to explain differences of space experience through the lifecycle. By this time it was more or less accepted that there would 'always be an element of mystery' about the reasons for such behaviour (Lee, 1966). It was precisely this 'element of mystery' which drew historians, geographers and demographers towards new approaches to understanding.

As both attitudes and methodologies have changed over the past two decades, scholars have increasingly turned to a wider range of evidence to try to understand the ways in which people actually behaved when they decided (or were obliged) to move. By the 1980s, scholars generally recognized that older deterministic models, let alone attempts to simulate probabilities, helped to define the more obvious and expected aspects of migration but took very little account of the behaviour of individuals and small socio-economic groups. The bureaucratic detail of Swedish historical records had begun to reveal the complex nature of mobility through lifecycles (Hägerstrand, 1982; Langton and Hoppe, 1992). The Swedish documentation has allowed historians to trace individuals from one station to another across lifespans of movement and to refine methodologies which are difficult to apply to other less precisely defined data. Elsewhere the low level of information available usually precluded such work, but it set people to look at sources which might reveal similar phenomena. Researchers used a wider range of archival evidence to identify subtle differences of relationship between distance and behaviour over time. Greater awareness of the ways in which individuals behaved over a lifetime of changing locations began to allow the search for variation in terms of mobility rather than migration (Lawton, 1979; Baines, 1985). The significance began to emerge of 'circulatory flows' of mobile individuals who, while appearing in only one or two locations in decennial census returns, nevertheless moved around a sequence of locations between home and 'back to home' or followed 'chains'. It also became apparent that both behaviours often followed the pre-established patterns of earlier movers who were linked by kinship, neighbourhood or trade with those who came before. Some made moves along a personal migration path as they followed the stages of their career. Again attempts were made to classify all these different movements in terms of local migration, chain migration, circular migration, and career migration (Tilly, 1979). Clark and Souden (1987) introduced an element of motivation into their very similar model of migration, measuring levels of movement (locomotion) in terms of these four categories outlined above using both physical and mental dimensions of 'distance' and 'definitiveness'. They thereby expressed a more subjective degree of separation from the place of origin.

Now the rise of increasingly subtle computer analysis of vital event registers and the refined use of complementary notarial and other archival sources have made it possible to add a new dimension to such analysis. Individual life histories and family behaviours began to emerge as useful complementary sources, making it possible to fit even the sporadic evidence from diaries, letters and family papers into a growing picture. As a result of such studies, things now appear to be ever more complex. The manichaean divisions between rural and urban, rich and poor, between

INTRODUCTION

dysfunction and opportunity are being shown to provide only crude templates. In the face of growing evidence of individuals and groups of sentient decision makers operating in environments of real choice, the older models and analogies, which implicitly assumed that people are physical objects blindly responding to the machinations of a universe of physical determinants, appear ever more threadbare. Whole strata and substrata of movements are gradually being revealed which blur the crude distinctions of earlier scholarship. Such movements may be more difficult to explain and predict but they are closer to the reality of experience.

The most obvious casualty has been the earlier distinction made between the *mobility* of individuals travelling backwards and forwards between locations in the interests of family or work and the definitive *migration* of families or individuals to new work and a new home. Migrants are now shown to be involved in patterns of mobility, frequently connecting with their place of origin, even when the place of origin is removed by a generation or more. At the same time, mobile workers may have been away from their homes for periods long enough to seem footloose until they reveal themselves as tied to their home place by a web of interconnections which may eventually manifest itself in the form of long-term investment in property and a place of retirement. These movements were interwoven with family histories and craft or occupational behaviour which evolved to meet the challenge of changing times. New groupings also emerged to serve new opportunities. These in their turn inter-layer with regional and inter-regional networks of movement. What is revealed is that purposive mobility and migration intertwined into skeins which weaved back much further than the nineteenth century. Moreover, patterns of behaviour were closely tied to changing circumstances. While some migrant behaviour was as desperate and footloose as it still is today, the social and commercial structures of the pre-industrial period did not end with the first factory and the first steam train: the more fortunate remained part of older networks and while there were clearly those who followed more random trajectories, as the chapters of this book reveal, even the poorest and most disadvantaged frequently followed worn pathways. Even they carried forward intensive and extensive networks which evolved to connect families, kin, acquaintances, craft and occupation groupings in a widening system of places.

In this set of studies, which is the first of its kind for some time, individual life tracks are used to add dimension to the evidence for such processes. Rather than the considerations of earlier aggregate migration studies and even the more recent attempts to model mobility across the 'stations' of a lifecycle, all the chapters explore much more interesting, if much messier, behavioural perspectives. They reflect the improving techniques of linking data from vital event registers, censuses and other registration documents with apprentice books, guild and craft records, legal and court documents, diaries and biographies. It is the imaginative use of sources which has led to fresh insights into the processes of movement. The chapters cover a range of examples of such processes at work over a time span which concentrates mainly on the roots of such movements.

Through all the chapters the extent and persistence of movement, of mobility rather than migration, in modernizing Europe are evident. The accent is very much on individuals, families and kin groups: people 'on the move' both in time and space. We see them passing from one stage to another in their lives as they move to fill in niche spaces in a farming landscape, back and forth to town, within the urban matrix, across regional networks which use towns as depots and stopping off points. The studies reveal a culture which was adapting to the effects of urbanization, and which continued its intimate connection with the workings of what early classifiers would have called the pre-industrial world and what Tonnies defines as the *gemeinschaft* society. Though seldom overt, everywhere in the pages of this book we see evidence of the ways in which family networks were orchestrated, debts bonded, reciprocities engaged through the processes of mobility. Systems of reciprocity and support which reach back into the early modern period even when much in the society and economy reflected the rising spirit of capitalist individualism. In some areas this culture persisted well into the nineteenth century and beyond. Indeed, so impressed is one historian by the evidence of carefully instrumented changes in location that he refers to the whole pattern of behaviour as a 'culture of mobility' (Reher, 1990). It is a culture which, as the chapters here demonstrate, affected individuals, work groups, trades and genders differently at different points of their lifecycles. All the chapters reflect the interplay of several quite different sources and approaches (personal testimonies, diaries, notarial records, factory lists, statutory enquiries, charity reports, family papers) as well as more orthodox demographic sources (vital event registers and censuses). Most dwell on individual case studies to grapple with the complex character of individual actors and to develop their arguments. Most challenge conclusions based on anodyne aggregates.

The first two chapters, by Smyth and by Fontaine and myself, are much to do with the ingenuity of what might otherwise be considered as traditional communities in their relations with a changing world, where 'name on the land' inheritance behaviour would ostensibly seem to fix the people in the static relations of traditional society. William Smyth's essay confronts the issue of rural immobility in post-Famine Ireland. He shows that this picture, formed from the classic work by Arensberg and Kimball, totally misrepresents the fluid situation in which land is one dimension of a matrix of changing roles, and puts forward a complex set of strategies for managing the use of niche spaces through generations of social and economic change. It is a set of relations instrumented by mobility and migration which is cast against a background of movements to the New World, but which takes place in an active rural economy. Laurence Fontaine and I also dwell on the ways in which matrices of debt, obligation and credit generation become part of a system of considerable commercial enterprise for Alpine rural families which, over generations, built impressive networks across pre-industrial Western Europe, giving a different perspective to simplistic notions of the relations between centre and periphery and the significance of crisis out-migration. The essays of both Josef Ehmer and John Langton dwell on the particular characteristics of worker groups. For Langton it is the mining families of south Lancashire during the period of rapid increase in coal production in the eighteenth century. He explores the ways in which this highly dangerous work attracted so much labour through the instruments of unstable and highly differential pay, whereas social solidarity created a tradition of mutual support for the unemployed. Here the linkages of work, movement and information between pits aided the development of a strong regional rather than a purely local culture, putting into perspective the trade union records which, when used in isolation, suggest much longer-distance migration behaviour. Josef Ehmer draws attention to another aspect of the organized mobility of skilled labour, this time in nineteenth-century central Europe, where an industrializing economy drew on the much longer and deeper tradition closely related to the phenomenon of the tramping artisan. Through the nineteenth century such artisans retained the culture and traditions of the craft guilds. The latter's records reveal the highly institutionalized, strictly controlled character of extremely mobile artisans. Here it is the volume of such movement which is staggering. In this case, like that of the Alpine example, increasing statism and bureaucracy eventually restricted the free flow of such labour.

Diana Ascott and Fiona Lewis show how imaginative and rigorous deployment of the techniques of family reconstitution and record linkage can embrace a variety of sources (vital event registers, wills, port books, apprentice records) to tease out the migration histories of those who settled in eighteenth-century Liverpool. Their chapter stresses the ways in which mobility behaviour transcends the Clark and Souden categories referred to above. They show how 'career' mobility can also be 'local' and 'circular' and how 'career' moves might also prompt 'chain' movements among kinsmen. They also show how women often had distinctive agendas which were not encapsulated by such male-orientated categories.

In two chapters on female migrant behaviour, Antoinette Fauve-Chamoux summarizes her work on eighteenth-century Rheims, drawing attention to the opportunities and restrictions on the life of migrant women at different points in their lifecycles, while Jacinta Prunty shows how poor women struggled to survive in nineteenth-century Dublin. Prunty uses charity and orphanage records to trace and vividly describe the movements of a sample of Dublin's poorest women between 1868 and 1875. Both case studies illuminate the essential desperation which characterized the extreme mobility of these lives on the margins of existence. Finally, using the family histories assembled by numerous genealogists and family historians, Colin Pooley and Jean Turnbull challenge the orthodox view of direct stepwise migration from smaller to larger towns in the urban hierarchy. They assemble a data set of over 8,500 residential moves made between 1750 and 1930 by 2,251 individuals who had in common a point of origin and/or destination in Lancashire and Cheshire. As with all the other chapters in this book, the imaginative use of an alternative source casts much clearer light on the processes of movement to reveal much more complex circulatory behaviour than the standard models derived from census and registration sources might suggest. Here, too, the detailed migration histories of individuals and families bring the statistical evidence to life.

Clearly there is much left to do to identify and explore the rich veins of human experience in the past: to develop satisfactory methodologies which link together sources that are so variable between periods and locations. We can only hope that the chapters in this volume provide not only fascinating insights into the possibilities for such work, but also the ways in which such new approaches add fresh dimensions to the study of the motives and behaviour of people on the move. Rather in the way that a higher magnification microscope reveals that below the limpid surface of a drop of pond water there is a frantic world of activity, it is now clear that below the surface of the moving tide of aggregates which seemingly obey the 'laws' of migration, men and women, and social and economic groups followed their own much more complicated agendas. These agendas involved activity which was not as clearly purposive as might be suggested by the word 'circulation'. They were the product of a gamut of time-specific choices which reflect the individuality of human behaviour and its variable capacities for bloody-mindedness. People take or make opportunities, make mistakes, react either to private whims or to growing desperation. They strike out alone or using an unseen network of kin and acquaintances to make what otherwise appear to be random shifts. All this fascinating noise and babble is a far cry from the laser-like movements along predictable pathways towards ever larger towns revealed by aggregates of census data.

REFERENCES

BAINES, D. (1985), *Migration in a Mature Economy: Emigration and Internal Migration in England and Wales 1861–1900*, Cambridge.
CLARK, P. and D. SOUDEN (1987), *Migration and Society in Early Modern England*, London.
GRIGG, D. (1977), 'E. G. Ravenstein and the "laws" of migration', *Journal of Historical Geography*, III, 41–54.
HÄGERSTRAND, T. (1982), 'Diorama, path and project', *Tijdschrift voor Economische en Sociale Geografie*, 73, 323–39.
LANGTON, J. and G. HOPPE (1992), *Flows of Labour in the Early Phase of Capitalist Development: The Time Geography of Longitudinal Migration Paths in Nineteenth Century Sweden'* (Historical Geography Research Series), IBG, London.
LAWTON, R. (1979), 'Mobility and nineteenth century British cities', *The Geographical Journal*, 145, 206–24.
LEE, E. S. (1966), 'A theory of migration', *Demography*, 3, 47–54.
MABOGUNJE, A. (1970), 'Systems approach to a theory of rural urban migration', *Geographical Analysis*, 2, 22.
RAVENSTEIN, E. G. (1885), 'The laws of migration', *Journal of the Royal Statistical Society*, XLVIII, 167–227.
RAVENSTEIN, E. G. (1889), 'The laws of migration', *Journal of the Royal Statistical Society*, LII, 214–301.
REHER, D. S. (1990), *Town and Country in Pre-Industrial Spain: Cuena 1550–1870*, Cambridge, 299–307.
STOUFFER, S. A. (1940), 'Intervening opportunities: a theory relating mobility and distance', *American Sociological Review*, V, 845–67.
TILLY, C. (1979), 'Migration in modern European history', In *Time, Space and Man: Essays on Microdemography*, Stockholm.
VRIES, J. de (1984), *European Urbanisation 1500–1800*, Cambridge, Mass.
WOLPERT, J. (1965), 'Behavioural aspects of the decision to migrate', *Papers of the Regional Science Association*, 15, 159–73.
WRIGLEY, G. A. (1967), 'The simple model of London's importance in changing English society and economy 1650–1750', *Past and Present*, 37, 44–70.
ZELINSKY, W. (1970), *A Prologue to Population Geography*, London.
ZELINSKY, W. (1971), 'The hypothesis of the mobility transition', *Geographical Review*, 61, 219–49.

Chapter 2

NEPHEWS, DOWRIES, SONS AND MOTHERS: THE GEOGRAPHY OF FARM AND MARITAL TRANSACTIONS IN EASTERN IRELAND, c.1820–c.1970

WILLIAM J. SMYTH

Much of the literature on family farming in Ireland has been concentrated on the small farm culture of the west. This study focuses on the bigger farming world of the east and south-east. It also takes a long time perspective which stretches from the beginning of the nineteenth century almost to the close of the twentieth. Ireland's population in 1800 was five million – the same as today – but three-and-a-half million people fewer than existed on this island in 1845. This study also engages both a period when landlordism was still a dominant force in Ireland (i.e. up to c.1900) and an era when farming proprietorship subsequently became universal. It also straddles one of the most traumatic events in Irish history – the Great Famine of 1845–51 – when one million excess deaths occurred and over one million emigrants/refugees fled the country.

Pre-Famine Ireland was characterized by a ramshackle property structure dominated by landlords and a great variety of leaseholders. Close on thirty per cent of total agricultural output was used to pay rents (Mokyr, 1983, pp. 81–102). One-third of all tenant farmers occupied holdings greater than 20 acres (12 ha). These bigger farmers were dominant in the most profitable eastern and south-eastern regions of the country. However, labourers, cottiers and small-holder farmers then made up a population of four million, or close on half the total population in 1841. These groups were to be found everywhere on the island but the greatest concentrations were in the north-west, west and south-west. Not surprisingly, the Great Famine wreaked havoc amongst these classes.

While recognizing these diverse regional experiences, the Great Famine generally left behind a denuded and simplified rural landscape and a rapidly reducing and restructured society. Extreme caution in property transfers made for late marriage or no marriage, thus helping to mark out Ireland as a demographic exception in the western world. The other side of this property equation was emigration. Up until 1846, emigration was generally seen by most local communities as a social evil. Yet, by 1855, two million people had fled the country. By 1891 two out of every five persons (38.3 per cent) born in Ireland were living outside the country (Akenson, 1993, p. 54). In 1841 the equivalent figure was a tiny 6.2 per cent. The central concern of this case study, therefore, is to analyse how the 'stronger' farming society – most of whose members stayed at home – negotiated issues of marriage, migration and inheritance amongst its family members over this lengthy, often traumatic and always complex period.

Arensberg and Kimball (1940, p. 109) describe the attitudes towards family land in Ireland as appearing to make for a very specific relationship between the farm family and the land:

> Historically all the sons and daughters were provided for on the land and where possible this is still the ideal situation but the close identification of family with one particular plot of land and the difficulties of land division fostered through three generation of agrarian agitation and land reform have prevented this. One son ordinarily is to be settled on the land.

Thus continuity is achieved and the family keep the name on the land in a system where marriage, economic control and family reorganization and inheritance are linked in a social structure which appears to be highly resistant to change. Inheritance is linked with match-making and the marriage of the heir when the parents 'retire to the west room' and other members of the family, having acquired their share of the family fortune, 'must travel' (i.e. emigrate), if they have not already left the holding. One daughter may or may not marry into an adjoining farm in the neighbourhood. Arensberg (1937, pp. 37–40) would see the situation where another farmer's son marries into a farm with an only daughter or where a nephew or some other relation inherits the farm from a childless couple or bachelor as 'makeshift' devices overcoming the structural difficulties in these family households. He emphasizes the centrality of the match in the transfer of the family holding from one generation to the next and the recrystallization of the roles of all members of the family after the marriage of the heir. Yet the question whether Irish family farming is so stable, as Arensberg and Kimball infer, or is characterized by more complex internal changes in equilibrium needs to be addressed more carefully.

The objective of this paper, therefore, is to test, and modify if necessary, the Arensberg and Kimball model of the continuity process in family farming in Ireland. We do this by focusing, not on a western small farming community, but on a transitional region between the west and the east in Ireland, where the medium-sized farm of 40–100 acres (20–40 ha) is the dominant type. Arensberg and Kimball's west Clare is ecologically more homogeneous and characterized by a more egalitarian small farming culture. South-west Tipperary is much more diverse geographically, is more socially differentiated and characterized by deeper levels of social change. The first part of the chapter briefly attempts to outline the changing distribution of farm units in the parish of Clogheen-Burncourt since the early nineteenth century. The second section analyses the specific details of inheritance patterns, examining in particular the status and rights of sons, nephews, mothers and daughters and others in this process and looking also at the nature of the interrelationships between marriage, wills and inheritance. Finally an attempt is made to summarize how the changing territorial lattice of farms is matched to the changing lifelines of farmers, daughters, sons, and families. It should be stressed that throughout these latter two sections, the specific behaviour patterns of the medium-sized farm group will receive particular attention.

Technically, the study area comprises a single parish unit in south-west Tipperary. But as the essay progressed, it emerged that the proper area of study must correspond to the effective social field of the rural community being analysed. This, therefore, involves one in a consideration of the wider territorial and social frameworks within which the system of family farming in one parish is embedded (see Fig. 1). It is, therefore, more appropriate to view such a parish community and its plurality of farm nuclei as the local nodes of a complex web of territorially structured relationships which ultimately encompass the nation and the globe. The parish study must also be set against the backdrop of the transformation of the Irish economy over the past two centuries – especially the sharp oscillations in the relative dominance of either a predominantly pastoral or a mixed farming regime. For the purposes of this chapter, powerful forces of economic transformation and the increasing openness of the Irish economy are taken as given: the focus of the chapter is rather on how these transformation have been mediated through and by the property and family systems of the parish and its locality.

This map of the migration field of the parish in this century (Fig. 1b) also highlights the global dimension, raising a whole series of questions about how – in a given rural community with a limited number of 'territorial domains' (farms) and a limited number of 'livelihood positions' (jobs) – different strategies in the utilization and transfer of both local land resources and occupational skills have meant that there may well be fewer vacancies to be filled in each generation and an increasing number of candidates competing to occupy such 'niches' in the local community. It is helpful her to consider strategies of occupation and property exchange in terms of a multi-dimensional game board (in which society, economy and geography all contribute parameters) and to envisage actors occupying 'niche' spaces. Mobility can then be defined in terms of a series of well-considered moves within an overall strategy in which decision makers are always responding to changing circumstances. The central goal of the game is the reproduction of the social system and the associated enhancement of family status within that system. The game board of the play comprises the many farms, other forms of property and other niches, jobs and privileges pertaining to this specific board. The players in the system command highly differentiated power bases and include landlords and their agents, big farmers, small farmers, shopkeepers, husbands and wives, sons and daughters, artisans and labourers. The field of play is constituted by the kinship and marital networks which loop and interlock across the game board landscape. And in each generation, each family has to cope with a new disposition of actors on the board (see Bourdieu, 1976, pp. 117–44).

The area under consideration comprises the modern Catholic parish of Clogheen-Burncourt in south-west Tipperary. Co. Tipperary occupies a transitional location in Ireland between the east and the west and may be described as a hybrid county in physical, economic and cultural terms. The parish area (see Fig. 2) is also characterized by similar transitional characteristics including the wide range of land values from the poorest land on the mountain edges to the north and south through an intermediate region of medium quality land as one moves from the west to the rich farms

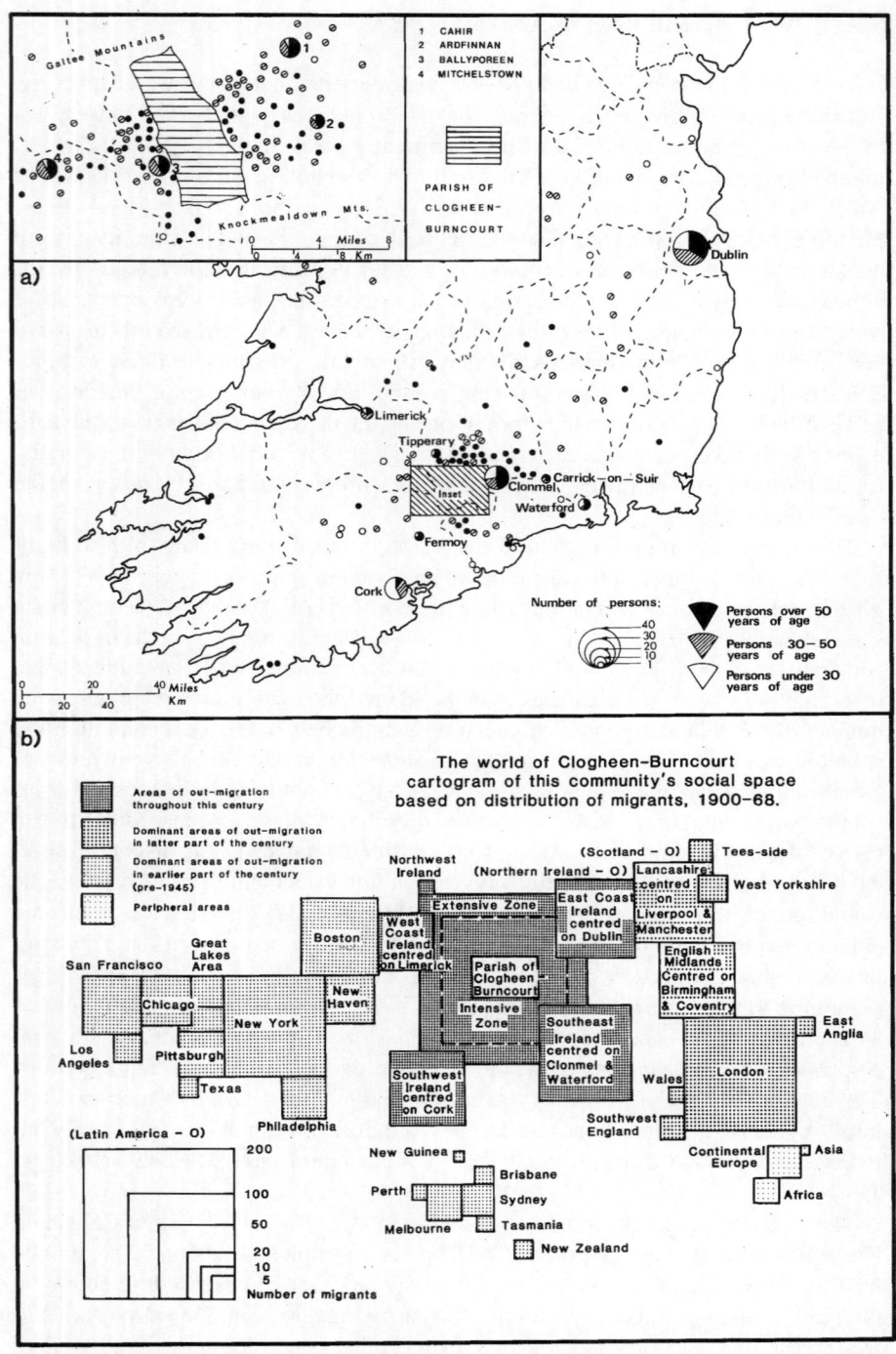

Figure 1 (a) Destination of migrants from the parish of Clogheen-Burncourt *within* Ireland, 1900–68; (b) Clogheen-Burncourt's global migration field, 1900–68
Source: Questionnaire survey by author 1966–68.

of the eastern part of the parish. Located as it is between the Galtee and Knockmealdown ranges to the north and south, the parish can be simply described as comprising 22 'lowland' or 'valley' townlands with richer limestone soils and 18 poorer 'mountain' or upland townlands fringing the Old Red Sandstone area. Townlands are one of the oldest landholding and administrative units in Ireland, developed strongly in the period 800 to 1200 and usually comprise an area of around 300 acres (120 ha). In this long-settled area, climate and ecological factors generally have favoured a pastoral grassland regime, with dairying the predominant mode, although both a mixed cattle/cash cropping economy and a dairying/tillage economy overlap on the eastern and southern edges of the parish respectively. Cattle, as a mobile form of property, therefore constitute a central motif in this culture. The population of the parish today is 1,600, about the same as its mid-seventeenth-century population. It therefore needs to be stressed from the beginning that what we are examining here is a long-occupied area with an already differential social structure at the beginning of the seventeenth century which became even more diversified during the eighteenth century and by 1821 was characterized by a very complex and highly stratified social structure. We are therefore dealing with an old culture characterized by both subtle strategies in the manipulation of territories such as farms, and the handling of these resource units within specific family and social structures.

THE TERRITORIAL (OR 'GAME BOARD') MATRIX

It is necessary to realize that from c. 1830 to c. 1900 the landowning system of the parish was still dominated by large estate landowners. Since the beginning of this century, these estate-structures have been gradually dismantled and the former tenant-farmers have become independent owner-occupiers. In terms of the territorial management of land units, we are therefore dealing with two rather different periods: the landlord era, when the estate system sought to regulate landholding and tenurial structures, and secondly, an era of farmer proprietorship when these broader estate systems of land management no longer had any active role in influencing family farm patterns. Taking a longer view, however, this whole period can be interpreted as one where the gradually increasing power of a leaseholding tenantry came to sap, weaken and eventually dismantle the superstructure of landlordism, thus revealing and unravelling the complex networks of relations and power structures that had developed underneath and beside what was to turn out to be a rather brittle upper crust of colonial accretions.

Figure 2 provides us with a useful benchmark from which to project the development of the farm units both backwards and forwards in time. This map represents a composite picture of the pre-Famine landscape, using the 1835 Tithe Applotment books (National Archives, Dublin), the 1839–41 Ordnance Survey first edition six-inch maps and the earliest of Griffith's Valuation Surveys for 1847 (Dublin, 1851, pp. 1–143: Valuation Office). It needs to be stressed that this composite map must be seen as portraying the culmination of a phenomenal expansion of the population in the previous half century or more; the population of the parish trebled, for example, between 1766 and 1841 to reach a total of 7,200 (Census of Ireland 1841). Our only

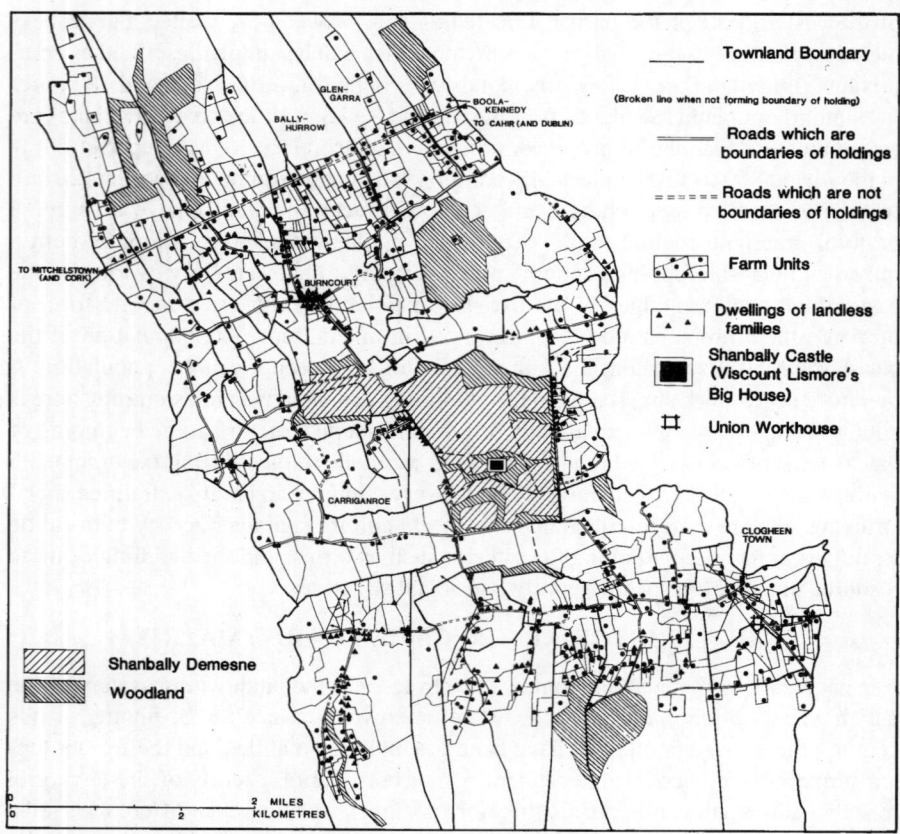

Figure 2: Distribution of farm-holdings c. 1841
Sources: Tithe Applotment books, first edition Ordnance Survey six-inch maps and first draft of Griffith's Valuation, Ely Place, Dublin.

concern here is to give some indication of the trajectories (or life paths) of the specific farm units which have evolved over the previous century or so.

From 1815–20 onwards, we note a transitional phase – one of reorientation of policy and farm amalgamation on the part of the landlords and one of increasing competition for land between the bigger grazier farmers able to swing back reasonably quickly to the now growing pastoral economy and the still proliferating small tillage farmers and even more desperate labouring population. Approximately one-third of the total number of rural households were landless cottiers in 1821, while a further 63 per cent of all holdings on the largest estate in the parish were under 15 acres (6 ha) in size (Smyth, 1983, pp. 19–21). In these difficult years from 1815 to 1845 a delicate balance was struck between surging demographic pressures on the one hand and the goals of the landlords (supported by the better-off farmers) to consolidate holdings on the other. From the 1780s, leasing policy was increasingly geared towards the elimination of middlemen, the introduction of rich Catholic farmers, the rationalization of farm-holdings and the introduction of strict rules in relation to subdivision. The landlords were thus seeking to enforce impartible inheritance systems, particularly on the lowlands, but there were problems of monitoring and enforcing such regulations in a rural culture which had evolved subtle ways of obscuring the real tenurial situation in a townland. There was also a deliberate attempt to deflect population pressures onto the peripheral mountain townlands which came to bear the brunt of these demographic pressures from the latter part of the eighteenth century onwards. This was particularly true of the Galtee mountains where there is much cartographic, townland, family name and folklore evidence to suggest intensive colonization from the 1780s onwards. Subdivision of farm units was far more characteristic of the mountain townlands. One surrogate measure of the scale of subdivision may be the contiguous holdings of equal size with the same family name which occur in the same townland in the Tithe Applotment books. Whereas there were no examples of this on one half of the lowland townlands by 1835, there were at least four examples of such subdivisions in each of nine Galtee mountain townlands by 1835. And the greatest density of dwarf holdings was on the still middlemen-administered townlands of the Cahir Butler estate in the north-eastern townlands of the parish. The delicate equilibrium between lowland consolidation and moorland deflection was shattered by the Famine, thus opening up the fragile small farm communities to colonization by the adjacent bigger farmers, a process that has continued ever since. This highlights a sharp difference between the fate of smaller farmers living in close juxtaposition to large commercial farmers and the more egalitarian small farm communities elsewhere, and in western Ireland in particular, where sharp differences in farm size structure only accelerated during this century.

Table 1 summarizes the changing number and size of farms in the parish since 1835. The pre-Famine landscape was characterized by a remarkable range of farm sizes, from the numerous dwarf holdings on the edges of the roads and moorlands to the 1,174 acre demesne of the landlord. Even at this peak of the farming population it is relevant to note that all holdings are still locked into and partially administered within the townland framework. The landlord's private farm alone transcends these ancestral boundaries – symbolizing the lack of congruence between the estate-administered landholding system and the hidden forces of territorially-based kinship and neighbourhood systems which struggle for expression within and between these townlands. However, the overwhelming numerical dominance of the groups of small-holders with less than 30 acres fails to reveal that these small-holdings were very much concentrated on the poorer lands and that the larger farms dominated the long-settled fertile central townlands, comprising as they do over two-thirds of the settled area of the parish (see Fig. 2).

Table 1: Number and size of farms, parish of Clogheen-Burncourt, 1835–1974

		1835	1851	1901	1967	1974
1–5 acres	(<2 ha)	122	55	15	3	2
5–30 acres	(2–12 ha)	278	150	71	34	27
30–50 acres	(12–20 ha)	56	47	49	48	46
50–100 acres	(20–40 ha)	27	30	32	47	50
100–200 acres	(40–80 ha)	11	16	20	18	18
200+ acres	(+80 ha)	4	4	4	6	7
Total		498	302	191	156	150

Sources: 1835: Tithe Applotment Books
1851: Griffith's Valuation
1901: 1901 Mss. Census of Ireland
1967: Author's own survey
1974: Author's own survey.

The contrasts in the pattern of farm occupation between the period of the Tithe Survey (National Archives, Dublin, 1835) and Griffith's Valuation (Dublin, 1851) – a time span of only 16 years – are as sharp as the differences between the 1851 picture and what prevails today. There was obviously a dramatic reduction in the holdings under 30 acres and even a 16 per cent decrease in the 30 to 50 acre farm group. In contrast, the increase in the larger farm groups was far less dramatic since it required the amalgamation of many smaller holdings to bring a *single* small-holding into the 30 to 50 acre category. Here again a bald statistical summary fails to reveal significant areal contrasts with the 1835 pattern. The longer-settled small farm communities of the southern townlands reveal a certain level of stability up to 1851, for the greater proportion of holdings under 30 acres survived the Famine period intact (see Fig. 3). In the mid-nineteenth century these small farmer families continued to cultivate their small plots of oats and potatoes, rear a cow and a few pigs and goats and cut (and often sell) turf from the mountain bogs. They were also either permanently employed as labourers or domestic servants by the bigger farmers in the valley or hired themselves out as seasonal workers in East Limerick or South Tipperary during the harvesting seasons. A long-established ecological rhythm, tight-knit kin and neighbourhood structures, local job opportunities and seasonal migration thus enabled these small-holders to consolidate their precarious position, at least for the time being.

In contrast to the gradual disintegration of the southern small farm communities which took at least a hundred years to be accomplished, the social structure of the northern small farm zone was completely shattered by the crisis of the Famine and associated events. This was especially true of the townlands of the north-east which were still part of the middlemen-administered Cahir estate. By 1841 these townlands were dominated by a high proportion of pauperized tenants subsisting on small plots of often recently colonized inferior land who increased their meagre subsistence by selling turf and turf mould from the mountain to the lowland farmers and villagers.

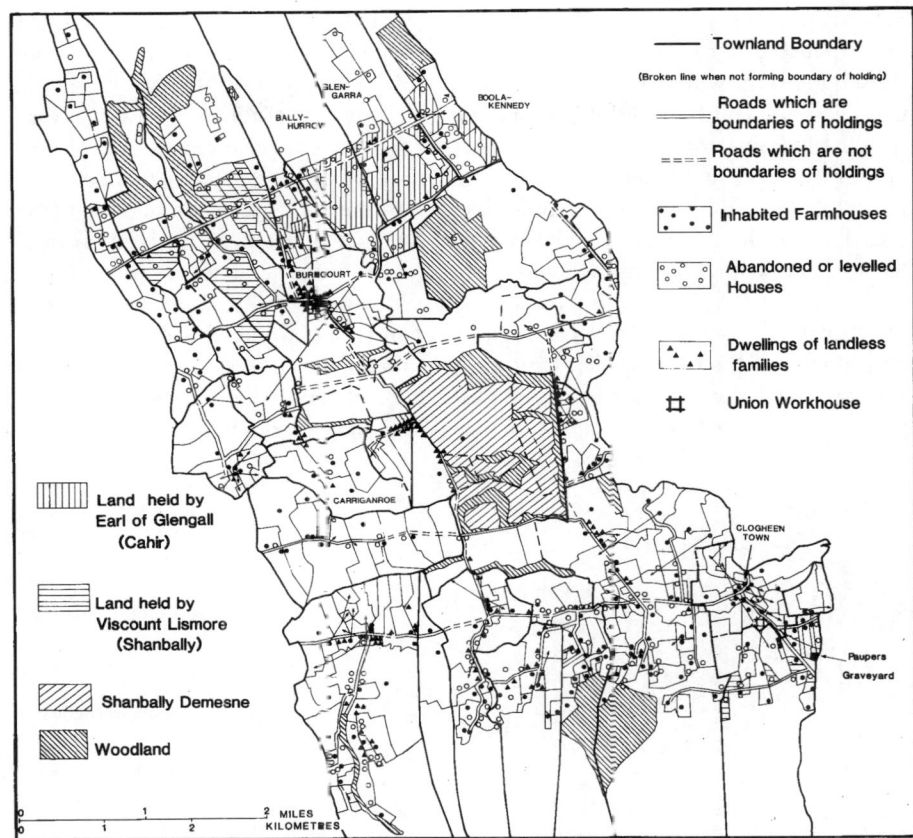

Figure 3: Distribution of farm-holdings 1851
Sources: First edition Ordnance Survey six-inch maps and official Griffith's Valuation publication, 1851.

That changes were inevitable here due to the Famine crisis could be expected. The completeness of the transformation, however, points to the role of the landlord who seized his opportunity to possess these lands. Apart from positively discriminating in favour of a few surviving tenants, he demolished the remaining holdings and their farmhouses. On the central Shanbally estate, the landlord – if in a more cautious and unobtrusive manner – also capitalized on this traumatic period by using the specific regulations of the Poor Law system to further rationalize farm structures in some transitional townlands. Landowners, therefore, intervened in very specific ways to determine the form of society that emerged after the Famine.

The century and a half since 1851 has witnessed a pattern of cumulative change in the distribution of both farm-holdings and farm families. Fields and farm-holdings have been added to some farms, while others have disappeared. These processes of amalgamation and consolidation have seen the disappearance of a total of 172 holdings ranging in size from 2 to 130 acres (52 ha), and the pre-Famine class structure underpinned by a majority of small-holders has equally been transformed. The more substantial farm with over 25 acres (10 ha) and especially over 50 acres (20 ha) is now the dominant type of holding in the parish as it is also in the wider East Munster–South Leinster region. The simplification of the class structure is completed not only by the current decline in the small-holder group and the 75 per cent decline in the number of cottier-labourer families but also by the almost total elimination of the artisan class who throughout the latter part of the eighteenth and first half of the nineteenth century still comprised close on five per cent of the rural population.

The most striking feature of the map showing the spatial distribution of these holdings today (Fig. 4) is the relative emptiness and uniformity of this countryside as compared with its teeming diversity in the earlier nineteenth century. The second striking feature of the map is the blurred nature of the divide which now distinguishes the bigger farming central zone from the formerly dominant small zones to

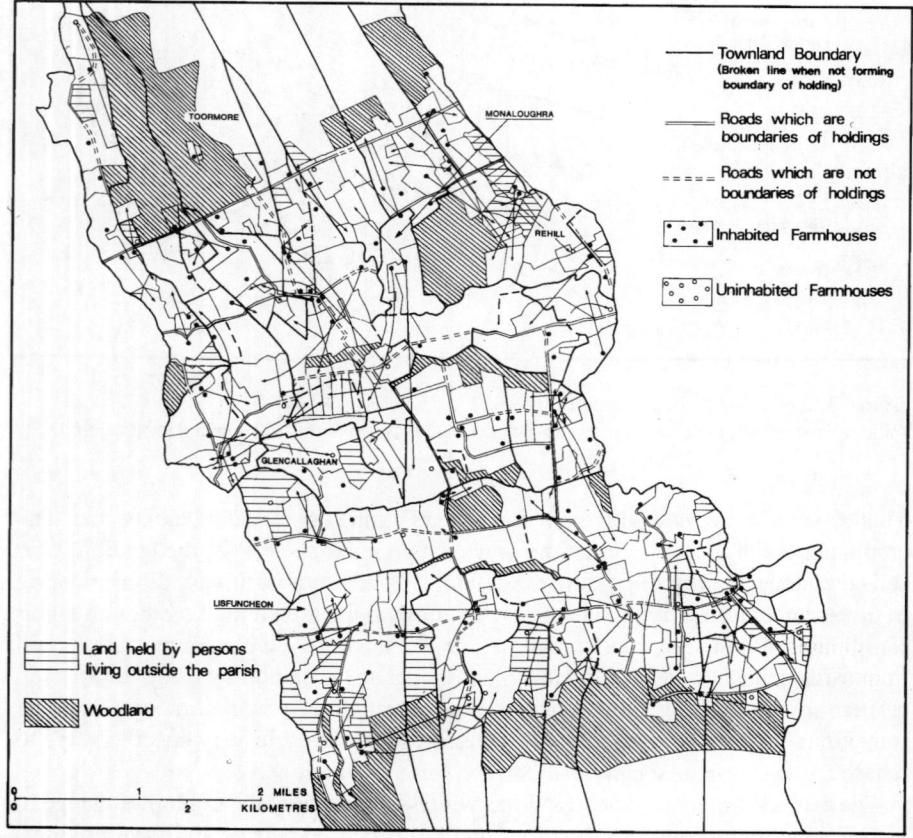

Figure 4: Distribution of farm-holdings c. 1970
Sources: Valuation records, 6 Ely Place, Dublin and author's own surveys 1966–68 and 1974.

the north and south. The relative stability of the central area may be contrasted with the other zones where substantial changes have taken place. The result of these changes is a landscape and society dominated by the medium-sized and larger farm groups. A final distinguishing feature of the pattern is the significant increase in the level of fragmentation of holdings which has occurred since the mid-nineteenth century. Today, there are 80 holdings worked by farm families who live at varying distances from these uninhabited 'outside' farms. Many of the medium and larger farms therefore comprised a total of two or three holdings. This fragmented distribution of land ownership patterns has been intensified by the actions of the State Land Commission which endeavoured to enlarge the size of some smaller holdings by the subdivision of both large untenanted farms and the central demesne. These trends indicate that land ownership and occupation are no longer locked within a townland or estate framework but now operate in a looser and much enlarged setting.

The analysis has been deliberately confined up to this point to the structure and distribution of the farm-holding units themselves. We now turn to the changing distribution of farm families. An examination of the tenant ledger of the central Shanbally estate from 1817 to 1840 (Smyth, 1969, pp. 166–68) provides the first key to our understanding of the degree of continuity which has characterized the former tenants and now owner-occupiers. Of the present total of farm families now living within the former estate boundary, close on one-third have exhibited a tenacious capacity to retain control of and retain their name intact in the same farmstead since at least 1817. An analysis of Griffith's Valuation from 1851 reveals that about half of the present-day families can trace back their name on the land for at least 140 years. However, these powerful examples of continuity are more than a little misleading. If, for example, we look at the total number of farm families in occupation in 1851, only 21 per cent of that group have survived and 79 per cent have since ceased to occupy their holdings.

To more fully understand the processes of continuity and change, Figure 5 indicates the number of occupiers to each holding between 1851 and 1974. It should be noted that what Figure 5 measures is the number of changes that have taken place in the *names* of families who have occupied each holding since 1851. Consequently, many name changes which have taken place within the extended kin group are represented on the map. The capacity of the 'comfortable' or 'strong' farming family to survive and continue in occupation of the same holding over a number of generations is obviously greater than that of the 'struggling' small-holder. This feature is illustrated by the distribution of holdings which have exhibited either no change in name or only one change in name since 1851. Thus the relative stability of the larger farm boundaries in the central townlands is complemented by a definite stability in the farm families who occupy these townlands. Thus size of farm and quality of land have enhanced the prospects of continuity. The stability also hints at the long-established capacity of these families to find vacant positions in town and countryside for their sons and daughters and so not threaten the patrimony. And here the crucial role played by labourers, servants, nephews and nieces in tiding the bigger farms over difficult parts of the lifecycle needs to be recognized. On one such farm, where a kind of kin-based continuity

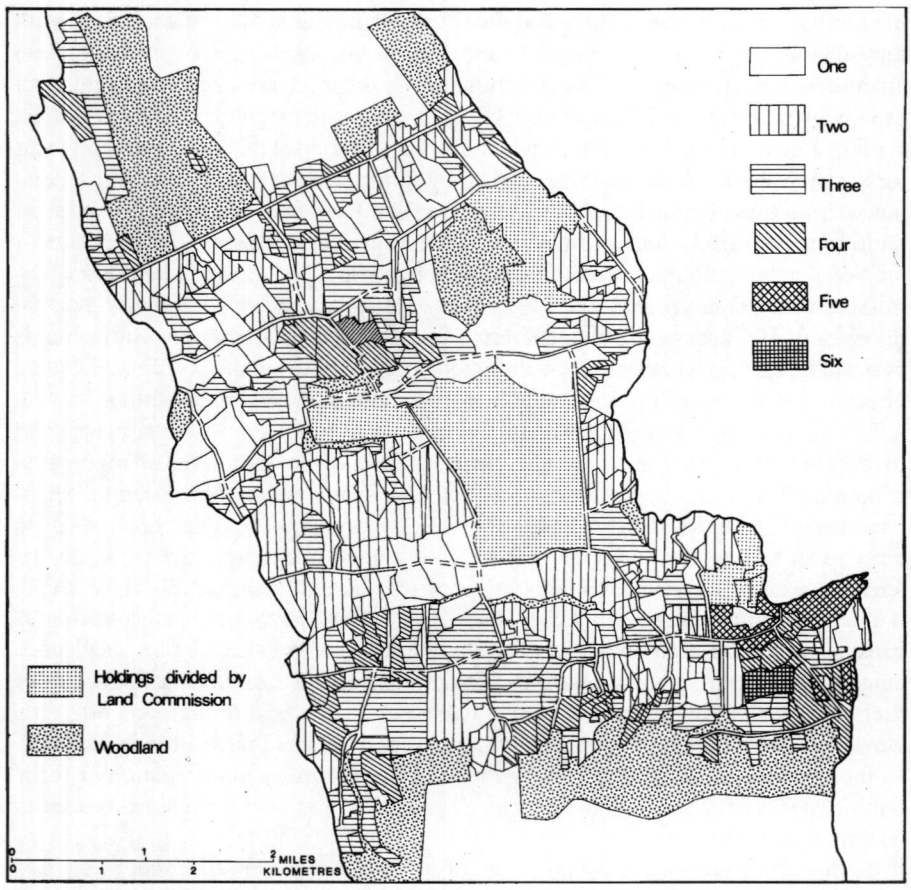

Figure 5: Number of changes in the *names* of families occupying each holding since 1857
Sources: Valuation records, 6 Ely Place, Dublin and author's own surveys 1966–68 and 1974.

has been achieved, no child has been born to that holding in over a hundred years.

The distribution of holdings which have seen three or more changes also reflects the influence of farm size, quality of land and other interesting features. Because of the planned demolition of small-holdings in the northern small zone prior to 1851, it is in the southern zone that the long drawn-out processes of small-farm family erosion are most conspicuous. It is also noticeable that islands of poorer land in some central townlands also seem to have made for difficulty in the maintenance of the family name on the land. The greatest numbers of changes in names have taken place in the vicinity of the town and the villages where more commercial attitudes to the land and a far higher turnover of shopkeeper-farm families have made for a higher percentage of changes.

Farm families increasing the size of their holdings are most relevant here. The bigger farm families were especially active in this process, and of the 119 farm families who failed to add to the size of the holdings, the vast majority belonged to the under-15-acre group who had neither the economic capacity nor the political influence which facilitated increases in the size of family holdings at this time. Thus it was the long-established often grazier families with extensive kinship connections locally in town and countryside and with good relationships with the estate administration who exhibited the greatest initiative in expanding the size of their holdings both before and indeed after the Famine. One can cite numerous examples of this process – it is sufficient to note that one farm family of 250 acres occupies and controls a territorial entity which in 1818 sustained at least eight farm families. And these families were not only successful in expanding their own territorial domains but also in settling at least some other sons and daughters on other farms as well. Their expansion took place at the expense of the contracting distribution of other farm families – some already dying out because of a failure to attract a bride 'as backward places breed few fortunes', while folk tradition indicates that others sold their plots for the passage money to America. The folk memory of the residual small-farm communities still identifies today the acquisitiveness of the bigger farming class and it still distinguishes the families who increased the size of their holdings by what were deemed to be dubious methods as opposed to the families who 'bought the land fair and square'. It would appear then in the decade of and following the Famine, as the overarching power of the landlord regime weakened still further, that many traditional social obligations lost their particular sanction. Rural communities such as this one saw the rise of wealthier families who shouldered aside their less successful neighbours and moved to some extent to fill the power vacuum left both by the decline of the cottier/small-holding class on the one hand and by the disintegration of the landlord class on the other. To understand how a kind of equilibrium was established in the central townlands and how marginalization came to characterize the small-farming uplands, we must now address the issue of family, kinship and marital strategies.

THE KINSHIP NETWORK AND THE GRID OF INHERITANCE
Learning the rules of the game

Quite clearly the landholding structure of a society dominated by medium-sized farms (20–40 ha) is characterized by greater internal changes in structure than allowed for by Arensberg and Kimball (1940, pp. 127–41) for the small-farming communities in Co. Clare. We must now seek to identify more precisely the processes by which land is transferred between the generations. In particular, we need to identify – in a society committed to the maintenance of occupation on ancestral land – the processes by which sufficient vacancies arise to allow for the greater circulation of individuals and properties both within and between kin groups. We are, therefore, ready to explore the ground rules of the inheritance game, what kind of 'hands' (i.e. opportunities) different families were dealt in the game and, given these rules and opportunities, with what skill did the families play the game.

In the period between 1851 and 1900, the great majority of land transfers took place within the boundaries and the codes of the extended kin groups. The valuation and parish records and the remnants of the folk memory allow one to be fairly confident about the general trends illustrated in Figure 6. Of all transfers within the kin group in this period around 52 per cent involved transfers of family land to the son who married; a very impressive 23.5 per cent of land transfers in this period involved the farmer's widow; 6 per cent went to a son who remained a bachelor, 5 per cent to the only daughter, 4 per cent to an unmarried brother and/or unmarried sister and 9.5 per cent to a nephew, niece or other relative.

By contrast some very significant changes occurred in these time-space alloca-

Nature and direction of land transfers within the kin group
a) 1851-1900 :

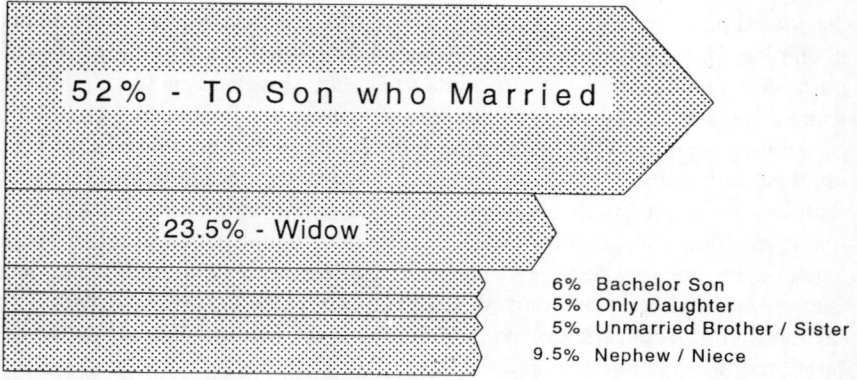

b) 1901-1974 :

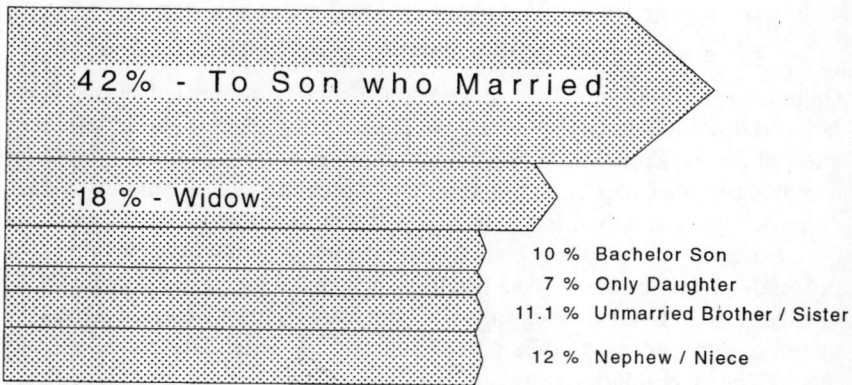

Figure 6: Recipients of land transfers (a) 1851–1900 and (b) 1901–74
Sources: Valuation records, 6 Ely Place, Dublin and author's own surveys 1966–68 and 1974.

tions in the period 1901 to 1974. Of all transfers to kinsmen since c.1901, only 42 per cent involved a direct line of succession to a married son, 18 per cent to a widow, 7 per cent to an only daughter, 10 per cent to a bachelor son and 11 per cent to a bachelor brother and/or sister, while 11 per cent of the transactions saw the nephew or niece take the reins of power. Thus over this period, the married son and widow have lost over 15 per cent of the administrative 'ground' and the main beneficiaries have been either unmarried members of the immediate family or members of the extended kin group. Likewise across almost all categories, there has been some expansion in the average length of time over which any one kin member would ultimately control the farm enterprise – the most noticeable increases belong to the married son/father and the unmarried son who gain an additional 4.2 and 4.0 years respectively in the length of their 'reigns'.

It is therefore the male heir – whether married or unmarried – who still dominates the farm transfer process. In the published material on rural communities in Clare and elsewhere, it would appear that there was no established pattern in the choosing of an heir who was to succeed to the holding (Arensberg and Kimball, 1940, p. 127; Freeman, 1968, p. 158). In this part of south-west Tipperary, although the pattern is still quite varied, it is quite clear that there is a strong preference for the eldest son as heir (see Table 2). A brief analysis of the changes in heads of households between the 1901 and 1911 census schedules also indicates an ever more emphatic preference for the eldest son at the turn of the century (Smyth, 1969, pp. 265–73). The evidence of wills for the same period would seem to concur with this pattern.

Table 2: Patterns of succession on existing farm-holdings, 1967

Succession by eldest son	42
Succession by only son	14
Succession by intermediate son	18
Succession by younger son	11
Succession by only daughter (married)	3
Succession by only daughter (single)	3
Succession by daughter (although the family contained sons)	3
Joint succession by bachelor(s) and/or spinster(s)	12
Inheritance by nephew	14
Inheritance by niece	5
Inheritance by other relative	2
Holding acquired by purchase	7
Land Commission holdings	16
Total	150

Source: Author's own survey 1967.

In this last generation then, on the elementary family farm, about half of these holdings passed to the eldest son. Amongst the intermediate sons, it is the second eldest who is more favoured – and in ten of these instances, the eldest son had already been established on another holding, thus showing that there is still regularity in the pattern but also indicating that the inheritance preference system is not a totally inflexible one. It is also relevant to note that of the eight nephews who moved into the parish in this generation, five were also eldest sons. The notion then of non-patterned succession on Irish farms may need to be dramatically revised, and similar research for counties as far apart as Donegal, Meath and Mayo confirms this general preference for the eldest son (Curry, 1968, pp. 66–88). There is therefore an old tradition of not only continuing the family name but also of handing back 'the farm to the grandfather's name' since the eldest son is almost invariably called after his paternal grandfather. The old people thus see the name on the land established in true tradition and the 'immortality' of the family is symbolized in the recurring Christian names in alternate generations. In south-west Tipperary, succession by the youngest son is confined to the smaller farms. Unlike the larger farmer who attempts to strike a balance between the freedom to advantage one heir on the one hand and ensure equality of treatment to most if not all other members of the family on the other, the smaller farmer has no such freedom; he/she does not have sufficient land and capital or the kin and psychological resources to do this. On many smaller farms, it is not now a question of selecting an heir but rather one of adapting to the migration histories of such small-farm families. The farm is therefore often inherited by the only available son – usually the youngest – who has not migrated out of the system altogether.

The most critical feature of this aspect of succession is the importance of inheritance by the eldest son. Here we have a factor which may make for either late marriage or no marriage at all, two conditions which could affect the nature of the continuity. The eldest son belongs to the land – the land inherits him. In early Irish society, the eldest son was under certain obligations towards his brothers and sisters, and since 'he was the stem of the family until his brothers came of age, he was responsible for them in law and the assertor of their rights' (Coghlan, 1933, p. 81). Since all members of the family are, in theory at least, entitled to equal shares within the familistic system, the eldest son who acquires or is about to acquire the family holding is under an obligation to other members of the family and is responsible with his parents or in their absence for placing such members of the family in positions equal to if not of greater status than his own. In many early twentieth-century wills, this son's specific responsibility to provide the remaining members of the family with a 'trade' is emphasized. Thus the parents and the inheriting son are caught in the classic dilemma of equality and patrimony – of trying to solve the twin goals of settling most if not all sons and daughters (or brothers and sisters) in good positions, while keeping the ancestral farm intact to perpetuate the family name. Traditionally the time-period in which other members of the family could be settled was often a lengthy one. The brothers and sisters who remained on the farm and who were not 'provided for' might have presented almost as difficult an obstacle to the inheriting son's marriage as the ageing parents who did not relinquish control.

The precise nature of the timing of the transfer to the son and the nature of the controls exercised by the parents in this process also needs to be assessed. Numerous descriptions of the interplay of dowry, family and land analyse in detail the role of the father and to a lesser extent the mother in the choosing of the bride-to-be for the heir. One-half of the chapter on 'Family Transition at Marriage' by Arensberg and Kimball (1940, pp. 123–43) deals with the transformation of the roles of both the 'old' and the 'new' couples following the marriage of the heir. This may well have been very characteristic of authentic small-farm cultures where sons and daughters married at a younger age and the proportion of three-generation households was almost certainly greater. The above pattern may have been more characteristic of Clogheen-Burncourt parish over the latter part of the nineteenth and the early decades of the twentieth century; for example, 13.9 per cent of the households in this parish were of the three-generation type in 1901, but in 1974 this proportion had fallen to 8.2 per cent. A detailed analysis of the role of parents in relation to the marriage of the heir in this last generation therefore reveals a rather different situation to that in Co. Clare. Of the total of 66 marriages, 30 marriages occurred while only one parent was still alive while 29 occurred at a time when both parents were deceased. There are thus only seven instances where it could possibly be inferred that both parents exercised some direct influence on the selection of the incoming partner. However, in the other marriages, we should not lose sight of the negative controls exercised by the parents. That as many as 29 out of 66 marriages took place after both parents had died hints, among other things, that the old couple may have acted as a stumbling block to the marriage of the heir. Most particularly, the fact that 30 per cent of the total number of households in the parish comprise bachelors/spinsters over 35 years of age is also relevant to this argument. But here as elsewhere one has to recognize that the objective economic conditions of the farms may be acting as even more powerful constraints to marriage. In addition, many young farm women voted with their feet and emigrated out of the locality and the system.

In 20 out of 30 marriages the surviving parent was the mother. As in some other European countries, it is customary in Ireland for most farmers to leave the holding to the widow for her lifetime. It should be stressed that this pattern is not a recent phenomenon; it shows up as emphatically in the valuation records for the nineteenth century as for the twentieth. The traditional patterns of later marriage, the discrepancy in the ages of husband and wife and the greater life expectancy of the female all combine to enhance the power of the black-frocked widow. One is almost tempted to describe the Irish farm family as being strongly patriarchal in its external manifestations and tending towards the matriarchal within the homestead. The widow therefore often tends to control the farm economy and more particularly the farm finances until at least the marriage of the heir. In 10 out of the 20 marriages, a settlement was drawn up protecting the rights of the widow while transferring the farm to the inheriting son. In the other nine marriages the evidence available would suggest that effective legal control was retained until the widow died.

The most striking feature, perhaps, that an examination of the wills reveals – particularly for the earlier part of the century – is the strictness of the provisions which accompany the inheritance and the nature of the controls then operative in this society. To take just two examples, a son is not to get full possession until he has suitably married 'a girl of means' of not less than two hundred pounds, while another son does not inherit until he marries and his wife brings in 'a fortune' (dowry) which the executor shall deem in proportion to his stock and holding (Willbooks, 1850–1902). Thus, the character of kinship control, the degree of family loyalty requested and the overwhelming importance of the interests of the family group as a whole, as opposed to the individual's own desires, are emphasized.

Both the valuation records and the wills also indicate the consistency with which a certain proportion of farms are inherited by only daughters or nephews, and this is another feature relevant to the circulation of land and families. Inheritance of a farm by an only daughter, therefore, reverses the normal flow of the sexes in what is essentially a patrilocal society. A marriage settlement is also arranged in these circumstances with the incoming husband now responsible for bringing in a substantial fortune, for the family of the daughter must be compensated for the loss of the name of the land. The Irish term 'cliamhain insteach' – 'the relation coming in' – is how the country people still describe this movement. The translation of the Irish term would suggest that in many cases a cross-cousin marriage is again characteristic of such alliances which cut right across the grain of the normal pattern of family/land succession. The reversal of roles in this context is borne out by the fact that one-quarter of the only daughters who married and brought up a family retained full title to the land long after such a marriage transaction.

It is also relevant to observe the consistent significance of the nephew and the niece in the overall inheritance pattern. The uncle/nephew dyad and uncle/niece axis would seem to be a classic feature of this rural culture, and quite a number of permutations can evolve from this linkage. Powerful loyalties between the mother's brother and the sister's younger son represent one dimension of this equation which may have consequences in the inheritance pattern. It is not a unilateral system but rather a bilateral or cognatic one where blood relations on either side can inherit the farm – and so come from the 'mother's people' as well as the 'father's people'.

Inheritance by the married son after a period of administration by the widow represents, therefore, the main pathway by which land is transferred from one generation to the next. Land, however, may also descend along the branches rather than the main stem. Here it is relevant to note that about one-quarter of the total number of transactions in the second half of the nineteenth century involved inheritance by an only daughter, bachelor son/brother/spinster or nephew/niece. In the twentieth century this proportion increased significantly to make up over two-fifths of the total. The probabilities of only daughters or nephews/nieces inheriting land have increased only slightly – the real transformation has occurred amongst the categories of bachelor son or bachelor brothers and spinsters. This transformation is also reflected in the contrast in the composition of households between 1901 (Mss. Census, National Archives, Dublin) and 1974 (Table 3). For our purposes, the main consequence of the increase in incomplete households is the probability of a greater proportion of land eventually passing out of the hands of the nuclear and extended family.

Table 3: Structure of farm households, 1901 and 1974

	1901	1974	Percentage change
Three-generation households	13.9%	8.2%	−5.7%
Two-generation households	65.0%	49.7%	−15.3%
Parents/ no children	9.4%	9.5%	+0.1%
Bachelor/spinster >35 years of age	7.3%	27.0%	+19.7%
Siblings under 35 years of age	4.4%	5.6%	−1.8%

Sources: 1901: Mss. Census of Ireland
1974: Author's own survey

Although it is not possible to document all farm sales in the parish since 1851, an inspection of the valuation records would indicate that between 15 and 18 per cent of the total number of transfers since the mid-nineteenth century involved the alienation of family lands via sales, while the remainder involved the transfer of farms within the extended kin group. Of the present-day farm families, 67 per cent have occupied their holdings continuously over the generations since at least 1900. During the same period, 86 farm families have become extinct, including 49 belonging to the under-30-acre group, 23 to the 30–50-acre group, 9 to the 50–100-acre group and 5 to the group with over 100 acres. Apart from these extinct families, ten others have sold their holdings and moved out of the region. Thus the balance between families on the land has continued to change. However, much of this change has been concentrated in the small-farm zones. Even if the families of bigger holdings die out, both the size of the farm and its capacity to ensure economic viability usually mean that such a holding remains attractive enough to be either inherited or purchased and maintained as an independent economic and social unit.

The disappearance of 96 farm families in the twentieth century, however, has not resulted in the establishment of a similar number of new families on the land. Only in 30 instances between 1901 and 1974 did the sale of such farm-holdings bring a new family to the townland concerned. In all other cases the land was inherited by a near relative and/or incorporated through purchase into an adjacent farm. Excluding the sale of plots of less than 5 acres, an analysis of approximately 80 farm sales in this century will help to clarify the processes of change and amalgamation. In 10 per cent of these sales, it was the ageing bachelor(s) and/or spinster(s), the childless couple, or widow who had seen 'the name lost to the land' at the public auction or the private sale. A further 10 per cent of these farms were sold by an inheriting nephew or niece who – already in occupation of a viable holding and living at a considerable distance from the inherited farm – elected to sell this land. In addition, it is invariably the bachelor or spinster – unable to work the holding in old age and with no kinsmen available to assist – who is obliged to sell the farm piecemeal. This process is still characteristic of some 'terminal' farmsteads and has long been a factor in the piecemeal changes in farm and field boundaries. A further 10 per cent of the sales were associated with shopkeeping families – the 'gombeen' men and women of the Irish novels – who, often acquiring lands from terminal households on the credit system, soon release such holdings back onto the land market. A further 10 per cent of the farm sales relate directly to sales by nuclear families in difficult economic and familial circumstances. Failure to maintain a viable economic enterprise and the related failure to reproduce heirs were therefore responsible for over three-quarters of the total number of sales in the twentieth century. The concern with continuity and the social disgrace which normally follows the sale of a family farm ensure, therefore, that land generally only passes out of the family because of their incapacity to provide or find an heir. The loss of status associated with the selling of a farm is above all epitomized by the nuclear farm families who sold out. Thus declassed, they migrated out of the region and never returned.

The above analysis also hints at the significance of the distant relative in inheriting land. Even within the sphere of the selling and purchasing of land, kinship relationships do not cease to act as powerful controls on behaviour. If a family was forced to sell land and members of the extended kin network could not be expected to 'redeem' the farm by financial loans, then it was expected that the relations in the locality should be afforded preferential treatment if they desired to purchase the holding. The bachelor farmer who sold the family holding with nephews living on nearby farms was roundly condemned by all sections of the rural community: 'He was wrong to do it. He had a right to leave the farm to some of his nephews who were always good to him' (Smyth, 1969, p. 190). By the unwritten laws of family tradition he was obliged to pass on the land to the nearest kinsmen, but he failed to respond to the coercive charter of the kinship code.

Consequently there are a number of examples where the purchaser of the farm was related to the previous owner-occupier. This was already clearly a feature of transactions in the mid-nineteenth century when the sale of the 'interest' or 'good-will' of a farm by one tenant farmer to another most often involved kinsmen, and failing that, near neighbours in the same townland. Overall, since it is the terminal household which is generally involved in the selling of a farm – indicating that there is no near relative to inherit it – such land is not only alienated out of the immediate family but also out of the extended kin group. The land is thus released into general circulation and freed from the constraints of kin rules.

We have now identified the major processes by which land is transmitted over generations in this community. We have also noted the mechanism by which land travels along the main stem of the patrilocal family and we have noted the strategies by which land flows out along the various branches of the extended kin group. In the situation where land is passed both laterally to brothers and sisters and down to a bachelor son, there are increasing probabilities that a proportion of such farms will eventually pass out from under the grip of the kin group. Farm amalgamation and farm sales obviously emerge in such situations. Likewise the significant proportion of land which devolves on nephews, nieces, cousins and only daughters also introduces further key variations in the matching of the land with the lifelines of the rural population.

Underlying all these processes and giving a certain coherent pattern to the actual filling of the vacancies created is the existing class structure in the countryside. Farm families on different size farms behave differently in relation to their involvement in the processes of land acquisition and transfer. Whereas small-holders with less than 30 acres (12 ha) make up 18 per cent of the total number of farm households, this group only manages to acquire 7.1 per cent of the farm vacancies which arise via the processes of purchase, inheritance and marriage to an heir (or heiress). Similarly, the small medium-sized farm group (30–50 acres [12–20]), while making up 31 per cent of the total number of farm households, still only succeeds in capturing 21.9 per cent of the extra-familial 'niches' in the system. In contrast, and dominating the whole picture, are the medium-sized and, to a lesser extent, larger farm-holders. The farm group with 50–100 acres (20–40 ha), while making up 34 per cent of the total number of farmers, manages to amass almost half of the total number of farm opportunities which have arisen in this last generation. It is among this group that we find the classic 'landfast' families – as we do to a slightly lesser extent amongst the larger farmers who, making up 16.9 per cent of the total number of farm households, still manage to acquire a 21.4 per cent share of the wider farm 'market'.

It is, therefore, clear that families in the 50–100-acre group have by far the largest kin groups living locally in farming. As Hannan (1979, pp. 140–41) has argued, the larger the kin group, the greater the local resource base which that group can control and the greater the number of people that group can manage to settle locally.

Decisions to stay locally therefore appear to depend on three factors:

(i) the opportunities for brothers to inherit or buy land locally,
(ii) opportunities for and willingness of sisters to marry local farmers and
(iii) the extent of local concentration of the wider kin group, a factor which appears to increase the commitment of the kin group to the locality.

The number of migrant siblings is then best explained as a residual – those having to travel after all available local positions have been filled.

The reverse of this equation also holds. The larger the number of emigrant kin, the weaker the local kinship structure, the greater the poverty of local kin-based opportunities and the greater cultural contact with emigrants. Given that we have identified the medium-sized farm group with 50–100 acres (20–40 ha) as providing the most successful farm opportunities, our focus for the remainder of this chapter will be on the behaviour of this specific group in playing the game.

THE MATCH-MAKING PROCESS, OR 'PLAYING THE GAME': Practices and strategies of medium-sized farm-holders in matching farms with farmers and sons with brides

For the purpose of analysis, up to now we have separated the trajectories through time of farm units on the one hand and the lifelines of the heirs and purchasers of these farms on the other. To synthesize these two strands, we must examine what the country people themselves do to link farms and families together. They and we have to work out the best strategies for establishing lateral connections so as to marry the farms to new lifelines. Thus the farm family itself ensures the process of social reproduction and, in a wider sense, the social reproduction of the rural social system as a whole. Here we examine the skills of the farm families in playing the game, given the variations in both farming resources and family size and structure. It is proposed to examine these processes by looking in particular at the territorial basis of the marriage field and to analyse the circulation of males into non-paternal farms which become vacant because of the defects in the family farm transmission system as identified earlier in this chapter.

The ritual and drama of the 'match' and those interlocked processes noted by Arensberg (1937, pp. 37–45) for the western region when the heir marries and succeeds to the holding, when all other family roles are reorganized and recrystallized and when other sons and daughters must disperse and migrate, are processes which are often widely separated in Clogheen-Burncourt. In the century between c.1845 and 1945, members of families from medium-sized farm groups grew up in a social and economic environment which saw the family act as a cooperative group enterprise where father, mother, sons and daughters played distinctive but complementary roles. Each member of the family may have laboured for years on the farm with little recompense in building up a reserve of family wealth. Each member claimed his/her share of the accumulated wealth when the opportunity for acquiring or marrying into a farm arose or when some other job opportunity arose in the locality or region. Each came to share in the culture of the group, was concerned to ensure the reproduction of that kin group and was intimately aware of the strategies and rules – the hidden assumptions – that went with the process.

For previous generations and particularly before the transformation of social habits in the 1930s and 1940s, it was usually the father in his contacts with relations and neighbours at the fair, weddings or funerals who 'got word of a possible match'. Traditionally it was the eldest daughter who was to be dowried first and the father might send a 'friend' or neighbour of his to 'put in a word' or 'draw down a match' with another farmer who was known 'to be on the lookout for a wife'. However, in the farming community in the 1970s, patterns of contract between the sexes had changed. 'Today they make their own matches' is how the older people describe modern courtship practices.

In the earlier context, courtship might be continued for a number of years before the son could marry, but one of the most striking features of the rural community was the almost complete absence of sexual intimacy before marriage. Since 1865, only 15 per cent of what is a relatively small total of premarital pregnancies actually occurred amongst members of the farming community. While the males who were responsible for the relatively low illegitimacy rates are unknown, only 11.5 per cent of the females concerned were drawn from the farming community. Thus, not only age at marriage but also general sexual behaviour was tightly controlled in and for this powerful property system. Sexual behaviour must be interpreted in terms of the overriding importance of the goals of a familistic farm system and the kind of marriage that system has entailed.

Courtship for men was therefore focused on 'seeing how good a woman she was in the line of business and in minding the purse and how much of a dowry she might be able to bring in'. Although the institution of the match had become discredited by the 1950s, most of its ramifications still remained. Immediate and extended kin controls are still operative in the farming community. The qualities and demographic structure of the groom's family and his own personal characteristics are examined; likewise the size of the farm and the quality of his land will be scrutinized. A farmer's status is, in part, based on the size of his farm and the quality and quantity of his stock and, as in early Irish society, his farm is still described as 'a place of so many cows'. *It is always the farmers' ambition to see their daughters marrying into a farm of equal if not of larger size than that they were born on.* The family of 'old stock' and 'good blood' with a long history of occupation and a 'long-tailed' kinship network which includes family members who have achieved higher status in the world outside as priests, teachers, nuns, doctors or creamery managers is most highly favoured. As has been outlined for many other European cultures, the specific marriage of any one member is strongly influenced by the entire matrimonial history of that family. The attitudes and values of the groom and his family are similar. The standing of the girl's family, the size of the farm, her kinship connections and above all her perceived managerial competence within the home and the farmyard will be carefully measured. The size of the dowry may also be a critical factor. The function of the dowry or its modern equivalent in terms of new occupational skills and level of education obtained may have changed but little on a majority of farms. A farmer's wife summarizes the situation for the early 1960s:

> 'I was below in the home place working with my brothers and sister. Her fortune was to get her into the convent. That was her dowry going into the convent and although it is not necessary, they expect it from you if you can afford it. I was at home when my brother got married and his wife brought in so much money. I could get married then into a good farm for I also had some money coming to me out of the farm. If my brother hadn't provided me with this money out of his wife's dowry and otherwise it would affect my chances of a good marriage. If you fail to provide a dowry you are letting down the family name and the neighbours would say "she hadn't much of a fortune, she hadn't enough to marry into such a farm". I brought £1000 into this farm but if I didn't have it I don't know what would have happened here, but it is doubtful if there would have been a marriage. It is a tough system but I think it is dying slowly. People are becoming more aware of the fact that it is more of a deal, a bargain rather than a real marriage. But to a certain extent it is necessary; supposing Tom [her brother] brought in a girl with no money, what was I going to do, where was I going to get a fortune? Yet things are becoming more like the town. What education you have and what occupation you had before marriage, these things are beginning to count. You know, it's easier for a nurse [to] marry into a farm than for an ordinary farmer's daughter.' (Smyth, 1969, p. 254)

Thus, this summary acknowledges the function of the dowry, proceeds to describe the changes which are taking place, but still emphasizes its functional role in marriage, inheritance and family reorganization.

Furthermore, the majority of farmers and, even more so, their wives wish to provide a daughter with a suitable dowry or its equivalent, for not only is it a mechanism which facilitates the transfer of the family land to the son, enables the parent to retire (if alive) or a sister or brother to leave the farm but it is also an instrument which asserts and maintains the rights of both the woman and her kin group in relation to the farm which she marries into. The frequent description that 'she paid dearly for that farm' illustrates this latter feature and also highlights the sacrifices which thrifty farmers make to establish their sons and daughters on other farms. The marriage therefore is an alliance of near equals – and its full significance lies in the kinship it creates. In a sense the old dowry system was a powerful quantitative measure of all the subtleties that made up the relative ranking of families in a locality. Today the incoming brides almost invariably insist on the groom's title to the land before they will marry, just as under the landlord regime families struggled to clear arrears in rent and safeguard their lease so as to clinch the proposed match. The country people therefore see the dowry as a symbol of the independence and equality of the woman who marries into a farm. Her dowry has established her on a farm where she has equal rights and where she plays as vital a role as the husband in the economy. If she survives him, as she generally does, it is she who will normally inherit the land and govern its administration until she dies or a son marries. The numerous farm families where the brother or sister lives out their life of celibacy into old age may, amongst other things, reflect the failure of such families to find a mate of acceptable standing in the community. That the family name is more important than the life of the individual is often strikingly illustrated in the country marriage; it is often more apparent when the individual does not marry at all, for the family name will even be allowed to become extinct rather than be allowed to be 'tarnished' by an unacceptable alliance. In this community then, the establishment of a woman on a suitable farm almost invariably means putting her into a farm further east in an area of better land and larger farms. The fierce centring of the family's ambition in the farm and occupational status of their sons and daughters produces a circulation system for brides – the marriage field – which is powerfully shaped by an agro-economic, hypergamous ethos.

The shape, size and dynamic character of this marriage field can be illustrated by an analysis of the spatial patterns exhibited by brides moving into farms in the study area (Fig. 7a). From 71 documented examples, 56 per cent of the brides who married into farms within the sample area originated from adjacent western parishes – areas characterized by generally poorer land and a higher proportion of smaller farms than found in Clogheen-Burncourt. The adjacent eastern parishes only contributed 24 per cent to this movement and, almost invariably, wives originating from the generally larger farm area of south-east Tipperary were marrying into the bigger holdings within the parish. The remainder of the brides (20 per cent) were born within the parish area. The nature of the bridal drift into the parish, reflecting the struggle for greater security and higher status by members of families with smaller farms, both contrasts with and complements the movement of farmers' daughters who originated from the parish of Clogheen-Burncourt and who married into farms outside the

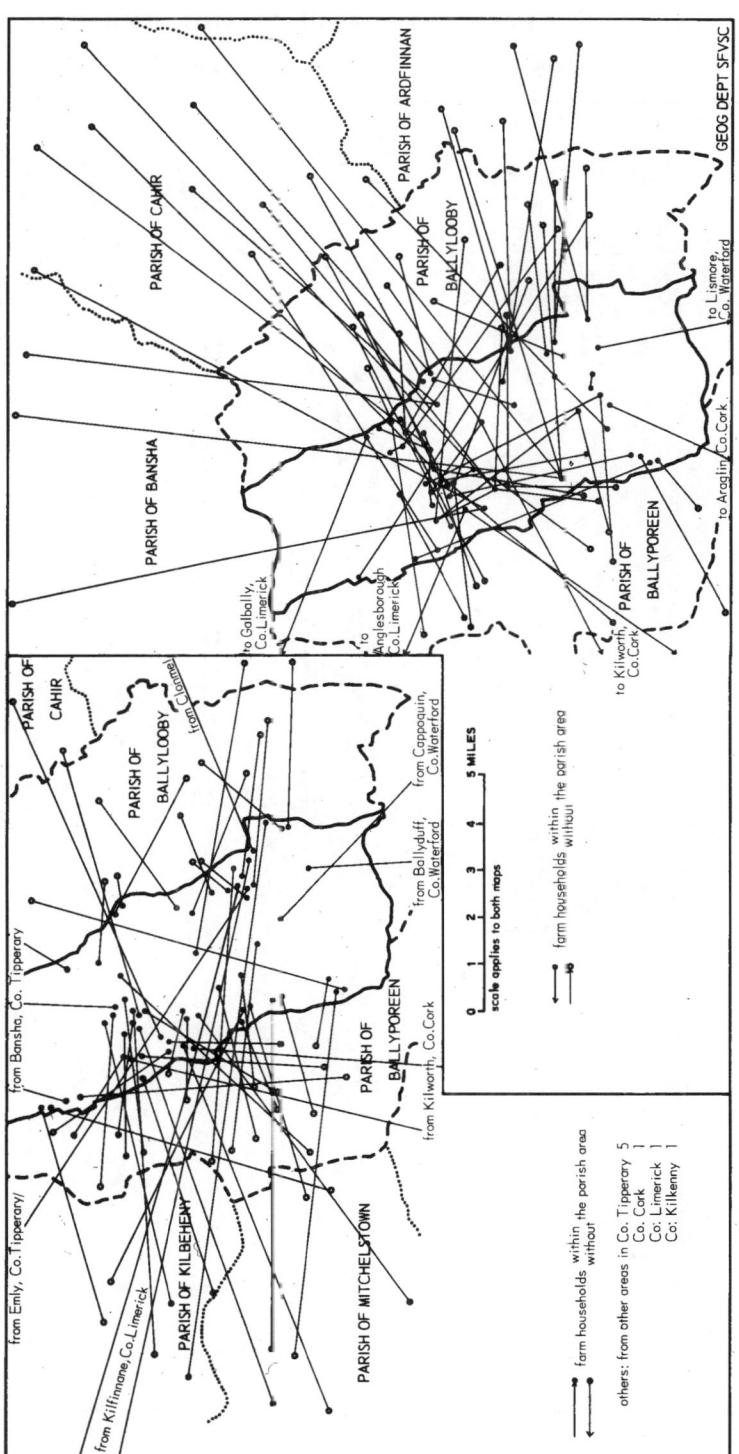

Figure 7: Movement of brides (a) marrying *into* farms *within* the parish, and (b) marrying into farms *outside* the parish of Clogheen-Burncourt.
Source: Author's own questionnaire survey, 1966–68.

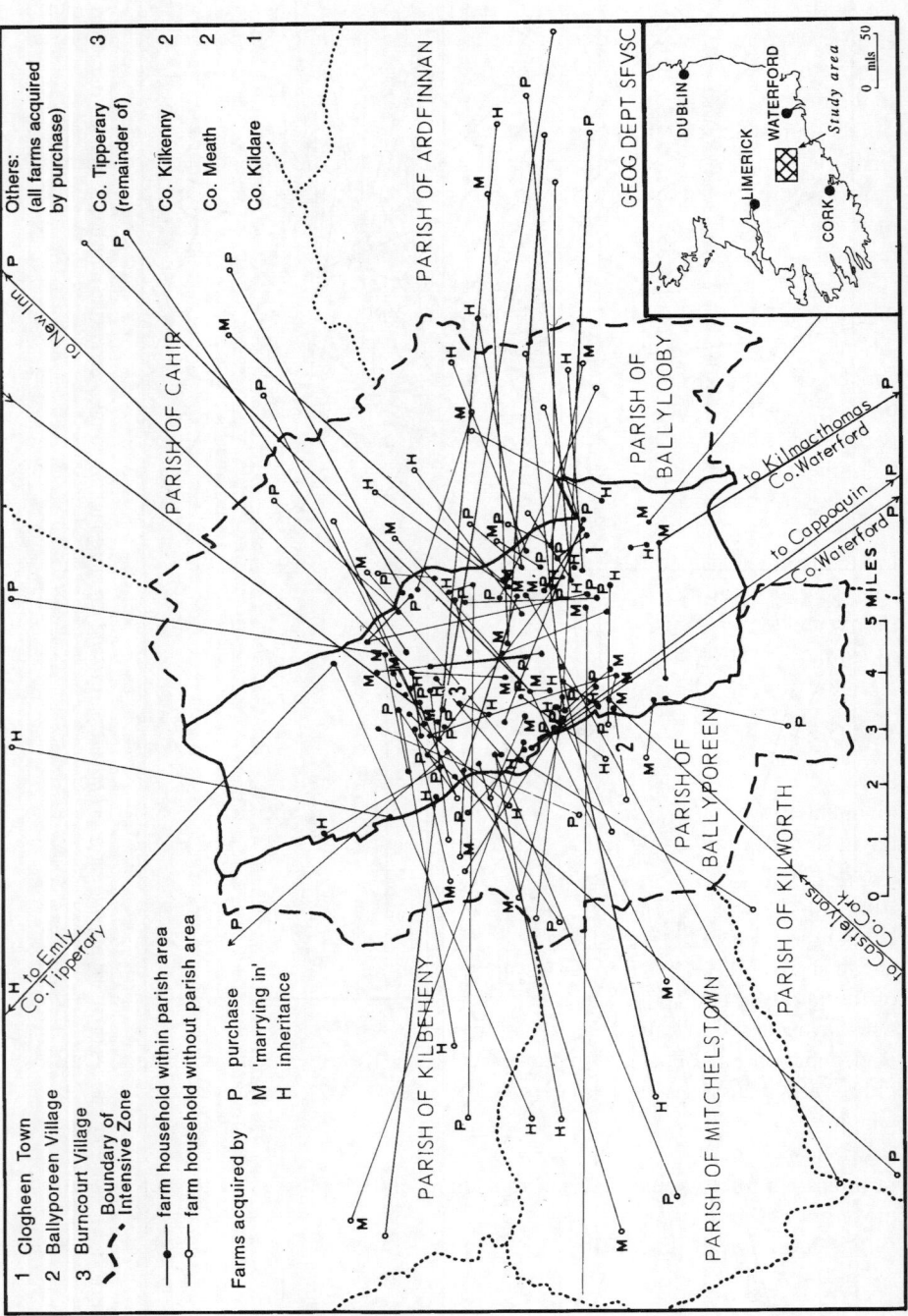

Figure 8: Movement of male farm occupiers into non-paternal farms, 1900–68

parish (Fig. 7b). Almost two-thirds of this latter group have moved into the eastern/ north-eastern parishes which have bigger farms while only 34 per cent have moved westwards. As farmers' daughters climb up the agricultural ladder as they move east, so their counterparts in the medium-sized farming region continue the same trend.

The shape, size and dynamic character of the marriage field likewise underlie the territorial structure of the movements of male farm occupiers into non-paternal farms. Figure 8 illustrates this movement, with the inheritance of a farm from a kinsman, marrying into a farm with an only daughter and the purchase of a new farm representing the three critical strategies for filling vacancies in the system. Not surprisingly, almost two-thirds of the total number of male farming movements in this generation have taken place within the limited confines of the three parishes of the intensive zone. Of the 118 examples which could be documented, 27.2 per cent concerned native-born farmers moving within their own parish area while an additional 37.2 per cent involved the movement of farmers to and from the two adjacent parishes. Another layer of connections stretches to an outer ring of parishes, also identified in the marriage field. The remaining 7.5 per cent of the total number of male farming movements reflects the far flung connections of big farming families.

The attitudes, values and behaviour patterns of farm families at the crucial periods in life histories have now been described and the general factors affecting continuity analysed. One can best summarize the specific relationships between the Irish farm family and the land by a brief analysis of two case histories of families with holdings of from 50 to 100 acres and one case study from the small-farming world of under 30 acres (Smyth, 1969, pp. 273–84).

The Quirk family[1]

Here we have a classic example of the long-tailed 'landfast' family. An adjoining townland to the Ballyknockane farm in Doughill-Ballylooby parish is called Quirkstown, so the family name is as old and as characteristic of the area as the townland names whose origins date back to at least the early medieval period. This family, from an original farmstead of 33 acres, became established in three different townlands in the next generation, and from these three farmsteads at Kiltankin, Lisfuncheon and Ballyknockane have expanded and flourished, the overwhelming majority of the family members remaining in farming. The only exceptions are the women who have entered religion, and the single priest. However, new attitudes and patterns of occupation have become characteristic of the younger families. Daniel Quirk's family at Kilcaroon is a clear example of the new influences in educational trends which have and will continue to change the pattern of continuity. Whereas Daniel Quirk himself had come from a family of twelve, of whom eleven had remained in farming, his own family has seen four members, by process of further education, move out of the farming world yet stay in Ireland.

The Quirk family originally belonged to the townland of Kiltankin in the adjacent western parish of Ballyporeen where in the mid-nineteenth century they occupied a

---

1 All the family names used in this section have been changed to protect the identity of those concerned.

farm of 33 acres. Very little is known of this generation of the Quirks, although present family traditions suggest that the majority of them 'went foreign', i.e. to America. The heir, John, married a farmer's daughter from an adjoining townland in the 1860s and would appear to have had a family of six – four sons and two daughters. One son migrated to the United States while one daughter died at a relatively young age. The other four remained in farming, and while three married, a remaining brother worked on the farm all his life and remained single. The youngest son, Thomas, married into a well-known and old-established family in the townland of Lisfuncheon in the parish of Clogheen-Burncourt in the 1890s: his sister, Mary, married into a 60-acre farm in the townland of Ballyknockane in the eastern parish of Doughill-Ballylooby a few years later, while the eldest son, James, married on the home farm in 1909.

From this home farm in Kiltankin the eldest son of the next generation, John, married into a nearby farm but had no family and the farm reverted to 'the wife's people'. His sister, Hannah, remained single on the farm while the other son, James, inherited the family holding and had two sons, Here, the elder son, James, married a farmer's daughter from Kilbeheny parish in 1945 and has one son, while the other son was established on a purchased farm adjoining the other Quirk farmstead in Lisfuncheon in 1946. He too has married but has no family.

On the other Lisfuncheon farm, which contained and still contains 90 acres, Thomas Quirk had a family of 12, 7 sons and 5 daughters. Of the sons, the eldest, John, married into a farm in Kiltankin in 1932, the townland from which his father had originated, and had an only daughter who has since married another farmer from the townland of Shanrahan. This farmer had already purchased a holding and now owns and works the Kiltankin farm from his own farm at Shanrahan. The second eldest son, James, married a farmer's daughter from Mitchelstown parish in 1940 and had two sons, who are both at home working on the farm with their widowed mother. The third son, Thomas, inherited the aunt's farm in Ballyknockane since she had no family. Having worked on her farm from his early youth he inherited the holding, which was held in trust by his father until 1945 when he married a farmer's daughter from Newcastle parish, south-east of Ardfinnan parish. He has an only daughter who is working on the farm. The next brother, William, in the Lisfuncheon family, had also worked on the Ballyknockane farm with his brother Thomas, but then purchased a farm in Ballyhale, County Kilkenny. He, however, married another farmer's daughter from Ballyknockane townland where he had worked. He has three sons and a daughter. The daughter, originally a nurse, has married a bank clerk in the town of Clonmel. One son has inherited the farm but is single; two other sons have migrated to England.

The next brother on the Lisfuncheon farm, Daniel Quirk, who, because of the large number of sons on the home farm, worked for a period in other areas of south Tipperary as a farm labourer, married into a farm of 37 acres in the adjoining townland of Kilcaroon. He has one son and five daughters. The son has remained on the farm working with the father, while of his five daughters, the eldest has become a nun, another is a nurse in Cashel Hospital while another, also a nurse, has married a farmer from a nearby townland in Ballyporeen parish. Two other daughters who had worked in the Civil Service in Dublin have married an accountant and an electrician in the city. Of the remaining brothers on the Lisfuncheon farmstead, one remained working on the farm but died at a relatively young age, while the other, the youngest in the family, received further education and moved out of farming.

However, during this protracted period when the sons were being established or establishing themselves in farms, changes were also taking place amongst the five daughters of Thomas Quirk on this Lisfuncheon farm. The eldest, Kathleen, became a Sister of Mercy and is now in a convent in Clonakilty, County Cork. The second daughter, Joan, was married in 1922 to a farmer with 80 acres in the eastern Bansha parish, and of her family of eight, one son has migrated to the United States and the eldest daughter has become a nun in England, while three other daughters and two sons have all married into farms in the Bansha locality. The eldest son is still single and living on the home farm. Aileen, the next daughter on the Lisfuncheon farm, has married a farmer in Ballyknockane townland where, as we have already seen, her aunt had lived on a farm which her brother Thomas inherited. She has had four sons; one is a priest, two have remained at home working on the farm, while the fourth, after a period at secondary school, has migrated to England.

Another daughter of the Lisfuncheon farm, Martha, married in 1924 into a farm of 90 acres in the townland of Castlegrace, which is also in Ballylooby-Doughill parish. Of her family, the eldest son is married and living on the home farm, another son has married into a farm within the same parish, and her only daughter has also married into a farm in Ballylooby-Doughill parish. The remaining daughter on the Lisfuncheon farm, Bridget, married in the late 1920s into a 100-acre farm in Ballyclerihan parish, north of Clonmel, and of her family, one daughter has become a Presentation nun in Thurles, another is a nurse in Clonmel Hospital while the two sons are working on the home farm.

With the exception of Daniel Quirk's family at Kilcaron, all the other Quirk families exhibit almost all the facets of continuity in family farming. Sons have married into various sized farms; all the daughters have moved eastwards onto better farms. Again, the extended kinship network has been used, as with Thomas at Ballyknockane, while farms have also been purchased. Likewise, one notes the inter-relationships between kinship groups and neighbourhoods. The Quirk family of Lisfuncheon had originally come from Kiltankin and one of the Lisfuncheon sons married into a farm in Kiltankin. Likewise, a son of the Kiltankin family inherited a holding from an aunt in Ballyknockane, his sister married a farmer in the same townland, while his brother, who purchased a farm in County Kilkenny, also married a farmer's daughter from the same townland. As already demonstrated, one relationship, whether through kinship or marriage, often creates another.

The Fitzgerald family

The Fitzgerald family of Ballyhurrow illustrates a similar capacity to expand and diversify, but also demonstrates other adaptive strategies exhibited by families from medium-sized farms.

In the mid-nineteenth century the Fitzgerald families occupied two holdings in the townland of Monaloughra, each with 27 acres, and it would seem that an original farm of 54 acres had been subdivided at some period previous to 1851. Michael and Patrick Fitzgerald occupied these two farms respectively, while another sister had married into an adjoining farm in the townland of Ballyhurrow. Michael Fitzgerald married and had no family and the farm passed to a nephew of his wife. The farm in Ballyhurrow contained 38 acres in 1851, but it would seem that this family was obliged to give up its holding to the estate because of its inability to pay the rent. However, tradition maintains that it handed the key of the homestead to the Fitzgeralds of Monaloughra, thus indicating to the estate management and to the community that they desired their relatives to occupy the holding. Thus, Patrick Fitzgerald of Monaloughra occupied the Ballyhurrow farm too and increased the size of this farm to 69 acres on the acquisition of smaller holdings in the vicinity. Patrick Fitzgerald had only one son, Michael, who married a farmer's daughter from another townland in the parish, Toormore, in 1883. There were nine in Michael Fitzgerald's family, six sons and three daughters. His farm now totalled 93 acres.

The eldest son, Thomas, inherited 'the mother's place' in Toormore, a farm of 53 acres but which included only 30 acres within its boundaries in 1851. As with the Quirk holding at Ballyknockane, so this 'outside' farm at Toormore was worked by the family as a unit for 12 years before Thomas Fitzgerald inherited the farm in 1925 and married in 1927. He had two sons, the eldest of whom married in 1965, while the other brother is still single and working on the farm.

The second son of the Ballyhurrow farm, William, left the farm after a number of years and established a butcher's shop in the village of Ardfinnan, six miles east of Clogheen. He married a farmer's daughter from the adjacent parish of Doughill-Ballylooby and also acquired a medium-sized farm in the Ardfinnan locality. His only son now owns the butcher's shop and the farm. The eldest sister in the Ballyhurrow family, Joan, married into a farm of 70 acres in the Ardfinnan locality, through her brother's connections. Of her family, one son inherited the home farm and one son has become a priest, while of the three daughters, one inherited a farm from a paternal uncle, another married into a farm in the locality and the third, formerly a nurse, married an insurance agent in Dublin.

The third son on the Ballyhurrow farm, David Fitzgerald, 'served his time' in a grocery-public house in the nearby town of Cahir and later succeeded in buying a shop of the same character. He married a farmer's daughter from Newcastle parish and had three sons and three daughters. Two of the sons have remained single in the shop while the other son is married on a farm inherited from 'his mother's people' in the parish of Balyclerihan. Of the daughters, one has become a nun, one has married a hotel owner in Cahir and the other has married a shopkeeper in Clonmel. The fourth son from the Ballyhurrow farm, Andrew, became a priest, and worked as a curate in England, while the second daughter, Margaret, married into an upland farm of 50 acres in Toormore. Of her family, however, only one, a son, remained in farming, while the other five, two sons and three daughters, migrated to England.

The fifth son, James Fitzgerald, from the original homestead at Ballyhurrow, married into a farm in the townland of Glencallaghan within the parish of Clogheen-Burncourt. Of a family of two, the only son remained on the home farm, while the only daughter is a teacher in Dublin. This farm has been enlarged since James Fitzgerald married in; an adjoining holding has been purchased and the farm now exceeds 60 acres in size. Anne, the remaining daughter on the Ballyhurrow farm, married into a rural public house and small farm in the townland of Rehill, but the public house has long been closed and the family has acquired land both by inheritance and purchase within the townland. However, only two sons remain at home, while five emigrated, three to England and two to the United States. Finally, the sixth and youngest son of the Ballyhurrow family, Peter, inherited the original homestead, married, and his two sons, both single, now work the farm together.

Thus, the Fitzgerald family exhibits the same commitment to the land as the Quirk family, and expansion is achieved by purchase, inheritance and by 'marrying into' farms. Again, the inter-relationships between neighbourhoods through kinship connections is illustrated by the sister who married into a farm in Ardfinnan after her brother had established a shop there. Likewise, one notes the movement of another daughter into a farm in Toormore, where her mother was born and where her brother had inherited the maternal holding. However, the Fitzgerald family displays a greater range of the values and patterns of activity which characterize the families of the medium-sized group. Not only did they increase their holdings in the mid-nineteenth century, but they continue to do so, as, for example, James Fitzgerald in Glencallaghan. It is also important to note that inheritance of land is not confined to the paternal side of the family; there are three instances of sons acquiring land from their 'mother's people'. Besides, the Fitzgerald family shows the traditional attachment of many farming families to the public house, the butcher's shop and the grocery. However, it exhibits a higher level of social mobility by its greater representation in religious occupations. However, note the differences between the destinies of the two families in the poorer upland townlands of Toormore and Rehill. These farms are situated on the poorer land and the greater number of the siblings in this generation have emigrated.

This contrast between the patterns of continuity on the bigger Fitzgerald farms on the better land as opposed to that of their two smaller farms on the poorer land is best illustrated by a case study of one small-farming family, the Hanrahans.

The Hanrahan family

Thomas Hanrahan of Boolakennedy occupied a holding of seven acres in 1851. Of this man's family, six migrated to the United States while two remained in farming. The daughter, Elizabeth, married into a small farm of 20 acres in the adjoining townland of Toorbeg. There was only one son in her family, who married in 1914. His only son sold this small farm in 1966 and now works with the County Council. Thomas Hanrahan's heir, James of Boolakennedy, married a small farmer's daughter from the adjacent townland of Cullenagh and had a family of five sons and four daughters. Their eldest son, Thomas, remained on the home farm but never married. Two other sons, Patrick and Michael, and the four daughters, Margaret, Alice, Eileen and Bridget, emigrated to America during the first years of the twentieth century. Another son, John, married on the home farm a small farmer's daughter 'from up the mountain' in Coolgarranroe. Of his family of four, the sons, John and William, have emigrated, one to New York and the other to Birmingham and the small farm is still worked by the widowed mother, while her eldest daughter Mary has married a creamery worker and also lives with her family on the home farm. The other daughter Eileen has married a mechanic who lives in the adjoining parish of Ballyporeen.

Dermot, the youngest son of James Hanrahan's Boolakennedy family, worked as a shop assistant at Ballyhooly Cooperative Creamery for a period and in 1939 married into a farm of 30 acres in the townland of Glengarra. He still retained ownership of the farm to the age of 75 and had increased the size of the farm to 46 acres by qualifying for a Land Commission divide. He had a family of six, the eldest of whom is a lorry driver in the locality and lives on the farm, the second eldest inherited the home farm while the third and fourth sons work in London as an electrician and bulldozer driver respectively. Another daughter returned from nursing in London to attend to the ageing father, while the youngest daughter became a nun.

The contrast with the patterns outlined for the medium-sized farms is striking. In the place of stability and durability are emigration and change. 'It is the lonesomest history you ever heard' is how Dermot Hanrahan described it. This was, and is, the pattern for the majority of the smaller farms in the more remote and poorer townlands'. For some small farmers the struggle is too much and they capitulate (e.g. the man who sold his farm and went to work for the County Council). Again, one notes that there is no male heir for the Boolakennedy farm where the sons have left farming, pushed out by the rushy fields that could provide a means of subsistence in the nineteenth century but which offer little attraction when the emigrant ship and the wage packet have become a reality in such small farming communities. One notes the relative stability of the family from the bigger farm at Glengarra, but here also emigration is characteristic for 'the Hanrahans are bred to travel'.

This detailed analysis, therefore, takes us out of the confines of the parish and involves a consideration of circulation over a much more extensive area, where durable bonds of kinship, marital and occupational connections are created and maintained. This relatively tight community information field, as shaped by marital, farm and other transactions, thus provides and represents a territorial base for social and economic relations of an enduring kind. The influence exerted by each of the spouses is clearly very important to the overall family marriage strategies. Over each generation female marriage connections continue to stretch the boundaries of the community information field while the movement of male farmers throughout all the area stabilizes and indeed anchors the local kin-based interaction patterns. It is the woman who is most often responsible by her marriage for establishing close and stable relationships between areas and neighbourhoods with which her father may only have had business contacts. In a real sense it is a woman who often creates and intensifies social relationships between localities and neighbourhoods. It is the man who solidifies these connections and creates new opportunities in turn. For example, the purchase of a farm may depend on information provided by the married sister in the locality where the farm is to be sold. The balance between east and west, therefore, is maintained by the farmer's sons. 'His mother's people' come generally from the west while his sisters and paternal aunts generally marry further east. By inheritance, marrying in, and by farm purchases, the sons move in all directions throughout the whole region and so solidify and enhance the overall structure. They in turn may create or identify new opportunities for their sisters or daughters in the region. This means that every matrimonial alliance in the family has a bearing on every future marriage.

As a comparison of Figures 7 and 8 shows, there is therefore a striking similarity in the overall spatial structure of male and female movements within the farming community. The social or community information field can thus be interpreted as a localized yet complex communication system. The intricate lattice of networks can be seen as lines of communication along which flows a continual stream of information about all aspects of local life and particularly about the vacancies in the system – farms for sale, meadows for letting, and, crucially, mating and inheritance opportunities.

The contrasts with the linkages of kin groups of smaller farms are often quite striking. Unlike the bigger farms where the establishment of one member of the family may lead to the provision of an opportunity for the next, in the small farming zone where there is often nobody left but the youngest son, there is no such extensive kin network to fall back on for 'they have all gone foreign'. And when one analyses the 'pioneering' character of the bridal movement and its drive to expand into the better lands, one must also note the progressive desertion of the small farming edges where the great proportion of bachelor-spinster farms are now concentrated. Thus, a kind of equilibrium is maintained by an upward spiralling process of interactions on the better farms of the central townlands while a downward cumulative process further erodes in each generation the increasingly marginalized small-farm holding. The overall occupational and geographical distribution of members of the different status groups in Ireland and elsewhere highlights the cumulative consequences of differential access to crucial resources such as land, capital and information, the varying aspirations and differences in educational, migrant and occupational linkages of these groups, combined with uneven patterns of accessibility to new sources of expertise.

These territorial patterns have also quite a historical depth as well. Obviously factors of population density, farm size, and related changes in modes of communication do affect the patterns of 'intervening bridal opportunities'. However, a comparison of marriage patterns c.1910 to 1940 with marriage patterns over the decade 1865 to 1875 reveals no striking transformation (Fig. 9). The proportion of brides not born within the parish was reduced by 12 per cent (from 54 to 42 per cent), but this reduction has been complemented by an almost equivalent intensification of links with the adjoining parishes. There seems to be little change in the connections maintained with the outlying group of parishes over this last century. Certainly the territorial basis of community life in Clogheen-Burncourt has been

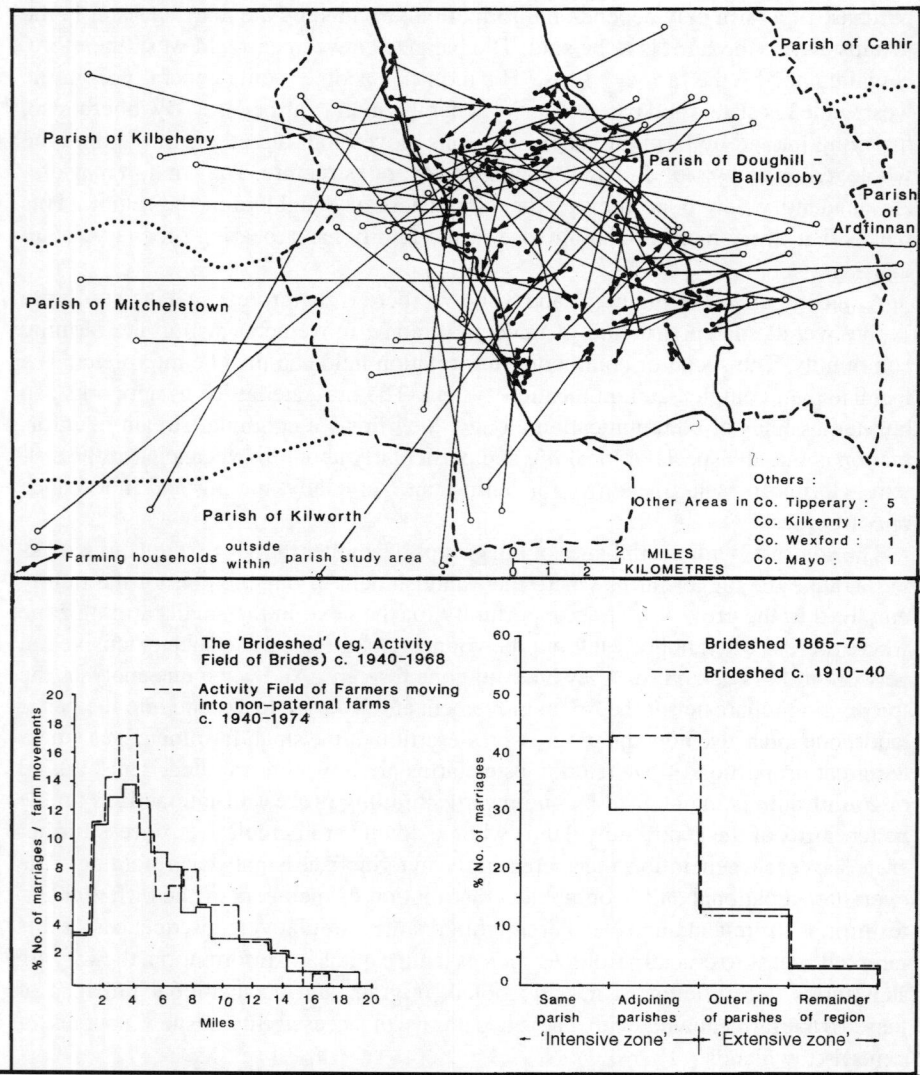

Figure 9: (a) Movement of brides into and within the parish of Clogheen-Burncourt, c. 1910–40; (b) Comparisons of activity fields of males and females, c. 1940–74 *and*, 'bridesheds', 1865–1875/c.1910–1940

Sources: Parochial records, Clogheen presbytery and author's own survey 1966–68.

more stable and has covered a more extensive area than was initially allowed for at the beginning of this chapter. There may well be a deeper structure to this territorially-based system of exchanges of brides, properties and other goods, involving reciprocities stretching back over generations linking groups of loosely paired kin groups and localities, thus giving this territorial structure its own inner logic.

SUMMARY

The way in which farms, heirs and brides are matched, mis-matched and not matched in each generation is a very complex business. In this chapter, we have been concerned with farm-unit and lifeline trajectories since c. 1820. The period 1820 to 1850 was a critical transitional phase for it saw the rural society of this southern parish begin to slowly pivot around on its hinges and face in a rather different direction. In attempting to evaluate the critical changes in this period, are we seeing here a search for a new equilibrium – a new equation between land resources and family systems – or are we seeing the re-emergence of a system of property management and control which, allowing for the changed demographic and economic contexts, was quite similar to an earlier and equally strong pastoralist phase in the economy?

These readjustments and reorientations were taking place when the estate system was directly involved in influencing landholding and, indirectly, inheritance patterns. Under the landlord regime, the evidence is quite clear that the maintenance of the family name on the land was a central ambition of the majority of leaseholders in the region. Lifetime transfers within the family, the marrying-in process, the succession to land by a nephew and indeed the subletting of land by the widow or incomplete household were also seen by the estate administration as quite acceptable practices both in pre-Famine and more particularly post-Famine times. Equally relevant, the right of the tenant to sell his 'interest' or 'goodwill' in a holding – usually to either kinsman or neighbour – was also quite characteristic and was accepted, with reservations, by the estate administration.

It is also relevant to note that 40 per cent of the total number of changes in occupation between c. 1818 and 1840 would seem to relate to the failure of incomplete/joint households to maintain viable economic holdings. It should therefore not be assumed that, in this era of high marriage rates, this pattern of nuptiality extended uniformly across the different social strata. Whereas about 75 per cent and 60 per cent of the male labourers and small-holders respectively were married before reaching 30 years of age in the decade prior to 1821, this figure dropped to around 42 per cent for the farmers with over 30 acres (12 ha) who dominated the better lands of the central townlands. There were therefore significant demographic differences between the two groups, and farm vacancies – as with the post-Famine model – could also then arise because of family failures to reproduce.

While recognizing the validity of the above trends, it also needs to be stressed that estate policy, however, was not conducted to facilitate such affectionate kin arrangements. It is quite clear that the main estate in the parish sought to have as much freedom of choice as possible in the re-allocation of leases and in the amalgamation of lands. At one level then, one could view the local and regional 'agrarian combinations' at this time as reflecting a battle between firstly, reforming landlords seeking to optimize productivity and profits by positively discriminating in favour of the better tenants, and secondly, kinship and locality systems which tried to blunt the effects of the operation of free market forces, sought to peg back rent levels and above all sought to establish the right of the sitting tenants to occupy what were deemed to be ancestral lands. On another level, however, these combinations as much reflect the internal conflict between competing kin, locality and class groups as they sought to maximize their own positions in a changing environment.

Through the leasing policy, landlords could and did effect a number of changes in land occupation where kin and locality rules were overridden and the most suitable tenant rather than the nearest relative or neighbour was seen to be patronized. There was thus a profound gap between a system which asserted its right to manage the occupation of holdings via a competitive leaseholding system which made for a much greater mobility in tenurial occupation patterns, and a system where traditional rights to land were not a product of a written agreement with a landlord but were rather based on the 'nearness' of one's kinship (or locality) ties with the existing occupier(s). Estate policy therefore assisted in both the pre-Famine and post-Famine decades in accelerating the processes of rationalization and consolidation and therefore helped to activate or support the goals of those farm families who were already advantaged by better land, kin and political resources. Ironically, it was the members of this same group, which had benefited most from the landlords' rationalization policy, who delivered the final blows to the crumbling estate structures in the 1880s.

Thus, slowly developing over the previous century or more, these interlocked yet highly competitive family groups came to dominate completely after 1900 without the intervening effects of estate management policy and at the end of a half-century of transformation in Irish agricultural patterns which had increasingly favoured pastoral production. One could, perhaps, suggest that out of this dialectic came a modified inheritance system whose field of operations was not narrowly defined by the boundaries of a few townlands but rather extended itself to incorporate the full range of opportunities and possibilities which derived from membership of loosely organized extended kin and locality groups. Such an inheritance system insisted both on the maintenance of the integrity of the ancestral holding and the settlement of (most) other sons and daughters in positions of equivalent status whether on other farms, in towns, in seminaries or convents or overseas. In this context, it should also be stressed that these processes of farm consolidation and sibling settlement were not carried out in an aggressive, individualistic way but were rather carried out by families acting together with much family pride (in Irish: 'mortas cine') and self-confidence, adapting to and seeking to benefit from changing economic conditions but achieving these goals by maintaining and strengthening existing kinship and neighbourhood ties.

However, the advancement and success of such extended kin groups were very much dependent on the failure of other families and kin groups to achieve identical goals. Both long-established strategies and the particular crises of the nineteenth century had enabled some kin groups to achieve and consolidate positions of dominance locally. In contrast, other families for a complex of reasons were left behind in the modernizing surges which characterized both centuries and emigration became the main and indeed often the only strategy availably for the dispersal of siblings and sons and daughters on such farms. Although this pattern was heavily overladen by significant variations in the level of control exercised over land and other local resources, shifting patterns of supremacy and subordination evolved over the generations. The cumulative consequence of such shifting alliances was to reinforce linkages with, or alienate particular families from, the circulation of farms, brides, jobs and privileges which in effect determined the changing distribution of farming and other vacancies and consequently of family opportunities.

The strategy of the Clogheen-Burncourt farmer is to increase the size of the family holding outwards by acquiring adjacent or neighbouring farm units. This 'expansionist territorial policy', and the related tensions between competing kin groups, have very deep roots in Irish kinship and landholding strategies. Mobility in the Irish scene does not relate to farm families as a whole as in Devon (Williams, 1963, p. 48) and elsewhere in England but to the individual members of families. This pattern includes the high mobility of many individual women. The movement of males into non-paternal holdings illustrates one side of the processes of continuity in the region. In this relatively stable landholding system, the association of the family name on the land means that there is little if any mobility of farm families per se, but the imperfections of the family as a means of ensuring biological continuity and other historical, social and economic factors enable a relatively large number of farmers' sons to be established on non-paternal farms. The matrimonial space created by the females helps to shape, complement, underpin and enhance such patterns and strategies.

Most if not all means are justified in protecting the patrimony and thus a wide variety of practices are acceptable. In the still highly cohesive Irish kinship system, the nephew, niece and son-in-law are essential instruments in making for family continuity in family farming. These processes operate in a bilateral way, and even if the family name is not maintained on the land, the land is kept 'in the family' – that is, within the range of the countryman's recognized kin. Examples of cross-cousin or cross-brother/sister marriages are also variations on this pattern, as were the traditional preferential rights of the kinsman to have first option in purchasing another kinsman's holding. It is the strength of this bilaterally extended kin group which gives this society its resilient cellular character and enables many family holdings to survive and perpetuate themselves in difficult situations. Overall, however, it has been the growing dominance of the medium-sized farm groups which has most shaped the system. A process of replacement and renewal proceeds from the middle levels both upwards and downwards in this society as these more vibrant kin groups expand both at the expense of other depleted kin groups and indeed at the expense of their own remote and weaker kinsmen and women.

REFERENCES

AKENSON, D. H. (1993), *The Irish Diaspora*, Belfast.
ARENSBERG, C. (1937), *The Irish Countryman*, London.
ARENSBERG, C. and S. KIMBALL, (1940), *Family and Community in Ireland*, Cambridge, Mass.

BOURDIEU, P. (1976), 'Marriage strategies as strategies of social reproduction', in R. Forster and O. Ranum (eds), *Family and Society: Selections from the 'Annales'*, Baltimore.
COGHLAN, D. (1933), *The Ancient Land Tenures of Ireland*, Dublin.
CURRY, J. (1968), *Ballycastle: A Social Geography of a North Mayo Parish*, unpublished MA thesis, Department of Geography, University College, Dublin.
FREEMAN, T. W. (1968), *Ireland: Its Physical, Historical, Social and Economic Geography*, London and New York (second edition).
Griffith's Valuation Surveys, 1847 (1851), Valuation Office, Dublin.
HANNAN, D. (1979), 'Displacement and development: class, kinship and social change in Irish rural communities', ESRI Paper No. 96, Dublin.
MOKYR, J. (1983), *Why Ireland Starved: A Quantitative and Analytical History of the Irish Economy 1800–1850*, London.
SMYTH, W. J. (1969), *Clogheen-Burncourt: A Social Geography of a Rural Parish in South Tipperary*, unpublished PhD dissertation, National University of Ireland.
SMYTH, W. J. (1983), 'Landholding changes, kinship networks and class transformation in rural Ireland: a case-study from County Tipperary', *Irish Geography*, **16**, 16–35.
Willbooks, 1850–1902, National Archives, Dublin.
WILLIAMS, W. M. (1963), *A West Country Village: Ashworthy*, London.

Chapter 3

MOBILITY, KINSHIP AND COMMERCE IN THE ALPS, 1500–1800

LAURENCE FONTAINE and DAVID SIDDLE

A well-known characteristic of the mountain regions of southern Europe in the pre-industrial period was the regular movement of young migrants who left each winter to seek work in the lowlands and returned in the spring as the snows melted. This response became an established and lasting feature of the economies of upland areas from the period of demographic recovery following the Black Death. For most scholars the iconography of such movement helped to define the human ecology of mountain areas. In conditions closest to the margins of existence, the main function of such migration, it seemed, was to ease the pressure on subsistence – though those returning might be expected to bring back a little capital to help pay taxes (Dupâquier, 1988; Braudel, 1966, pp. 33, 42, 46, 272–74; 1979, pp. 78, 79; 1990, pp. 244, 301, 302, 509, 510; Le Roy Ladurie, 1966, pp. 98–102; Hufton, 1974, p. 72; Poitrineau, 1981; Perrel, 1966; Moch, 1983, pp. 33, 34; Viazzo, 1989, chs 1–6).[1]

Recent demographic research reveals that this regular movement was certainly significant, leaving its mark on the periodicity of marriages and births, as young men left in the autumn and returned again in the spring. In some circumstances it may also have regulated fertility (Maistre and Maistre, 1986, p. 101; Jones, 1990; Reher, 1990, ch. 3). It seems at least reasonable to infer, however, that such seasonal movements were no more than a minor brake on increasing population. When harvests were good, these healthy mountain environments, perhaps isolated from the worst effects of epidemics and plagues which affected lowland areas, developed demographic regimes characterized by relatively high nuptiality, potentially high fertility, good life expectancy and relatively low death rates (Jones, 1990; Collomp, 1988; 1984, pp. 145–70; Viazzo, 1989, pp. 215–19).[2] While it is wise to remain cautious about this kind of generalization, these populations certainly had the potential to expand quite rapidly during periodic ameliorations of climate, especially where they were encouraged (or unrestrained) by seigneurial authority. Here they could clear new land for cultivation and increase the size of their animal herds and flocks, eventually to press against the new ecological margins that the more temperate conditions had exposed. In these circumstances any change in environmental regime – a sequence of poor harvests or long winters – created acute stress which could not be sustained merely by seasonal migration strategies. This was especially true when lowland

---

1 Viazzo provides the most wide ranging discussion of the issues relating to Alpine migrations.
2 Viazzo (1989), pp. 215–219, is at pains to point out that fertility levels varied, with lower values on all demographic variables as altitude increases.

areas themselves were affected by a more general malaise and could not sustain the seasonal influx.

Detailed analysis of weather patterns and harvest dates have revealed that mountain ecosystems were highly vulnerable to climatic changes and their carrying capacities were therefore intrinsically unstable (Le Roy Ladurie, 1972, pp. 128–43; Phister, 1983, pp. 291–97).[3] Subsistence crises were probably endemic and conditions generally worsened with the rapid advance of the Little Ice Age from the late sixteenth century and particularly from the end of the seventeenth century (Phister, 1983, p. 292). The problem could be exacerbated by economic stagnation or by conflict between states and the consequent need to increase taxation. Peasants sold off stock and land to meet the increasing burden but eventually, instead of a seasonally adjusted flux of the young, poorer families were left with no option but to sell off their remaining animals and abandon their holdings. In these circumstances, the normal dynamics of seasonal migration were overtaken by crisis out-migration, rising to a climax in the eighteenth century (Hufton, 1974). Poitrineau (1981) has in fact argued that the crisis of subsistence produced by the Little Ice Age in the Alps, the Pyrenees and the Massif Central in the eighteenth century was crucial in changing the social and economic behaviour of the upland communities that had previously long adjusted to the fluctuations of opportunity by the use of temporary migration.[4] As a response to persistent hardship, it seemed that migrants, attracted by the potential opportunities of the growing towns, increasingly stayed away for good. Remittances dried up and communities suffered.

There is strong circumstantial evidence for such a hypothesis. The court records, day books, cadastral records and notarial entries of southern mountain Europe indicate that for many, particularly in French-speaking areas, *absent du pays* became *absent du pays pour longtemps*.[5] Growing urban and metropolitan centres of the eighteenth century provided a new centrifuge which attracted an influx of street traders, pedlars, and entertainers. Indeed, it seemed that it was from this miserable flotsam that the emergent urban proletariat was forged (Hufton, 1974; Roche, 1987, ch. 2; Dupâquier, 1988, pp. 114–24). There is no reason to doubt that in bad times the traditional seasonal workers (on which lowland economies began increasingly to rely) turned into a horde, often referred to by contemporaries as 'beggars, petty thieves, and scoundrels'. The dramatic and often socially disturbing character of such infusions attracted the attention of authorities, and historians have naturally been drawn to their accounts. Certainly the later years of the seventeenth and the first two-thirds of the eighteenth century provided the most dramatic of these periods of collective trauma, and its impact on mountain societies in the Pyrenees, the Massif Central, the Jura and the Alps was severe (Poussou, 1970, p. 63; 1966; Guillen, 1982;

---

3 Phister's paper is a summary of his monumental work on the excellent Swiss weather observations (Phister, 1984). See particularly Vol. 1, pp. 144–49.
4 This is the thesis he presents throughout the book.
5 Reference will be made later to the richly detailed archival records of the kingdom of Savoy, but similar indications occur widely in the village records of Provence and the Alpes Maritimes. See also Poitrineau (1981), p. 45; Dupâquier (1988), pp. 104–16.

Perrel, 1964; Nicolas, 1964; Guichonnet, 1948; Rambaud and Vincienne, 1964; Nadal and Giralt, 1960). It is easy to pick up the disparagement with which such migrants were treated from the official records of receiving areas, and it is an attitude reflected in the tone of scholarly treatment of such evidence (Poitrineau, 1981, pp. 51, 61–65). It is this interpretation which allowed Braudel (1966, p. 46) to refer to mountain areas as 'human factories' (*fabriques d'hommes à l'usage d'autrui*), pumping out their surplus populations to clutter the highways and fill the streets and alleyways of the growing towns. Their numbers certainly increased during the seventeenth and particularly the eighteenth century (Poitrineau, 1981, pp. 25–68).

This impression of a regular seasonal overflow punctuated by perhaps lengthy periods of total haemorrhage was further encouraged by historical anthropologists who concentrated attention on the basically subsistent (*closed corporate*) upland societies whose isolation left them constantly teetering on the edge of ecological and demographic breakdown.[6] If one adds to the picture of bad seasons and crop failures indicated above, the growing power of emergent centralized states to extract taxes, the pressure of church and petty nobility on the peasant population and the influence of a widening economy to depress local cereal prices, then the argument for the pattern of upland migration gradually dominated by immiseration is not difficult to sustain. It also makes it possible to interpret migration behaviour simply in terms of an increasingly permanent exodus of the upland poor which eventually made up an increasing proportion of the proletariat of the growing towns. Such a view still dominates interpretation of the character of mountain economies by European historians.[7] This attitude obtains even among regional scholars who draw on local archival sources.

The historians of Savoy, for example, provide striking local evidence for this pattern of responses. They are almost unanimous in two opinions: the generally poor state of the local economy in the seventeenth and eighteenth centuries and the significance of crisis out-migration as a dimension of that condition (Devos and Grosperrin, 1985, pp. 497–501; Guichonnet, 1975; Veyret, 1972; Maistre and Maistre, 1986, pp. 24–31; Nicholas, 1978, Vol. 2, pp. 559–75; Vermale, 1911).[8] The case for a fragile economy is in fact a strong one. Agriculture was stagnant and could not sustain population increases. New higher yielding crops such as maize and potatoes did not begin to appear until the end of the eighteenth century. The effects of shortened seasons of the Little Ice Age outlined above, may have been partly responsible for the sequences of bad years spasmodically until the end of the 1780s. The periods 1709–12, 1739–41, 1766–74, 1778–80 and 1788–89 were particularly bad, causing

---

6 This notion of communities living as near as possible to conditions of a closed homeostatic system was developed by anthropologist E. R. Wolf from experience first in tropical highlands. See Wolf (1955; 1957; 1986). His work with Cole on Alpine closed corporate communities is to be found in Cole and Wolf (1974). See also Burns (1961; 1963); Netting (1981), though more demographically respectable, is strongly in this tradition.
7 This is the main thesis of Moch (1983).
8 It should be noted however that Guichonnet (1975) and Veyret (1972) challenge the view that the Savoyard diaspora was quite so dramatic.

marked fluctuations in grain prices (see Fig. 10) (Devos and Grosperrin, 1985, p. 500). Nicholas identifies the latter half of the century as being characterized by cattle plagues, storms and floods and long winters producing a 'profound misery' (Nicholas, 1978, p. 574). Military activity, including the invasion by Spain during the 1740s, increasing taxation by both church and state added to the general malaise. Most significantly, the tax on all land introduced after the Grand Cadastration of 1728–30 (*Cadastre Sarde*) trapped peasants in a new form of expropriation (Bruchet, 1894; 1896b; Guichonnet, 1955; Veysierre et al., 1981). From the mid-sixteenth century, state taxation on salt was the chief source of revenue and it had proved rather easily avoidable. In a region where peasant ownership of land was almost universal, the tax on land was immediately more effective. It raised state taxation levels for all families by at least 18 per cent. These were added to those other taxes of the church and local nobility which contributed a further 10 per cent to their burdens (Bruchet, 1908). Indeed, Maistre and Maistre (1986, p. 30) argue that taxes absorbed 44 per cent of the net annual agricultural revenue in this period. According to Bruchet (1908), the resulting disaffection was the main cause of crisis emigration and was in fact instrumental in the abolition of noble privilege in 1756.

There is little or no evidence that the local economy expanded to meet the challenges of such changes. Urban centres in Savoy showed few indications of advance through industrial or commercial activity during the century (Devos and Grosperrin, 1985, pp. 515–25), though Nicholas demonstrates an upturn in prices of land, fatstock and grain in the last three decades of the *ancien régime*. This he attributes less

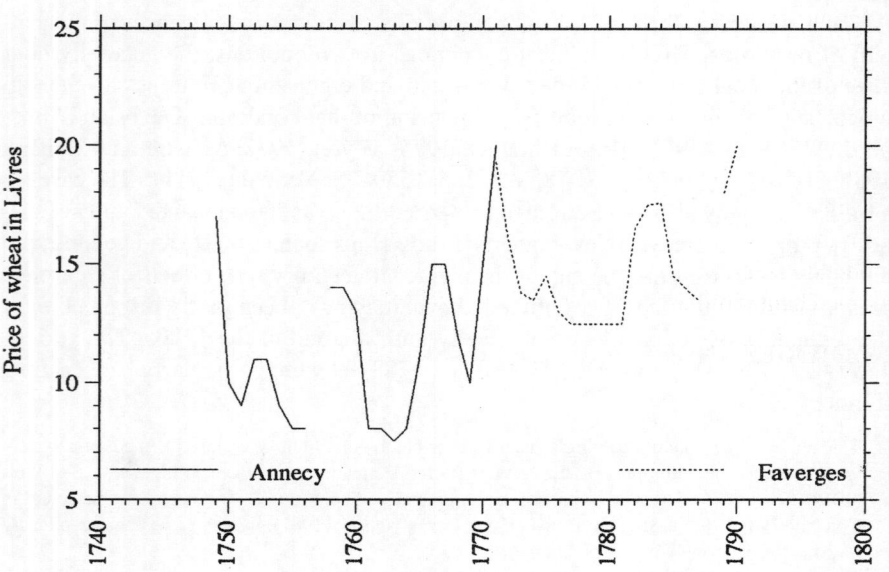

Figure 10: Wheat price series for Annecy and Faverges, Savoy, 1740–1800
Source: ADHS.6C

to the abolition of feudal dues, as Bruchet does, than to the reduction of interest rates by a fifth to 5 per cent (Nicholas, 1978, pp. 707–09). He argues, however, that this merely produced an increase in population and that these reforms were not sufficient to change the general character of a stagnant economy (Nicholas, 1978, pp. 494, 710–11). So there seemed plenty of reasons to justify out-migration figures of the kind first quoted by Bruchet and often repeated by local historians, of up to 40,000 Savoyards a year moving in and out of the country during the latter part of the eighteenth century (Bruchet, 1894, p. 256). Though usually admitting the difficulty of giving a true estimate of the effects of out-migration, a general consensus is that no less than 10 per cent of the male population of Savoy was involved in out-migration at any one time during the seventeenth and eighteenth centuries.[9]

Clearly, local situations were always going to be exaggerated when the aim of reporters was a reduction in the burden of taxation. Some population historians have certainly challenged this very gloomy picture of a shattered ecological equilibrium and a general diaspora of the dispossessed (Guichonnet, 1975; Lichtenberger, 1975, p. 7; Veyret, 1972, pp. 80–83).[10] The purpose of this chapter is to show that this perspective represents a very limited view of the dynamics of pre-industrial Alpine economies. Indeed there are some indications that a good deal more money was circulating in the local economy than the circumstances outlined above should allow. It might be argued that an increase in land prices of never less than 25 per cent and doubling in some areas over the course of the century, accompanied by a similar rise in the value of cattle sales in the local markets after 1760, could not merely be the product of the abolition of seigneurial dues and a reduction in interest rates. Nor was this due to the wealthier elements in village families buying up the land from those who sold out to pay taxes (Nicholas, 1978, pp. 744–48). Indeed, these discrepancies remain sufficiently marked to appear contradictory. Our examination of the evidence of probate inventories and dowry settlements, family and business archives, both in Savoy and Dauphiné, indicate that the picture of closed peripheral mountain economies in a delicate balance with limited local resources and prey to demographic crises is very partial. We turn first to the indications of increasing capital wealth as evidenced in dowry and probate records for Savoy. We then turn to an examination of the argument for a spread of commercial activity in and through mountain areas, of the links with lowland and urban regions and the role of particular merchant families and kinship networks as instruments of this process.

DOWRIES AND PROBATE INVENTORIES AS INDICES OF WEALTH

If more wealth were circulating in the peasant economy as a whole than appeared in official statistics, then it would be surprising if this economic behaviour did not reflect itself in the composition of dowries and in probate inventories. Used with circumspection, this evidence can give a much clearer view of the state of peasant family

9 Maistre and Maistre (1986), pp. 16–19 indicate that in some upland parishes the proportion of permanent out-migrants reached almost 50 per cent of the population at this time.
10 Viazzo (1989, pp. 38–45) provides an excellent summary of this critique and outlines the demographic implications of such reservations.

economies than that provided by taxation (Daumard and Furet, 1959; Daumard, 1962). Two aspects of dowry provision signal changes in wealth: the quality and number of items in the trousseau and the capital sum given to the husband (or husband's family). In Savoy, the giving of dowries was a universal aspect of marriage contracting (Devos, 1975a; Chevallier, 1953; Perouse, 1914). What is more, all contracts were recorded by notaries and entered into the annual registers (*tabellions*) which were kept in the administrative centre of each district (*mandement*). For the eighteenth century, most of these carefully indexed registers survive.[11] For the poorest families, or in the case of widow remarriage, goods in kind (a goat, sheep or cow, sometimes even a house) were offered instead of money, but in most cases capital sums were included. These reflected the prestige of the family of the bride.

It is useful to begin by comparing the dowry data for the *mandement* of Faverges with those for Thônes presented by Nicholas.[12] Nicholas, whose main concern was not peasant incomes but social status as a whole, nevertheless examined (amongst other items) 266 peasant dowries for the rural and largely upland *mandement* of Thônes in the sub-Alpine limestone region of northern Savoy (Haute Savoie) for the five years 1721–25 and 251 dowries for the period 1781–85 (Nicholas, 1978, pp. 60–62, 780). For the first period he distinguished a mean dowry of 265 livres, with 92 per cent of all dowries being less than 500 livres.[13] A dowry of 200 livres represented the value of four cows and two goats. Only when a peasant owned twice that number of animals, Nicholas suggests, was he achieving a level of modest ease (*aisance*). On the basis of the evidence for adverse conditions outlined above, he argues for, at most, a steady state in peasant fortunes between 1720 and 1780 and that only the changing economic circumstances of the last decade of the *ancien régime* increased the mean value of dowries to 350 livres (though 89 per cent were still below 700 livres, which by then 'marked the lower level of *aisance*' [Nicholas, 1978, p. 780]). Even a casual preliminary examination of dowry arrangements for the *mandement* of Faverges, immediately to the south of Thônes, indicated that things were not so simple.[14] There were too many well-founded peasant dowries in the 1740s and 1750s to conform with Nicholas' judgement. Accordingly a full search was made through the well-indexed records of the nine parishes of Faverges. The 3,000 marriage contracts (1700–89) which were tabulated and analysed[15] revealed a rather different picture. In the first place, despite the impact of immiseration and the rising tide of crisis out-migration, the number of marriage arrangements recorded in the notarial registers actually varied very little over the period, from a mean of 42 per annum for the first decade of the century to 38 per annum in the period between 1780 and

11 Archives Départmentalese de Haute Savoie (ADHS) Series 6 C.
12 Evidence used by Nicholas (1978, pp. 60–62, 780) but only for the first quarter of the century.
13 One livre Piedmont was worth slightly less than the French livre at this time (see Vermale [1911] p. 334).
14 The *tabellions* for Faverges are in a continuous series from 1700 to 1789, with one missing volume – the one for 1756.
15 Faverges, Viuz, Giez, Cons, St Ferreole, Marlens, Hery Ugine, Serreval, Montmin. The area of the district spans the Bornes and Bauges massifs to the east of Lake Annecy and includes the trench (*cluse*) separating the two massifs, a very similar range of environments to that of the *mandement* of Thônes.

1790 (see Fig. 11). Here is at least some evidence to support Guichonnet's argument for a less than universal impact of crisis out-migration. Indeed there would seem to be quite dramatic changes in the dimensions of economic life during a century of apparent stagnation. After bumping along a baseline of 200 livres for the first two decades of the century, the five-year moving mean lifts exponentially, riding out variations in the mid-1770s and 1780s to a peak in 1790 of more than double this amount.

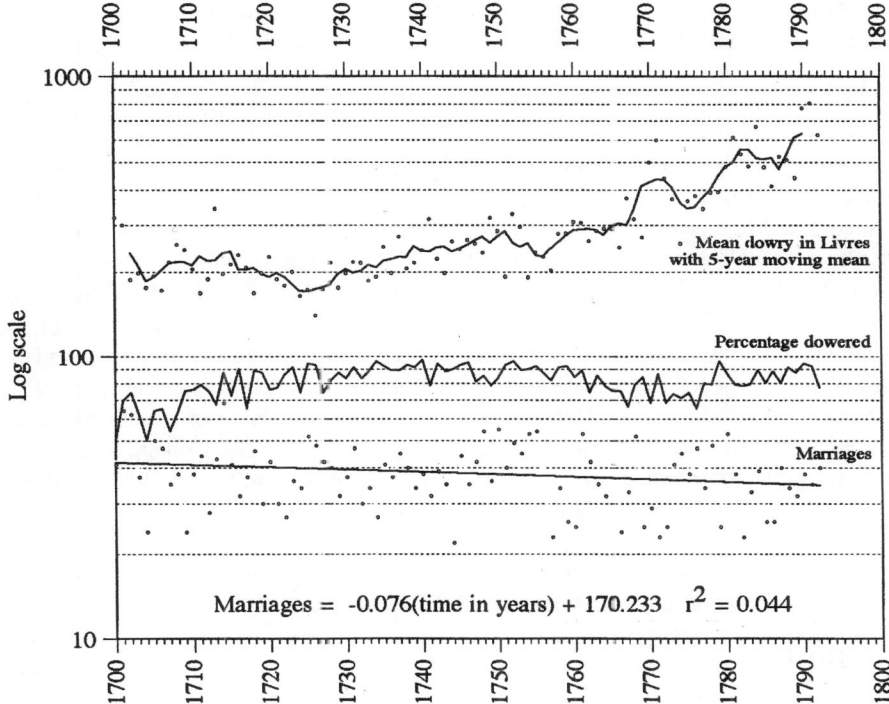

Figure 11: Marriages and dowries in Faverges, Savoy, 1700–92

This opportunity to increase marriage endowments was available, it seemed, to an increasing proportion of the population even during the period of major taxation overload, as it coincided with a drop in the percentage of dowried marriages with less than 100 livres to negligible proportions well before the last decades of the *ancien régime* (see Fig. 12). In fact, apart from these very poorest, probably landless peasants, it would seem that during a period when differences between richer and poorer elements might be expected to increase, the opposite appears to be the case. Indeed, the dowry record reveals that considerable changes occurred in the relative affluence of poorer and richer peasants.[16] At the beginning of the century, almost half the

---

16 Rules governing status were strictly defined in Savoy in the eighteenth century. Titles were always noted in any contractual arrangement. Until the last decade of the century, peasants were distinguished by the title '*honorable*' or '*honnêtes*' (Nicholas, 1978), p. 66.

marriages recorded no money as part of the transaction, there was a large proportion of poor peasant marriages (donating a cow, a sheep, a goat, or dowries of less than 100 livres) and very few raised dowries of over 400 livres. This markedly skewed distribution accords well with Nicholas' data for Thônes. But Nicholas did not examine the data for the next 55 years and at least in the *mandement* of Faverges this picture changes rapidly after 1730. In 1750, not only were there very few who were unable to raise money for a dowry but the distinctions between the well-off and the less well-off had begun to disappear. By 1760 the statistical distribution was almost normal (see Fig. 13). Average dowry payments show a similar trend. Thirty-year cohorts of running means reveal that for each period after the first third of the century, the increases were significant and exponential. It seems clear that not only was more capital available but also it was more widely spread in the local economy much earlier than other sources would lead one to believe. Given the political, economic and environmental circumstances already outlined above, of local economic stagnation and bad harvests, it seems reasonable to infer that the only possible source of capital accumulation of this kind was through the remittances of migrants. More direct indications of this kind of investment are, by their very nature, difficult to come by in official records. But from the evidence cited here it seems possible to challenge the view of Devos (1975a) that in the eighteenth century only the nobility and *haute bourgeoisie* could afford bed curtains, imported silks, fine lacework and pieces of jewellery. Early in the century, few peasant trousseaux included items of real capital value and fewer still of these items were from outside the local region. Indeed, peasant dowries in the early eighteenth century seldom contained items of clothing which did not fit within the local subsistence regime. In these

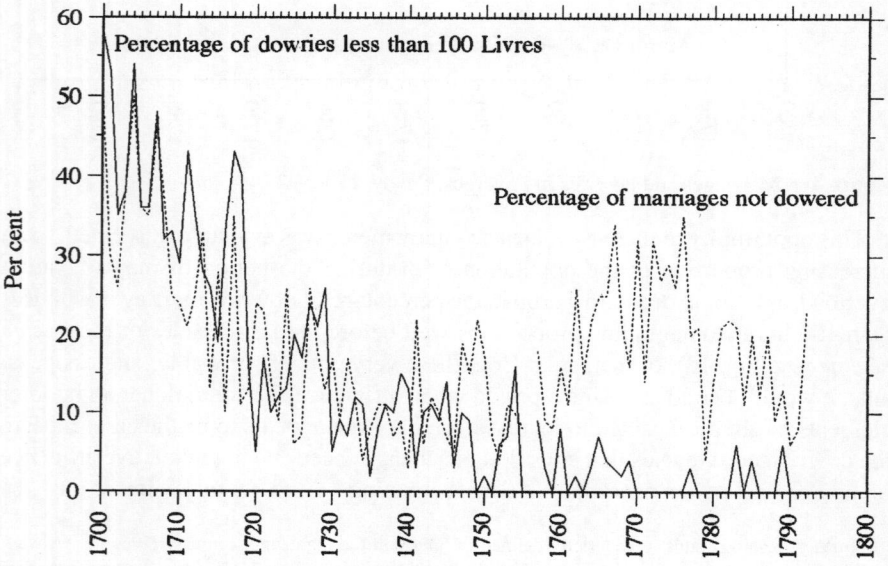

Figure 12: Marriages and dowries in Faverges, Savoy, 1700–92

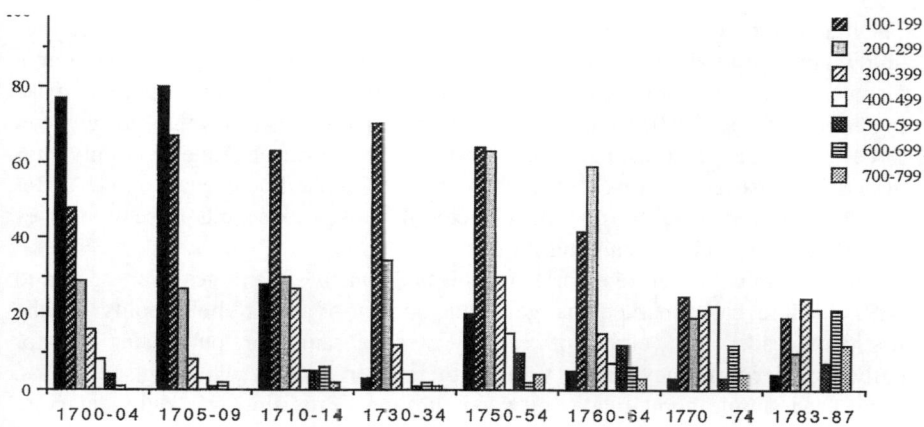

Figure 13: Dowry distributions, Faverges, 1700–87

circumstances, clothing was usually identified by the notary as country 'best clothes' of local origin (*du pays*). They comprised woollen items in the traditional dark blues of country cloth (*commun[e]*), some linen under-garments and traditional head-dresses with perhaps some hand-made lacework and a few home-made lace collars and handkerchiefs. Sometimes there was a distaff (*tour à filer*), perhaps a spinning wheel. Many of these items were handed down, part used, from mother to daughter.

This basically enclosed subsistence world may have characterized the dowries of peasants during the earlier part of the century, but by the 1750s the occasional peasant trousseau was already presenting clothing items of foreign origin. Specific items of adornment were described, like the Faverges dowry of 1753 which specified 'a gold and sapphire broach and a gold pendant imprinted with the name of Jesus' (though in this case in lieu of payments in cash).[17] Thirty years later such features were almost commonplace. Very few items, apart from woollens, were of local origin and trousseaux tended to be much more colourful, less utilitarian. There were foreign styled floral satins, flannels ('*de Paris*'), muslins and serges ('*de Londres*', '*de Vallence*'). Dyed cloths brought a splash of colour to what must otherwise have been a drab uniformity. There were Indian cottons in light blue, claret, red, strawberry, or with floral decoration. Not unusually, trousseaux now contained silver broaches and gold bracelets. These might even be decorated by a sapphire or a ruby.[18]

Peasant probate inventories also reflected the changing circumstances of ordinary life during this period of apparent economic crisis. Here the evidence is admittedly more scanty. Because the whole system of inheritance was designed to minimize the risk of emotionally and legally expensive post-mortem disputes over possessions, official inventories of peasant material possessions were undertaken only rarely.

17 ADHS, 6C, Tabellion de Faverges, 1753, f. 32
18 ADHS, 6C, Tabellion de Faverges, 1784, ff. 79, 84, 129, 205, 310; 1785, ff. 225, 240, 248.

They tended to be associated with three events: the early death of a head of household which left affairs in the hands of his wife as the guardian of young children; a dispute between partitioners; and as a precaution against dispute at the point of making a will (Devos, 1980, pp. 109–22). Moreover, such inventories that survive tend to be circumspect as to actual value. Normally the worth of property is only suggested in subsistence terms ('new', 'good quality', 'mediocre quality', etc.). But even with these caveats, the overall character of peasant household possessions does provide a clear guide to changing fortunes.

Close examination of inventories for the *mandement* of Faverges over the period 1697–1792 revealed marked changes in the content of peasant households.[19] In the first two decades of the eighteenth century, most peasants were purchasing little for daily use. Nor were they adding value to their inheritance by acquiring such items. They used simple home-made softwood furniture. Provision was rudimentary (a long table with a bench, a pair of wooden chairs, a locked wooden box for papers and clothes). Plates and eating implements were also predominantly made of wood. Simple cooking items were of iron. Copper pots and pans were rare and pewter and brass rarer still, even though Faverges was an area of regional specialization in the manufacture of such items. Again Devos suggests that, as a general rule, such items were not appearing regularly in peasant inventories until the last quarter of the eighteenth century, a view that finds support elsewhere (Devos, 1980, pp. 109–12; Tardieu, 1964; Garden, 1967, pp. 153–73). Yet the Faverges peasant inventories increasingly regularly reveal the appearance of more substantial hardwood furniture (wardrobes, armoires and substantially curtained bed frames) and higher grade metal items of good value as early as the middle years of the century. The main point here is that if this hidden capital was available for prestige activity of this kind, one may also perhaps assume that it was available for investment in other enterprises. We must assume that migrants or their remittances may have been bringing a new dimension to the economy much earlier than the end of the eighteenth century.[20] It is here that we must turn to the growing evidence from research on family papers and other notarial sources for the widening network of commercial activity: the circulation of capital generated by migrants which linked mountain economies with wider economy. It is increasingly clear that this played a much more significant part in defining the nature of upland societies than has hitherto been assumed.

---

19 ADHS 6C. There was an average of little more than two inventories per annum in the annual *tabellions* of Faverges for the period 1697–1792.

20 Bruchet (1894) p. 258, quotes a visitor to Magland in northern Haute Savoie: 'Magland is a big village, well built and very agreeably situated, the inhabitants for the most part exercise a profession as traders or merchants in Switzerland or Germany, coming back after a number of years to live surrounded by the symbols of their success [*auprés leurs pénates*] having brought back with them the fruits of their labour. The general appearance is one of an ease and comfort rarely seen around Geneva among the peasantry, where houses are generally miserable, the inhabitants besotted with wine.' See also Nicholas (1978), p. 937; Marriot and Baud (1987) p. 281; Devos (1975b); Rosenberg (1978), p. 52, makes the point that remittances were not so much the product of poverty as a means of combatting it.

REMITTANCES, COMMERCE AND THE DEPLOYMENT OF CAPITAL IN MOUNTAIN ECONOMIES

Most writers have assumed, with Braudel, that the bulk of remittances to mountain areas were the product of the petty savings of the urban poor, 'banding together in their urban ghettos' to save their pittances to pay family taxes at home (Braudel, 1990, pp. 244, 301, 32, 509–10), and there are accounts of this kind in official records of upland regions (Devos, 1975b, p. 295). What we are seeking here is some positive indication that migration produced changes of fortune in the society as a whole.

The argument presented here is that this positive change was brought about by elite peasant families who, over many generations, developed a sophisticated involvement in the macro-regional economy. It was essentially an economy based on trade in easily portable luxury items which developed out of the growing importance of overland trade routes. Its instrument was the population mobility endemic to mountain societies. What we will describe is a set of commercial relations which from the thirteenth century to the eighteenth century developed an increasingly complex web of connections over much of lowland Europe.

George Duby (1968, p. 146) has shown that until the twelfth century the high Alpine valleys were largely avoided for settlement. Economic expansion in the period before the Black Death is evidenced in the growth of towns, the development of maritime trade and expansion in new foodstuffs and clothing. From this time the products and skills of mountain areas became important: wood for shipbuilding, wool and leather crafts, exotic herbs and liqueurs were all the products of areas previously regarded as marginal. Mountain communities organized themselves to respond to these new demands. Livestock breeding grew alongside new practices of grassland irrigation and especially both short- and long-distance transhumance. Mountain populations increased. Barcelonette, for example, in the Ubaye valley is credited with a population of between 3,000 and 4,000 in the thirteenth century, which was half the size of Nice at this time and a third of that of Toulon. Similarly, La Grave, which is situated at 1,400 metres close to the Lauteret pass, was more populous than Bourg d'Oisans which commanded access to the valleys and fertile lands (Duby, 1984; Allix, 1929).

As the wider economy expanded into mountain regions, fairs sprang up to service the trade between mountain and lowland regions. Many mountain valley communities found themselves alongside new trade routes for lighter luxury goods between southern and northern Europe, which expanded with the growing sophistication of a developing bourgeoisie in north-western Europe during the Renaissance (Jardine, 1996; Braudel, 1979). Long mule trains carried their valuable cargoes of silks, carpets, precious dyes, indigo, gold and silver thread along any Alpine route where guides could guarantee passage throughout the year, pausing only for the worst days of winter. Merchants did everything to avoid tolls and customs charges. The more isolated the route, the more profitable it was and even remote valleys saw the benefits of the growing traffic in luxury items. Within such a developing socio-economic system, migration was not simply a 'seasonal safety valve', or 'a response to a crisis of subsistence', the product of 'overpopulation' spilling out of 'closed corporate communities' when times were hard. We would argue that the mobility of men living in these mountain regions was at least as much the product of expanding economies and that they were opportunities which they themselves engendered. If some of the more desperate crises of subsistence produced poor migrants who were footloose and apparently feckless, the iconography of this diaspora draws attention away from the much more coherent process of entrepreneurial activity which operated among better placed peasant families.

It is clear that, from an early period of development, social and economic stratification of Alpine communities took place to the advantage of elite families: clans of long-surviving lineages who seemed to operate in a web of kin relationships. It was a system of mutual support and advantage which increasingly separated such kin groups from the poorest families who made up the most vulnerable crisis-prone elements of mountain society: the land-short potential vagrants who were the bane of authorities. This positive economic activity was the product of the inner workings of the most successful aspect of survival strategy among upland societies: the articulation of debt bonding alliances. This process was one which was intimately linked with the development of sound marriage strategies associated with large households operating within successful and persistent lineages (Fontaine, 1992c; Siddle, 1986a; 1986c; Collomp, 1972). This in its turn is closely related to flexible systems of inheritance. Nominally impartible, much inheritance behaviour in fact came to reflect the position of the family in the commercial network at the time of transfer of property. In Auvergne for example, in many families all the male heirs were engaged in profitable commercial activity. Here a system evolved in which the youngest daughter became the heir! This did not, however, lead to instability. Mountain areas were characterized by peasant freeholding and here the incentive to build a patrimony was strong. In areas where only one or two children could technically 'inherit the property', all the others were still involved in its survival and development. Moreover, the peasant economies of pre-industrial Alpine societies combined all these elements with private ownership of land, mixed farming and a well-defined system of both *inter-vivos* and *post-mortem* transfers of land, property and capital. These usual interchanges between families and in the market place, a subtle blend of customary and statutory law, were mediated by the ever-present notary. This structure of the written law, based on Roman practice, was bolstered by a high level of pragmatic literacy on the part of both contractors and witnesses (enhanced and encouraged by those involved in the wider commerce). It was the framework for a developing experience of commerce, at first local and then eventually regional and macro-regional in character (Fontaine, 1993; Siddle, 1986d).

The system of records, with copies for the family and for the registers of each local administrative region, formed the basis of complicated arrangements of debt and loan, contract and sale and of marriage strategy in which alliances were often played out over a century or more of intricate deals. Working with the day books (*journaliers*) of land transfers for a village community, family papers, account books and notarial records, it has been possible to demonstrate the complex strategies of inheritance, trade linkages and associations which allow for long absences, especially of junior sons. Their place in the process was to earn capital in the wider economy which could be invested in family enterprises or in land on their eventual return to their home communities. Detailed examination of this successional behaviour and the deployment of functional literacy leaves one in no doubt of the importance of commerce in the development of successful elite lineages (Siddle, 1986b).

There is strong evidence, moreover, that these practices were common in most European mountain areas. As Le Play was the first to point out, it was the inheritance systems of those areas largely in southern upland Europe (he specifies the Pyrenees, Massif Central, Bavaria, Switzerland, Italy and Spain) which most encouraged this form of economic activity and others have taken his work further by examining the behaviour of families in the Basque Pyrenees and in Béarn (Le Play, 1871, pp. 30–31; Chiva and Goy, 1981; 1986; Fauve-Chamoux, 1995; 1987; Bourdieu, 1972). Indeed, if kinship and lineage bonding lay at the heart of all mountain economies, perhaps this was especially true in those areas of southern Europe where the old Roman written law was reinforced by notarial practice. Here, attendant levels of literacy encouraged inter-generational loan and deed bonding arrangements to reinforce links of marriage, god parentage and kinship. It was within this context of successful lineages and impartible inheritance that trading activity became a vital mechanism for patrimonial success, releasing active individuals for long periods into a wider economy. Evidence is now accumulating to suggest that this was a process which grew in significance as the spatial economy of Europe developed, changing its character from that of a local and regional dimension to one which was national and eventually international (Fontaine, 1993, 1996).

THE WIDENING SPATIAL NETWORK OF COMMERCIAL ENTERPRISE

It is now possible to propose the process of inter-generational advancement which characterized the more successful family lineage from mountain areas. This process may have had its earliest beginnings among the structural organization of the seasonal migrants who traded the most basic skills of the temporary worker (haymakers, fruit-pickers, cleaners) or managed the long-distance movement of flocks. But such behaviour soon came under the influence of individual entrepreneurs who managed the deployment of a regionally skilled workforce. It was they who came to control the mountain passes and the trade routes from Venice to Spain and the Baltic. It was a tradition that was established in many areas by the fifteenth century (Poitrineau, 1981, pp. 97–147; Fontaine, 1993, 1996).

Alongside the trade routes which developed through the mountain regions, the more successful family groups also began to specialize in certain craft items for sale in the lowlands. Kinship networks reinforced a strong tendency towards regional and even micro-regional specialization.[21] At first, these specialists were based on local

---

21 Poitrineau (1981) deals with the macro-regional dimension of this phenomenon. Detail for Savoy is provided by Maistre et al. (1992), pp. 11–25. They quote a large number of local sources.

skills: flax combers from the Auvergne, masons from Limousin, millers from Chablais, ironmongers from areas close to centres of manufacture or repair and recycling: Faverges, Sallanches, Magland, and Saint Sigismond. These skills developed in response to the market opportunities in lowland areas which upland merchants identified through their migration chains. Gradually another stratum of pedlars (*petits colporteurs*) developed who traded in smaller items of greater value: items of adornment, lacework, silks, handkerchiefs, that could be locked into a portable box. Less casual in their trading behaviour, they established networks and a clientele. Soon they were also trading in pamphlets and tracts, becoming part of the system of increasing circulation of information – some of it distinctly subversive (Zemon-Davis, 1987; Darnton, 1984). If you were to avoid falling foul of the authorities (and for this reason, if no other), it became important to know what you were selling. The incentive to develop basic levels of literacy, which began in the contractual system of village life, opened up the world of simple bookkeeping and accounts. It became possible to develop local depots for goods and eventually some of these became retail outlets in the bigger and growing towns.

Gradually, as successful fathers passed on businesses to sons, trading contacts developed and locations established where larger stocks of trading items and eventually (as banking became more reliable) capital could be stored. Accumulations eventually produced a focus of trading activity in a town which was expanding. Regional specializations developed: choclatiers, confectionery makers, café proprietors from Biella and the Grisons in Switzerland, masons from Lake Como and Tessin and from the valley of Haute Giffre in Savoy who dominated the building trade in Turin and Geneva, literate scribes and booksellers from Briançon (Kaiser, 1985; Levi, 1990; Moch and Tilly, 1985; Fontaine, 1992b). These literate and mobile dealers in chap books and tracts were regarded as highly subversive in the *ancien régime* (Darnton, 1984).

The development of literacy and business skills was often encouraged in their home villages by successful returning migrants who invested in schools, allowed more intelligent operators to become fixed location traders, employing members of their own kinship network as itinerants, as they or their fathers had been themselves (Siddle, 1986d; Maistre et al., 1992). As they prospered they eventually became members of the merchant class in their adopted towns and the focus for an increasing network of contacts – providing for their families in their home villages. Indeed, many made donations to the home churches – adding to their own status with their relatives and often returning to build extensions to a family house and retire to enjoy the fruit of their hard work. As they did so they changed the shape of social and economic relations in the local communities, shifting the balance of power between families and generations. Clever sons first went into the church and eventually advanced in other careers. Sometimes this process appeared spectacular. Baud refers to Alexis Bouvard from Contamines in Savoy, who left the commune as a peasant in 1785 at the age of 18 to become a member of the French Academy of Science and Director of the Paris Observatory in 1843 (Marriot and Baud, 1987, p. 392). The Maistres have used family records to define this dramatic process of advancement for the families of Nancy-sur-Cluses in the high Alps of Savoy. This small village itself produced several major bourgeois families in Strasbourg (Maistre and Maistre, 1986; Maistre et al., 1992).

Detailed analysis of the activity of these city merchants with migrant backgrounds reveals a structure of commercial organization operating on two levels. The first level is a product of kinship and marriage alliances which support a family banking system which often extended, through shops and warehouses, over a vast geographical area. The second level was the intricate deployment of links with the migrant community. This was extremely hierarchical and used the temporary labour migrants, from home villages Credit and loan arrangements cemented these bonds of familiarity, dialect and community (Fontaine, 1991. 1992a; 1992b). Archival sources provide a fascinating insight into this inter-generational process through which individual mountain families established their extensive trading networks, using kin and cousinage to consolidate and extend them first regionally and then internationally through southern and western Europe.

The Giraud family, for example, was originally from La Grave in Oisans (Dauphiné). By the seventeenth century, it was part of a Protestant commercial network which operated over Switzerland, northern Italy and southern France with centres in Lyons, Geneva, Mantua and Perpignan.[22] Jean Giraud, like his father before him, had a shop in Lyons. His father-in-law had a shop in Geneva. Together they were a segment of a much larger network of inter-related families with origins in the same Dauphinois micro-region: the Bérards, the Delors, the Horards and the Vieux. These men were not modest merchants. The Delor family from Mizoen had been established in Geneva for over a century and Antoine, Gabriel, Luc and Etienne Delor, all small-scale merchants, were all accepted as citizens in 1572. Another member of the family, Georges, was recognized as a burger of Geneva in 1597. By the seventeenth century Thobie Delor was a burger of Lyons and an influential member of the Consistory.[23] Village notarial archives reveal that other family members were established in Burgundy, in Italy and along the route between Spain and Germany. An intricate family banking system consolidated capital and each member contributed the best part of his inheritance to the business network. For example, Jean Giraud, his uncle and his widowed sister all placed large sums of money in the Giraud trading enterprise. The uncle deposited 6,000 livres, the sister her dowry, the pension left her by her late husband and the endowment for her children for whom Jean was the guardian. Jean Giraud regularly paid out the interest due and kept an accurate account of how much money he was managing for different members of the family.[24]

22 Archives Départmentales d'Isère (ADI), 1J 1102, *Livre de raizon apartenant à Moy Jean Giraud de Lagrave où est contenu mais affa res emparticulier. Comance, le 17 janvier 1670 à Lion ...* The *raizon* (account book) unfortunately covers only some of his business affairs. These are normally inscribed in four volumes: a main book of transactions (*le raizon*), a confidential record of his dealings with his business associates (*livre secret*), a log book (*carnets de voyage*) and a book relating to dealings with mountain communities of his region (*livre de la Grave*).
23 Archives Départmentales de Bouche de Rhone (ADBR), série B. 8 mai 1690. Martin (1986); Arnaud, 1875.
24 ADI, 1J 1102.

Endogamy was the vital cog in a mechanism which protected the banking system and tied everyone involved into the commercial enterprise. The only compromises in this rule of endogamy were the result of deals struck to gain access to the markets of countries in which they settled. All the above families were Protestants but it is possible to describe similar networking among Catholic families. These networks were characterized by flexibility. They were able to form, disband and re-form in response to commercial forces, vital events (deaths, marriages, births) and the relative fortunes of the members. Specific partnerships lasted for between one and four years. Merchant activity focused on both loans and merchandise.

Few of the group studied here invested in land or domestic property in either their home villages or in countries in which they resided. At one level they relied on bonds, promissory notes and other credit relationships. But they also owned well-supplied shops. According to the inventory made following Jacques Bérard's death in Lyon in 1690, he ranked as one of the richest merchants in the town. The shop contained fabric, clothing, braid and ribbons, and the value of this merchandise was estimated to be 43,000 livres. The combined capital of letters of credit in his chest in the bedroom totalled a further 19,000 livres, making a staggering total of 62,000 livres.[25]

The nature of the network in operation is revealed by the letters of credit. Of the 53 accounted for in the deed box, 34 were signed by men of northern Dauphiné.[26] The account books of Jean Giraud show similar features. Of the letters of credit from 54 shopkeepers along the route from Italy to Spain owing him a total of 11,000 livres, many are northern Dauphinois names. He also recorded his dealings with his home village. When he left La Grave after the Revocation of the Edict of Nantes, 42 debtors owed him a total of over 9,000 livres. It is clear that he traded in items from both the lowlands and the uplands: a horse for Michel Girard; a 'small bale of silk' for Pierre Pic; a mule to Martin Berthieu. For all these men he acted as sponsor, supplier but also their banker (some had accounts in credit in his books) and he took it upon himself to pay the debts they owed to others.

So Giraud stood at the centre of two systems of relationship: the kinship network for wider trade and the village relationship for whom he was a major creditor. In Lyon he was a major merchant but his home and family properties were in his village, to which he returned for short periods. Sometimes the context was not general merchandise but specialist trade. Some mention has been made earlier of the functional need for literacy (the need to draw up accounts and read bond notes drawn up by notaries) and the development of that specialism in mountain villages. The trade in chap books, tracts and pamphlets carried in a pack or in panniers developed into a trade in books. Many of them were banned by the authorities, which made them all the more desirable, and their circulation was eminently suited to the forms of enterprise described above. Perhaps the most impressive were the families of one small Dauphinois village near Briançon who came to control a network of bookshops and book traders which extended from France to Spain, Portugal, Italy and Germany (Fontaine, 1992b).

25 ADBR, série B, 8 mai 1690.
26 ADI, 1J 1102.

The extent of this often illicit trade is made clear by François Grasset, the old chief bookkeeper to the Geneva publishing house of Cramers, who wrote to the director of their bookshop in Paris in 1754:

> The book trade in Spain, Portugal and also for many towns in Italy, is entirely in the hands of the French, all of whom come from a village in the valley of Briançon in the Dauphiné. In Spain, these hard working, sober and efficient people almost always pass this trade from father to son and deal only with their kinsmen ... not only is the book trade in their hands but also the commerce in maps, stamps, timepieces, linen, chintz, stockings, bonnets etc.[27]

One can trace how, despite the dispersion of families and political and religious problems, the ties between mountain families which were formed in the sixteenth century still persisted in the nineteenth.[28] Even the conflict between Protestants and Catholics, which despite the Edict of Nantes (1598) divided both villages and families in the seventeenth century, failed to fracture the commercial links between trading relatives. In fact, the network of merchants from northern Dauphiné which formed around the families of Giraud, Delor and Bérard, was not even broken by the Revocation of the Edict of Nantes in 1685 which unleashed a fresh wave of persecution of Protestants; it was merely restructured. Eventually it was to be reconstituted in the eighteenth century with the printing works in Geneva at its core.

The commercial network was built on a system in which the the fixed points (depositories) of the bookshops were intimately tied through kinship to a radiating network of pedlars. It was this connection, based on blood and trust, which allowed the Briançonnais to conquer an important part of the book trade of southern Europe. They not only opened over a hundred shops (spread throughout Spain, Portugal, southern France and Italy), and dealt with the great Swiss publishers (Fontaine, 1993, ch. 3), but even opened their own printing works, always working as part of a linked system. It is possible to estimate that at the very minimum, they controlled a quarter of the market between them. In the case of Italy and Portugal, this represented almost all the 'new' books circulating during the period of the Enlightenment.

These networks were based on both the adaptability of the circuits and the mobility of the people who operated through them. At the core was the network of shops, each one susceptible to the vagaries of commerce or the biological hazards which left a firm without a head, but supporting the essential commercial functions and facilitating the dispersion of families between the towns and ports of the Mediterranean lowlands and the villages of the Alps. The flexibility of these circuits allowed the circulation of books and merchandise between these regions without reliance on traditional routes and outside the predictive control of the authorities.

Operating together with the network of shopkeepers were the varying flows of temporary migrants. At first there were activities closely related to the family

---

27 Bibliothèque Nationale, Ms. fr. 22130, fo. 37, novembre 1754.
28 ADI, H. 963–968 (Livre de raison de Jean Nicolas, père et fils, de 1647–1677); ADI, IJ 1102 (Livre de raison de Jean Giraud, marchand de la Grave); private archive, the Gravier family; Martin et al. (1977); Maignien (1913); (1883–84), pp. 220–24.

economy which attached young pedlars to their households for many years in a kind of apprenticeship. Then there were the long-distance seasonal migrations. 'Every year', wrote Malesherbes, '[they] descend from their mountains to take their job lots of books to Lyon and elsewhere, even carrying them as far as Cadiz or Sicily.' In 1757–58, responding to complaints from the publishers against the cheap jack hawkers and with the aim of arresting the pedlars who carried banned works, the Spanish government instituted a general inspection of publishers. All this did was to attest to the diversity of the foreign trade in books which deprived the Spanish publishers of business in both the town and the countryside.

Finally, alongside the traders who travelled abroad were the men who came down from the mountains to Provence and Languedoc each year and, among the pots and pans and haberdashery of their more legitimized trade, spread books and pamphlets. According to one authority from the period, it may be that more than five hundred traders came each year to Avignon, and the Paris publishing house of David wrote in 1754 that 'more than two hundred people from the mountains of Dauphiné' came down ostensibly to service the fair at Beaucaire. According to the Paris publisher, it was they who were primarily responsible for the diffusion of pirated editions from Avignon. They certainly sold a wide range of books, ranging from works of piety, morality, law and history to poetry and political tracts. For the official guardians of public morality a good deal of this material could fall within the category of banned works, even those which to a modern eye would appear entirely innocent. The demand for such works increased during the eighteenth century (Darnton, 1984).

To preserve both flexibility and adaptability, each family concern made sure that business knowledge was widely understood within the family. This lack of specialization made it possible for attested 'haberdashers' within the extended family to hide prohibited works within their stocks. There was in fact a rich interplay of reinforcing factors which embraced the widespread distribution of family members and their network of communication. It was a subtle interplay of market constraints, the demands of cooperation, together with the weak linkages in the chain of policing and other aspects of institutional control, which both allowed them to operate and strengthened the bonds of confidentiality and trust between members of the circuit. In fact these haberdashers, booksellers and pedlars created a service network during a period of general commercial expansion which enriched both the elite families in the mountain villages and their clientele.

Below this upper level of operation were the pedlars who carried merchandise from shop to customer. Here too there was a hierarchy. At the top were the travelling salesmen who did not have a shop. Often they were also referred to in the archives as 'merchants', absent according to the rhythm of the seasons; they were certainly among the richest inhabitants of their home villages. The notarial records reveal the essential role they had in linking lowland shop owners and the field they served. The incredible variety of portable merchandise in the inventories of shop owners reveals the character of this traffic. Travelling merchants also kept village and lowland merchants in contact through this winter trade, providing work for other migrants, acting as middlemen for merchants who visited their home communities more rarely.

These pedlars became pivots of the village migratory system. They were held tight into the commercial relationship with shop owners in the towns and were themselves tied into debt relationships with fellow villagers. At the bottom end were the poor pedlars who carried almost all they owned on their backs. Jean Albert from Villard d'Arène for example, who died on his rounds, left 270 livres' worth of goods in the lowlands and 267 livres' worth of debts. In the village his furniture was valued at a mere 50 livres.[29] The value of Pierre Gonnet's goods came to 139 livres. His debts were 240 livres and the city merchant on whom he depended wasted no time in seizing his remaining assets to cover his debts.[30]

The remainder of this village population, the majority, were supported by the elite class and their intermediaries. They supplied them with credit and took on village manpower to service their trading networks. The merchants paid villagers to look after their flocks and herds and farm their village lands. They sold on their cloth and rural handicraft items made in the winter months. They provided liquid capital to help pay taxes and raise dowries. Through these arrangements everyone was linked into the wider economy whether or not they were merchants or pedlars. The support offered to the poorest elements was one function which did not often appear in the records. Only rare glimpses reveal the character of such activity. In seventeenth-century Clavans the inhabitants justified their refusal to accept a change of tax collector on the grounds that the present incumbent gave the poor animals to overwinter and in this way enabled them to pay their taxes.

So it would seem that the more affluent trading migrants from mountain areas became part of an ever wider economy, and it was along the channels that they created that the new patterns of demand began to flow. It is they too who created the means to satisfy that demand by the money they fed into the local trading networks.[31] How then do we relate this argument to the evidence for a broadening base of well-being revealed by dowries in eighteenth-century Savoy, and by implication in other similar Alpine regions? Much of the explanation for this phenomenon seems to be associated with the changing composition of a population which was responding to two different sets of forces. Crisis migration clearly represented the failure of the poorest participants in the local economy, unable to cope with peripheral location and a difficult environment. At the other extreme, the economic migration instrumented by the successful peasant lineages represented the sound management of local networking, reinforced through generations, enlarging such networks and providing positions for kinsmen within the widening structure. This went with long experience of trading and trafficking. But because it mainly involved the more prosperous and well-placed peasant families with large households and kinship networks and reflected investment and development over many generations, one is left to speculate on the extent to which it drew in others who were less well placed in the web of patronage and obligation.

29 Archives Départmentales de Haute Alpes (ADHA), 1E 4839, 18 mai. 1684
30 ADHA, 1E 16 octobre 1684 and 19 mars 1685.
31 ADI, 4E 26 GG9, 13 mars 1668.

This form of successful commercial behaviour among lineages had wider implications, especially in circumstances where debt bonding and networking were such an integral part of both survival and success. Although merchants began to abandon the villages even before the nineteenth century, the fluid social and economic situation which developed in the long years of the *ancien régime* created a dynamism which allowed at least some mountain areas to continue to prosper through the nineteenth-century despite the apparently damaging impact of out-migration on a scale which might otherwise have destroyed whole regions, let alone single communities. The evidence considered in this chapter suggests that while crisis out-migration may have removed some elements of the poorest strata of peasant society – those who disappeared into the urban milieu and had no reason to return – this probably created the space to allow those more prosperous elements to acquire land and animals for further investment in craft and trade activity. But if the dowry evidence is taken into account, it seems that this local activity was less important than the widening network of trading contacts, from which a wider range of people remaining in the peasant society seems to have benefited, providing capital and links with urban and commercial worlds well removed from this apparently isolated peripheral region. If the strategies deployed by the more successful families involved a complex association of inter-generational wealth flows through debt bonding, god parentage and marriage alliances, the whole structure of these relationships was reinforced and developed through the deployment of migration remittances and savings. The families of those who remained part of these networks were thus poised to take advantage of proto-industrial and industrial developments which were to alter the character of the local economies of mountain areas in the nineteenth century.

Author's note: The evidence relating to Savoy has previously been published (see Siddle, 1997).

REFERENCES

ALLIX, A. (1929), *L'Oisans au Moyen-Age: étude de géographie historique en haute montagne d'après des documents inédits suivie de la transcription des textes*, Paris, 150–51.

ARNAUD, E. (1875), *Histoire des protestants du Dauphiné, XVIe et XVIIIe siècles*, 3 vols, Paris, Vol. 1 499–510.

BOURDIEU, P. (1972), 'Les Strategies matrimoniales dans le système de reproduction', *Annales ESC*, **72**, 1105–25.

BRAUDEL, F. (1966), *La Méditerranée et le monde Méditerranée à l'époque de Phillipe II*, 2nd edn (2 vols), Paris.

BRAUDEL, F. (1979) (trans S. Reynolds), *Civilisation and Capitalism Vol. 1: The Structures of Everyday Life*, London.

BRAUDEL, F. (1990) (trans. Sian Reynolds), *The Identity of France: People and Production*, London.

BRUCHET, M. (1894), 'Notes sur émigration des Savoyardes', *Revue Salésienne*.

BRUCHET, M. (1896a), 'L'Emigration des Savoyardes originaires du Faucigny au XVIIIe siècle', *Bull. historique et philologique*, 815-32.

BRUCHET, M. (1896b), *Notice sur l'ancien cadastre de Savoie*, Annecy.

BRUCHET, M. (1908), *L'Abolition des droits seigneuriaux en Savoie: 1761–93*, Annecy.

BURNS, R. K. (1961), 'The ecological basis of French Alpine peasant communities in the Dauphine', *Anthropological Quarterly*, **34**, 19–35.

BURNS, R. K. (1963), 'The Circum-Alpine area: a preliminary view', *Anthropological Quarterly*, **36**, 130-55.
CHEVALLIER, L. (1953), *Recherches sur réception du droit romain en Savoie des Origines à 1789*, Annecy.
CHIVA, I. and J. GOY (eds) (1981, Vol. 1) and (1986, Vol. 2), *Les Baronnies des Pyrénées*, Paris.
COLE, J. W. and E. R. WOLF (1974), *The Hidden Frontier: Ecology and Ethnicity in an Alpine Valley*, New York.
COLLOMP, A. (1972), 'Famille nucléaire et famille élargie en Haute Provence au XVIII siècle', *Annales ESC*, **27**, 969-75.
COLLOMP, A. (1984), 'Tensions, dissentions, and ruptures in the co-resident domestic group in seventeenth and eighteenth century Haute-Provence', In H. Medick and D. W. Sabian (eds), *Interest and Emotion: Essays on the Study of Family and Kinship*, Cambridge, 145-70.
COLLOMP, A. (1988), 'From stem family to nuclear family: changes in the co-resident domestic group in Haute Provence between the end of the eighteenth century and the middle of the nineteenth century', *Continuity and Change*, **3**, 65-81.
DARNTON, R. (1984), *The Literary Underground of the Old Regime*, London.
DAUMARD, A. (1962), 'Structures sociales et classement sous professional l'apport des archives notariales au XVII et au XIX siècles', *Revue Historiques*, January-March, 139-54.
DAUMARD, A. and F. FURET (1959), 'Méthodes de l'histoire sociale: archives notariales et la mécanographie', *Annales ESC*, 676-93.
DECHAVASSINE, M. (1967), 'Les rapports entre le Valais et la vallée du Giffre', *Revue Savoisienne*, **2**, 195-207.
DEVOS, R. (1975a), 'Le contract de marriage à l'époque moderne – XVII-XVIII siècles', In 'Recontres d'Initiation aux mèthodes', *Practiques aux Mèthodes Historiques*, Academie Salésienne, Annecy.
DEVOS, R. (1975b), *Histoire d'Ugine*, Mémoires et documents publiés par l'Academie Salésienne, Tm. XLVIII, Annecy.
DEVOS, R. (1980), 'Les Inventaires après décès', In Devos et al. *La Pratique des documents anciens: sources et méthodes de l'histoire de la Savoie II*, Archives Départmentale de la Haute Savoie, Annecy, 109-22.
DEVOS, R. and B. GROSPERRIN (1985), *La Savoie de la Reforme à la Révolution Francaise*, Rennes.
DOUVILLE, G. (1968), 'L'apport de l'Auvergne et Massif Centrale dans le peuplement de la Nouvelle France', *Cahiers des Dix*, Montréal, **33**.
DUBY, G. (1968), *Rural Economy and Country Life in the Medieval West*, London.
DUBY, G. (1984), 'L'état de la vallée de Barcelonette au moyen âge', *Sabença de la Valeia*, Barcelonette.
DUPAQUIER J. (1988), *Histoire de la population française, Vol. 2. De la Renaissance à 1789*, Paris, 99-143.
FAUVE-CHAMOUX, A. (1987), 'Fonctionnement de la famille-souche dans les Baronnies des Pyrénées avant 1914', *Annales de Démographie Historique*, Paris, 241-62.
FAUVE-CHAMOUX, A. (1995), 'The stem family, demography and inheritance: the social frontiers of auto-regulation', In R. L. Rudolph (ed.), *The European Peasant Family and Society: Historical Studies*, Liverpool, 86-113.
FONTAINE, L. (1991), 'Family cycles, peddling and society in upper Alpine valleys in the eighteenth century', In S. Woolf (ed.), *Domestic Strategies: Work and Family in France and Italy*, Cambridge, 43-68.
FONTAINE, L. (1992a) 'Les Alpes dans le commerce européen', *Itinera*, **12**, 130-52.
FONTAINE, L. (1992b), 'Les Vendeurs de livres: réseaux de libraires et colporteurs dans l'Europe du Sud (XVIIe-XIXe siècles)', *Istituto Internazionale di Shone Economica Francisco Batni*, Prato, Serie II, **23**, 'Produzione e commercio della carta del libro serc. XIII-XVIII', Florence, 631-76.
FONTAINE, L. (1992c) 'Droit et stratégies: la reproduction des systèmes familiaux dans le Haute Dauphiné (XVIIe-XVIIIe siècles)', *Annales ESC*, **6**, 1259-77.
FONTAINE, L. (1993), *Histoire du colportage en Europe XVe-XIXe siècle*, Paris (translated as *History of Peddlers in Europe*, Cambridge, 1996).

GARDEN, M. (1967), 'Les inventaires après décès: source globale d'e histoire sociale lyonnaise ou juxtaposition de monographies familiales', *Cahiers d'Histoire*, 153–73.
GUICHONNET, P. (1948), 'L'Emigration alpine vers le pays allemande', *Revue de Géographie Alpine*, **36**, 553-76.
GUICHONNET, P. (1955), 'Le cadastre savoyard de 1738 et son utilisation pour les recherches d'histoire et de géographie sociale', *Revue de Géographie Alpine*, **43**, 255–98.
GUICHONNET, P. (1975), 'Le développement démographique et économique des régions alpines', In *Le Alpi e l'Europa*, Vol. 2, Bari, 138–96.
GUILLEN, P. (1982), *Travail et migration dans les Alpes français et italiennes*, Grenoble.
HUFTON, O. (1974), *The Poor of Eighteenth Century France, 1750–1789*, Oxford.
JARDINE, L. (1996), *Worldly Goods: A New History of the Renaissance*, London.
JONES, A. M. (1990), 'Exploiting a marginal European environment: population control and resource management under the ancient regime', *Journal of Family History*, **16**, 363–79.
KAISER, D. (1985), *Fast ein Volk von Zuckerbäckern Bündner (Grabünden) Konditoren, Cafetiers und Hoteliers in europäischen Landen bis zum Ersten Weltkreig. Ein wirtschaftsgeschichtlicher Beitrag*, Zurich.
LE PLAY, F. (1871), *Organisation de la famille selon le vrai modèle*, Paris.
LE ROY LADURIE, E. (1966), *Les Paysannes de Languedoc*, Paris.
LE ROY LADURIE, E. (1972), *Times of Feast, Times of Famine: A History of Climate since the Year 1000*, London.
LEVI, G. (1990), 'Carrières d'artisans et marché du travail à Turin (XVIIIe–XIXe siècles)', *Annales ESC*, **6**, 1351–64.
LICHTENBERGER, E. (1975), *The Eastern Alps*, Oxford.
MAIGNIEN, E. (1883, 3e serie) (1884, 2e part), 'L'Imprimerie, les imprimeurs et les libraires à Grenoble du XVe au XVIIIe siècle', *Bulletin de L'Académie Delphinale*.
MAIGNIEN, E. (1913), 'Les Nicoas, libraires à Grenoble: 1608–1681', *Petite Revue des Bibliophiles Dauphinois*, **IV**.
MAISTRE, C. and G. MAISTRE (1986), *Emigration marchandes Savoyardes aux XVIIe–XVIIIe siècles – l'exemple de Nancy-sur-Cluses*, Académie Salésienne, Annecy.
MAISTRE, C., G. MAISTRE and G. HEITZ (1992), *Colporteurs et marchands savoyards dans l'Europe des XVIIe et XVIIIe siècles*, Académie Salésienne, Annecy.
MARRIOTT, J. V. and H. BAUD (1987), *Histoire des communes Savoyardes, III. Le genevois et Faucigny*, Annecy.
MARTIN, H. J., M. LECOCQ, H. CARRIER and A. SAUVY (1977), *Livres et lecteurs à Grenoble: les registres du Libraire Nicolas (1645–1668)*, 2 vols, Geneva.
MARTIN, O. (1986), *La conversion protestante à Lyon (1659–1687)*, Geneva, Paris, Droz, 50–65.
MOCH, L. P. (1983), *Paths to the City: Regional Migration in Eighteenth Century France*, London.
MOCH, L. P and L. A. TILLY (1985), 'Joining the urban world: occupation, family and migration in three French cities', *Comparative Studies in Society and History*, **27**, 33–56.
NADAL, J. and E. GIRALT (1960), *La Population catalane de 1553–1717: immigration francaise*, Paris.
NETTING, R. M. (1981), *Balancing on an Alp: Ecological Change in a Swiss Mountain Community*, Cambridge.
NICOLAS, J. (1964), 'L'Emigration des Mauriennais en Espagne', *Actes du Congrès des sociétés savantes de la province de Savoie Moutiers*, September, 72–85.
NICHOLAS, J. (1978), *La Savoie au 18e siècle: noblesse et bourgeoisie*, 2 vols, Paris.
PEROUSE, G. (1914), *Etude sur les usages et droits privés en Savoie au milieu du XVI siècle*, Chambery.
PERREL, J. (1964), 'Aspects de l'émigration bas-limousine en Espagne aux siècles passés', *Bulletin de la société des lettres, sciences et arts de la Corrèze*, **LXVIII**, 31.
PERREL, J. (1966), 'Une région d'émigrations vers Espagne aux XVIIe–XVIIIe: le plateau de Roche de Vic (Corrèze)', *Le Bas Limousin: histoire et économie*, Tulle, 183–98.
PHISTER, C. (1983), 'Changes in the stability and carrying capacity of lowland and highland agrosystems in Switzerland in the historic past', *Mountain Research and Development*, **3**, 291–97.
PHISTER, C. (1984), *Das Klima der Schweiz von 1525–1860 und die seine Bedeutung in der Gesichte*

von Bevolkerung und Landwirtschaft, 2 vols, Berne.
POITRINEAU, A. (1981), *Remues d'hommes: les migrations montagnardes en France au XVIIe et XVIIIe siècles,* Paris.
POUSSOU, J. P. (1966), 'Aspects de 'immigration pyrénéene à Bordeaux au milieu et à la fin du XVIIIe siècle', *Bulletin de la société des lettres, sciences et arts de Pau,* 4e série, **1**, 99–116.
POUSSOU, J. P. (1970), 'Les mouvements migratoires en France et à partir de la France de la fin du XVe siècle: approches pour une synthèse', *Annales de Démographie Historique,* 11–78.
RAGGIO, O. (1991), 'Social relations and control of resources in an area of transit: eastern Liguria, sixteenth and seventeenth centuries', In S. Woolf (ed.), *Domestic Strategies,* 20–35.
RAMBAUD, P. and M. VINCIENNE (1964), *Les transformations d'une société rurale: la Maurienne, 1561–1962,* Paris.
REHER, D. S. (1990), *Town and Country in Pre-industrial Spain,* Cambridge.
ROCHE, D. (1987), *The People of Paris: An Essay in Popular Culture in the Eighteenth Century,* Leamington Spa.
ROSENBERG, H. (1978), *The Experience of Underdevelopment in a French Alpine Village: From the Old Regime to the Present,* Michigan.
RUDOLPH, R. L. (ed.) (1995), *The European Peasant Family and Society: Historical Studies,* Liverpool.
SIDDLE, D. J. (1986a), 'Articulating the grid of inheritance: the accumulation and transmission of wealth in peasant Savoie 1561–1792', In M. Matmuller (ed.), *Wirschaft und Gesellschaft in Berggebeiten,* Basle.
SIDDLE, D. J. (1986b), 'The transmission of wealth in peasant Savoy' *Itinera,* **5/6**, 123–82.
SIDDLE, D. J. (1986c), 'Inheritance strategies and lineage development in a peasant society', *Continuity and Change,* **3**, 333–61.
SIDDLE, D. J. (1986d), 'Cultural prejudice and the geography of ignorance: peasant literacy in southeastern France, 1550–1790', *Transactions of the Institute of British Geographers,* **11** (NS), **4**, 19–28.
SIDDLE, D. J. (1997), 'Migration as a strategy of accumulation: social and economic change in eighteenth century Savoy', *Economic History Review,* **1**, 1–19.
TARDIEU, S. (1964), *La Vie domestique dans le Maçonnais rural pré-industrial,* Paris.
VERMALE, F. (1911), *Les Classes rurales en Savoie au XVIIIe siècle,* Paris.
VEYRET, P. (1972), *Les Alpes,* Paris
VEYSIERRE, B. et al. (1981), *Le Cadastre Sarde de 1730 en Savoie,* Annecy.
VIAZZO, P. (1989), *Upland Communities: Environment, Population and Social Structure in the Alps since the Sixteenth Century,* Cambridge.
WOLF, E. R. (1955), 'Types of Latin American peasantry: a preliminary discussion', *American Anthropologist,* **57**.
WOLF, E. R. (1957), 'Closed corporate communities in Meso-america and central Java', *Southwestern Journal of Anthropology,* **13**, 1–18.
WOLF, E. R. (1986), 'The vicissitudes of the closed corporate community', *American Ethnologist,* **13**, 325–9.
WOOLF, S. (ed.) (1991), *Domestic Strategies: Work and Family in France and Italy,* Cambridge.
ZEMON-DAVIS, N. (1987), *Society and Culture in Early Modern France,* Cambridge.

Chapter 4

PEOPLE FROM THE PITS: THE ORIGINS OF COLLIERS IN EIGHTEENTH-CENTURY SOUTH-WEST LANCASHIRE

JOHN LANGTON

Coal production started to increase early and quickly in south-west Lancashire. Growth was staggered in timing from one sub-region to another, largely according to when they were joined by cheap transport routes to Liverpool and the Mersey (Langton, 1983). The west and north (see Fig. 14) were largely stable, though coal moved from the former area along the Leeds and Liverpool Canal to Liverpool after 1744 and collieries in the latter held part of the landsale market in Preston and beyond (see Table 4). The first sub-region to grow strongly was the south-west around the town of Prescot, the nearest part of the coalfield to Liverpool, to which it was joined by a continually improved turnpike road after 1732. The south fuelled the Cheshire salt industry throughout the century, but output rocketed after the Sankey Navigation brought complete water access via the Weaver into Cheshire and the Mersey to Liverpool in 1757. Output grew even more during the last quarter of the century in the centre around Wigan, linked to the Ribble estuary by the Douglas Navigation in the 1740s, then directly to Liverpool by the Leeds and Liverpool Canal in 1774. The region's coal output grew more than ten-fold between 1720 and 1799 and trebled in the last quarter of the eighteenth century – much faster than in Britain as a whole.[1]

Table 4: Estimated annual outputs of the sub-regions of the south-west Lancashire coalfield, 1720–99 (in tons)

	1720	1740	1760	1773	1799
West	1,500	2,000	2,000	2,000	8,000
North	6,500	7,500	7,500	8,000	8,000
Centre	13,400	20,000	29,000	36,000	380,000
South	7,500	8,000	115,000	125,000	200,000
South-west	16,000	50,000	55,000	60,000	100,000
Total	45,000	87,000	208,500	221,000	696,000

Sources: Based on accounted colliery outputs and estimates for other collieries working at each date. Figures for the three main sub-regions in 1740, 1760, 1773 and 1799 are taken from Langton (1979), p. 154. Others were calculated for this chapter by the same method. For more detailed information on the numbers and sizes of collieries, see Langton (1979), pp. 83–89 and 136–55.

1 National coal output increased about five-fold in the eighteenth century, and less than doubled during the period 1775–1800. The south-west produced more than half of the Lancashire total, which was 2.7 per cent of Britain's output in 1700 and 9.3 per cent in 1800 (Flinn and Stoker, 1984, p. 26).

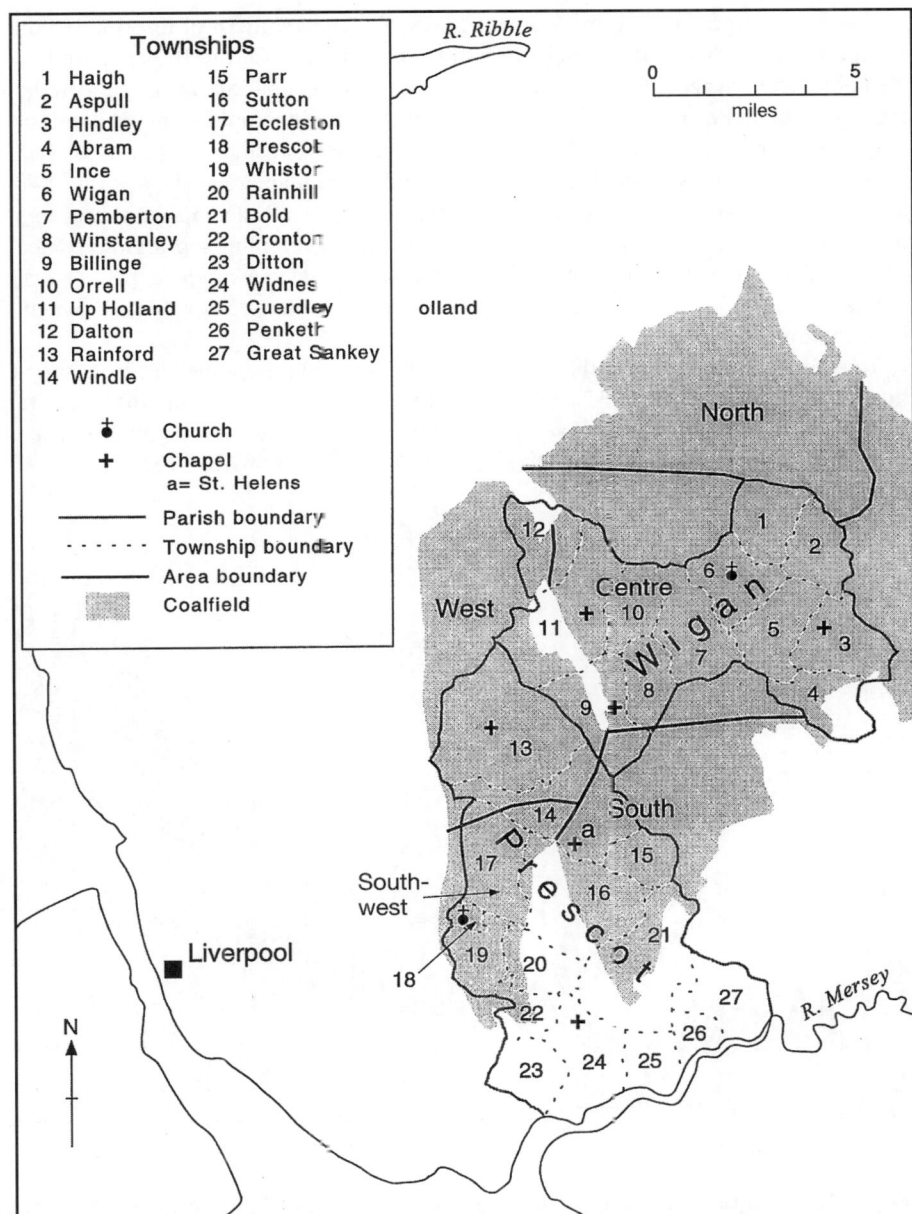

Figure 14: The south-west Lancashire coalfield, showing sub-regions and Prescot and Wigan parishes and their constituent townships

These big surges needed many more miners. Different sources of information on manpower yield different estimates of numbers and trends. Of the 10 parish and 12 chapel registers serving the coalfield, 9 do not include occupations at any time in the eighteenth century. In some of the rest, occupations are incomplete, intermittent, or begin late. However, both occupations and townships of residence appear early in those of Prescot parish church and St Helens and Up Holland chapels (see Fig. 14), and by the last quarter of the century they exist in nearly all the baptismal registers of the two big parishes covering a large part of the developing sub-regions of the coalfield.[2] Despite its limitations Figure 15 shows what we might expect: quick bursts of colliers' children's baptisms coming with the onset of rapid development, then abating somewhat.

To estimate numbers of colliers from these figures requires some heroic assumptions. If the birth rate were 35 per 1,000 and each married collier supported a wife and three-and-a-half children, five-year moving means of the baptism total indicate 115 married colliers in 1722, 200 in 1763, 349 in 1773 and 697 in 1797.[3] However,

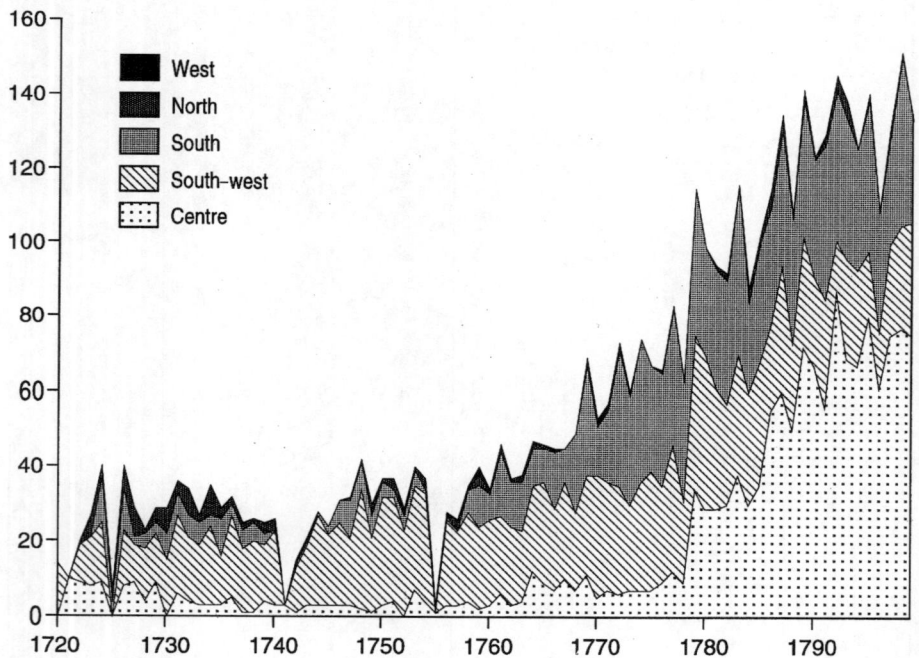

Figure 15: Numbers of colliers' children registered in coalfield sub-regions, 1720–99

2 The registers of Eccleston parish church and Douglas Chapel, serving the townships in the extreme north-west of the coalfield, also contain occupations for large parts of the eighteenth century. Generally, marriage records contain relatively few occupations, even in registers where they are almost complete in baptism and burial entries.
3 There are too few occupations in the registers around 1740 for a reasonable estimate.

given that colliers could be as young as 12,[4] that marriage did not usually occur until the mid- to late 20s,[5] and that colliers generally died young,[6] there might have been as many again who were unmarried. In addition, there were the married colliers who neglected parochial registration. If all these factors remained constant, manpower needs increased by a factor of between three and four, much less than the increase in output, which suggests that registration became more defective over the period.[7] Another way to estimate the colliery workforce is through the ratio between the numbers of baptisms registered annually for colliers resident in Orrell (the most important mining township on the coalfield in the 1790s), and the number of hewers[8] recorded in the Land Tax Assessments of Orrell between 1783 and 1798 and in 1799. Multiplying the derived numbers by 2.5 to account for other mineworkers gives totals of 303 in 1722, 523 in 1760, 903 in 1773 and 1,828 in 1799 – a six-fold increase, although deteriorating registration would make the earlier totals overestimates and the rate of increase faster. Alternatively, manpower can be estimated from output and labour productivity, as in Table 5, where figures for later years are similar to those calculated from the Orrell ratio.[9] They increase much more rapidly than the total population of Lancashire, which grew faster than that of any other

Table 5: Estimated manpower requirements of south-west Lancashire collieries, 1720–99

	1720	1740	1760	1773	1799
West	10	10	10	10	20
North	24	27	27	29	20
Centre	48	71	104	129	950
South	27	29	280	313	500
South-west	59	179	196	150	250
Total	158	326	617	831	1,740

Source: Derived from accounted and estimated outputs of collieries. Outputs smaller than 10,000 tons per year were divided by 700 and larger ones by 1,000 to estimate the numbers of hewers employed. The different quotients allow for greater productivity at larger collieries, which were usually drained by steam engines, and therefore worked more continuously, and employed a local variant of the longwall system of getting. Hewer numbers were multiplied by 2.5 to estimate the total colliery labour force (Langton, 1979, pp. 85–89, 148–53, 255–59).

4 John Goolding of Wigan, coal-getter, aged 12, registered as a Papist in 1767 (Worrall, 1980, p. 55). Of 57 Roman Catholic colliers in the region, 4 were younger than 18. 18 were under 30, and the average age was 36.
5 During 1740–99, the average age of 69 colliers at the baptism of their first child was 27 years and 4 months (Langton, 1979, p. 200).
6 The average age at death of married colliers was probably in the 40s (Langton, 1979, pp. 200, 293).
7 Krause (1965) suggests that to estimate births, baptisms should be inflated by about 15 per cent from 1700 to 1780 but by 41 per cent in the 1810s because of increasing under-registration from c. 1790.
8 Hewers, or getters, cut coal from the seam faces.
9 In 1767, 7.76 per cent of the region's population were committed Roman Catholics, so the 57 colliers listed in the Return of Papists suggest a total of 735 (Langton, 1998; Worrall, 1980).

county in the eighteenth century.[10] Indeed, the more-than-ten-fold increase surpassed that of Liverpool,[11] the fastest growing English city in the eighteenth century, and paralleled the population of industrializing south-west Lancashire as a whole.[12]

To understand how the dangerous and uncertain job of coalmining could attract workers in such numbers when Liverpool, other towns and other industries beckoned nearby, we need to know how work in the pits was organized and remunerated.

PIT WORK AND PIT WORKERS

Annual outputs of individual pits ranged from a few hundred tons at single-pit small collieries to over 5,000 tons a year at large canal-side collieries in the 1790s, with up to ten pits each. Until the end of the period each pit was worked for only three to five years before abandonment, and most collieries lasted for under a decade, although a few in the south-west, south and centre operated throughout the century (Langton, 1979, pp. 85, 147–48). The median number of hewers per pit was four, though it averaged five at the biggest coal collieries at the end of the period and reached over eight at cannell collieries (Langton 1979, pp. 88, 150).[13] A hewer worked for piece rates, out of which he usually paid one adult or two child drawers to move coal in baskets from the face to the pit-eye. An auditor kept accounts and supervised sales, and labourers on day wages stacked and loaded coal on the surface, wound things up and down the shaft, and did underground jobs other than hewing and drawing. Altogether, there were 10 to 15 men per pit.

Men underground worked separately from those in other pits at the same colliery, unseen by authority and largely unsupervised, completely reliant on each other for safety and success. This 'miner's freedom' (Goodrich, 1926) bred fierce independence and comradeship among colliers, who were 'the arrantest knaves in nature',[14] implacably 'bigoted in their own opinions' about how their job should be done.[15] These traits were intensified by the method of reckoning used. A hewer was paid so much for each full basket of unadulterated coal delivered by his drawer, on whom he relied to ensure that an accurate tally was kept by the auditor, who was liable, acting for the coalowner, to under-record baskets or claim that some were not full or

10 Parish register data suggest that the population of England and Wales increased by 57 per cent between 1701 and 1801, that of all industrializing counties by 93 per cent, and that of Lancashire alone by 191 per cent (Deane and Cole, 1964, p. 103).
11 From about 10,000 in 1720 to 77,653 in 1801 (Parkinson, 1952).
12 In Prescot parish church register, colliers' children comprised 19 per cent of all baptisms in 1720, 17 per cent in 1740 and 1760, 18 per cent in 1773, and 12 per cent in 1799. In St Helens chapel register they accounted for 20 per cent of baptisms in 1746, 15 per cent in 1760, 24 per cent in 1773 and 18 per cent in 1799. In Wigan parish church register they fell from 9 per cent to 4 per cent of total baptisms between 1721 and 1731, and rose from 5 per cent in 1778 to 11 per cent in 1799.
13 Cannell existed immediately to the east and north of Wigan. The best domestic fuel, it cost twice as much as ordinary coal by weight. 'Round cannell', carefully cut into large pieces, cost more than 'small cannell'. Hewing it must have needed different skills; only about half as much was got per hewer per year, at twice the pay rate per basket, compared with ordinary coal pits. Cannell-getters were distinguished from coal-getters in Wigan parish registers. No account was taken of lower productivity at cannell collieries in the manpower estimates.
14 Earl of Crawford and Balcarres (1934), p. 10. Spellings have been modernized in quotations.
15 John Rylands Library, Legh MSS/Box 59/Letter, Sergeant of Legh, November 10 1762.

contained too much stone to be allowed. Conversely, colliers could follow risky ploys to their own immediate advantage, but detrimental to the coalowner and perhaps life-threatening to other colliers.[16] Even with care, mining was very dangerous,[17] hewers were liable to be cheated, and all colliers in a pit could suffer if one was careless, devious or ineffectual.

A nucleus of men worked during most weeks of a year, but they were supplemented by a larger number who attended intermittently. Some came to help when work was relatively hectic; wildly fluctuating colliery outputs caused the workforce to rise and fall sharply.[18] However, many came sporadically in widely separated weeks, with no synchronization. Most of the occasional workers were day-wage men. In a 16-week day-wage account for Standish Colliery 1745–46,[19] only one man (the auditor) was paid for every week; four men worked from 13 to 15 weeks, but nine were paid for only one week (some of them may have been hewing for piece rates at other times). In a complete account for Skelmersdale Colliery in 1798,[20] 3 of the 24 colliers worked for 52 weeks. One was a hewer and two were day-wage men, one of whom was accompanied every week by his son. Four other colliers, three of them hewers, worked for 50 weeks, and another six for 40–50. Thus, half the colliers were full-time or nearly so, although the payment of some in pairs suggests that two young people or a father and son were doing a full week's work between them. The other 12 averaged 20 weeks each, including 6 men who worked more than half the year at the pit, and 5 who worked there for 5 or fewer weeks. The total of 680 man-weeks worked could have been done by 13 men: even in a medium-sized well-run colliery at the end of the period, twice as many men spent some time in a pit as would have been necessary if they had all worked full-time. This proportion excludes wives, sons and daughters acting as drawers,[21] and must have been much higher earlier in the century when work was less regular and continuous.

Part-timers might have been shuttling between different collieries, but many must have spent some weeks in the hay and corn harvests, or at general labouring (Samuel, 1977, p. 55). Wills and inventories show a few colliers with a bit of land, a loom or forge; others styled themselves as husbandman, skinner or shoemaker in leases or other coal agreements; some in the northern sub-region appeared in parish registers

---

16 Sending up unfilled baskets or stone mixed with coal, cutting coal from pillars supporting the mine roof or barriers left to dam back water in old workings, or failing to test for or dissipate gas.
17 The Prescot coroner held inquests on 19 colliery deaths from roof collapses, falls down shafts, flooding, and fire and choke damp between 1746 and 1789. Only one of the victims was older than 16, suggesting that inquiries were only made into child deaths (Bailey, 1934).
18 Coefficients of variation of annual output per pit for 12 long-running collieries range from 14 per cent to 67 per cent and average 36 per cent. For pits at large canal-serving collieries in the 1790s, they cluster at just over 20 per cent (Langton, 1979, p. 150).
19 Lancashire Record Office, RCSt/5.
20 Cheshire Record Office, EDC/5/1816–17, Rylance decd, 1816.
21 Women and girls were never listed in wage accounts. Their presence is revealed only in coroners' inquests and agreements about working practices. This must be because they acted only as drawers, who were not paid by auditors but by hewers for whom they worked. More likely, the hewer and his wife or children received a 'family wage' which was not divided up.

as 'farmer and collier', and some as 'collier-pauper' in the south. Whatever their other work, 'a man at the face has to know his place like a mother knows her young ones'.[22] Part-timers had to be fully trustworthy to the regular colliers and conversant with highly localized work-practices, terminology and conditions at the pit where they spent some of their time.[23]

Thanks to the way they worked and freedom from supervision, colliers had complete control over the recruitment of colleagues. Although formally men were taken on by auditors, 'the make-up of the work group was ... the miners' own; they chose their own mates' (Samuel, 1977, p. 56). Kinship and neighbourhood were the most reliable selection criteria, sometimes supplemented by Roman Catholicism.[24] A hewer could best guard against being cheated at the pit-eye by employing his wife or children (from the age of eight [Hair, 1968]) as drawers, and kin were likely to be most trustworthy as fellow hewers or underground labourers. If the chance arose for a collier to put a job or bit of extra income someone's way, he would keep it in the family if he could. Pit closure, injury, ill health from dust and soaking, or early death meant that colliers' nuclear families were bound to need assistance sometimes, probably often. A well-developed system of mutual aid among kin was the best guarantee. It was even more prudent for colliers than for other people to cultivate deep and widely extended kinship networks (Lord, 1993; Hann, 1999).

Where detailed records survive, they show pit workforces shot through with kinship. At Haigh Colliery in 1636 there were four male and three female Lowes, two women named 'Rothwell alias Lowe', and three male Rothwells – nearly half the labour force.[25] In 1737, the Wigan parish clerk recorded the burial of six colliers killed by gas at Haigh, five named Lowe. Three generations of families worked in particular pits in Ashton and Prescot.[26] Of the 20 men named in the day-wage account at Standish Colliery, 12 shared four surnames, and of the 24 named at Skelmersdale, 16 shared 6 names.[27] The hewers in Brook and Meadow pits at Kirkless Colliery

22 Quoted by Benson (1980), p. 55.
23 Many collieries still used the pillar and stall system of hewing, others variants of the longwall method; some were plagued with gas and water, others were not; some seams were under two feet thick, others up to seven feet, and some had solid rock roofs and floors, others loose 'dirt'; in the south-west night-time working seems to have been customary, but not elsewhere; basket sizes and systems and names of output measurements varied widely, as did whether men were supplied with tools, candles and earnest drink or money at hiring, and the regulations, if there were any, operating underground; the names of seams, tools and mining activities differed, and identical ones were pronounced differently in variants of dialect; each pit had its own noises and smells, and some were benign in one but harbingers of disaster in another. For how different conditions required different skills see Douglas (1977): e.g. 'men who had been used to lying flat and shovelling [in thin seams] all their lives found it agony getting used to kneeling up and working [in thicker seams]' (p. 210).
24 The Gerard household at Garswood was wholly Papist. An auditor and seven colliers were registered Papists at Garswood Colliery: about half enough, if the men were getters, to produce the 18,000 tons or so raised in 1767. Some of the 19 Papist colliers in neighbouring townships might also have worked at Garswood. Many other obdurately Catholic landowners probably also favoured co-religionists before they leased their collieries out (Worrall, 1980, pp. 68–69; Langton, 1979, p. 143).
25 Wigan Record Office, Haigh Colliery Orders, End B, Fols 8 and 9.
26 Lancashire Record Office, DDCs/3/39, and Bailey (1934).
27 Cheshire Record Office, EDC/5/1816–17, Rylance decd, 1816.

1792–96 included three Causeways, three Greens, two Millers and two Orrells.[28] It is also likely that, as at Haigh in 1636, some of those with different surnames were in-laws,[29] and that some wives, daughters and unrecorded sons were also present as drawers.

Strong bonds extended from the coal-face into a vast army of children at work with their fathers and part-time colliers. This latent labour force would allow a virtually immediate doubling or trebling of the number of fully-working pitmen (much more before collieries grew large and employment more regular), if enough work were available and it was well-enough paid.

COLLIERS' WAGES

'The outstanding characteristic of the wage system was its uncertainty. The miner lived on a roller-coaster ... [He] would never know what he would be earning the following week, let alone the following year' (Benson, 1980, p. 65). This was true even for hewers who worked every week: water, gas, floor or roof conditions changed as getting a seam proceeded; staunched demand put a temporary stop to production, and its sudden release dragged all men into day-wage work to clear stocks. Daily records show that hewers rarely worked six days a week at Winstanley in 1766, but they almost invariably all had the same days off in any week, suggesting that the pit was stopped, or that hewers were doing other work.[30] It was the same at Kirkless in the 1790s: on average one-quarter of the total days getting, at six per hewer per week, were lost, but three-quarters of this absenteeism occurred on days when no getting at all took place. The rest was due to one or two men who consistently hewed only a few days a week.[31] How much coal was cut in a day must have varied as much as how many days were worked.

Peaks and troughs on the roller-coaster of hewers' wages get giddier as we move from annual to seasonal to weekly cycles. Over a 42-week account for Moor Hey Pit in Winstanley in 1766, the hewers' average weekly pay was 6s 8½d; in particular weeks it ranged from nothing to 10s 6d. Over 36 weeks in 1774–75 at Kirkless Colliery's Engine Pit, the hewers' average weekly wage was 6s 3½d, ranging from 8d in the worst week to 11s in the best. Variation around the weekly average of £1 3s for hewers at Skelmersdale Colliery was apparently less: wages were paid every fortnight and weekly averages obtained by halving fortnightly payments even out some of the weekly variation. Even so, they ranged from less than 15s in the worst two weeks to £1 15s in the best. At all three pits there were deep troughs in wages in February and at harvest time between July and September (Langton, 1979, p. 208).

28 Wigan Record Office, Euxton MSS/6/24.
29 Matrilineal kinship links were probably much stronger than patrilineal ones: a widow's brothers and sisters would be more likely than her in-laws to look after her and her children.
30 Lancashire Record Office, DDBa/Colliery Accounts, 1766.
31 Wigan Record Office, Euxton MSS/6/24, 14.6 and 5/2. At Meadow Pit 1772–73, 24.8 per cent of hewing days were lost; only 5.8 per cent on days when all getters were not out. At Brook Pit 1772–73, equivalent figures were 25.7 per cent and 10.4 per cent; at Meadow Pit 1795–96, 23.4 per cent and 7.9 per cent, and at Peter Hilton's Pit 1799–1800, when 17 per cent of days were lost, one-third of the total was due to one man. All work stopped for one day at Christmas and two at New Year.

Day-wage men's earnings would fluctuate less because their work was more predictable, but more because of less regular attendance. At Standish in 1745–46 only the auditor averaged more than five days a week; two other men averaged more than four days, but half averaged only one or two days during the (usually few) weeks they attended. Of the 14 day-wage men at Skelmersdale in 1798, five averaged six days in the weeks they worked, and only two less than four days. Day-wage men's earnings thus rose and fell like hewers', at less than one half of the level (Langton, 1979, pp. 117–18, 201–03, 206–07).[32]

The wild variability of wages was intrinsic to a set of employment characteristics which gave colliers a very distinctive culture. It accentuated the need for short-term mutual aid between kin and neighbours,[33] and compounded the impact of the collier family's normally ragged, drenched and coal-blackened bodies and clothing to bring minimization of regular weekly commitments for such things as friendly society subscriptions, house rent, or repayments on loans for furniture and clothes. In consequence, wages were often far higher than was necessary, ensuring that some kinsman or neighbour was always able to give help when another needed it. Meagre home comforts and the fatalistic fecklessness and proclivity for 'treating' one another encouraged by dangerous clannish work gave the alehouse a prominent place in colliers' lives. Frequent spare cash funded the violent drunkenness for which pitmen – and probably, as later, their womenfolk (Douglas, 1977, p. 213) – were notorious. At Prescot in 1750, 'taking one week with another, it is supposed that the colliers lose one day in each week at the alehouses',[34] and in 1804 the region's colliers were said to 'idle half the week in the ale houses, which is to [them] enjoyment'.[35] The relationship of danger at work, intermittent attendance, varying wages and domestic neglect with frequent drunkenness ran both ways in a culture in which there was little correspondence between average wages and what would now be construed as 'standard of living'.[36]

The wage and attendance figures demonstrate some other important aspects of colliers' pay. It rose sharply, more than doubling, in the late eighteenth century (Langton, 1979, pp. 201–09). Drunkenness and absenteeism were explained at the time by extravagant wages.[37] Certainly, in so far as valid comparisons can be made, it seems that colliers were paid more in south-west Lancashire than in some other coalfields (Flinn and Stoker, 1984, pp. 388–89), and than other menial workers locally.[38] It seems that already, as in the nineteenth century:

32 A hewer's wage probably included pay for his drawer(s).
33 There is no evidence that hewers in a particular pit pooled and shared out their earnings equally, as in Durham in the nineteenth century (Douglas, 1977, pp. 221–24).
34 King's College Cambridge, Prescot MSS/1/V/38, p. 36.
35 *Remarks on the Salt Trade ... in reference to the Weaver Navigation the Coal Trade and the Revenue Laws* (1804), pp. 23–24.
36 Not all colliers matched this stereotype. Some were devoutly religious; a few progressed to auditor, colliery engineer or coalmaster, and 16 left property in wills, worth from next to nothing through £13 and £2 per year from a piece of land to £36.
37 See notes 34 and 35.
38 Day-rates in the Lancashire hay and corn harvests in 1768 were similar to colliery day-wages at Haigh

> Collier lads get gold and silver,
> Factory lads get nought but brass.
> Who'd get married to a two-loom weaver
> When there's plenty of collier lads?
> (Benson, 1980, p. 79)

This is implied by the tenacity with which pitmen stuck to their job. Seventy-one men were entered as colliers at least once during their lives in the chapel registers of Up Holland before the 1770s.[39] Altogether there are 232 entries for these men, 224 with occupations, 84 per cent of which are collier; less than 2 per cent are non-mining jobs recorded after a man had first been registered as a miner. In St Helens register between 1720 and 1800, 147 men were recorded as collier at least once in their lives. Of their 747 entries, 606 contain occupations, of which 92 per cent are collier. Most of the 5 per cent which are other occupations entered after a man had first been registered as a collier were labourer or pauper in their burial entries. If they were still physically able to do the job, it was rare for men to leave the pits.[40] It was also usual for colliers' sons to follow their fathers – and through a high rate of endogamy,[41] their maternal uncles – into adult employment at the pits. Eleven St Helens colliers married other colliers' daughters, only 3 of whom definitely married men with other jobs, and 39 were sons of colliers, compared with 8 whose fathers definitely had other occupations.[42] The

in 1749 and Winstanley in 1766, and day labourers' rates in 1794 were about two-thirds of colliery day-wages in Orrell in 1795 and Skelmersdale in 1798. The highest paid craftsmen got 2/10d per week, barely higher than colliery day tally men, in the 1790s. Flatt masters on the Sankey Navigation earned £90 a year in 1792, more than an average hewer's wage in the 1990s but below the highest, and wages at St Helens copper works in 1805 were lower than colliers' a decade earlier (Langton, 1979, pp. 203, 294–95).

39 Reliable family reconstitution is made impossible by the incompleteness of the registration of individuals' life-events in particular chapel registers, and by the commonness of particular names among colliers. The 71 registered in Up Holland shared 48 surnames, and there were 4 Andertons and Unsworths. The 153 registered in St Helens shared 73 names; 4 were called Sumner, 7 Houghton, 8 Marsh, 9 Adamson, 13 Cartwright and 17 Greenough. Partial reconstitution is aided by the inclusion of occupations and townships of residence in the registers of these chapels from 1699 and 1720 and the publication of indexed copies (Brearley, 1968; Dickinson, 1968 and 1972).

40 There are 12 burial registrations with occupations for men who were at some time colliers in St Helens: 7 were still colliers when they died, 3 in their 30s and 2 in their 60s. Three who had moved out of the pits were over 60, one of them a labourer of 88; the other 2 died as paupers aged 37 and 45, suggesting that they were disabled before they died. Of the 57 Catholic colliers, 5 were over 60, the eldest 72 (Worrall, 1980).

41 It is difficult to reconstruct colliers' marriage patterns because of the commonness of particular surnames and forenames within families, the comparative rarity of occupations in marriage registers, and the probability that the parish church was a more tempting venue for marriage than the chapel where other vital events were registered. To counter the last problem, the marriage registers of Prescot parish church (with occupations 1722–53 and after 1778) were searched for the colliers who registered other events at St Helens. Twenty were married at St Helen's and 12 at Prescot. Forty-eight other colliers from Eccleston, Sutton, Windle and Parr who married in Prescot are completely absent from St Helens registers, as are the 13 Catholic colliers of the district, though two of the seven colliers with Catholic wives did register.

42 Like their marriages, most colliers' births cannot be traced in the register where their own children were entered, and some which can occurred before occupations begin. It was customary at Worsley, to the east, for all colliers' sons to be taken on when they were old enough at their fathers' pits and paid wages even if there was no work for them to do (Mather, 1970, pp. 324–25).

attractions of mining were unrivalled as far as colliers and their children were concerned: the work some of them did on absences from the pits was supplementary, not a search for preferable work. Given its danger and other disadvantages, this suggests that no other job could match its wages.

Piece and day rates seem to have been highest where development was fastest (Langton 1979, p. 201–02),[43] and colliers probably knew about pay at many collieries through kinship networks. But this information must have been irresolvably equivocal: not only did earnings vary from week to week and year to year at every colliery as well as between them, but they differed widely between men in the pits of a single colliery, and even those in the same pit. The average weekly pay of 17 men who worked for day wages for at least one week at Skelmersdale in 1798 varied from 6s 8d to 18s 6d; the total annual pay of the 11 specialist day tally men, who did no hewing, varied from £2 2s to £13 7½d. The average weekly pay of the 14 men who spent some time at getting ranged from 4s to £2 7s 1½d ; the total annual earnings of the six specialist getters who worked for 36 weeks or more ranged from £27 1s 6d to £124 3s 6½d. A 'big hewer' could earn double the next best-paid getter in his pit and four times the worst-paid (Langton, 1979, pp. 206–07).

THE SPATIAL MOBILITY OF COLLIERS

We would expect the direct impact of these aspects of wages and working practices on the mobility of colliers to be profound, but in a number of conflicting ways. A man with a getting place in a pit would be likely to stay there. So would his only or eldest son, who could expect to succeed him as a hewer – sooner rather than later with high rates of mortality and injury. If a colliery expanded by digging extra pits, or a new one opened nearby, the large latent local labour force would be sucked powerfully in. Some journeys to work were a few miles long (Langton, 1979, p. 295) and colliers were far more concentrated in particular parts of Wigan and what became St Helens than there was colliery employment for them. These circumstances would be conducive to a residentially stable labour force, and so might the importance of kin in colliers' lives and stricter operation of the poor and settlement laws (Taylor, 1976).[44]

On the other hand most colliers, especially youths and part-timers, would be likely to move if hewing or closer to full-time day work became available elsewhere, and the short lives of pits and many collieries meant that getters must sometimes migrate to continue their lucrative job. At the outset, new collieries did not have established

---

43 Probably because coal prices reflected the strength of demand, and wages were (roughly) kept in proportion with prices. The comparison of wages is fraught with danger because *rates* of pay were not necessarily paralleled by *earnings*, and because the incidence of fines for bad work varied from colliery to colliery, as did whether earnest money, drink and tobacco were given on hiring, or compensation to injured men or colliers' widows, and whether tools and candles were provided free.

44 People who could not support themselves were entitled to poor relief from their place of 'settlement', generally their own or their husband's parish of birth or one in which he had subsequently earned the right by completing an annual contract of employment. In northern England the units of organization for poor relief were townships, not parishes. The abandonment of bonded hiring, in which colliers contracted to work for a coalmaster for a year, in south-west Lancashire in the mid-eighteenth century was probably because it gave a right to settlement.

family labour groups to confine entry to relatives, but as they expanded to full capacity over a number of years, early in-migrant workers could draw them in from their places of origin, and so knit the kinship networks of colliers stronger and push them further than the five or so miles which was the norm in rural England (Lord, 1993; Hann, 1999). As well as information to prompt migration, they offered material support to pitmen who moved out of their home townships, and thereby countered the effects of the settlement and poor laws. In any event, it is questionable whether stricter use of the law necessarily dampened mobility. The prevention of an in-migrant from establishing a settlement, forcing him to return to his township of origin if he became unemployed, or his widow and children if he were killed and she did not quickly re-marry,[45] would encourage the retention of family contacts in places of origin, but would not prevent movement in the first place.[46] For these reasons, we would expect a very mobile labour force, further enabled by nugatory domestic possessions and rudimentary housing.

Recruitment of kin, high wages, and lifetime persistence and generational succession in mining would also affect mobility indirectly through other demographic parameters. If the industry were stable, successive generations would have to await the death of earlier ones before getting regular hewing or day work. This would keep the average age at marriage high[47] which, with the short lives of colliers, would make their families small[48] and ensure that all sons could follow their fathers into mining. If the industry were expanding, very young men could move into regular work, pulling the age at marriage down[49] and family size and the rate of reproduction up.[50] Because boys barely into their teens worked as getters and colliers favoured their kin in recruiting extra labour, the impact of expansion in coal output on the demography of collier families was dramatic, quickly increasing the latent labour force, to man further expansion. Again, the effect on mobility would be two-edged: on the one hand the amount of in-migration needed to work extra pits would be diminished, but if expansion in an area ceased, out-migration would be necessary for children to enter the pits.

---

45 The early death of colliers left many widows, who seem often to have married other pitmen. Of the 69 St Helens colliers married in Prescot parish church 1722–52 and 1778–1799, nine wed widows.
46 Taylor (1991) argues that it was common for home-townships to send relief payments to overseers of the poor in the township to which the person concerned had moved, rather than for him to return.
47 No age at marriage is calculable for colliers in Up Holland, where the industry was quite stable during the period for which entries were abstracted, but the average age of 30 colliers at the baptism of their first child was nearly 30 years, suggesting an average age at marriage of about 28.
48 The average number of baptisms for 68 Up Holland colliers was 3.3, with an average interval of 2.4 years. Incomplete registration makes the first figure an under- and the second an over-estimate.
49 In St Helens, where output was buoyant in the first half of the eighteenth century and expanded rapidly after 1757, the average age at marriage of 25 colliers was 24 years and six months; that of 13 of their wives was 24 years and three months; that of 11 colliers' daughters who married colliers was 22 years and six months; and that of 15 colliers' daughters who did not definitely marry colliers was 28 years and nine months. Omitting two second marriages, 22 Catholic colliers were on average 1.95 years older than their wives.
50 The average number of baptisms per collier family in St Helens was 4.24, and the average interval between baptisms 2.35 years. There is no reason why registration should be less defective than in Up Holland.

There is no Lancashire survey like that which shows 30 per cent of north-eastern pitmen changing colliery from year to year (Gill and Burke, 1987, p. 42). However, various snippets of evidence indicate what we would expect: some geographically stable families within a whirl of movement by others. Of the 57 colliers listed as Papists in 1767, 26 had spent the whole of their lives in the townships where they then lived, and although none of those in townships near St Helens registered any events at their local Anglican chapel, they had names in common with other colliers there. Information on length of residence is available for 17 Catholic collier couples.[51] Six of the eight non-migrant husbands had wives who had also spent all their lives in the same township. In six couples the man moved to the township where his wife had always lived (one of the two migrant wives went to join a widowed mother-in-law). Thus, amongst the Catholics, only 5 of 17 colliers' wives had not spent the whole of their lives in one township: 12 husbands had moved to join their wives' kin in the pits.[52] Even though a wife took her husband's place of settlement if he became unable to work, matrilocal marriage was a logical response to the danger and earning pattern of pitwork, and a likely cause of collier migration. Of the three couples in which both partners changed township, two comprised husbands and wives who had moved at the same time, probably after marriage.

Statistics for the partially reconstituted collier families show similar patterns. Perhaps because non-Catholics were much thicker on the ground, township endogamy was even more prevalent: 20 of 79 St Helens collier couples were 'both of this parish'; in 43 the bride and groom were from the same township, and in 14 from adjacent ones. Only two couples came together over longer distances, which in neither case could have exceeded three miles. Many collier families formed dynasties in particular townships. In the Up Holland register, four called Unsworth clocked up 22 entries between them over three generations, all while resident in Winstanley. In St Helens, where the industry was larger and expanding, there were more dynastic families: indeed, colliers with the same name were so common that it is impossible to draw reliable family trees.[53] Three Adamsons accumulated 30 entries while resident as adults only in Parr, though one was born and died in Sutton; two other collier Adamsons were born and died in Sutton and registered 12 other times while living there, and four times from Parr. The Greenoughs also spanned three generations in Parr, where eight of them registered on 33 occasions. One of them was born and another died in Sutton, where another, born in Parr, had his own five children; another appeared five times resident only in Windle. Of the 13 Greenoughs, 10 lived in only one township while registering baptisms and burials of children, the three others shuttling between Eccleston, Sutton, Windle and Parr.[54] Of the 57 colliers

51 Man and wife were listed only if they were both Papists, and length of residence was omitted for some.
52 Although one entered his current township aged three, the others who moved to townships where their wives had always lived did so aged 20, 22, 23, 24 and 30, when their wives were 18, 18, 24, 23 and 30, suggesting that the men's moves were related to marriage.
53 For an attempt to do so for three families over four generations, see Langton (1979), p. 196.
54 Besides these two families there were 11 Cartwrights who registered 82 times between them; seven Marshes with 28 entries; seven Houghtons with 25; four Sumners with 32; and four Swifts with 26.

using Up Holland chapel, 5 moved twice between townships in the course of registering their childrens' events and 7 once; of the 29 for whom birth and adult entries are present, 14 were born in a different township from that in which they lived after marriage. All the townships registered were clustered together to the south-west of Wigan. In St Helens, 21 of 44 were born and lived as adults in different townships; 28 changed their places of residence once as adults, 13 twice, and 4 three times. There were a number of stable families, each with members who moved around between neighbouring townships, plus other locally mobile individuals. However, in addition there were the 15 colliers in St Helens and 14 in Up Holland who registered only once, and the apparent abbreviation or intermittency of the life-courses of all but the negligible number whose births, marriages, children and deaths were all registered must have been at least partly due to geographical mobility, as they moved to townships served by other churches or chapels, as well as to negligent registration.

PATTERNS OF MIGRATION

Church registers only reveal the short moves which carried people between townships clustered around a particular place of worship, although as on the 26 occasions when colliers gave coalfield townships of residence to the east of Prescot parish in the St Helens register these might cross parish boundaries. They show considerable mobility within highly circumscribed areas, with a few transgressions at the fringes: between Sutton in the south and Whiston and Prescot in the south-west, for example, and Up Holland to the west of Wigan and Haigh to the east. Colliers who acquired engineering skills, as some from a number of the St Helens dynastic families did, were particularly mobile.[55] However, although supplemented by channels into the large reserves of part-timers, children, other kin and neighbours radiating from the pits, which drew locals in from jobs such as weaving, husbandry, labouring and so on (Langton, 1979, p. 197), these pools did not always provide all the labour needed. Sometimes, problems with water or fire beyond the experience of local colliers needed skills from elsewhere, and during the phase of most rapid growth around St Helens, a shortage of colliers and the introduction of longwall getting prompted newspaper advertisements offering housing and the recruitment of men 'who was all new to the work'.[56]

Of St Helens colliers registered in the second half of the eighteenth century, 19 per cent were born locally to fathers in less lucrative menial work. Judging from surnames, some of them may have been related to men already in the pits. Moreover,

---

55 At least 28 colliery steam engines were built in the region in the eighteenth century, most towards the end. Of the 31 men registered as colliery engineers between 1751 and 1799, 24 appear only once, itself a testimony to their incredible mobility. Thomas Tyther moved from Haydock to Whiston to Sutton during 1764–80; John Whittaker came from Norley in Cheshire to Orrell in 1764, then moved to Whiston and Prescot in the south during 1767–71, then back to the centre at Ince in 1783. George Nuttall's movements were more narrowly confined to the Wigan area, but he registered successive children at Aspull in 1790, Haigh in 1793, Wigan in 1795 and Leight in 1796 (Langton, 1979, pp. 192, 199).
56 John Rylands Library, Legh MSS/Box 59/Letter, Serjeant to Legh, November 10 1762.

the geographical distribution of surnames implies that kin networks stretched between most active mining areas of the coalfield, which could be used as conduits of recruitment to areas of rapid expansion. This inference is supported by 29 parish registrations of colliers said to be 'of' distant places (see Fig. 16). Four long migrations from outside the coalfield were recorded in this way, and 25 between different sub-regions.[57] Some were of more than passing significance: Giles Marsh, for example, moved 15 miles from Blackrod, 4 miles north-east of Wigan, at some time before 1729 to found one of the major collier dynasties of St Helens. This link stayed active: Moses Shaw of Parr was killed in a Blackrod pit in 1783.

The distribution pattern of poor law migrants to and from Parr, the most important mining township in the south, is similar and became only a little more extensive in the second half of the eighteenth century (see Fig. 15).[58] Thomas Greenough came to Parr with a settlement certificate from Ince in 1694 to join other Greenoughs already settled there,[59] and a Cartwright and a Sumner brought certificates to Parr from a Cheshire parish and Bedford township, Leigh, in 1731. Not all established themselves so successfully. Parr had a parsimonious poor relief policy (Harris, 1951, p. 121); many men and widows with young children were shuffled back and forth between Parr, Windle, Eccleston and Sutton (including Marshes and Cartwrights). For example, John Travers, collier, of Windle married Alice Arnott of Kirkby in Prescot in 1782; in 1791 he was dead and Alice was removed with five young children from Parr to Windle. A few were jettisoned further afield: Charles Simpson of Parr had daughters baptized in 1747 and 1749; the first was buried in 1748, and on his death in 1749 his widow and surviving seven-month-old daughter were removed to Hawarden in North Wales. Although neighbouring Sutton allowed paupers with rights to settlement elsewhere to stay if remissions were sent from their home parishes (Harris, 1951, p. 121), the Parr overseers were keen both to stop in-migrants gaining a settlement[60] and to eject them if they became, or threatened to become, paupers. They were not the only ones. In 1716 it was ordered that Joseph Lancaster, who came with his father 'out of Crossthwaite in the County of Cumberland to work at some coal works in Shevington', should be removed back to Crossthwaite with his wife.[61]

It was not only the high probability of injury or death coupled with the vigilance of overseers which made it difficult for long-distance in-migrants to get established.

---

57 Colliers registered in Eccleston parish church, off the north-western edge of the coalfield, probably worked in Wrightington to the south.

58 St Helens Reference Library, Parr Poor Law Papers/Settlement and Removal Orders, 1694–1802. This is the only large collection of township poor law records in the region. Few of the documents record occupations, but many of the names are identical with those of colliers at the time, and some can be linked with reconstituted collier families through date of death.

59 John Greenough, collier, of Parr, petitioned the magistrates for poor relief for himself, wife and seven children in 1698. Lancashire Record Office, QSP/823/17.

60 The employer of an in-migrant ironstone miner had to indemnify himself against the labour contract establishing a right of settlement, and many examinations were carried out to prove that the place of settlement of men working in Parr was elsewhere.

61 Lancashire Record Office, QSP/1099/3.

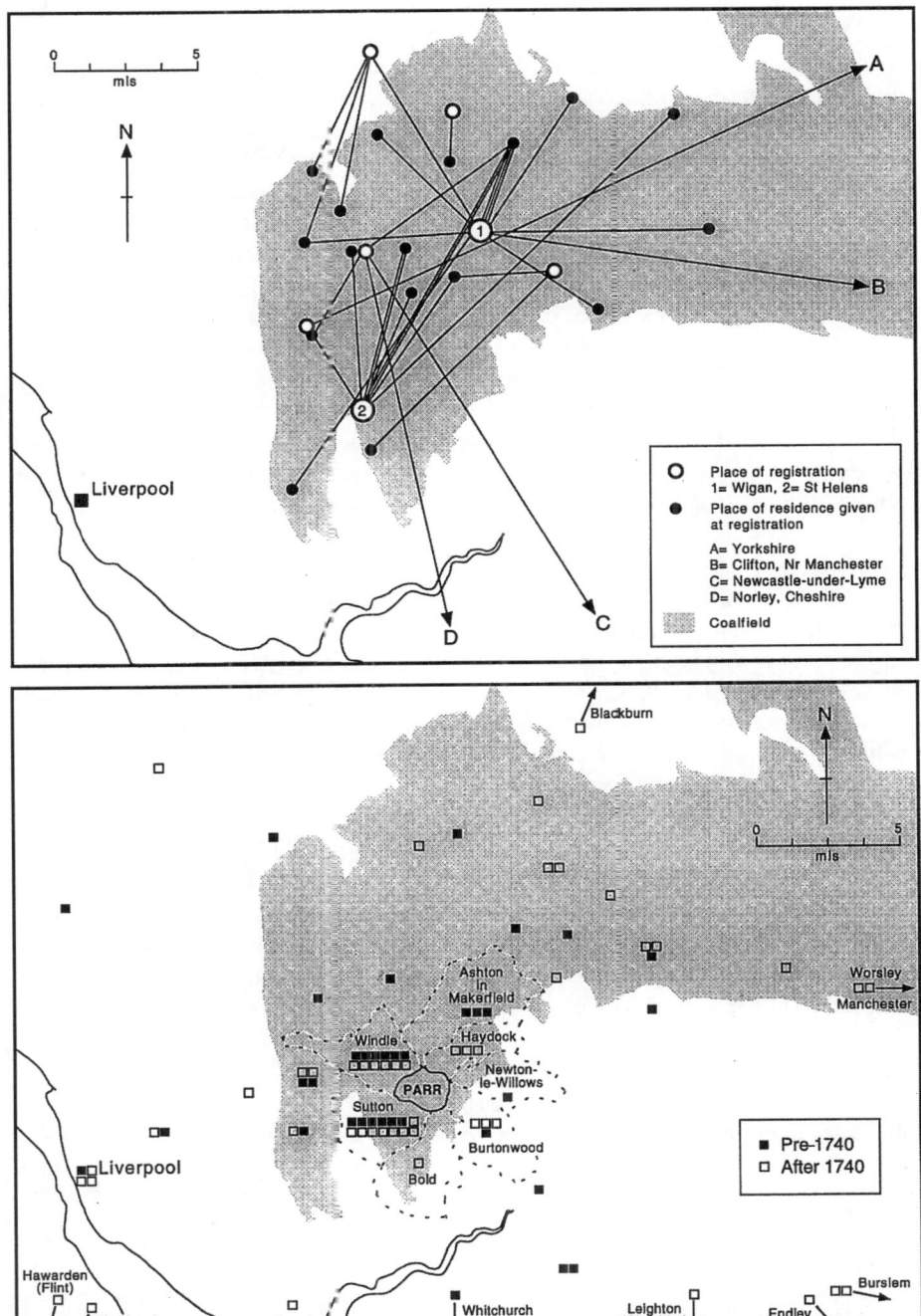

Figure 16: Colliers' mobility in eighteenth-century south-west Lancashire
Sources: (top) parish registers; (bottom) Parr Poor Law MSS.

Colliers treated strangers with suspicion, and auditors were loath to take them on.[62] When it was necessary, to deal with new problems, newcomers must have had difficulty in gaining acceptance. At some time in the early eighteenth century 'the three Rowley brothers of Shropshire' were brought to work the troublesome Tarbock pits of the Molyneux family of Croxteth.[63] Walton parish registered the burials of five Croxteth colliers between 1741 and 1745; all were unnamed, though one was called John Shropshire in the Bishop's transcript. No one had bothered to learn who they were. Perhaps this made it likely that people who did move over a long distance would do so again. The burial of Elizabeth, wife of Robert Lancaster, collier, of Yorkshire in Up Holland in 1713 suggests that Lancaster *père* must have moved across the river Douglas from Shevington, then off across the Pennines before his son was sent back to Cumberland.[64] The colliers brought from north-east England to deal with fires at Haigh in the same decade left no trace.[65] Even so, Welsh names crop up among St Helens colliers at the end of the eighteenth century, maybe through the supply of local copper smelters with ore from Anglesey.

CONCLUSION

A colliery labour force which was growing at an unprecedented and unparalleled rate seems to have been recruited largely from people already involved in coalmining, mainly within south-west Lancashire itself. Of course, care must be taken not to confuse lack of evidence for a phenomenon with its absence. However, even though most of the sources used here are biased towards recording geographical stability and short-distance movements of people, the nature of pit work, the composition of colliery labour forces, and the way they were paid, would lead us to expect that most miners would be recruited locally through networks of kinship and neighbourhood.[66] Notwithstanding the scale of expansion, people for the pits were largely produced by people from the pits. There was hardly a ripple of long-distance migration, but a surging maelstrom of short-distance movement among swiftly multiplying collier families and, where expansion was fastest, other local men drawn into mining, where they stayed. Occupational rigidity within and between generations of pitmen in the region combined with short-distance spatial mobility to provide

---

62 The steward at Haydock was unhappy with his 'strange' labour in the 1760s, and coalmasters in the north-east 'refused several strangers' in 1804 (Gill and Burke, 1987, p. 50).

63 Lancashire Record Office, DDM/4/21. South Lancashire's leading Roman Catholic family, they leased their mines to a Catholic coalmaster and may have recruited colliers through the widespread network of Catholic gentry. Catholicism might account for the brevity of the Croxteth colliers' burial registrations.

64 Elias Lloyd, collier at a Molyneux pit in 1732, had names which do not otherwise occur locally, and may have been the son of one of the men brought from Shropshire. He was a collier in Worsley in 1777, from where his eldest son moved to Hulton, then his great-grandson to Dukinfield, where his great-great-grandson was a pit sinker. I owe this information to Peter Lloyd, Esq, of Great Malvern.

65 Except, perhaps, the term 'marra', a Tyneside pit word still used in Aspull in the 1950s.

66 This was still so in the mid-nineteenth century when the Wigan census registration district, where over 25 per cent of adult males were coalminers, had remarkably few people born outside Lancashire. Census, 636; Lawton and Smith (1953), p. 276.

most of the manpower needed by new collieries, wherever they were opened on the coalfield.

This accounts for the survival of strong regional cultures through the English industrial revolution (Langton, 1984; Langton and Hoppe, forthcoming). Indeed, it demonstrates how regional culture could be *synthesized in* industrialization; how kinship and other ethnographic attributes were strengthened and almost undiluted from outside. Almost the whole stimulus of rapid economic growth reverberated within a surprisingly circumscribed population. This added cultural flavour by injecting large, if irregular and uncertain, doses of money into a small body of people whose lifestyle could hardly accommodate a rising 'standard of living'. However, it was readily able to produce not only greater drunkenness, gambling and idleness, but also an instant rapid demographic expansion through a rise in the rate and fall in the hitherto high age at marriage of colliers' children, who would then continue to multiply at compounding rates as long as new pit jobs continued to become available. It was new employment which brought population growth, not a rise in the wage level of the people employed, although the two must have been positively related. Although it was socially restricted and spatially circumscribed, labour recruitment and therefore the demographic impact of employment growth extended beyond the townships where new jobs emerged, across the whole coalfield. The relationship between economic development and demographic change was played out at a regional scale.

The interdependence of sources, methods and conclusions makes it inevitable that these findings are inimical with those of recent work on labour migration in the nineteenth century from trade union records, which reveals nationwide systems of circulation (Southall, 1991), and with those of historical demography *à la mode*, which shows a relationship between population growth rates and lagged levels of real wages in national aggregate series of vital events, supplemented by family reconstitutions which reveal no significant differences in fertility between a few small parishes with relatively low rates of population turnover.[67] The region studied here must remain unilluminated by the rigorous methods of modern historical demography: rapid population turnover in sprawling parishes studded by chapels makes systematic aggregate counting difficult and reliable family reconstitution impossible. But it was in such places where industry grew and its narrowly spread demographic effects occurred. Surely, like the drunkard who has lost his door key, we can only find what we seek by fumbling in the dark there, however brilliant the lamps now shining elsewhere.

---

67 Wrigley and Schofield (1981; 1983); Wrigley (1983); Wilson (1986). Perhaps the paramountcy of the value of full family reconstitution from parish registers is illusory. Ruggles (1992) shows that demographic statistics calculated in this way must be biased because of mobility even in agricultural areas.

REFERENCES

BAILEY, F. A. (1934), 'Coroners' inquests held in the manor of Prescot, 1746–89', *Transactions of the Historic Society of Lancashire and Cheshire*, **86**, 21–40.
BARKER, T. C. and J. R. HARRIS (1954), *A Merseyside Town in the Industrial Revolution: St Helens, 1750–1900*, Liverpool.
BENSON, J. (1980), *British Coalminers in the Nineteenth Century: A Social History*, London.
BREARLEY, A. E. (1968), *The Registers of the Church of St. Thomas the Martyr, Upholland, 1600–1735*, Lancashire Parish Register Society, **107**.
Census of Great Britain, 1851 (1954), Vol. II, London.
DEANE, P. and W. A. COLE (1964), *British Economic Growth 1688–1959: Trends and Structure*, Cambridge.
DICKINSON, F. (1968 and 1972), *The Registers of St. Helens Parish in Prescot ... 1713–1787 and 1788–1812*, Lancashire Parish Register Society, **107** and **111**.
DOUGLAS, D. (1977), 'The Durham pitman', In R. Samuel (ed.), *Miners, Quarrymen and Saltworkers*, London, 206–95.
EARL OF CRAWFORD AND BALCARRES (1934), 'Haigh Cannell', *Transactions of the Manchester Statistical Society*, Centenary Session, 1–23.
FLINN, M. W. and D. STOKER (1984), *The History of the British Coal Industry, Vol 2. 1700–1830: The Industrial Revolution*, Oxford.
GILL, M. and M. BURKE (1987), 'Coal miner mobility: north east England in the early nineteenth century', *Journal of Regional and Local Studies*, **7**, 35–54.
GOODRICH, C. L. (1926), *The Miner's Freedom*, New York.
HAIR, P. E. H. (1968), 'The Lancashire collier girl, 1795', *Transactions of the Historic Society of Lancashire and Cheshire*, **120**, 63–86.
HANN, A. (1999), *Kinship and Exchange Relations within an Estate Economy: Ditchley, 1680–1750*, (DPhil Thesis), Oxford.
HARRIS, J. R. (1951), 'The Hughes Papers: Lancashire social life, 1780–1825', *Transactions of the Historic Society of Lancashire and Cheshire*, **103**, 113–28.
KRAUSE, J. T. (1965), 'The changing adequacy of English registration, 1690–1837', In D. V. Glass and D. E. C. Eversley (eds), *Population in History: Essays in Historical Demography*, London, 379–93.
LANGTON, J. (1979), *Geographical Change and Industrial Revolution: Coalmining in Southwest Lancashire, 1590–1799*, Cambridge.
LANGTON, J. (1983), 'Liverpool and its hinterland in the late eighteenth century', In B. L. Anderson and P. J. M. Stoney (eds), *Commerce, Industry and Transport: Studies in Economic Change on Merseyside*, Liverpool, 1–25.
LANGTON, J. (1984), 'The industrial revolution and the regional geography of England', *Transactions of the Institute of British Geographers*, Series 2, **9**, 145–67.
LANGTON, J. (1998), 'Continuity of regional culture: Lancashire Catholicism from the sixteenth to the nineteenth centuries', In E. Royle (ed.), *Regional Identities: Essays in Honour of John Marshall*, Manchester, 82–101.
LANGTON, J. and G. HOPPE (forthcoming), 'Patterns of migration and regional identity: economic development, social change and the life-paths of individuals in nineteenth-century Western Östergötland', In D. Postles (ed.), *Naming, Society and Regional Identity*, Leicester.
LAWTON, R. and W. SMITH (1953), 'The West Lancashire coalfield', In W. Smith (ed.), *A Scientific Survey of Merseyside*, Liverpool, 268–77.
LORD, E. (1993), 'Communities of common interest: the social landscape of south-east Surrey, 1750–1850', In C. Phythian-Adams (ed.), *Societies, Cultures and Kinship, 1580–1850*, Leicester, 131–99.
MATHER, F. C. (1970), *After the Canal Duke*, Oxford.
PARKINSON, C. N. (1952), *The Rise of the Port of Liverpool*, Liverpool.
RUGGLES, S. (1992), 'Migration, marriage, and mortality: correcting sources of bias in English family reconstitutions', *Population Studies*, **46**, 507–22.

SAMUEL, R. (1977), 'Mineral workers', In R. Samuel (ed.), *Miners, Quarrymen and Saltworkers*, London, 1–97.
SOUTHALL, H. (1991), 'Mobility, the artisan community and popular politics in early nineteenth-century England', In G. Kearns and W. J. Withers (eds), *Urbanising Britain: Essays on Class and Community in the Nineteenth Century*, Cambridge, 103–30.
TAYLOR, J. S. (1976), 'The impact of pauper settlement', *Past and Present*, **73**, 42–74.
TAYLOR, J. S. (1991), 'A different kind of Speenhamland: nonresident relief in the industrial revolution', *Journal of British Studies*, **30**, 183–208.
WILSON, C. (1986), 'The proximate determinants of marital fertility in England 1600–1799', In L. Bonfield, R. Smith and K. Wrightson (eds), *The World We Have Gained: Histories of Population and Social Structure*, Oxford, 203–30.
WORRALL, E. S. (1980), *Returns of Papists 1767: Diocese of Chester*, Catholic Record Society, Occasional Publications, **1**.
WRIGLEY, E. A. (1983), 'The growth of population in eighteenth-century England: a conundrum resolved', *Past and Present*, **98**, 121–50.
WRIGLEY, E. A. and R. S. SCHOFIELD (1981), *The Population History of England, 1541–1871: A Reconstruction*, Cambridge.
WRIGLEY, E. A. and R. S. SCHOFIELD (1983), 'English population history from family reconstitution: summary results, 1600–1799', *Population Studies*, **37**, 157–84.

Chapter 5

MOTIVES TO MOVE:
RECONSTRUCTING INDIVIDUAL
MIGRATION HISTORIES IN EARLY
EIGHTEENTH-CENTURY LIVERPOOL

DIANA E. ASCOTT and FIONA LEWIS

Evidence from a variety of sources suggests that in the pre-industrial period, the population of England was highly mobile, often over short distances.[1] Much of this movement was in-migration to towns and was fundamental in engineering sustained population growth and the supply of labour necessary to maintain the manufacturing, trading, and service sectors of the early urbanizing economies.

This chapter seeks to give a flavour of the potential for multiple source analysis when exploring migration issues. It draws upon the findings of a recent research project seeking to explore 'The Liverpool Community and Urban Growth, 1660–1750'.[2] That investigation employed multiple record linkage to construct detailed biographies of individual townsfolk and to reconstruct their associations within the widest social and occupational base. Set against the findings of aggregate studies of Liverpool to date,[3] four detailed case histories will be presented to demonstrate migration and mobility characteristics at the experience level of the individual, and of the individual's interaction and connectivity with others.

LIVERPOOL

At the Restoration, it has been estimated that Liverpool had little more than 1,500 inhabitants. By the end of the seventeenth century, the population total had risen to approximately 5,000–5,500 and was to almost double in the first 20 years of the eighteenth century, and double again to reach 20–22,000 by the late 1750s.[4]

Analysis of parish register totals of baptisms and burials reveals that natural increase throughout the period was often slight, and between the mid-1720s and mid-1740s almost negligible. Indeed, the cumulative surplus of baptisms over burials between 1660 and 1760 amounted to slightly less than 5,500. In the same period, gross population expansion was of the order of 24,500, suggesting that barely 22 per

---

1   For a collection of essays on migration in the pre-industrial period, see Clark and Souden (1987). See also Pooley and Whyte (1991); Pryce (1994).
2   Funded by a grant from the Leverhulme Trust, this project was undertaken in the Department of Economic and Social History, University of Liverpool, by M. J. Power, F. Lewis and D. E. Ascott.
3   Langton and Laxton (1978); Rawling (1986), pp. 91–125, 180–90; Lewis (1994), pp. 10–12, 237–60. Also at the level of the individual, see Lawton and Pooley (1975).
4   Based on estimates calculated by Rawling (1996), note 5, p. 11; Baines (1852), p. 492.

cent of Liverpool's growth could be attributed to natural increase. The shortfall, almost an incredible 80 per cent, must have been supplied from elsewhere. Indeed, net migration into the town continued to account for well above 70 per cent of population increase until the final decade of the eighteenth century.[5]

In terms of charting the possible source of these migrants, a study of Liverpool and surrounding parishes, based on parish register totals of births and deaths and estimated population size derived from the 1664 Hearth Tax and the Notitia Cestriensis of 1717, is instructive. Prior to 1717, population surplus from neighbouring agricultural and coalfield townships was significant in fuelling Liverpool's growth, adding substance to the belief that the majority of migrants in this period emanated from within a relatively small catchment – usually 15 to 20 miles. After 1717, natural increase absorption in the neighbouring areas left little surplus potential for migration, with the result that Liverpool's migrants were supplied most probably from beyond the immediate south-west Lancashire hinterland (Rawling, 1986, pp. 180–90).

Evidence, both quantifiable and impressionistic, of this wider geographical catchment can be found in a variety of Liverpool sources. Analysis of Liverpool apprenticeship records, extant for the period 1707 to 1757, reveals that although the majority hailed from the hinterland, a significant minority came from places as disparate as the American plantations and Orkney.[6] References to places of origin, beyond the immediate area, as cosmopolitan as London, Dublin, Greenock, Antigua, and Virginia can be found also in the Liverpool parish register marriage records, particularly from the 1700s onwards.[7] Burial entries from the same period relating to single adult males show a proportion of similarly remote origins, as does testamentary evidence for those who had adopted Liverpool as their domicile but acknowledged movement from an original location.

To some extent, this migration evidence can be placed against the economic restructuring and labour demands of the town. Before the late seventeenth century, Liverpool was a modest port, contesting its position as a mere 'creek' of the customs 'port' of nearby Chester. Much of the traffic was local coasting or engaged in the considerable trade of the Irish Sea littoral. Potential port labour had geographical similarity, drawing upon sailors from the maritime communities of the Wirral peninsula, Cheshire, North Wales, the Isle of Man, Ireland and Scotland.

By the early eighteenth century, two developments were significant in altering the character of the port. Liverpool, with full customs autonomy, had entered into large-scale trans-Atlantic commerce, and an innovatory series of dock constructions were set in motion through Act of Parliament in 1708.[8] Strong trading connections were

5 Based on figures calculated by Langton and Laxton (1978), pp. 74–34.
6 Liverpool Apprenticeship Books. Lpl.R.O. 352 CLE/REG/4. See also an unpublished mapping by J. Langton reproduced in Rawling (1986), pp. 181–82.
7 See Lewis (1994), pp. 240–47. However, systematic analysis of only those marriage entries where both male and female partners' place of origin is stated is less revealing, providing again only a geographically limited picture of Liverpool's sphere of influence.
8 8 Anne, c. 12.

forged with the Americas, Europe and Scandinavia, and the maritime recruiting grounds were similarly extended.

Sailors and mariners were not the only migrants needed to maintain Liverpool's economic growth. In addition to pre-existing craft and manufacturing industries, amongst them clockmaking, tilemaking, and silk stocking weaving to name but a few, new and innovative commodity processing concerns were well established by the early eighteenth century linked to sugar and tobacco imports from the trans-Atlantic trade. Shipbuilding and, more dominantly, ship-outfitting provided a constant demand for carpenters, shipwrights, ropemakers, and sailmakers. Although the town's employment structure appears distinctly male-orientated, opportunities for female employment may have been opening up in the service and domestic sectors, which were both undergoing expansion (Lewis, 1994, Table 3.2, pp. 59–61, 64). However, in terms of documentary evidence, parochial registration and apprenticeship records provide no more than a glimpse of the movement and employment opportunities open to females, in particular single females, in the early eighteenth century.[9]

Whether relating to male or female, none of the findings from aggregate mono-sourced approaches to assess migrant origin does justice to Liverpool's importance as a terminal focus for migratory behaviour, nor as a nodal point in the circulation of local and national population movements by both land and sea. Liverpool was not only the destination for migrants but also a place from which others 'stepped out', a key feature of migratory movement overlooked in studies of the town to date.

To redress the situation, this chapter seeks to give some insight into not only the origin and destination of individuals moving both in and out of Liverpool, but also the motivation or even necessity behind such movements. As already suggested, the motive to move is implicit within certain source documents. More elusive, though, are the motivations to move not overtly bound up with economic opportunity or family formation, motivations that defy quantitative analysis but nonetheless were meaningful and to some extent shared by the contemporary population. None of these can be gleaned from a single source and very few without the mitigating behaviour of other people being taken into account. To unravel influences and motivations to move it would seem appropriate to follow two methodological strategies, in essence to break down aggregate studies to the level of the individual and to chart the behaviour of such individuals, and those with whom they interacted, through time.

SOURCES

Study of early eighteenth-century Liverpool is facilitated by the diverse array of information available. The nature of these data is summarized in Figure 17. Essentially, sources fall within one of three categories: longitudinal sources that extend

---

9   For analysis of female employment based on the Liverpool parish registers, see Lewis (1994), pp. 69–72. (Based on apprenticeship records, only one female apprentice, from a total of 701, was listed between 1707 and 1757.) For females' migration histories, the most favoured sources, Church court depositions, are not readily accessible for Liverpool at this time. For studies based on this source, see Clark (1979).

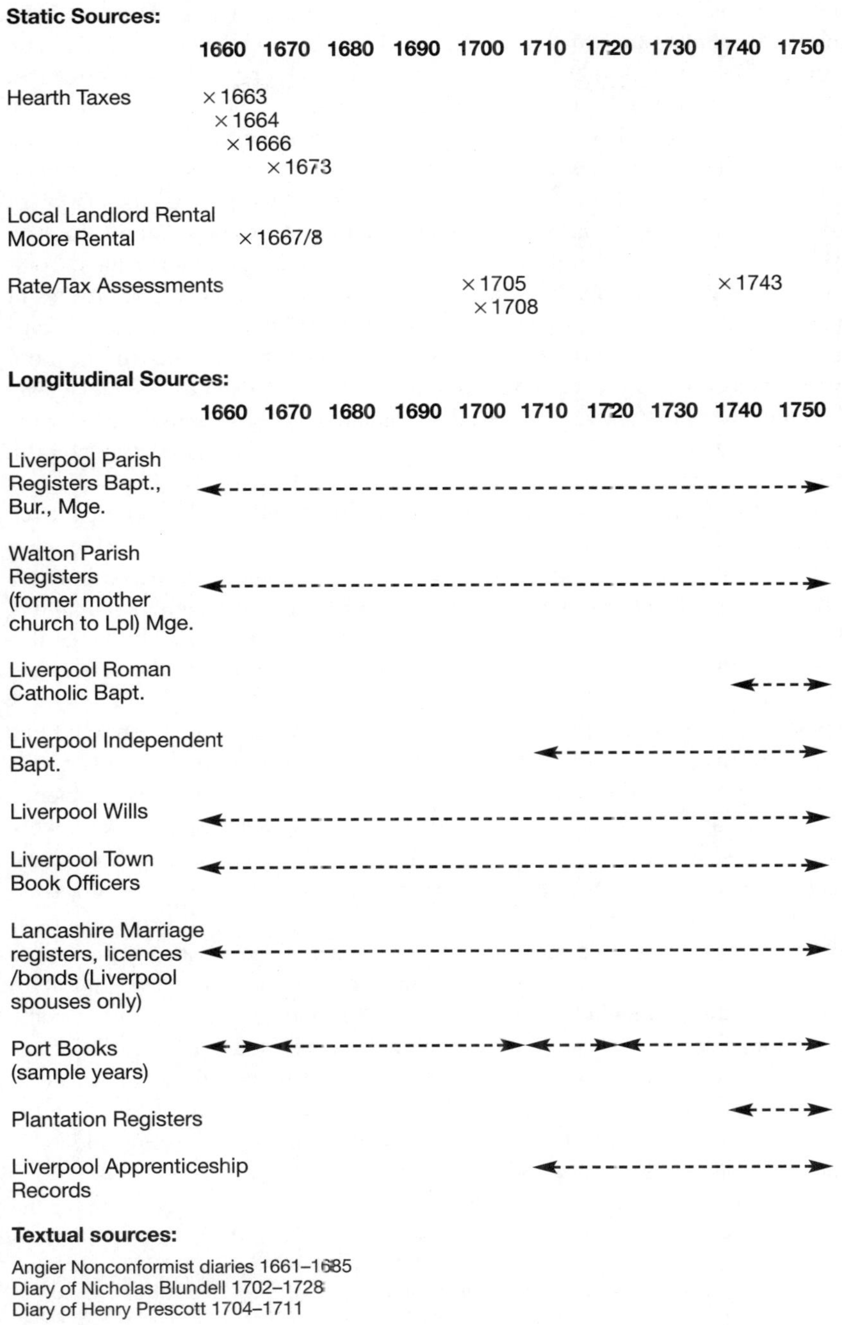

MIGRATION HISTORIES IN EIGHTEENTH-CENTURY LIVERPOOL

Static Sources:

	1660	1670	1680	1690	1700	1710	1720	1730	1740	1750
Hearth Taxes	×1663 ×1664 ×1666	×1673								
Local Landlord Rental Moore Rental		×1667/8								
Rate/Tax Assessments					×1705 ×1708				×1743	

Longitudinal Sources:

	1660	1670	1680	1690	1700	1710	1720	1730	1740	1750
Liverpool Parish Registers Bapt., Bur., Mge.	←--→
Walton Parish Registers (former mother church to Lpl) Mge.	←--→
Liverpool Roman Catholic Bapt.							←---→			
Liverpool Independent Bapt.						←-----------------------→				
Liverpool Wills	←--→
Liverpool Town Book Officers	←--→
Lancashire Marriage registers, licences /bonds (Liverpool spouses only)	←--→
Port Books (sample years)	←►←-----------►←--►←-----------→
Plantation Registers							←---→			
Liverpool Apprenticeship Records					←---------------------→					

Textual sources:

Angier Nonconformist diaries 1661–1685
Diary of Nicholas Blundell 1702–1728
Diary of Henry Prescott 1704–1711

Figure 17: Sources

over considerable time periods for example, the parish registers; cross-sectional sources that document information at one fixed point in time such as tax and rate assessments; and textual sources that offer descriptive or personal information. Diaries and family histories fall within this last category.

The construction of a detailed biography involves the identification of an individual within a number of sources and thence the linking together of pertinent information. The assessment of the greater significance of that individual's life then involves further linkage, principally through the reconstruction of extended family connections but also through the identification of economic and social relationships. Complex chains and webs of linked records are therefore constructed.[10] The process of compilation has to overcome problems commonplace within nominal record linkage such as mis-identification through common or shared names, assessment of the probability that a linkage is correctly made, and due weighting to all possible linkages.

To commence the linkage process, a foundation or base must be selected. Although the major longitudinal sources would seem the obvious starting point in terms of record coverage, these have certain problems. The wills are elitist and show gender bias, the Town Books, recording council office holders, similarly and even more extremely biased, and the parish registers simply too unwieldy. One solution lies in the cross-sectional sources which are date-specific and as inclusive, in terms of charting the social and economic characteristics of the recoverable population at a particular time, as the greater longitudinal sources. The cross-sectional sources also punctuate the period at regular and significant intervals: the 1660s, the 1700s, and the 1740s.

The source that captures the central period is the 1708 rate assessment, and this has formed the pivotal point for record linkage both backwards and forwards within the entire range of the database. However, the rate presents two key problems. Firstly, it is certainly not a fully comprehensive source, and secondly, it is unlikely that those individuals who are mentioned can be accounted for at both extremes of the ninety-year period. It is here that the construction of chains and webs of association built up from the individual biographies proves invaluable. It becomes possible not only to overcome the interruption of record linkage through omission or exclusion of an individual from a particular source, but also to evaluate the long-term legacy or implication of an individual's behaviour beyond a single generation or the time period imposed by the nature of a source. The construction of such 'information trees' provides not just straightforward record connections as found in genealogical mapping, but instead, complicated chains of record combinations that in terms of longitudinal coverage have been found in exceptional circumstances to identify six generations of a kinship network within our period.

The assessment of 1708 was undertaken for the purpose of levying a rate for the relief of the poor (Peet, 1908). The rate was 3d in the pound and was levied on prop-

---

10 Family reconstitution has already been attempted on the Liverpool population of this period: see Lewis (1994). The technique employed in this study builds upon the linkage strategy used in reconstitution but draws upon a far greater and more flexible record base than the parish registers alone, and therefore might be termed a variant of 'total' reconstitution. See Sharpe (1990), p. 43.

erty, stock in trade, and money at interest. The original catalogue of 2,903 separate mentions was rationalized to produce a listing of 1,308 individual ratepayers and tenants plus the Liverpool Corporation. By its very nature the rate excluded the poor. However, from the parish registers it is possible to gain an extremely crude impression of missing numbers based on the vital events for the year 1708. When rated personnel are cross-checked with these records, 47 per cent of adults appearing in the parish register in 1708 do not appear in the rate. From occupational information, the majority of these were sailors or labourers, two groups that were repeatedly under-represented.

Covering the full topographical extent of the town, the rate provides a virtual street directory of Liverpool in 1708. A total of 1,287 inhabited houses were documented within 34 streets, of which an original medieval and central one was Jugler Street. It was home and workplace not only to manufacturers and those in the service sector, but also to the town's butchers within the Shambles. In addition, mariners and a variety of others involved in port-related trades can be identified from the parish registers, as can the recently deceased (Figure 18). In sum, its rated personnel could be viewed as broadly representative of the town's early eighteenth-century population in terms of occupational diversity and social mix. For this reason, the mobility and migration experiences of a number of those listed under Liverpool's Jugler Street will be outlined in detailed case studies.

CASE STUDIES

William Holme

In the base source of the 1708 assessment, 'the executors of William Holme' were rated, either for stock or money at interest, in Jugler Street where William had been a tenant. This entry indicated his recent death and leads to an extant will.[11] The will, of 'William Holme, grocer', gave the following information (Figure 19, see especially the key): the beneficiaries were his wife, two children, and two brothers-in-law. Mention was also made of two of his wife's siblings. Linkage to the Liverpool parish registers added the baptismal dates of children, but no testator burial. However, clues in the will pointed to the immediate hinterland and his burial was found in Melling register, as were the burials of his daughter Mary and widow Sarah. There is no relevant parish register marriage record, but a search of the licences revealed the marriage of William to Sarah (Wright) and a re-marriage of Sarah (Holme) to John Aspinwall.

William's life stage when moving to Liverpool was either that of apprentice or single adult. His move can be taken as career enhancement, since there would have been limited opportunity to be a grocer in rural Melling. As tenant of a property in Liverpool which can be presumed the family home, William was not an early commuter. However, he did maintain an interest around his place of origin in both freehold and leasehold property. William returned to Melling to be buried 'among my

---

11 Of 33 executors cited in the 1708 assessments, only 17 wills (52 per cent) have survived Ascott, see (1996), p. 46.

BURGUS DE LIVERPOOLE IN COM̃ PALL LANCR.

An Assessmt. made on the Inhabitants of the parish of Liverpoole aforesaid for and towards the Releife of the Poor of the said Parish for the year Ensueing from Easter Tuesday the sixth Day of Aprill Ano Domiñ one Thousand seven hundred and eight.

Jugler Street

	£.	s.	d.
Mrs. Elizabeth Catterall, ye house she lives in and shops 4/- taken of pr. order for mentining her mother-in-law		......	
Thomas Peel, ye house he lives in	0	3	0
Mr. Ja. Townsend, the house he lives in [*Draper, S.N.R.*]			
id. ye shopp to Mr. Harrops	0	13	0
id. for Ellen Battesby			
Mr. Jon. Crane, ye house he lives in			
id. for Gawther Kerfoot	0	10	4
Gawther Kerfoot	0	1	0
Mr. Edmund Croston for Mrs. Hopkins	0	3	8
Mrs. Hopkins	0	1	0
execrs. Aldem. Bickesteth, p. Mr. Arthur Bold	0	4	4
Wm. Gryffeth, ye house he lives in [*Sadler, S.N.R.*]	0	4	0
Mr. Jon. Plumb, ye house he lives in & stock [*Attorney-at-law, S.N.R.*]	0	17	9
Wm. Rigby, Cooper		......	
Michael Short, Butcher	0	1	0
Mr. Jon. White [*Barber, S.N.R.*]	0	2	0
Jon. Gryffith, ye house he lives in	0	1	9
Mr. John Plumb, ye house he lives in		......	
Jon. Lawrenson, Taylor	0	1	6
Mr. Samuel Glover		......	
Mr. Wm. Moxon	0	1	0
The Corporation for ye Butchers' Shambles, and houses	2	0	0
Mr. Benjamin Branker for Mr. Rownson [*Grocer, S.N.R.*], and Mr. Moxon, houses, p. Mr. Cleveland	0	8	8
Mr. Robert Rownson	0	4	0
Mr. Wm. Leversage		......	
execrs. Mr. Carter, ye house Mr. Cowall lives in			
id. p. Mr. Saml. Glover	0	10	0
id. p. Mr. Aldridge			
Mr. Aldridge	0	5	0

Figure 18: Jugler Street
Sources: Annotations in square brackets by H. Peet, (1908). *S.N.R.* indicates St Nicholas Parish Register.

Richard Kenardy	0	2	6
Mr. Joseph Dannett, p. Mr James Richardson	0	5	0
Mr James Richardson [*Inn-keeper, buried 1708, S.N.R.*]			
execrs. Aldem. Bickesteth [*Buried June 20th, 1707, S.N.R.*] house & mill, &c.	0	8	0
Mrs. Williamson for Peter Mason	0	4	0
Peter Mason	0	2	0
Edward Carr, p. Tho. Charnock [*Saylor, S.N.R.*]	0	1	11
Widow Higginson, p. Andrew Davidson			
id. for Samuel Edwards	0	7	9
id. for Mr. Trotman, p. Liverstich [?]			
Andrew Davidson	0	1	0
Samuel Edwards	0	0	6
David Trotman		......	
Mr. Ra. Williamson for Mr. Jos. Shaw	0	7	6
Mr. Joseph Shaw [*Draper, S.N.R.*]	0	16	0
Mr. Nichs. Hatton, ye house he lives in & shopp	0	7	6
Philemon Lownes		......	
Mr. Tho. Ford, ye house he lives in [*Brazier, S.N.R.*]	0	9	6
Mr. Wm. Kennion	0	1	6
Alde. Sharples for Mr. Wm. Bickesteth			
id. for Mr. Ra. Prescott			
id. for Mr. Wm. Ranicars [*Draper, S.N.R.*]	1	9	9
id. ye house he lives in, Warehouse, &c. [*Alderman Cuthbert Sharples, buried Dec. 27th, 1707, S.N.R.; Mayor in 1699*]			
Mr. Wm. Bickesteth [*Grocer, S.N.R.*]	0	2	0
Mr. Ralph Prescott	0	3	0
Mr. Wm. Ranicars	0	3	0
Mrs. Anne Tarleton, p. Mr. Edwd. Leadbeater	0	9	4
id. for execrs. of Mr. William Holme			
Mr. Edward Leadbeater [*Inn-keeper, S.N.R.*]	0	3	0
execrs. Mr. Wm. Holme [*Grocer, S.N.R.*]	0	4	0
Mr. Jon. Sandiford, p. Mrs. Thompson	0	4	6
Mrs. Bridgett Thompson		......	
Mrs. Anne Rhodes		......	
Mr. Brown [Excers. Peter Altherton, Esq., *crossed out*]	0	10	4
id. for Mr. Nickallson			
Mr. Jno. Crumpton			
Andrew Davidson		......	
Samuel Edwards		......	
[D. Trotman *crossed out*] Mr. Matt. Nickelson	0	4	0
Mr. Jon. Browne		......	
Jno. Crumpton	0	2	0
Ellin Battersby	0	1	0
Mr. Taylor, Draper	0	6	0
Mrs.		......	
Jno. Cowall		......	

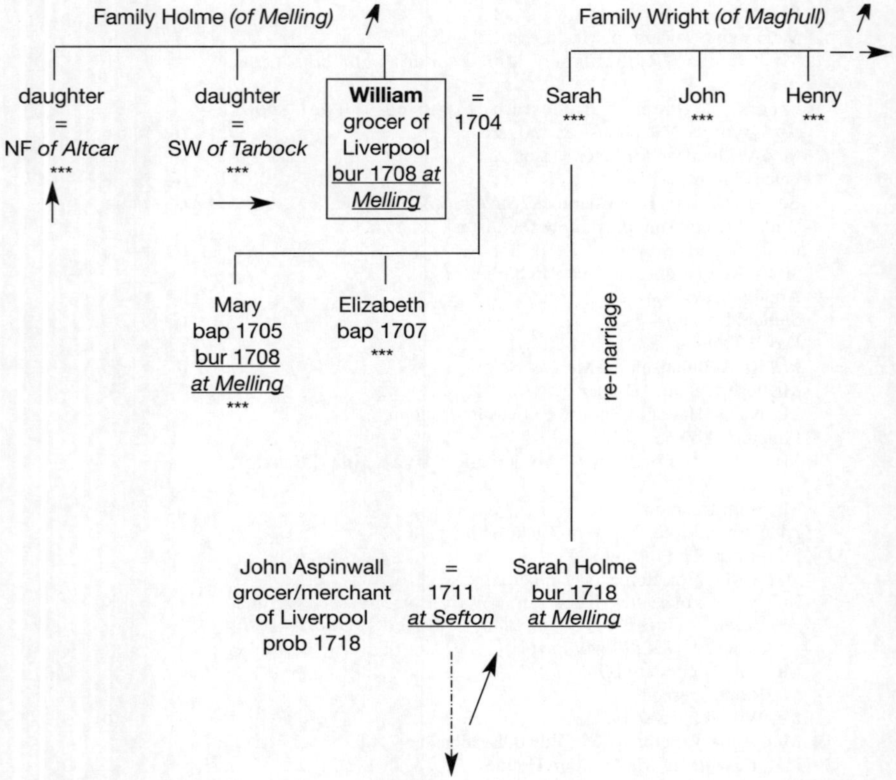

MIGRATION, MOBILITY AND MODERNIZATION

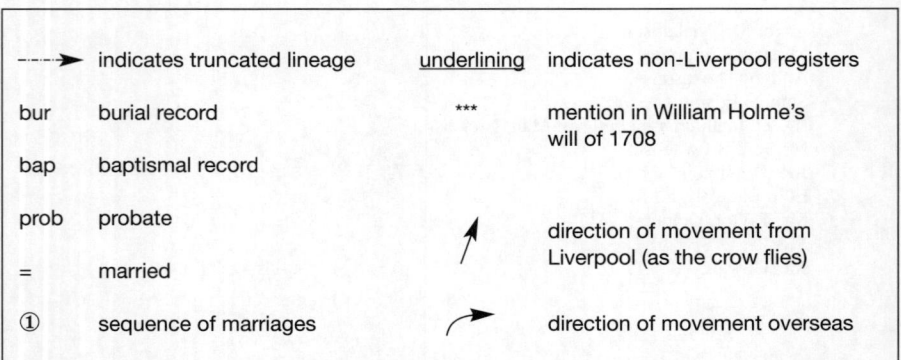

KEY TO FIGURES 19–23

----▶	indicates truncated lineage	underlining	indicates non-Liverpool registers
bur	burial record	***	mention in William Holme's will of 1708
bap	baptismal record		
prob	probate	↗	direction of movement from Liverpool (as the crow flies)
=	married		
①	sequence of marriages	↪	direction of movement overseas

Figure 19: William Holme

ancestors', as stipulated in his will.[12] The tie with home roots was such that his daughter, Mary, though christened in Liverpool, was buried in Melling, as was his widow, Sarah.

Methodologically, this is a prime example of the sum of the sources being much greater than the parts. Family reconstitution from Liverpool parish registers would have given only two child baptisms. However, by multiple record linkage testamentary evidence pointed to marriage licences and, more significantly, to the parish registers of Melling. The complete resultant linkage illustrates more than this fragment which has been abstracted to focus on William Holme.[13] From the web of linkages, there is evidence of relatively short-distance inward and outward migration by members of the family. Hinterland links were with Melling, Maghull, Sefton, Altcar, and Tarbock, all townships within 10 miles of Liverpool in the quadrant between north and east. William Holme's movement can be recognized as circulatory with a rural-urban-rural sequence, and as mitigating the subsequent movement, albeit only to interment, of both his daughter and his widow, who was at the time another man's wife.[14]

Anne Tarleton

The key individual was Mrs Anne Tarleton, the landlady of William Holme in Jugler Street. In 1708 she actually resided in what appears a widows' enclave, merry or otherwise, in Church Yard. The daughter of one mayor of Liverpool, Henry Corles, Anne was second wife and widow of another, Edward Tarleton. In the network which has been reconstructed, she could be described as the spider in the centre of a web of close kin who represent various migratory mechanisms (Figure 20).

One such mechanism, the taking up of apprenticeship, is considered to have been declining in this period other than in servicing the upper strata of urban occupations (Clark, 1987, p. 269). Such servicing is thought to have been typified by the sons of county families enrolling in mercantile apprenticeships. In mid seventeenth-century Liverpool the career ladder was frequently from mariner to merchant. This was the route of Edward Tarleton, Anne's husband, who was the grandson of minor landed gentry from three miles south of Liverpool. Deficient registration, the hiatus of the Interregnum, and the confusion of three possible parish registers, preclude the dating of vital events pertaining to Edward's parents, his first marriage and its offspring. However, Edward certainly became a Liverpool mariner/merchant, property holder, and civic dignitary. Growth of the family fortune in the Liverpool area enabled the eventual repurchase of the ancestral seat, Aigburth Hall, and subsequent relocation there by Edward's great-grandson, John Tarleton (1718–75).

12 Of the 1,769 extant wills for the period 1660–1760, 1,069 have been traced to burial records. Of those burials, 90 (8 per cent) have been traced to Anglican burial outside Liverpool. See Ascott, (1996), p. 134, Figure 4.4. Such numbers would be the tip of an iceberg. Not only were testators a minority but, as indicated in the Holme example, other family members might also 'migrate' from Liverpool for interment.
13 The greater linkage, incorporating the wider Aspinwall family, illustrates various facets of family occupational strategy as well as further migration evidence.
14 These three burials exemplify one aspect of the 'traffic in corpses' described by Schofield (1984).

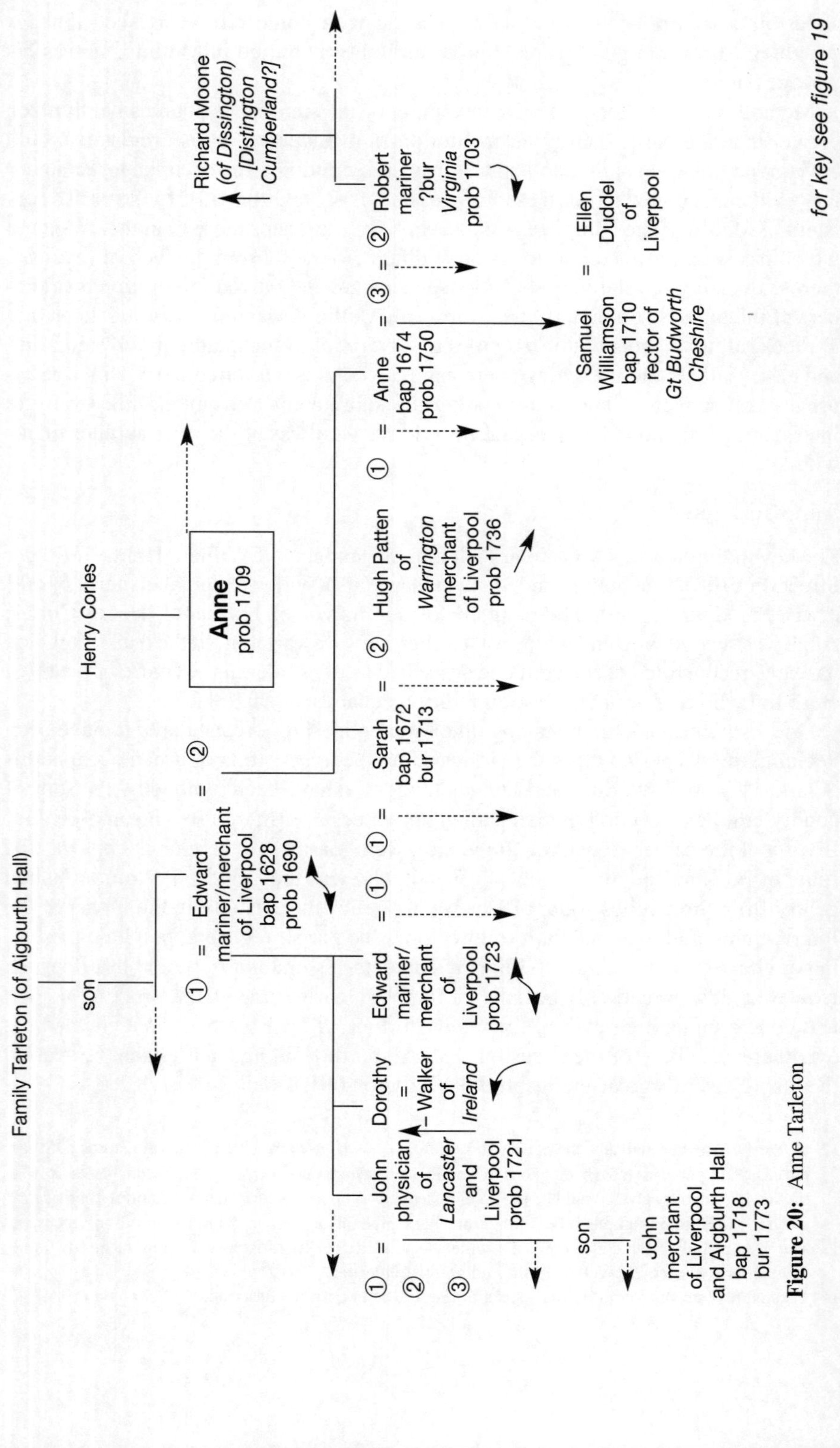

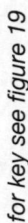

Figure 20: Anne Tarleton

A second distributary mechanism in population movement is attributed to the professions, which in this family were represented by a physician and a cleric. The physician, Dr John Tarleton, Anne's stepson, was an inter-urban migrant who achieved a circulatory pattern by returning to Liverpool from a practice in Lancaster. There could have been other motivations beyond career opportunity for the sojourn in Lancaster. The elusive constituent of personal feeling might be suspected since John, the eldest son of Edward, did not return to Liverpool until some time after his father's death, and was neither an executor nor a major beneficiary under Edward's will. Of course, his absence in Lancaster might explain exclusion from the former role, and prior provision might account for a lesser legacy. Such are the dangers of imputing motivation!

The Reverend Samuel Williamson, grandson of Anne, exemplified the redistributive function of the Church. He moved, for the education required by his calling, to Oxford, where he matriculated in 1728 and gained his MA in 1734.[15] After unknown moves for clerical advancement he was, in 1739, in the large rural parish of Great Budworth, Cheshire, as rector. However, he returned to Liverpool for his bride, Ellen Duddel, who was thus an urban-to-rural migrant by reason of marriage. A further female emigrant from Liverpool because of marriage was Anne's stepdaughter, Dorothy. From the will of her father, Edward, she is known to have been married in Ireland in 1690. Frustratingly there are no further indications of her movements.

Marriage has been suggested as a means of integration for urban in-migrants, as being substantially exogamous, and even where apparently endogamous, having at least one partner a recent in-migrant (Clark, 1987, p. 270). Substantiation for these points has been found in Liverpool,[16] and is illustrated here by the marital experience of two other women in the Tarleton family, who married migrants to Liverpool. These two, Sarah and Anne, daughters of Anne, also illustrate the high incidence of widowhood often associated with a port population. From their total of five marriage partners, the two women lost three mariner husbands. One of these was a stated, as opposed to suspected, in-migrant, Robert Moone, from Dissington (?Distington, Cumbs). His will is headed 'August 3rd 1703, Virg/a.' where he apparently died, as an involuntary emigrant. The second husband of Sarah Tarleton was Hugh Patten, described in the marriage record as 'merchant of Liverpool'. In fact he was the younger son of a mercantile family of Warrington, whence he had moved to Liverpool at the turn of the century. At his death in 1736, none of his ten children were living so his fortune returned to Warrington and many nephews and nieces. Although in both those cases marriage gave access to a Liverpool family of commercial and

---

15 Brasenose College, matriculated 1728, BA 1731, MA 1734 (Foster, 1891), p. 1575.
16 Analysis of Liverpool parish register marriage entries in the period 1660–1750 reveals that prior to the eighteenth century, at least 50 per cent of marriages recorded one endogamous partner. However, in the early decades of the eighteenth century, the proportion of endogamous partners, either male or female, showed marked decline, and from 1710 onwards, exogamous partners made up over 65 per cent of all marriages. For a review of marriage partner origin in Liverpool and the problems encountered in analysis of marriage migrant origin, see Lewis (1994), pp. 240–44.

political importance, in neither case was it 'rags to riches', since Moone and Patten were, respectively, from established rural and urban families.[17]

For several additional aspects of pre-industrial migration, Edward Tarleton junior, stepson of Anne (senior), can be termed the 'instrument'. Indentured servants were consigned to him, as a ship's master, for transfer to the North American plantations in 1698/99 (Elton, 1901, p. 184). Thus Edward made his contribution of indentured migrants during the year which saw arguably the highest total of unfree immigrants to the Chesapeake of the whole seventeenth century (Menard, 1980, p. 140). Edward also carried an apprentice across the Atlantic in 1704 to an English factor working in Virginia, himself representing another form of active relocation. There seems some ambivalence in the motivation of this apprentice, who was recruited only after a search and 'eventually persuaded' to sign articles in Liverpool (Bagley, 1968, p. 66). In classic migration terminology, the 'pull', of apprentice opportunity, needed the supplement of a strong 'push', from the local squire. Edward's own apprentices confuse the view of early eighteenth-century apprenticeship as a declining institution, restricted in catchment area, and essentially for superior youth to superior occupations (Clark, 1987, p. 269). Two apprentices, of only four in the extant records, came from within 10 miles and were respectively the sons of a rural craftsman and a yeoman. Their articles mention no trade. The third, a blacksmith's son from Kirkham in the Fylde, came 30 miles to be a sailor. The only gentleman's son, from Leeds, was apprenticed to Edward as a sailmaker. Edward was, in fact, a master on the cusp of transition between mariner and merchant.

The Tarleton network encapsulates exemplars of many aspects of migration which would be expected to manifest themselves in the late seventeenth and early eighteenth centuries. These include in-migration and emigration, both being illustrated over various distances, across different time spans, and for diverse reasons.

The Tarleton linkage also suggests ancillary causation for the apparent motive to move which was furnished by, for example, marriage or apprenticeship. Thus, while marriage was obviously causal to the emigration of Dorothy Walker, née Tarleton, from Liverpool to Ireland, the rationale for such a marriage could have been her father's frequent voyaging and trading to Ireland. Similarly, was there particular significance to the marriage and subsequent relocation of Ellen Duddel? Her marriage to the rector of Great Budworth seems the reason for the move and would be revealed as such in any single-sourced study seeking marriage horizons. However, this was less an isolated incidence of urban-to-rural migration than a return to her family's area of origin. In the same vein, one of the apprenticeships detailed above, that of the hesitant migrant to Virginia, is known to have had more complex motivation than simple economic advancement. Thus multiple linkage, in this case, demonstrates the possibility of discovering more of the mosaic of motivation, which presumably underlay any individual's migration decisions, than a single reference would expose.

---

17 This supports Clark's stricture against exaggerating marriage as a means of upward social mobility for urban newcomers (Clark, 1987, p. 271).

John Clieveland

'Mr Cleveland' of Jugler Street was in fact John Clieveland, merchant, alderman, and later Member of Parliament (Figure 21). The reconstruction of his connections demonstrates the pivotal nature of the 1708 assessment. John's family links backwards to the 1673 Hearth Tax and forward to the 1743 rate. He came to Liverpool to join his uncle, Richard, who was the first family member to move to the city. Richard Clieveland and his brother-in-law, Daniel Danvers, were both distance migrants of gentry origin, who came as entrepreneurs from London (Peet, 1908, pp. 32–33, 61–62). They were among '... the several ingenious men settled in Liverpool which caused ... trade to the plantations and other places ...'.[18] Richard and Daniel pioneered the new industry of sugar baking founded on West Indian imports. Family

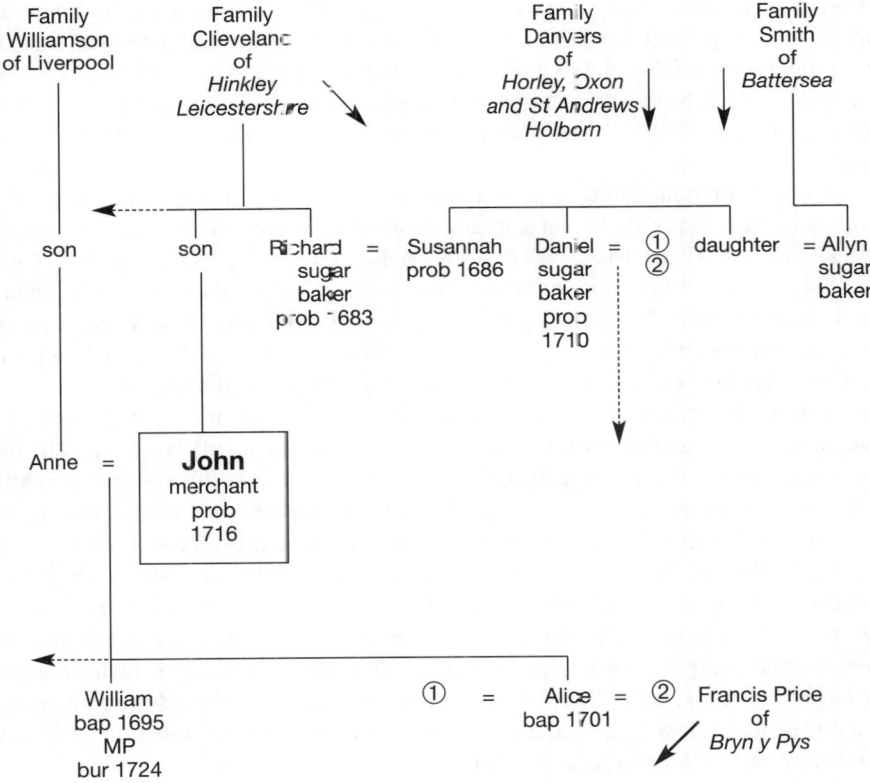

Figure 21: John Clieveland

for key see figure 19

---

18 10 and 11 Wm.III., c.36. The petition by Liverpool corporation to Parliament incorporated in the preamble to the act which made Liverpool a parish of itself distinct from Walton.

backing in the industry came from their affine links to the great London sugar baking family, the Smiths of Battersea.

Richard Clieveland had moved to Liverpool with his wife and daughter. Having no male heir, he adopted his nephew, John, who married into the old established Liverpool clan of Williamson. Of the three children of that union who survived to adulthood, the longest lived was a daughter, Alice. In her second marriage to a Welshman, the family of Clieveland physically left the town, while retaining control of John's bequest of real estate both within Liverpool and in the surrounding area.[19] These property acquisitions of John's expose the artificial constraints of a study founded on records 'of Liverpool'. Apart from property in the town, as listed in the rate, he died owning the Manor of Birkenhead together with 'divers messuages, land, and tenements' in four north Wirral townships, and a share in the saltworks at Dungeon Point, Hale, six miles up-river from Liverpool. Such detailed information, in this instance gleaned from John's will, is an erratic recovery, yet it is significant in highlighting the extra-Liverpool dimension of many financial and commercial activities, including property ownership. In a similar occasional way, personal connections outside the township can be reconstructed. For example, in the Clieveland family, education outside Liverpool might be suspected, and in fact the family had close Cambridge associations.[20]

Sessional migrant, rather than seasonal migrant, must be the description of a provincial Member of Parliament. John was the Whig representative for the borough from 1710 to 1713, as was his second son, William, from 1722 until his early death in 1724. The question of migration and office holding is also raised through a Clieveland apprenticeship. The father of this apprentice is described as 'of Wigan'. However, the said Bertil Entwistle was rated in 1708 for property in Liverpool and was in fact a leading light in Liverpool legal circles.[21] Thus, although technically a migrant, the boy was simply changing his abode within a familiar orbit. Obviously such instances cannot be discerned in a macro study and will only be revealed by the familiarity engendered in the reconstruction of networks. Although numerically small, such cases might constitute significant minorities within a certain stratum of the migrant community, and certainly serve to refine generalized conclusions.

The Clieveland linkage is illustrative of the motivation of distance migrants, entrepreneurship in a new industry, and the effect of marriage alliances. It is an example of a family which entered Liverpool, flourished there, and left within the generations spanned by this study, taking into absentee control appreciable amounts of Liverpool real estate. The leaving of Liverpool can be attributed more to demographic accident than design, in that the only surviving family member was a female who relocated to Wales after re-marriage.

19 Use of commercial fortunes to purchase landed estates and/or dower daughters marrying into county families is explored by Grassby (1978), p. 358.
20 John's grandfather, father, two uncles, and three cousins of various degrees (Venn and Venn, 1922), pp. 354–55.
21 He succeeded his father as Recorder of Liverpool, was also Vice Chancellor of the Duchy of Lancaster, and a node in the kinship network of legal families – Chorley, Entwistle, Peters, and Statham.

Matthew Nicholson

In the year when Matthew Nicholson was listed as a tenant in Jugler Street (Figure 22), he was described as a linen draper in the apprenticeship articles of James Percivall, a native of Warrington, and thus an inter-urban migrant. In 1708 Matthew was also importing linen from Ireland.[22] Previous mentions of Matthew were in 1705 when he was assessed as a tenant in Cook Street, and in 1704 when he married Dorothy Yates of Toxteth Park in the neighbouring parish of Childwall. There was just one baptismal entry in the Nonconformist register to confirm the family as Dissenters.[23] A child burial in 1721 records a street address giving further evidence of mobility within Liverpool. The Nicholsons were by then in Dale Street, whence Matthew himself and his wife Dorothy were buried in 1736.[24]

The only evidence of migration, as opposed to mobility, comes from the will of Matthew's eldest surviving son Samuel, which was written in London where he was lodging and maybe practising his profession of physician, for which he will have gained his education outside Liverpool. However, cross-referencing between the will of John Nicholson, 'the elder', and the wills of Matthew and his immediate family, confirms John as cousin of Matthew. In 1754 this John nominated, as one executor, his nephew William Lightbody. William, son of Adam Lightbody, husbandman of Nidsdale, Scotland, had been apprenticed to John Nicholson 23 years previously. This gives an indication of the Nicholsons' area of origin. The association between the Lightbody and Nicholson families provides an example of the way in which established kin in the town of destination, themselves of migrant origin, might offer various forms of aid to subsequent migrants within the extended family.[25]

Whereas all migration evidence for individuals cited in case studies above has been readily recoverable from within the combined data base records (Figure 17), Matthew Nicholson typifies the difficulty of retrieving information about Dissenters, who were grossly under-represented in the Anglican registers and barred from council membership if not all civic office. In the case of the Nicholsons, the information culled solely from record linkage within the data base of this study can be compared, or contrasted, with the genealogy from a published family history (Figure 23) (Nicholson and Axon, 1928). This book relates minutiae of the origin and immigration of Matthew, and much subsequent movement of family members.

The family history relates that Matthew was born in 1677, near the north coast of the Solway Firth at Blackshaw, Dumfriesshire, to a tenant of the Earl of Nithsdale. It

---

22 Liverpool Port Books. PRO E190/1375/8.
23 Baptismal register of Key Street Chapel, 1712. Unlike some apparently Nonconformist families who registered baptisms in both Anglican and Nonconformist registers, the Nicholsons recorded their marriages, burials, and only one baptism in Anglican registers. The missing baptisms may have been performed by Mrs Nicholson's cousin, the Dissenting minister in neighbouring Toxteth Park.
24 Mobility within the Liverpool township for this period has been assessed through the analysis of residence recorded in family reconstitution histories. This indicates that movement of families was relatively common and usually very localized. See Lewis (1995).
25 See Introduction in Clark (1984), p. 18; Cresy (1986); and, for a later period, Schürer (1991).

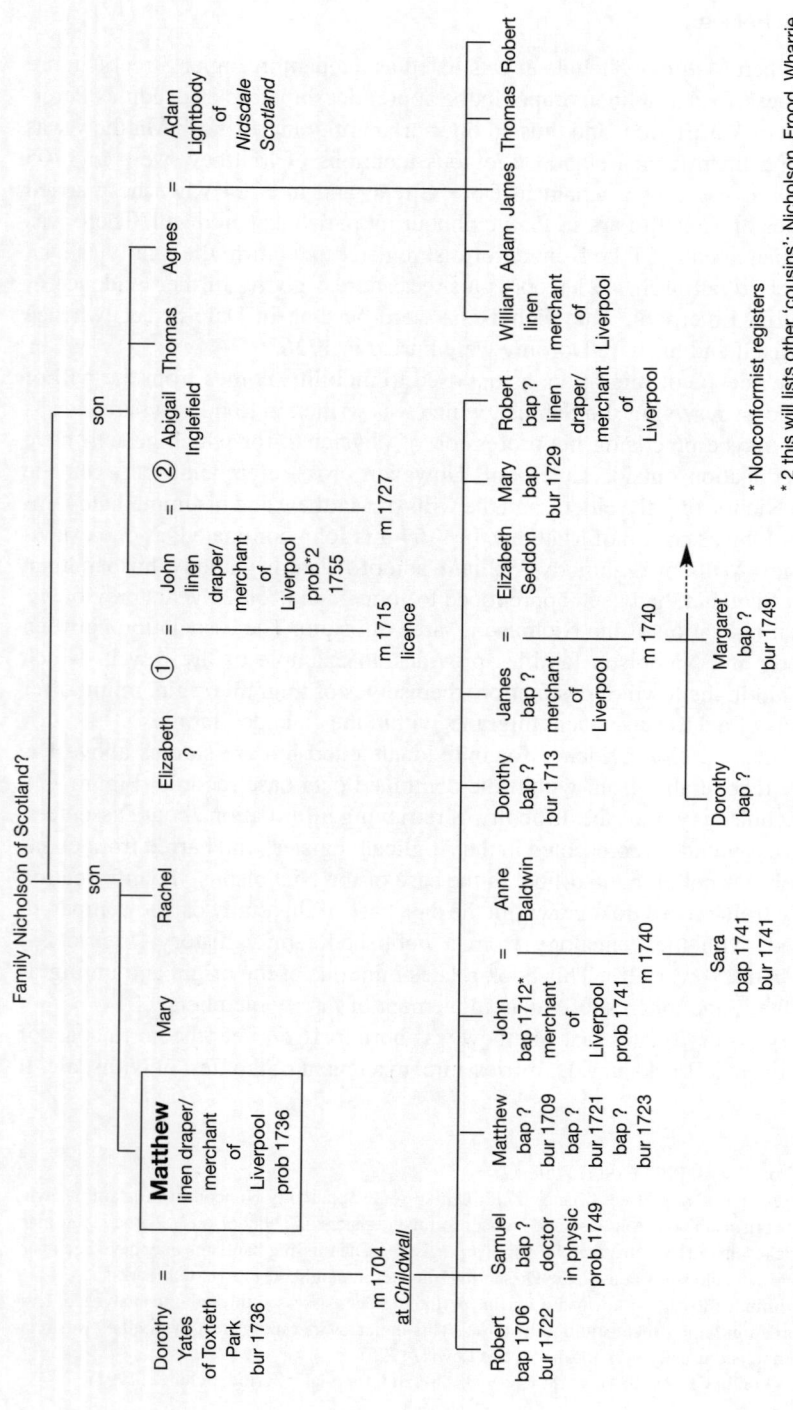

for key see figure 19

Figure 22: Matthew Nicholson – multiple record linkage

MIGRATION HISTORIES IN EIGHTEENTH-CENTURY LIVERPOOL 107

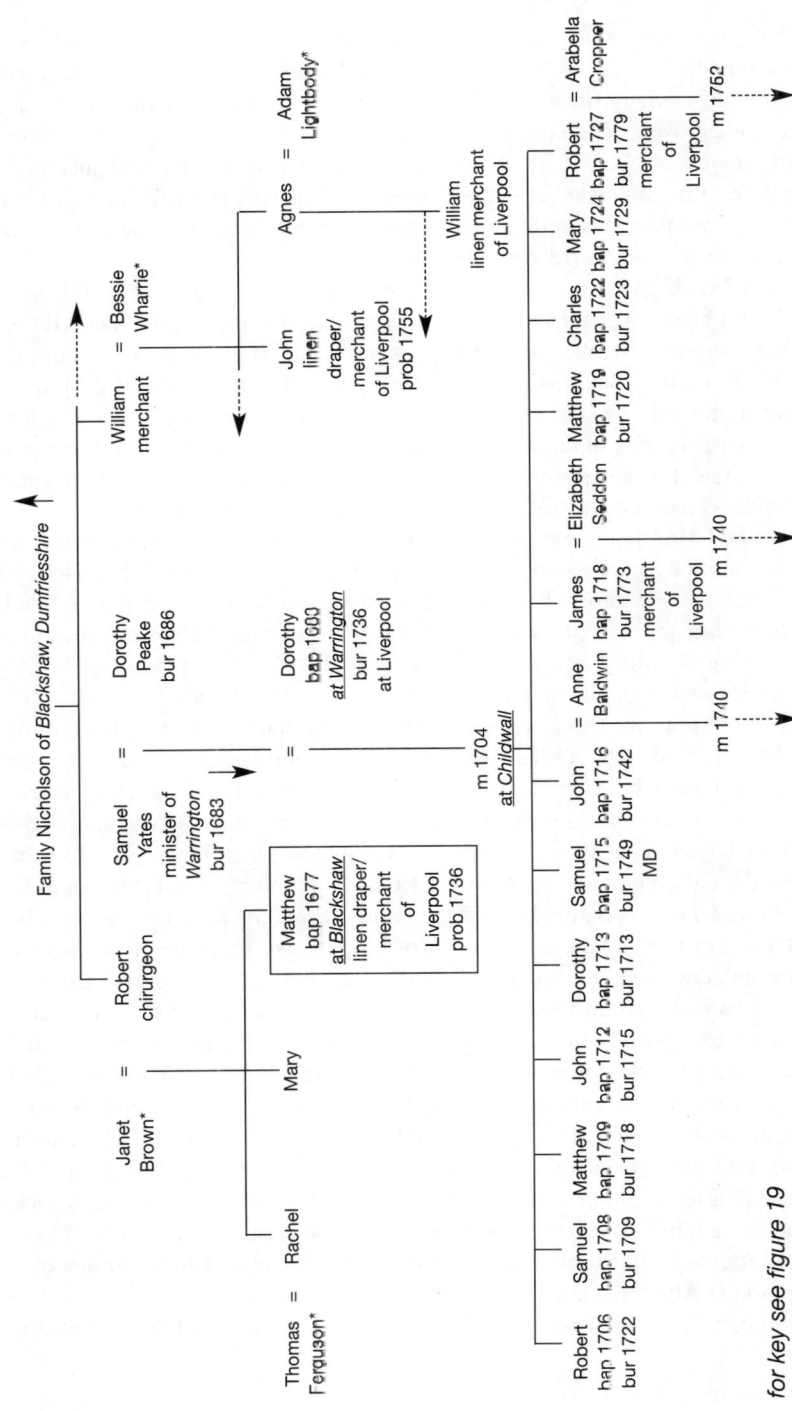

for key see figure 19

* cousins Brown, Wharrie, Ferguson and Lightbody all migrated from Dumfriesshire during this period to various places in Scotland, England and Ireland

Figure 23: Matthew Nicholson – genealogy from family history

suggests that, as a young man, he assisted one of the Blackshaw 'merchants', and would have travelled extensively in south-west Scotland and north-west England collecting and disposing of linen yarn. His first appearance in Liverpool records was as 'Matthew Nicholson, singlem[an], a traveller ... admitted free paying twenty pounds. Jurat Janny 26 1702'.[26] He obviously made a conscious career enhancement move, worth to him the cost of Liverpool freedom. This was possibly an informed decision following a previous trading visit to a place which he recognized as a developing node in the network of his chosen occupation.

A year later Matthew was married to a similarly mobile young woman. Dorothy Yates had been born in Warrington in 1683 as youngest and only surviving child of Samuel Yates, minister of the Dissenting congregation. He was dead within six months, and her mother also died before Dorothy was three. Dorothy had by then lived in Warrington and Wigan. She subsequently lived in Winwick as ward of her great aunt who was mother of the Reverend John Kenion, with whom Dorothy seems to have spent time after he became minister of Toxteth Park chapel in 1699. Hence Dorothy's address recorded as 'Toxteth Park' at the time of her marriage.

After marriage Matthew wrote home from business travels, on one of which in 1720 he was admitted a burgess and gild brother of Glasgow. His sons, John, Samuel, Robert and James, were similarly honoured a generation later. In fact Samuel and Robert, while on a journey of recuperation for the latter in 1748, were installed burgesses of both Dumfries and Glasgow. The travels of the boys had begun with boarding while attending Stand Grammar School in east Lancashire. Samuel's movement, inferred above from his profession and the place of writing his will, is related in the family history. He left Stand in 1731 and journeyed with cousin John Nicholson to London, where they lodged with another cousin. For John it was a business journey but for Samuel a pleasure trip, prior to study for the Nonconformist ministry. This began with a brief period in Warrington after which, in 1733, he became a student at Glasgow University where, true to undergraduate tradition, he overspent. From Glasgow, Samuel joined the famous academy at Kendal whence he was called home in 1736 by the last illnesses of his parents. A change of vocation to medicine meant education in Edinburgh with the intention of completion in Leyden. An MD was awarded there in 1741 after an interlude of study in Paris. There seems to have been a short period of practice in Liverpool terminating in professional disagreement. Samuel left the town and was mentioned only in March and April 1744 as visiting London, and in July and August 1748 on the journey to Scotland with Robert. Samuel was in London in November 1748 considering Bishop's Stortford, Nottingham and Liverpool as possible places to relocate his practice. In March 1749 he became so ill after a cold that he drew up his will and his youngest brother Robert was despatched to him in London. A slow recovery, convalescence in Kentish Town, and a tedious journey home took until June of 1749. At the end of July, Samuel died of consumption at Allerton, near Liverpool.

Of the younger Nicholson brothers only Robert actually relocated, for a brief trial

---

26 Liverpool Town Books. Lpl.R.O. 352/MIN/COU 1/5.

period at the age of 14. He spent some months in Manchester with a view to apprenticeship, but returned to serve his time with a Liverpool linen draper. In fact, after Stand Grammar School and different lengths of time at the Kendal academy, the brothers John, James, and Robert Nicholson pursued mercantile careers in Liverpool like their father and his cousin John. The youngsters travelled, individually or together, with the older men before their independent business journeying. In that journeying and in their business dealings they were associated with a plethora of 'cousins'. There had been successive waves of emigration from the Blackshaw area by at least two generations of Nicholsons and their affines, including the Lightbodys, as deduced above from record linkage. Established merchant relations were utilized in London, Liverpool, Dublin, Manchester, Whitehaven, and Wigan. At that time many merchants were their own travellers, and this family's itinerant mode of conducting business was also in the prevalent Scottish tradition.[27] As foreign immigrants prior to the Act of Union, the Scots might be expected to have maintained a specific support system. Such could be suspected in the case of the only apprentice listed as 'of Blackshaw, Scotland'. He was indentured in 1710 to William Crosbie, a young merchant of Liverpool like the Nicholsons and, also like them, staunchly Nonconformist. Their assistance in placing their compatriot seems highly probable.[28]

The motivation for Matthew Nicholson's mobility within Liverpool can be assessed from the multiple record linkage as a combination of a growing family and a prospering business. The tenure of his ultimate Dale Street property was leasehold, and, although the form of tenancy was not stated for either Cook Street or Jugler Street, tenancy 'at will' does not seem a likely tenure for a linen draper, still less for a merchant. For Southwark in an earlier period, tenancy 'at will' has been identified as the most likely form of property holding for those frequently mobile, but more especially for the habitual relocation of the 'lower orders' (Boulton, 1987, p. 214). However, Liverpool had an active market in leaseholds during the period under review, as well as a conspicuous custom of sub-letting. Certainly the merchant stratum of society appears to have maintained appreciable levels of mobility within the leasehold sector.[29]

Analysis of the migration patterns of father and sons, particularly Matthew and Samuel Nicholson, results in very different descriptions. Matthew essentially presents a single career enhancement move at the age of 25. However, the static impression, created by knowledge of this one career move in early manhood, is false in so far as Matthew was in almost perpetual motion in terms of business travels. There would be an even stronger impression of immobility in the merchants of the next generation who apparently never left Liverpool, although they took brides originating in the wider region. In fact they did travel frequently and extensively, not only within England, but to Ireland and to Scotland, where James and Robert actually became partners, with another Liverpool Nonconformist and a Lightbody kinsman

---

27 See Introduction in Clark and Souden (1987), p. 36.
28 This exemplifies assistance by established migrants of an earlier wave, reinforced by a denominational support system. See Corfield (1982), p. 105.
29 See Ascott (1996), pp. 253–4.

from Glasgow, in the foundation of the Hurlett Copperas Work in Paisley. Samuel made a succession of circulatory moves primarily motivated by various stages of education and career relocation. The actual places chosen for his education would have been influenced by his nonconformity. This not only applied to the training for that ministry, but also to medical training for which Oxford and Cambridge universities were closed to him. A first degree in Scotland would have been prompted by family origins, but Leyden University was customary for Protestant Nonconformists.

In common with biographic profiles created by record linkage, this published family history includes differing amounts of information on individual family members. The chronicled movements of any or all of the men, and of Dorothy Nicholson and other female marriage partners, have been recovered only if they occurred in extant family correspondence or record. Thus an apparently detailed published family history is not only subjective, but possibly as incomplete, in regard to inclusion of all the movements of family members, as an account compiled from multiple record sources. Yet it could be argued that both these avenues, to discovery of detailed migratory experience and characteristics, offer far greater insight than any aggregate study could offer.

CONCLUSION

The methodology adopted in this study, that is multiple source record linkage, has produced very positive results in recovering networks wider than the household or nuclear family. At the macro scale, it offers the potential to recover the intricacies of overlapping systems within the whole urban community, and enables longitudinal tracing of individuals' major migratory movements.[30] However, from the presentation of only four examples, it might be expected that little insight into the migratory characteristics of a population could be gained and still less of the motivations behind such moves. Nonetheless, as the case studies cited above indicate, the product of multiple source record linkage can bring together a wealth of detail rarely found outside the boundaries of biographical study. Indeed, although appearing to involve only four subjects from a total of 1,308 in the 1708 rate, the true extent of the networks centring upon these people actually involves, through time, over a thousand individuals. Simplification also underplays the extent to which the full complement of sources has been utilized in the creation of linkages.

From a selection of this size, no claim of universal typicality of experience within the total population can be made. Rather, these examples seek to give some flavour of the recognized, lesser known, and even unusual migratory characteristics discovered within a segment of Liverpool's population in the period. Omissions are nevertheless inevitable, in that more men than women are traced in detail, those of low

---

30 This study incorporates non-Anglican records and its most notable record linkages have resulted in establishing the origins and relationships of the expanding and commercially important Protestant Dissenters, particularly those of a Presbyterian or Independent persuasion, and the Quaker community, although the Anabaptists remain a largely unknown quantity. However, considering that the largest source is the Anglican parish registers, it is gratifying to have recovered such a significant proportion of those who did not record vital events in those registers.

status are not included, nor are the highly transitory. One of the main reasons for shortfall was that these groups left little or no impression on the record base. Even through the drawing together of relatively small amounts of information by record linkage, their behaviour cannot readily be discerned. The implications of this difficulty and the experience of these groups are touched upon below.

Motives to move were rarely singular but encompassed a variety of responses to or from stimuli. Broad generalizations are therefore awkward when using this methodology, particularly when attempts are made to ascribe moves to a single or dominant motivation. However, it may be possible to place the movements of individuals within a recognized framework for analysis. For example, Clark and Souden (1987) suggest a migration model based upon migration motivations open to the individual in the early modern period.[31] 'Distance' is plotted against 'definitiveness': the former not only in the physical sense but equally in the sense of cultural divide, the latter expressing the degree of separation from the place of origin. Between the axes are four 'clouds' of distinct but overlapping types of movement: 'local', 'career', 'circular', and 'chain'. 'Local' is essentially a migration field that centres upon a local area, whether a labour market or a geographical entity, and has been described by some writers as falling within an individual's knowledge- or action-space. Movement was therefore within a familiar orbit. In direct contrast to local movement, 'career' migration is defined by significant, or even total divorce from a familiar environment. Relocation is therefore an integral part of a chosen career path. 'Circular' migration involves a return to origins after a sequence of moves of indeterminate duration. Within this bracket could be long-term relocation as well as temporary residence, such as that for a season like the harvest. Classification of temporary relocation by business travel, or for health reasons or recuperative purposes, may also fall within this category, although such movement is often overlooked because of its seemingly more casual nature and absence of widespread documentation. Lastly, 'chain' migration describes how 'individuals move one after another, along a fairly determined path, taking advantage of established structures and contacts' (Clark and Souden, 1987, p. 16). Cultural as well as economic factors are often associated with such movement.

Historical analysis rarely lends itself to such straightforward categorization, either as a consequence of the source material or of the rationale behind the movement itself. Moreover, it is likely that individuals at different lifecycle stages will fall within the same abstract bracket although they may be moving for very different specific reasons. In terms of motivation, there can be wide variation contained within any of the categories and overlap is therefore the norm. Certainly, within the context of this study of Liverpool, few migrating individuals fall discretely within one category, and for this reason, no attempt has been made to quantify moves under particular headings.[32] Instead, the broad migrational categories have been

---

31 This draws upon Tilly (1979).
32 For an example of quantification of migration characteristics, see Pooley and D'Cruze (1994), pp. 355–58.

used as a base from which to view movement, and to assess, from individual experience, the prevalence and significance of particular moves and the motivations behind them.

Migration from a 'local' area has been recognized as one of the key mechanisms in fuelling the population growth of pre-industrial towns, and as aggregate analysis of Liverpool has shown, migration of this type was highly influential in the early eighteenth century. For this reason, it is perhaps inevitable that the majority of 'local' migrants had a further defining migrational characteristic that can be recognized in Clark and Souden's model. For example, the migration experience of William Holme might be described as 'local' and 'career', in the sense that ambition as a grocer took him from rural Melling to Liverpool. However, 'circular' must then be added to Holme's provenance since he returned to his family origins in Melling for burial. In overview, Holme's mobility was solely within a 10-mile radius of Liverpool, remaining firmly within a familiar geographical area. Therefore 'local' remains the defining characteristic. Yet, his experience is extremely useful in illustrating the human traffic both to, and from, the town. Indeed, from family reconstitution evidence for those marrying in Liverpool in the period 1691–1720 and recording at least two child baptisms, 48 per cent of adult females and 60 per cent of adult males cannot be traced to baptismal or burial entries in the parish registers. If absence of such vital event records can be taken as a crude indicator of presence elsewhere, then almost 50 per cent of the adult married population, arguably one of the most sedentary sub-groups within the population, were neither born nor buried in Liverpool.[33] The origin of these migrants and their motivation for movement to Liverpool has been variously assessed through aggregate study of sources and has been found to have a dominant local character. Perhaps more difficult is the analysis of movement from the town and the reason behind it. It is here that individual biographical profiles, such as that of William Holme, offer a fresh insight into the migratory machinations of the Liverpool population. The contribution of 'local' migration, whether assessed by aggregate study or individual approach, was the underpinning of the early eighteenth-century population structure, but as the experience of William Holme illustrates, motivations behind 'local' migration were more complex than a simple rural-to-urban relocation would indicate.

Liverpool, as a rapidly expanding town, offered all the expected urban career opportunities augmented by those of a fast developing port. The spur for many 'career' moves was therefore perceived economic opportunity in the expanding commercial environment of the late seventeenth and early eighteenth century. Early entrepreneurship within this setting can be recognized, for example, in the persons of Daniel Danvers and Richard Clieveland, who were drawn to Liverpool by the potential for furthering family success in an innovative industry, sugar baking. Mercantile activity, engendered by the port's rising authority, attracted interested parties from a wide catchment. A relatively local subject was Hugh Patten, who, recognizing

---

33 Lewis (1994), pp. 254–56. See also Souden (1984), pp. 20–22.

opportunity beyond the mercantile sphere in his native Warrington, relocated to Liverpool. However, not all career migrations to Liverpool or advancements within a chosen field were of such high profile. The four case studies are somewhat inadequate in highlighting the vast influx and subsequent career moves of craftsmen, tradesmen, journeymen and labourers, although an appreciable number of such individuals have been identified in the wider study. One exception to apparent elitism in the four cases was Matthew Nicholson, who came to Liverpool from Dumfriesshire as merely an itinerant trader, albeit specializing in linen. He rose to become an established linen draper and later merchant.

Longer-distance migration, still within the bracket of 'career', might be expected of professionals (Corfield, 1982, p. 103). Indeed, 'career' motivation was primary to the relocation of Dr John Tarleton. In a similar capacity Samuel Nicholson was at one point considering the alternatives of practising medicine in Bishop's Stortford or Nottingham in preference to Liverpool. Clergy were not always afforded such a choice of destination but, as in the case of Samuel Williamson, rector of Great Budworth, undoubtedly experienced migration during their careers.

Within the town economy were 'career' opportunities that might have prompted 'chain' migration. In aggregate studies the 'career' move of apprenticeship is a well-recognized example of this phenomenon. Key elements in the mechanism of 'chain' migration were structures for the succour of migrants (Clark, 1987, pp. 267–91). These can be recognized in a variety of forms. Kinship was one such form, and was evidenced in the apprenticeship of William Lightbody, who followed his Nicholson uncle from Scotland to Liverpool. Kinship links are not explicit in the Apprenticeship Books and are only recovered by multiple record linkage. Thus the kinship contribution to 'chain' migration, though known of, cannot easily be explored other than through the construction of networks. Apart from kinship support, community groupings such as religious denominations are known to have developed reception and support mechanisms. Such systems are more readily discovered in the later eighteenth and early nineteenth century when they became recognizably institutionalized. Thus, during the period under review, instances are difficult to identify in the absence of textual evidence, although, as the example of the Blackshaw youth illustrates, the assimilation of migrants by receiving communities was ongoing.

'Circular' is a form of migration nearly always recognized in conjunction with other categories described by Clark and Souden. Drawing upon the Liverpool evidence, and specifically the personal migration history of Dr John Tarleton, 'circular' might be added to 'career' in that he went from Liverpool to Lancaster and back again in the practice of medicine. In view of his social status as a professional, his circulatory movement falls within a particular sector, but circular movement could be manifest in very different forms and across all social strata. One well-recognized variant of circulation was the habit of harvest migration. This did not occur in Liverpool, but the maritime equivalent was the seasonal variation in trade and thus in shipping. For ships' masters, voyaging histories can be recovered, as in the cases of the Edward Tarletons, senior and junior. More elusive is the mainstay of the port economy, maritime migrants of more modest status, who left little imprint upon Liverpool's records.

As mentioned above, specialized forms of 'circular' migration can be recognized, often for relatively short periods and involving some element of temporary residence. Being Members of Parliament, the Clievelands, father and son, were 'sessional' migrants. In a similar fashion, education necessitated a circular movement for the Nicholson boys. These two examples highlight the possible differences in lifecycle stage that may be masked under a blanket term like 'circular'.

The models of migration and motivation cited above do not readily encompass the totality of the female experience. Women no doubt had their own agendas which can seldom be accurately defined in the absence of textual sources such as personal papers or diaries. The Nicholson women's correspondence provides a welcome exception to this dearth. Motives for women's movement were more often subsumed under those of their menfolk. Nonetheless, women filled a particular niche within the migration process. Marriage was a key mechanism by which families achieved economically-led mobility. Through marriage, the Danvers daughters unified entrepreneurial talents by constituting the bond between the sugar baking fraternity of Smith, Clieveland and Danvers. If 'marriage' can be taken as 'career', these women provided the motivational impetus for economic location and relocation in Liverpool. This may be an extreme example but it was not unique in Liverpool, and the phenomenon had impact upon both local and more distant migration fields.

In terms of career alternatives, women might have been expected to encounter a growing range of employment opportunities in the developing economy of Liverpool at this time, particularly in the domestic and service sectors. However, the adult sex ratio at burial in the period 1660 to 1750 indicates an almost consistent excess of male over female deaths (Lewis, 1994, p. 196, Table 6.13). Only between 1731 and 1740 did the balance of deaths suggest a surplus of women in the population, a characteristic commonly believed to typify the pre-industrial town. This imbalance may be rooted in the character of migrants entering the town, as a considerably greater number of males may have been drawn to Liverpool, attracted by the abundant and varied employment opportunities, particularly within the maritime sector. The implications for tracing female career moves are therefore greatly impeded. Indeed, in the greater database, only one female apprentice is recorded.

In terms of 'circular' migration, women display interesting variations on the theme. One form was the temporary relocation in a capacity of caring for other family members, whether local or distant. This was a role fulfilled in the Nicholson family by Arabella, née Cropper. Women also made prolonged supportive visits to one another, as Nicholson correspondence reveals. Such 'seasonal' movements, though apparently more casual than the equivalent male career-related episodes described above, were nonetheless circular relocations with distinct purpose. Without the constraints of their family responsibilities, women's mobility seems to have been more pronounced. Certainly there is evidence in Liverpool that in widowhood women were more likely to move than men. This movement could have been from choice as much as from the necessity to which it has usually been attributed. Due to this mobility, widows, especially poor widows, can be difficult, if not impossible, to link into networks of association.[34]

Just as the migratory motivations of most women can be only partially recovered, so the experience of certain other groups has not been recaptured through record linkage of the individual. One such omission will be those men who made a career move to become seafarers, most especially those who shipped 'before the mast', and were lost on voyage before making any mark on Liverpool. In the absence of crew lists, these individuals can be recovered only if leaving a will, which few ordinary seamen would have done.[35] Other 'missing persons' occur as individuals rather than groups. Both professionals and successful merchants might relocate to the capital or mark upward social mobility by physical mobility to landed country seats. However, while not recapturing the vagrant or subsistence migrants, the methodology employed has enabled penetration in the wider study beyond the wealthy elite to the 'middling sort' of craftsmen, and even to labourers. Indeed, by multiple record linkage, it has been possible to recover many elusive emigrants from the town, such as those relocating their wealth and themselves, or even consigning their corpses for removal.

Several of the movements classified by the abstractions above can be seen also as modifying or affecting the migration behaviour of others. William Holme was exercising an influence from beyond the grave, as regards the movement for burial of his daughter and widow. Matthew and John Nicholson sustained a close connection with their area of origin by contact with kin and return visits to Dumfriesshire. Thus they encouraged later migrants, whether related to them or not. They also fostered the maintenance of associations by the next generation who built on those connections when establishing works in Scotland with a Lightbody 'cousin'.

The role of women in mitigating the migration behaviour of others is perhaps the least likely role to be discovered by any but an approach at the level of individual networks of relationship. The reconstruction of the Danvers/Clieveland/Smith affine links are a case in which the female role is proved fundamental. Of course a woman's marriage may be influenced as well as being influential, which would seem the situation for Dorothy Tarleton, whose marriage may have been promoted by her father's maritime links with Ireland. In a different but related manner, the modifying of Liverpool migratory behaviour may have benefited from the acquired experience of regular maritime voyagers. Liverpool master mariners, through their prior experience or acquaintance, no doubt offered counsel or even assistance to migrants. Trans-Atlantic connections were utilized in various forms by or for, emigrants shipping from Liverpool. Those shipping with Edward Tarleton (junior) prove cases in point.

---

34 An imposed form of migration relevant to the latter group may have found expression in Poor Law removal orders. Unquestionably, Quarter Sessions records would afford the best prospect of identifying individual paupers, both male and female, in Liverpool during this period. Unfortunately, these records are beyond the remit of the present study.

35 Of the 447 seafaring testators known, or presumed, lost at sea, 84 (19 per cent) nominated no benefiting kin and indicated transience in Liverpool see Ascott (1996), p. 294.

In conclusion, this study has advanced beyond the mere identification of individual migrants, to the reconstruction of their history of movement and their personal motivations for mobility. It has been possible to perceive the interactions of individuals and consequent repercussions in terms of influences upon movement. Maritime influence was crucial for the distinct migration experience germane to Liverpool. That the place was a burgeoning urban centre was arguably secondary to its burgeoning port aspect, which apparently affected the catchment area for in-migrants, the sex ratio of those incomers, and the fluidity of the population character.[36] Significantly, Liverpool was a node both in the national urban hierarchy of migration and in the international context of population transfer. The port both extended its influence over the Lancashire hinterland and port communities elsewhere, and played an increasing role in trans-Atlantic emigration, while attracting a reverse flow of apprentices, marriage partners, returning factors and merchants. Motivations for movement to Liverpool were diverse, but motivations to leave Liverpool were, arguably, equally varied and important. Clearly, Liverpool was a society characterized by high population turnover and a complexity of migrational systems that are perhaps only revealed by analysis at the individual level.

---

36 The reflection of coastwise trading links in port in-migration, specifically culled from apprentice origins, has been remarked for earlier periods in Bristol, Great Yarmouth, and Ipswich. See Hollis (1948); Patten (1976), p. 129.

REFERENCES

ASCOTT, D. E. (1996), 'Wealth and community: Liverpool 1660–1760' (unpublished PhD thesis, University of Liverpool).
BAGLEY, J. J. (ed.) (1968), 'The Great Diurnal of Nicholas Blundell of Little Crosby, Lancashire', Vol. 1: 1702–1711, *Record Society of Lancashire and Cheshire*, **110**.
BAINES, T. (1852), *History of the Commerce and Town of Liverpool*, London.
BOULTON, J. (1987), *Neighbourhood and Society: A London Suburb in the Seventeenth Century*, Cambridge.
CLARK, P. (1979), 'Migration in England during the late seventeenth and early eighteenth centuries', *Past and Present*, **83**, 57–90.
CLARK, P. (ed.) (1984), *The Transformation of English Provincial Towns*, London.
CLARK, P. (1987), 'Migrants in the city: the process of social adaptation in English towns 1500–1800', In Clark and Souden (eds), 267–91.
CLARK, P. and D. C. SOUDEN (eds) (1987), *Migration and Society in Early Modern England*, London.
CORFIELD, P. J. (1982), *The Impact of English Towns 1700–1800*, Oxford.
CRESSY, D. (1986), 'Kinship and kin interaction in early modern England', *Past and Present*, **113**, 38–69.
ELTON, J. (1901), 'Liverpool lists of emigrants to America, 1697–1706', *Transactions of the Historic Society of Lancashire and Cheshire*, **53**, 179–88.
FOSTER, J. (1891), *Alumni Oxonienses: The Members of the University of Oxford 1715–1886: later series*, Vol. IV, Oxford.
GRASSBY, R. (1978), 'Social mobility and business enterprise in seventeenth century England', in D. Pennington and K. Thomas (eds), *Puritans and Revolutionaries: Essays in Seventeenth-Century History Presented to Christopher Hill*, Oxford, 355–81.
HOLLIS, D. (ed.) (1948), 'Calendar of the Bristol Apprentice Book, 1532–1569' (Pt. 1: 1532–1542), *Bristol Record Society*, **14**.
LANGTON, J. and P. LAXTON (1978), 'Parish registers and urban structure: the example of late eighteenth century Liverpool', *Urban History Yearbook*, 74–84.
LAWTON, R. and C. G. POOLEY (1975), 'David Brindley's Liverpool: an aspect of urban society in the 1880s', *Transactions of the Historic Society of Lancashire and Cheshire*, **125**, 146–68.
LEWIS, F. (1994), 'The demographic and occupational structure of Liverpool 1660–1750: a study of the parish registers' (unpublished PhD thesis, University of Liverpool).
LEWIS, F. (1995), 'Studying urban mobility: the possibilities for family reconstitution', *Local Population Studies*, **55**, 62–65.
MENARD, R. R. (1980), 'The tobacco industry in the Chesapeake colonies, 1617–1730: an interpretation', *Research in Economic History*, **5**, 109–77.
NICHOLSON, F. and E. AXON (eds.) (1928), *Memorials of the Family of Nicholson of Blackshaw, Dumfriesshire, Liverpool and Manchester*, private printing.
PATTEN, J. (1976), 'Patterns of migration and movement of labour to three pre-industrial East Anglian towns', *Journal of Historical Geographers*, **2**, 111–29.
PEET, H. (ed.) (1908), *Liverpool in the Reign of Queen Anne 1705 and 1708*, Liverpool.
POOLEY, C. G. and S. D'CRUZE (1994), 'Migration and urbanization in north-west England circa 1760–1830', *Social History*, **19**, 339–58.
POOLEY, C. G. and I. D. WHYTE (eds.) (1991), *Migrants, Emigrants and Immigrants: A Social History of Migration*, London.
PRYCE, W. T. R. (ed.) (1994), *From Family History to Community History*, Cambridge.
RAWLING, A. J. (1986), 'The rise of Liverpool and demographic change in part of South West Lancashire, 1660–1760' (unpublished PhD thesis, University of Liverpool).
SCHOFIELD, R. (1984), 'Traffic in corpses: some evidence from Barming, Kent (1778–1812)', *Local Population Studies*, **33**, 49–53.
SCHÜRER, K. (1991), 'The role of the family in the process of migration', in Pooley and Whyte (eds), 106–42.

SHARPE, P. (1990), 'The total reconstitution method: a tool for class specific study?', *Local Population Studies*, **44**, 41–51.

SOUDEN, D. (1984), 'Movers and stayers in family reconstitution populations', *Local Population Studies*, **33**, 11–28.

TILLY, C. (1979), 'Migration in modern European history', In J. Sundin and E. Söderlund (eds), *Time, Space and Man: Essays in Microdemography*, Stockholm, 175–97.

VENN, J. and J. A. VENN (1922), *Alumni Cantabrigiensis: A Biographical List of All Known Students Graduates and Holders of Office at the University of Cambridge, from the Earliest Times to 1900*, Pt. 1, Vol. 1, Cambridge.

Chapter 6

URBAN POPULATION AND FEMALE LABOUR: THE FORTUNES OF WOMEN WORKERS IN RHEIMS BEFORE THE INDUSTRIAL REVOLUTION

ANTOINETTE FAUVE-CHAMOUX

With a population of about 30.000 at the end of the eighteenth century, Rheims was one of the fastest growing towns in France and a large number of women were attracted to the opportunities for work afforded by the town's developing textile industry. It is the purpose of this chapter to use the evidence of family reconstitution, tax and census listings,[1] to reconstruct and present a view of the lives of women in the growing labour force of the town.

In a society where death rates were high and marriage was fundamentally both monogamous and delayed, not every mature woman could hope to either achieve this state or to retain it for a working lifetime. Indeed, so many of the working women of eighteenth-century Rheims were either single or widowed that married women constituted only half the adult female population (Fauve-Chamoux, 1983b). The significance of this relatively independent female labour force is one of the clearest features of a study of the population of Rheims through the seventeenth and eighteenth centuries. Research revealed that the proportion of women in the population reached a point when there were only 82 men for every 100 women (Fauve-Chamoux, 1994b). Following careful examination of the data and the archival sources, it is possible to identify quite different potential phases in life experience for urban women and, by defining them, to make important distinctions between seven different types of female employment which coincide with a potential seven stages in the lifecycle. In the first phase of working life there were two categories of women: *dowried young spinsters* who were likely to marry and *undowried young spinsters* who were not. Dowried women had a much better chance of becoming *married women and household managers (housewives)* and then of being either *young widows without children*, or *older widows with dependent children* and eventually *older widows without dependent children*. Undowried women might earn

---

. 1 The Rheims data bank created by Antoinette Fauve-Chamoux. Partly computerized, it includes nominative detailed parish registers of the vital events of all individuals with the patronym beginning with B in the 14 parishes and the several hospitals of the town (1668–1802). Tax listings and census information were also added and formed part of a general family reconstitution from the above data. For the census for 1802 we considered all households headed by individuals whose surnames began with the letter B: 12.8 per cent of the population of the town. The sample produced a total of 1,003 households.

enough to provide themselves with a dowry and move into the above categories. More often, if they survived, they became *older spinsters*.

In European early modern societies, women always outnumbered and outlived men and it is therefore not surprising that households headed by spinsters and widows were more numerous than those headed by bachelors and widowers. French towns were not exceptional in this regard (Fauve-Chamoux, 1986; Hufton, 1984; 1995; Wall, 1981). In the case of Rheims, this phenomenon was exaggerated by the nature of the dominant textile industry and its particular attraction for women. This factor also helped to define the social circumstances of this female labour force. It is important to note that within the traditional view of the role of women in industrializing society, only the third of the above stages could fit the traditional category of 'housewife' and that, as a consequence, the lives of many urban women were independent and often solitary. It is the aim of this chapter to dwell briefly on the lives of women in each of these categories in order to characterize the working life of each step in the female lifecycle.

DOWRIED YOUNG SPINSTERS

The unmarried proportion of the female labour force comprised women of mainly very modest means who were usually of rural origin (Fauve-Chamoux, 1994a), often living alone and faced with a market for their labour which was always volatile. Workshop labour was still the preserve of the men in most branches of early industry. Indeed, the textile industry as a whole was still predominantly male and remained a domestic industry where the workers plied their trade together, working all hours in a common room. Two distinct types of work were, however, open to young spinsters from the age of about fifteen. First there were the girls who worked as servants or shop assistants, lodging in the home of an employer. Second, living in more or less the same areas were the girls who took in piece work at home or in lodgings, with the aim of supplementing their dowries. Many of these young women were quite literally spinsters. To some extent these piece-work girls were outside the male-dominated structure of textile working during this period. This was as true of the towns as the countryside, where such activity might more readily be classified as proto-industrial. Only the preparation of the wool (washing, carding, dye-soaking) was conducted outside the home, and that only when the weather was fine. In these circumstances the women and children worked under the putative authority of the male head of household, when there was one.

UNDOWRIED SPINSTERS

If most women who raised or were given dowries worked in the family home until the time of marriage, not all women living at home managed to raise dowries and for some the only alternative was to find service in the house of a patron. Sometimes these were members of the family who would keep a careful watch on their charges. Census listings reveal more often than one might believe that servants were related to their employers. Nevertheless, a serving girl, freed from the autocratic authority of her father, often enjoyed at least a small measure of relative autonomy. It is impossible to calculate precisely what proportion of women had experience of paid work outside the home in the period of their lives when they were young and unmarried. It is probable that some girls were able to live away from home or in a family enterprise for a brief apprenticeship without leaving a specific trace in the records. Agencies did exist to recruit girls to specific tasks. The *Bureau des Recommanderesses* in sixteenth-century Paris, for example, was specifically established to recruit wet nurses. But the choice of servants was normally the product of word of mouth. In provincial towns, with strong rural-urban links, it was more common to use this grapevine of information. In Rheims, this was literally the case. A young country girl, coming to town, could easily find employment with someone who owned vines in her home village.

With rising migration, however, increasing numbers of women were not fortunate enough to find the support of a family structure. Often the position of the younger daughters of larger or poorer families was fragile and became more fragile as the eighteenth century progressed. Given the production system which favoured the family unit, how can we identify the relationship between these young single women and the world of work? Theoretically, in the first stage (that of domestic service) a young unmarried woman without capital (i.e. without a cowry) worked for as long as necessary to accumulate her portion. The end of employment of this kind was marked by the day of marriage. Such women preferred to live in the house of their employers, male or female, until that day, as the best means of saving their portion. They were meanwhile 'in service'. Although controlled and subordinate, in some ways they were in a less dependent position than a girl who continued to live in the house of her parents. They were, at least in principle, under the protection of the house for their board and employers were held responsible for their servants. This responsibility extended to bed as well as board, and until the eighteenth century the law was very much on the side of the servant made pregnant by the employer (Fairchilds, 1984; Gutton, 1981; Maza, 1983). If one examines the depositions made by unmarried mothers in this period (and servants made up a good proportion of their number), often enough the children of such unions were incorporated into the family economy of the employer. This became less common as social practice changed. Things tended to deteriorate in the Age of Enlightenment. In these circumstances, there were those unmarried mothers whose limited life chances set them on a downward spiral. These were not necessarily women who were overtaken by some dramatic tragedy but those who made a slow descent into the gutter. So often it was a precarious parenthood which was the start of the decline. Such was the situation of Marie-Anne Blavier, the daughter of Marie Henry.

Marie-Anne Blavier's mother was a widow who had married again when she was 40. She did not marry particularly well, for her husband, the son of Didier Blavier, was quite poor. She bore him one child, Marie-Anne, who was 13 years old when her mother died in hospital, aged 58, in August 1790. Her father had abandoned them before this date and she had no news of him. Orphaned and with no brothers and sisters, she had only her knowledge of spinning and her distaff to support her. Every day she looked for casual work in the rue Flechambaut. It was at an address here that she became pregnant at the age of 19. Her illegitimate daughter, Françoise, was born in the alms house in October 1795. She was immediately abandoned to charity and the often less-than-tender ministrations of a wet nurse. The baby died six weeks later. Two further daughters were born in similar circumstances in 1798 and 1799. Marie-Anne never saw them again.

There is evidence that in parallel with the loosening of constraints on tracing fathers of illegitimate children, the conditions for caring for such children changed dramatically during the century. If Marie-Anne had been admitted to the same alms house 50 years earlier she would have been closely interrogated about her partners. Indeed, before 1750, all the natural fathers were traced (Fauve-Chamoux, 1983c). Perhaps because of the social and political upheaval, which in itself created more situations to be solved, 50 years later no one cared any more who the father might have been. In the period from 1779 to 1792, only 0.4 per cent of genitors were found. It seems clear that, during this period, the abandonment of illegitimate children became institutionalized. Of these infants, 80 per cent fell into the hands of wet nurses recruited by the administrators of the foundling institutions.

What we do not know, though we may surmise, is whether Marie-Anne's pregnancies were due simply to loose morals or to prostitution. What is certain is that spinster women like her led precarious lives. Most of the illegitimate children were produced by these casual day labourers and they were almost certainly under-enumerated in the censuses. There is plenty of evidence of the rural origin of most of this social flotsam of potentially industrious women. As some of them continued to seek out towns where they had family ties, the tide of migration increased and, as the capacity of informal social systems failed to cope with the influx, so did the levels of destitution.

Beggary reappeared in pre-Revolutionary times. It reached such a level that by 1768, 'mounted constabulary ... comb out vagrants and outlaws and escort them to Châlons, where the strongest men are condemned to row in galleys and crippled ones or women to be shut up in the confinement of a vast place precisely opened for this purpose'. In a contrary move, 'carders and spinners from the near countryside' (which may be interpreted as a euphemism for starving poor people from adjacent pre-industrial villages) came into town to sack the merchants' granaries in a frumentary riot (Fauve-Chamoux, 1993b). In many ways the increasing number of women in this group provide an index of the social disjunction which accompanied rapid economic change.

MARRIED WOMEN (HOUSEWIVES)

Most women, both in towns and in rural areas, were married with a dowry from a father or brother and they left the domestic hearth for the first time on their wedding day. Restricted to the home, they escaped the vulnerable if relatively free stage of domestic service and jumped directly from the status of young girl to wife. Once married, persistently pregnant and surrounded by a brood of children, she was very much part of the economic unit of her husband. These women often continued to do economic work, but usually they disappeared from documentary sources and their situation remains difficult to interpret. While the children were some security against the penury of old age, they were an absorbing distraction from directly useful labour. The economic cost of children is still a very fraught topic (Fauve-Chamoux, 1981; Reher, 1995) and we should distinguish between the behaviour of rural and urban families in this matter. In the towns of the *ancien régime*, mothers were more often than not obliged both to work at their trade and to 'perform their duties as a wife'. Both activities were increasingly put before the vital interests of the children. Whether or not women perceived the significance of their behaviour, they were often socially obliged to follow the common urban practice of the times by putting their babies out to wet nurses who lived in the countryside. The work of ordinary women was difficult to disassociate from their domestic activities in that both economic and domestic activities were both contributions to the joint patrimony of the couple. But the more economically productive the mother, the more likely she was to be able to pay the wages of a village wet nurse to look after her nursing children. The return to maternal values, perceived by some to be characteristic of the new *sentiments* spread by the Enlightenment, was in fact restricted to a small circle of the intelligentsia. In this sense the literature is misleading (Fauve-Chamoux, 1983a; 1985). The truth is that as more and more women became involved in the economy, increasing numbers of children were put out to the often less-than-tender care of wet nurses. The practice continued in eighteenth- and nineteenth-century France both in large and small towns, where infant mortality remained high. The practice is evident even until the beginning of the First World War (Fauve-Chamoux, 1989).

In addition to the benefit of labour which a working wife brought to the new household, she also brought a dowry. This patrimony consisted of both possessions and capital, often deployed, if possible, as regular income deriving from interest from loans. For a woman these were the only measure of insurance against an old age of increasingly uncertain dependence on her children. Against this background of information, the position of the wife in an economically active urban family becomes much clearer. Indeed, when we explore the changing fortunes of a family of artisans, the participation of a capable woman (wife, daughter, sister, mother) was crucial to the success of a business. Let us examine another case.

In the year 1802, Marie-Anne Cornette, a spice bread maker, was living in the centre of Rheims with her husband Pierre Billet, nine years her senior, and six of the nine children she was to bear him. They had been married 24 years and lived quite well. Pierre was a gingerbread merchant and the household paid a capitation of between 20 and 50 livres, which, in the period before the Revolution, placed them in the category of the *petite bourgeoisie*. They had two live-in domestic servants, both from the same village in the Champenois, and with the same name; they were probably sisters. Marie-Anne's father-in-law came from the little town of Fismes, the first stage post on the road to Paris. It was he who had founded the business and, with the help of Pierre and two other sons who worked as spice bread makers in the same house, he watched it flourish. Father and son now lived separately but in neighbouring houses, so that when her mother-in-law died in 1799, Marie-Anne probably took over responsibility for the economy of both households. This, then, was clearly a hard-working artisan's wife, but one who had a good status from her work and lived quite well.

When widowhood occurred for such women, they had to adapt to new economic conditions and most of them tried to re-marry as soon as possible. This was clearly not always possible, or even desirable, and some women actually chose to remain mistresses of their own fate. These were usually those who came from strong family backgrounds with deep roots in crafts or trades. To be born in a trade helped women to maintain social status and they benefited from the strong socio-professional ties which were consolidated through generations, drawing on reciprocities and debts which could be activated when necessary.

YOUNG WIDOWS WITHOUT CHILDREN

The young widows were always likely to be in a stronger position than those with children. These young widows, when they had some capital, carried into widowhood a better set of options than the older spinsters. Indeed, in a period when things were generally improving for women, especially in a situation where they were in a majority, these young widows who were not absorbed in childrearing constituted a considerable economic force. If her husband died when she was young, a widow was not automatically precipitated into a stage of surrogate spinsterhood. Marriage conferred a status of independence which she retained as a widow, even as a young woman of between 20 and 25. So if young widows did not remarry it was not always because they found it difficult to find a husband. It was sometimes because they did not find it necessary. For a woman left relatively well-off, widowhood was no bad condition. A widow only worked if she had a need. She often only re-married if her income was not sufficient to support her, or if the family occupation demanded. Re-marriage was often a 'privileged choice' for young widows (Cabourdin, 1981). Indeed, in the life history of many such women, the years of widowhood (free from the burdens of childbearing) frequently exceeded those in the married state (Fauve-Chamoux, forthcoming). These women were often the entrepreneurs of some trade. Most of them, in pre-industrial Rheims, belonged to the textile sector.

YOUNG WIDOWS WITH CHILDREN

Widows with children and some business opportunities sought a way to provide for themselves and their children, usually by bringing the skills and capital gained in a previous trade, often shared with the dead husband, into a new marriage partnership. Sometimes families went through quite complicated mechanisms to retain and build a family business out of the ruins imposed by demographic accidents. Women were absolutely crucial to the successful contrivances which followed an early death. Let us look at the case of the Boudaille family.

In 1763, Jacques Boudaille, second son of a master butcher, Gérard I, had a butcher's shop in the parish of St Etienne. He died at the age of 36. His widow, burdened by four small children and reduced opportunities, was lucky in that she married again, 11 months later, to a man from Château-Porcien where she went to live, relinquishing the shop and the main part of the resultant capital to Gérard II Boudaille, the oldest brother of her deceased husband. Eventually, the main butchery passed to Gérard II's eldest daughter, Marie-Jeanne, married to Pierre Beuzard, a butcher from the Ardennes who became the putative inheritor of the trade. Marie-Jeanne died at the age of 39, herself leaving four small children, so that her husband also re-married quickly. He married a young butcher's widow from the neighbouring shop and found himself in charge of two establishments. An astonishing arrangement then took place. Pierre kept one shop with his new wife and two of his daughters aged 19 and 20, and left the other shop (with a young servant and a day labourer of 69) in the charge of his youngest daughter, aged only 15, Benoite, listed already as a professional 'butcher girl' in the 1802 census.

OLDER WIDOWS WITHOUT CHILDREN

Ursule Thomas was widowed in 1792. Her children had died before her widowhood. She was 51 years old at her husband's death and inherited his weaving workshop, a very modest one: taxes were only two-and-a-half pounds yearly. But she revealed herself such a very active and business-minded widow, even in the very midst of revolutionary turmoil, that she met with some success, being able to transform this workshop into a small factory with some hands as weavers, until she designated herself as a '*fabricante*' in 1802. We might relate this relatively late success in trade to her capacity to organize a family-based workshop, to which her stepbrothers contributed as hand workers. But she had no direct heir. This literate woman, born in Juniville, near Rheims, in the heart of local textile proto-industry, had married at the advanced age of 35, after a long period very probably spent as a servant. Four children were born to her between 1777 and 1783, of which none survived, the first one dying at birth, the later ones while being wet-nursed. Ursule, who did not re-marry despite being well off, advanced at the same time in old age and in solitariness, though she may have chosen this status for herself. In many ways this was a case of relatively prosperous widowhood, although deprived of direct descendants. Things were often not always so good for older widows without children.

OLDER WIDOWS WITH CHILDREN

It might be assumed that a fecund marriage was the best insurance against an indigent old age. But with urban infant mortality rates, exacerbated by poor child care, taking away half the children born alive, much still depended on chance. With Anne Marlette, widowed when 42 years old, we come across a much more common situation than that of Ursule. Born in 1711, married when 24 years old, she probably worked together with her husband Jean-Baptiste Bruyen, a weaver, and maybe for some neighbouring workshops: she had specialized in 'finishing' wool textiles. Despite this she nevertheless bore children almost incessantly until her husband died in 1753. Anne Marlette was pregnant for practically all her married life, bringing forth 11 children between 1736 and 1753. But only three of them reached adult age – two girls and a boy. This fate is very similar to that of the siblings of her own husband, born to a poor family of urban weavers at a time when living conditions for such working people were very hard. Jean-Baptiste indeed had been the only survivor of 12 brothers and sisters, and of those the longest surviving brother had only reached the age of seven, as we read in the parish registers of Confirmation. For his household also, living conditions were precarious, at a time of crisis in the textile business. Apparently, work came in with no regularity at all. Poverty is indicated by the fact that taxation on the family income remained at the lowest possible level between 1730 and 1751. No surprise then that Jean-Baptiste Bruyen did not die at home in 1753, but at the poor house of the Hôtel-Dieu, like all indigent people. His widow lived thereafter with her three children, until 1773 when Jeanne, the eldest child, married, followed in 1774 by her brother Philippe, who left his mother's household and his father's weaving loom to set up his own business as a shoemaker. Anne Marlette, now 63 years old, remained then with her youngest daughter, Nicole, who did not marry, maybe for that reason. Mother and daughter went on working together with increasing difficulties, until 1790 when the mother died in her seventy-ninth year, the daughter following her seven years later, when 54 years old, still a spinster.

Widowhood clearly aggravated already existing poverty in the working classes for these widows left in charge of children (Henderson and Wall, 1994; Kerzer and Laslett, 1995). Anne Marlette's taxation halved as soon as her husband died. It is a clear indication that her income manifestly spiralled down, when the needs of her household were still there with Jeanne, the eldest child, 16 years old, Nicole not yet 10 and Philippe 6. Unlike some shopkeepers' widows, who specialized in their husbands' trades or crafts, these women in the textile working business had few opportunities to re-marry in a sector undergoing a generalized crisis. When we analyse how and for how long widows survived their widowhood, living children, even if they were not always in a position to help much materially, were a positive factor to take into consideration, if only for their presence. Of course, the case described here is the best conceivable situation, for a working-class widow. In the case of Anne Marlette, already ageing, work-tired, and in need of care, her chance was the presence of her single daughter Nicole. But this permanent family attachment also had a cost: Anne Marlette maybe only attained a very old age at the price of her daughter definitely remaining a spinster.

Elizabeth Regnault, who is another example of a weaver's widow, is a case very similar to that of Anne Marlette. She lived through very similar hard conditions, but with seemingly one advantage: she was a very late widow. Her husband died at the age of 60, in 1762, after 32 years of marriage. But she was still poor. For, like Anne's spouse, her husband also died at the Hôtel-Dieu. Of her seven children, only two survived their father. The eldest son, Louis, also a weaver, had already married. Apparently, Elizabeth lived with her younger son, aged 27, until he married eight years later in 1770, only to become a childless widower himself almost immediately. He waited four years to re-marry – an unusual lapse of time which suggests that he went on co-residing with his mother. He took his second wife in 1774. Three years later, after the birth of her son's first child, Elizabeth herself died in the Hôtel-Dieu. It seems that none of her children were in a position to help her.

OLDER SPINSTERS

Here we come to the final category of female workers in Rheims. In many ways they were vital to the processes of emergent capitalism. Older spinsters were often unable to rely on their immediate families for support and were desperate to find work to survive. They provided a veritable reserve army. The increasing number of young widows with dowries and inheritances on the marriage market made things more difficult for these older spinsters, and by the time they reached what might be termed a 'certain age' (between 35 and 40), the spinsters lost all hope of finding a spouse. This was precisely the kind of flexible labour reserve which suited the developing textile industry, faced as it was by frequent crises of price and variable demand.

A large number of such women came from domestic service. For servant women who were unable or unwilling to marry, there came a time when they passed from the stage of young spinsterhood to the stage of developing their own household as a single person. Most women left their first essentially temporary job as they reached their thirties. Often they did so after bearing an illegitimate child. As we have seen, many of the unmarried mothers remained unmarried. The unmarried mother who raised daughters who in their turn became unmarried mothers was to become a more common feature of the nineteenth-century industrial revolution than the century of Enlightenment when infant mortality was very high, particularly for the illegitimates (Fauve-Chamoux, 1983c). The main point is that with or without children, these women rarely stayed in the home of the employer after thirty years of age. Some lived alone, many joined another female, often a relative, to set up an independent household (Fauve-Chamoux, 1993a).

Suzanne Boudaille, a 30-year-old single dressmaker, was doing quite well, working together with her sister, Hélène, aged 31 in 1802. The reasons for doing so were both emotional and economic. Live-in companions of better-off women often took up dressmaking as an occupation. If it became common for all 'good wives' during the nineteenth century to know how to knit and sew, this was not the case in the *ancien régime*. It was then a specialist craft and trades associated with dressmaking were the most practical for women, demanding time and patience in a period before sewing machines. Specialist needlework did not demand a particular location but it was imperative to live close to clients wealthy enough to provide their own materials. Working-class women made their own clothes or bought them second-hand. It was a flexible option which allowed intelligent women the opportunity both to create and to copy styles. The majority of dressmakers paid two livres as annual tax at the end of the eighteenth century. A third paid more. In 1789 there were 243 female dressmakers in Rheims of whom 12 were living with a sister. They were generally unmarried. Some women seem almost to have actually chosen this relatively lucrative form of independence. Such may have been the case for Gérarde Bruyant, for example. Although the daughter of a master oil merchant, she lived as a single needle woman until her death in 1742 at the age of 55. Though she registered as from her mother's parish of St Timothée, she lived in the more fashionable urban parish of St Pierre for her work and paid the relatively high rate of three livres of annual tax for the privilege.

A similar case seems to have been that of Henriette Bruyant, a dressmaker in her fiftieth year at the time of the census in 1802. She was of good family, her grandfather being a respected grocer in St Pierre who was well enough off to employ a permanent live-in servant. His wife had borne him 13 children and he had been able to establish his three sons as tradesmen. Their children had gone on to become respectively wine merchants and a municipal notable, always a sign of upward mobility. Two sisters had made good marriages. Mademoiselle Henriette, on the other hand, seems to have taken to her role as working spinster and pursued the craft of dressmaker in the fashionable rue St Hilaire (and some time later rue de l'Oignon) not far away. The fact that an upwardly mobile family seems to have accepted this status for one of its female members is interesting.

Although such cases are worthy of attention, showing that it was possible to make a decent living as a single elderly woman, as we have seen, the path of downward mobility and early death was the more probable fate of the elderly spinster, just as it was for the unmarried mothers and the widows of poorer workmen without a trade outside textiles.

CONCLUSION

This chapter has concentrated on the economic and social implications for women with their changing roles in the urban social and economic structure of a rapidly developing textile town. It has drawn on a body of previous statistical research using the approaches of historical demography. Here, however, the same evidence has been viewed in rather a different way: to point to the harshness of living conditions for lower-class women, especially spinsters and widows. In such a town as Rheims nearing the end of the eighteenth century, this group comprised broadly half of the female adult population.

The study considered a period of increasing social and economic disturbance. The French revolutionary turmoil disrupted the traditional nets of church-administered aid and relief. It was followed by one of the worst economic crises in the textile proto-industry which nurtured about half of the population. At the same time, the side effects of female-dominated rural-urban migration amplified. The consequent unbalanced sex ratios in Rheims further contributed to disturb a socio-economic system which was strongly based on the family unit. The increase in female labour in the textile industry led to enhanced infant mortality as a product of wet nursing.

The case studies presented tend to confirm the growing harshness of these changing circumstances. They also depict the wretched precariousness of survival for these women, especially for the widows whose new status almost automatically implied at least halving their standard of living, even for the poorest. Work opportunities became rarer, except for the youngest childless widows, and hopes for a second life with another man diminished. Infant mortality produced considerable emotional pressure, as with the father quoted above who was the sole survivor of a family of 12 children and who himself saw the death of 8 of his 11 children! Of course charities, such as the Church, had traditionally developed over centuries with the help of prominent members of the community or municipality in institutions such as the Hôtels-Dieu. But these were increasingly thought of as death-traps and admittance into such institutions was stamped as a sign of absolute destitution. Outside the Hôtels-Dieu there only remained the lonely disintegrative forces of family breakdown. Behind all this was the shadowy presence of the illegitimate children, whose filiation was not worth enquiring after because, where charity had found a place for them, 80 to 90 per cent were in any case to die at the hands of wet nurses.

These women in the poorer parts of Rheims may represent the situation in every expanding town in eighteenth-century France, struggling to maintain the necessary resilience to go on living and even to reach old age. This account perhaps provides some insight into their lives and the web of social and economic relations in pre-modern urban France just before industrialization.

REFERENCES

CABOURDIN, G. (1981), 'Le remariage en France sous l'ancien régime (seizième–dix-huitième siècles)', In J. Dupâquier, E. Hélin, P. Laslett, M. Livi-Bacci and S. Sogner (eds), *Marriage and Remarriage in Populations of the Past*, London, 273–86.

FAIRCHILDS, C. (1984), *Domestic Enemies, Servants and their Masters in Old Regime France*, Baltimore.

FAUVE-CHAMOUX, A. (1981), 'Les aspects culturels de la mortalité différentielle des enfants dans le passé', *Congrès de Manille*, UIESP, Liège, 341–61.

FAUVE-CHAMOUX, A. (1983a), 'La femme devant l'allaitement', *Annales de Démographie Historique*, Paris, 7–22.

FAUVE-CHAMOUX, A. (1983b), 'The importance of women in an urban environment: the example of the Rheims household at the beginning of the Industrial Revolution', In R. Wall, J. Robin and P. Laslett (eds), *Family Forms in Historic Europe*, Cambridge University Press, 475–92.

FAUVE-CHAMOUX, A. (1983c), 'Rémois et rémoises d'ancien régime', *Histoire de Reims*, Toulouse, 193–228.

FAUVE-CHAMOUX, A. (1985), 'Innovation et comportement parental en milieu urbain (XVe-XIXe siècles)', *Annales, ESC*, **5**, 1023–39.

FAUVE-CHAMOUX, A. (1986), 'La femme seule, une réalité urbaine: l'exemple de Reims au début du XIXe siècle', *Mémoires de la Société d'ACSA de la Marne*, 295–305.

FAUVE-CHAMOUX, A. (1988), 'Les structures familiales en France aux XVIIe et XVIIIe–siècles', In J. Dupâquier (ed.), *Histoire de la population française*, Vol. 2, Paris, PUF, 317–47.

FAUVE-CHAMOUX, A. (1989), 'La famille et le petit enfant en France au XVIIIe siècle: modèles et réalités', *Actes du Congrès international des Lumières*, London, 1683–89.

FAUVE-CHAMOUX, A. (1993a), "Per la buona e la cattiva sorte": Convivenze nella Francia preindustriale', *Quaderni Storici*, **83**, 457–502.

FAUVE-CHAMOUX, A. (1993b), 'Household forms and living standards in pre-industrial France: from models to realities', *Journal of Family History*, **18**, 135–56.

FAUVE-CHAMOUX, A. (1994a), 'Female mobility and urban population in preindustrial France (1500–1900)', In A. Eiras-Roel and O. Rey Castelao (eds), *Les migrations internes et à moyenne distance en Europe, 1500-1900*, Santiago de Compostela, CIDH, 43–71.

FAUVE-CHAMOUX, A. (1994b), 'Female surplus and preindustrial work: the French urban experience', In S. Sogner and A. Fauve-Chamoux (eds), *Socio-economic Consequences of Sex-ratios in Historical Perspective, 1500–1980*, Milan, 31-50.

FAUVE-CHAMOUX, A. (forthcoming), 'Veuves et veuvage en France préindustrielle', *Quaderni Storici*.

GUTTON, J-P. (1981), *Domestiques et serviteurs dans la France de l'ancien régime*, Paris.
HENDERSON, J and R. WALL (eds) (1994), *Poor Women and Children in the European Past*, London.
HUFTON, O. (1984), 'Women without men: widows and spinsters in Britain and France in the eighteenth century', *Journal of Family History*, **9**, 355–76.
HUFTON, O. (1995), 'Women without men: widows and spinsters in Britain and France in the eighteenth century', In J. Bremmer and L. Van den Bosch (eds), *Between Poverty and the Pyre: Moments in the History of Widowhood*, London.
KERZER, D. and P. LASLETT (eds) (1995), *Aging in the Past: Demography, Society, and Old Age*, Berkeley.
MAZA, S. C. (1983), *Servants and Masters in Eighteenth Century France: The Use of Loyalty*, Princeton.
REHER, D. (1995), 'Wasted investments: some economic implications of childhood mortality patterns', *Population Studies*, **49**, 519–36.
WALL, R. (1981), 'Woman alone in English society', *Annales de Démographie Historique*, 303–17.

Chapter 7

MOBILITY AMONG WOMEN IN NINETEENTH-CENTURY DUBLIN

JACINTA PRUNTY

INTRODUCTION

Geographical studies of nineteenth-century Irish urban centres have been dominated by concern with morphology and the built fabric, with attempts to reconstruct the social geography of individual towns and cities heavily dependent on property valuation records, health and housing reports (Royle, 1991; Martin 1988; Aalen, 1992; McCullough, 1989). The compilation of topographical information, most notably in the *Irish Historic Towns Atlas* series,[1] provides a firm foundation on which to build geographical studies, but the lack of census data at the household level prior to 1901,[2] such as is available for most British cities in the form of census enumerators' books, greatly hinders the follow-through stage of effectively 'peopling the [Irish] past' (Lawton, 1987). The search for alternate city-wide sources which provide detail on all residents, rather than on the property they occupy, is still in its infancy.[3] In terms of mobility, recent nineteenth-century research has concentrated on Irish overseas migration flows rather than on movements within Ireland, with the exodus precipitated by the famine holocaust (1845–c.1851) understandably dominating the discussion (McKay, 1990; O'Sullivan, 1995). The experience of the overseas Irish in such places as Liverpool, Manchester, Bristol and York has also received some very close attention, but such studies cannot be replicated in Ireland in the absence of household census data (Letford and Pooley, 1995; Busteed and Hodgson, 1994; Large, 1985; Finnegan, 1982; Swift and Gilley, 1999). Against this background, a gender perspective on geographical mobility in nineteenth-century Dublin is practically non-existent.

Yet the question of mobility, assessed from a gender standpoint, is essential to any reconstruction of the social geography of the nineteenth-century city. Residential mobility is 'the mechanism whereby the character of social areas is maintained or changed' while social areas themselves 'provide the context in which individuals

---

1 *Irish Historic Towns Atlas*, eds. John H. Andrews, Anngret Simms, Howard Clarke, Raymond Gillespie (Dublin: Royal Irish Academy), published to date: Kildare (1985), Bandon (1989), Kells (1990), Carrickfergus (1986), Mullingar (1992), Athlone (1995), Maynooth (1996), Downpatrick (1997), Bray (1999).
2 Household census material for Ireland, stored in the Public Record Office, was destroyed during the bombing of the adjoining Four Courts during the Civil War, 1922. As an example of how the earliest surviving data for Ireland (1901) may be used see Murnane (1988).
3 See Fahy (1984) where the distributions of pawnbrokers, perfumers, taverners, and private, charity and boarding schools are among the many variables used in an attempt to differentiate status areas.

make decisions about their residential location and subsequent mobility' (Dennis, 1984, p. 250). It has been argued that mobility, or its opposite, persistence, can be used as a key indicator of the stability of communities; by reworking this argument to include a gender perspective, it can be maintained that the distances over which men and women move, the differing sources of their information, the vacancies they examine and the particular destinations they choose may all be used to define the geographical limits of varying types of 'community' (ibid.). In the search to define 'geographical spaces' which are 'also relevant social spaces' (Anderson, 1982) it is essential to move beyond property assessment into the more complex human realms of school and church attendance, kinship networks, household structure, type and length of tenure, occupation and journey-to-work, and where persons seek assistance in times of crisis such as illness or widowhood. The necessity of a gender perspective in such matters is indisputable; female employment in domestic service, and male involvement in dock labouring for example, will greatly influence choice of residence, while the role of women as the primary child-care providers has enormous repercussions for patterns of mobility.

This study focuses purposely on women, as the more neglected area of research, beginning firstly with an analysis of contemporary reports on mobility, and extracting whatever gender-specific information is possible. The second section requires the mapping of changes of address of 60 individual women, based on a sample of case histories (1868–75) drawn from the Register of St Brigid's Orphanage, Dublin. This reconstruction of individual mobility patterns, in conjunction with personal details covering the process behind the movements (also extracted from the orphanage records), is similar to the method employed in several British studies where information gleaned from personal diaries has been used to reconstruct individual and family patterns of mobility.[4] The use of individual records always prompts the question of whether such patterns can be taken as representative of types of individuals. In this Dublin study, the relatively large sample size, considering the nature of the material, makes it more likely that the pattern which emerges is typical of the class and gender represented, viz., poor Catholic women with children, who were resident in Dublin city at the time of their application for relief.

EVIDENCE FOR MOBILITY AMONG WOMEN

The extant Census of Ireland material for the period 1841–91 is largely limited to printed reports, from which very generalized evidence for mobility can be extracted. Summary tables such as those enumerating the number and sex of emigrants from Irish ports, for example, are available from 1 May 1852 (Table 6). In the case of Dublin, the tables cover emigration from both the city and county.[5] The numbers of females emigrating during the period 1852–80 ranges from a high of 2,186 in 1864

---

4 Dealing with studies utilizing both census enumerators' books and individual diaries see Lawton (1987); Dennis (1984); Pooley and Lawton (1988), pp. 165–68; Lawton and Pooley (1992), pp 127–33.
5 For example, *Census of Ireland 1881*, Province of Leinster, County and City of Dublin, Table XXXVIII.

Table 6: Emigration from the county and city of Dublin, 1 May 1851–21 March 1871

Years	Males	Females	Persons
1851	2,277	1,901	4,178
1852	1,516	1,516	3,032
1853	1,218	1,268	2,486
1854	1,158	1,174	2,332
1855	867	1,096	1,963
1856	1,023	1,020	2,043
1857	737	699	1,436
1858	1,192	850	2,052
1859	1,309	1,399	2,708
1860	1,547	1,419	2,966
1861	1,104	931	2,035
1862	2,732	1,218	3,950
1863	1,592	1,309	2,901
1864	2,561	2,186	4,747
1865	2,412	2,043	4,455
1866	1,318	1,260	3,078
1867	1,397	1,052	2,449
1868	1,299	897	2,196
1869	1,375	990	2,365
1870	1,511	1,209	2,820
1871	214	121	335
Total	30,959	25,568	56,527

Source: *Census of Ireland 1871*, Table XLI.

to a low of 303 in 1876. In the early 1850s more than half the total enumerated were female; in 1877 and 1878 women were again in the majority, but for most of the period females averaged 46.3% of the total returned. The total numbers of emigrants fluctuated greatly from year to year, the post-famine downward spiral of the early 1850s reversed by a marked increase in 1864, with the smallest numbers recorded during the mid-1870s. There is some gender bias in that female numbers did not fluctuate quite as widely as male numbers, but the difference is not substantial. Such emigrant tables prove to be of minimal use, except perhaps to underline Dublin's important role as a through port for passenger traffic, to confirm that women made up a substantial portion of cross-channel migrants, in some years exceeding half of those recorded, and to highlight significant annual fluctuations in the volume of migration affecting both men and women.[6]

A more useful census table is that detailing the birthplaces of persons enumerated in the counties and cities of Ireland. Although the numbers for Dublin city

---

6 Before even the most tentative conclusions could be drawn, it would be necessary to examine the Dublin pattern in relation to trends in all Irish ports, whilst changes in the methods of data collection and classification over time must also be considered.

and county are again compounded together, it is nevertheless possible to discern the broad outlines and gender breakdown of the migration pattern to the city in the later nineteenth century (Figure 24). Almost 62 per cent of Dublin's population of 418,910 in 1881 was born within the city or county; 7 per cent was born in Great Britain or 'abroad' or at sea; while the remaining bulk of 31 per cent was drawn from every county in Ireland but most notably from those adjoining Dublin. The southern neighbour, County Wicklow, was by far the most important source of migrants, contributing 21,700 persons, almost as many persons as counties Kildare and Meath together. County Wexford was also an important source

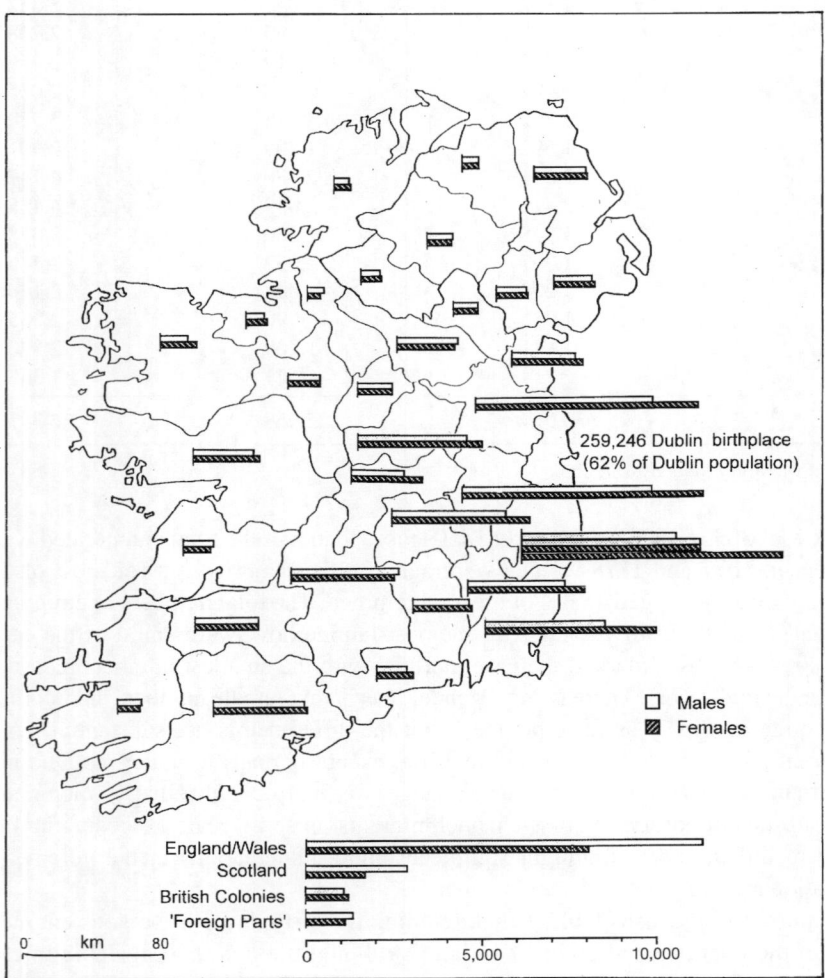

Figure 24: Birthplaces of persons enumerated in the city and county of Dublin, 1881
Source: *Census of Ireland 1881*, Table XXIII.

of newcomers, while the flow of persons from the densely-populated, most urbanized and mostly Protestant northern province to Dublin was relatively light. Women outnumber men in mostly instances, most spectacularly in County Wicklow; the possibility of domestic service in the city and suburbs was largely responsible for this. However, even if other factors such as population density, level of urbanization, and socio-economic status (standard of house accommodation, literacy, occupation) for each county were brought into the equation, only the most tentative and generalized statements could be advanced about Irish migration flows to Dublin.

The large number of soldiers garrisoned in the city throughout the nineteenth century contributed to the gender imbalance among Dublin residents born outside Ireland evident in Figure 24. In 1861 military personnel quartered in Dublin city numbered 2,638, in 1871 the number was 2,356, in 1881 it had risen to 3,439. Among army personnel posted to Dublin a small minority were of Irish birth, with 67 per cent returned as natives of England and Wales, 5 per cent as natives of Scotland, and 2 per cent classed as 'born abroad' in the 1871 returns.[7]

The debate which surrounded the extension of the English 'New' Poor Law (1834) to Ireland in 1838, and subsequent inquiries into its operation, revolved around the issues of mendicancy and mobility (Prunty, 1998 pp. 210–18). It was repeatedly claimed that Dublin, with its 'superior wealth and population', acted as a magnet to the mendicant classes from all over the country. The attractions of 'a richer harvest ... augmented by the donations of casual visitors' along with the 'numerous charities' and the 'known benevolence of its inhabitants', served to 'lure' the destitute (Nicholls, 1838, p. 88). The great dearth of alternatives especially in the period preceding the Poor Law left many with little option but to resort to urban centres and especially to Dublin; it was obvious even to those most critical of the city's beggars that 'there is no other place where the needy, or the famishing, will be sustained' so that 'nearly the whole tide of wretchedness and want must of necessity pour in upon Dublin' (ibid., p. 89). While the exact number, origin and gender breakdown of the city's mendicant population were always disputed, the preponderance of women was undeniable: nine out of every ten beggars it was claimed were female, from the 'young widow or the deserted wife, with two or three helpless children' who 'professes her willingness to seek, but her want of success in her endeavours to obtain work', to the huckster who 'urges on your attention the claims of a sick husband or children', to the 'aged female' who seeks relief as 'unable any longer to maintain herself'.[8]

As the ratepayers of each Poor Law Union had to support those relieved within its workhouse, the admission of vagrants from outside the union boundaries, and the question of 'settlement', i.e. residency requirement before relief would be granted, repeatedly surfaced as contentious issues. From the 1840s to the 1870s the question of removal of Irish and Scottish paupers from the workhouses of England and Wales

7   *Census of Ireland 1871*, Province of Leinster, County and City of Dublin, Table XXVII
8   *Report upon Vagrancy and Mendicity in the City of Dublin*, Appendix C, Part II, *Poor Inquiry (Ireland)*, 1836, p. 27a*.

dominated the debate.⁹ The Liverpool authorities claimed that the city's position as 'a kind of terminus for all parts of the country' resulted in an inordinate number of persons resorting to their workhouse for relief. About half the inmates were Irish, including 'persons landing directly from the steamer and applying at the workhouse for relief'.¹⁰ Among the flow of arrivals from Ireland, it was alleged, were women who travelled to Liverpool Union Workhouse to have their babies, and then returned home.¹¹ In Leeds, efforts to implement the 'law of removal' which allowed the authorities to forcibly return Irish migrants to an Irish seaport or, from 1863, to the union of their place of birth, met with considerable criticism; the case of Bridget Parker, an Irish washer-woman working in Leeds, was cited as an example of the harshness and even illegality with which such matters were dealt. On falling ill this woman had been admitted to the infirmary of the Leeds workhouse; within days 'she was taken from her bed so hurriedly as to be only half dressed' to the police office and removed, under an incorrect warrant, to the union at Ennis, the place of her birth.¹² The question of mobility among the Irish poor was thus a cross-channel matter, made possible by the growth in cheap steamship fares.

Charity sources also testify to very high levels of in-migration to Dublin city throughout the nineteenth century. Margaret Aylward, a Catholic activist who established the first city branch of the Ladies' Association of Charity of St Vincent de Paul in 1851, with the purpose of relieving the 'sick poor', repeatedly highlighted the position of both men and women driven to the city slums from many parts of the island (Prunty, 1999). Typical was a widow in Greek Street, 'not so fluent in English as in her native Irish', and heading a family from the country, 'one among the many who have been swept away out of their little holdings into the back lanes of the city'.¹³ The Association for the Relief of Distressed Protestants claimed the support of its co-religionists from all over the country, 'on the grounds that many of the persons relieved have been from the Provinces, who have been assisted in their struggles to obtain employment in the Metropolis, whither they have come in search of it'.¹⁴ Summarizing the situation in Dublin city in 1918 P. C. Cowan, a government inspector appointed to inquire into the housing of the working classes, described the city as 'the rest house or alms house to which people broken in health, character or fortune come from all over Ireland to shelter or hide themselves, or to take advantage of its numerous hospitals and almost innumerable over-lapping charities' (Cowan, 1918 p. 14). Critical to the question of mobility was the continued downgrading of

---

9 Settlement and Poor Removal Committee of the House of Commons 1847; Settlement and Poor Removal Committee of the House of Commons printed report, 1855; *Report from the Select Committee on Poor Removal*, 1878–79 (282),. Vol XIII, 1879 (hereafter *Poor Removal*, 1879)
10 Evidence of Mr Ebenezer Wilkie, *Poor Removal*, 1879 (282), Vol XIII, 1879, p. 99, q. 1811
11 *Poor Removal* (1879), Evidence of Mr French, p. 43, q. 818
12 *Poor Removal* (1879), Evidence of Mr French, p. 43, q. 1822; Evidence of Richard Bourke, p. 82, q. 1511
13 *Ladies of Charity of St Vincent De Paul, First Annual Report*, 1852, p. 16
14 *Twenty Eighth Annual Report of the Association for the Relief of Distressed Protestants*, 2 February 1865, p. 12.

former one-family residences to tenement dwellings, as the better-off abandoned the city for the attractions of the suburbs. A recurrent complaint by charity workers, medical officers, ratepayers and clergy alike was that a large part of the city 'abandoned by the independent' was now 'almost exclusively the abode of the struggling poor', 'penniless families' crowded into every room, with 'no wealthy residents at hand to visit and relieve them'.[15] The subdivision of houses in the older parts of the city was well underway at the time of Whitelaw's census and survey (published 1805), so that from 30 to 50 individuals per house was a common occurrence, with up to four separate families sharing a single room (Whitelaw, 1805, pp. 50–51). By 1894 the city's medical officer of health stated unequivocally that 'one third of the people of Dublin live in single room tenements, in which they eat, drink, cook, sleep and often carry on their work for a living'.[16] In the complex web of property holding in the Dublin slums, with perhaps five owners to one tenement house, along with immediate lessees, tenants, subtenants, and occupiers, weekly and even daily tenancies were common. Such a fluid structure, when the minimal furnishings of these apartments is also taken into account, made changing one's address the simplest of matters, especially if the move was within the immediate district. In these instances social and economic ties were hardly stretched, let alone severed. As the century proceeded the tenement structure became even more widespread and entrenched, as the once-aristocratic north city Gardiner estate lost out to the shift of 'fashionable society' to the south-eastern Fitzwilliam/Pembroke sector, a move that was greatly hastened by the bankruptcy of the Gardiner estate administration at mid-century. When asked in 1885 to account for the downgrading of the parish of St Mary's, which included much of the Gardiner district, a local priest replied simply that 'fashion has a good deal to do with it', as families require 'modern appliances' not possible in old houses and 'as the people can get fresh air, and everything outside in the suburbs, with lower taxes, they go there'.[17] While there is ample statistical evidence of appalling housing conditions in the tenement dwellings, with a wide range of case studies which testify to the hardships experienced by individual women, hard facts on turnover of occupancy for men or women are impossible to ascertain, let alone data which would allow individual changes of address over time to be traced. Compelling evidence for widespread homelessness among women and children in Dublin is available, but is similarly qualitative rather than quantitative. The promotional literature for female night refuges highlights this situation. A zealous Protestant woman, Mrs Ellen Smyly and the evangelical missionary society the Irish Church Missions were heavily involved in the provision of dormitory accommodation for 'grown girls, from fifteen to twenty years of age' in Luke Street (near Townsend Street). The young women this home targeted were 'so destitute as to have no settled place of abode', placing them at considerable risk (*Them Also*, 1866, p. 32). Catholic activists launched a major public campaign in 1861 to establish a night refuge for

15 *Twenty Seventh Annual Report of the ARDP*, 11 May 1864, p. 6
16 *Report on Public Health, Dublin Corporation Reports*, 1894, no. 136, p. 27
17 Robert Conlan, evidence to *Third Report of H.M. Commissioners for Inquiring into the Housing of the Working Classes* (Ireland, 1885) c-4547-I, qs. 23,237–23,300; see also Prunty (1998).

homeless women and children, 'wherein the comfort of a clean bed of straw, would be afforded to all poor females and children who would present themselves before a certain hour at night, with a ticket from a clergyman or respectable householder'.[18] Its promoter, Dr Spratt, appealed to the public to consider the hundreds of women who spend the nights 'forlorn and deserted by all' in open hallways, under archways, and in 'the roofless garret, the foul and fetid cellar, the filthy and crowded lodging'. The destitute younger woman was again the principal concern, those who were refused permission to shelter in the police stations 'because there was no charge against them' and 'unable to bear up against the cold and hunger, succumb and lose their virtue'. This asylum was located in Brickfield Lane in the Liberties, in what was originally Pleasant's Tenter House where poor weavers 'tentered' their cloth before sale; it was later an auxiliary workhouse of the South Dublin Union. All those using what was to become known as St Joseph's Night Asylum were initially put off the premises in the morning, but by 1884 when it could accommodate a total of 200 persons per night, it sought to open a laundry to generate an income and also provide work for the girls without homes 'who are allowed to stay all day' (Barrett, 1884).

At the other end of the social spectrum, the steady outward movement of the well-to-do to the self-governing townships of Pembroke, Rathmines and Rathgar (south side) and Clontarf (north side) had repercussions for all classes, but especially for the large number of poorer women for whom domestic service was practically the only sphere of employment. The 1881 census returned 49,623 females 'of specified occupations and positions' in Dublin city; of these 32 per cent were entered as 'domestic indoor servant', followed in order of magnitude by dressmaker/tailoress/seamstress (20 per cent) and dealers in provisions and 'general or unspecified commodities' (8 per cent).[19] This army of domestic servants was directly affected by the increase in commuting distance which accompanied suburbanization, while the many live-in positions multiplied the difficulties of women workers who had responsibility for children or other dependants. The scale of suburban development can be judged crudely from aggregate population figures: in 1871 22 per cent of the city's population of 314,666 lived outside the municipal boundary; in 1891 30 per cent of a total population of 349,594 were suburban residents.[20] The demographic and denominational situation can be appraised from a fundraising campaign in 1862 to erect a Catholic church in Rathgar, launched out of concern for 'the condition of numerous domestics located in the Protestant families of the neighbourhood'; these women 'find it not infrequently all but impossible to reach the parish church even for Mass upon Sundays, and return home within the few moments allotted to them for that purpose'. The new church was intended 'to console and encourage them in their pious struggles and lessen as much as possible the perils they encounter by multiplying for them the opportunities of religious observance'.[21]

18 Fundraising circular, John Spratt, Dublin Diocesan Archives [hereafter DDA], file 335/5, priests, no. 163, 1860.
19 *Census of Ireland 1881*, Table XIXa
20 *Yearly Summary of the Weekly Returns of Births and Deaths in Dublin*, 1877 Table I; 1891 Table VI.
21 Fundraising leaflet, DDA, 26 March 1862, 340/3 file 111 no. 1.

It is possible to trace changes in the city's built fabric, such as the conversion of existing housing stock into tenements, the erection of institutional buildings, and the spread of new terraces throughout the suburbs, by comparing entries in *Thom's Official Almanac and Street Directory* from year to year, and by close reference to the accompanying six-inch directory maps (produced by the Ordnance Survey). However, no occupiers are named for the many premises listed as 'tenements', inmates of institutions are completely ignored, and among the better-off classes the head of household, usually male, is the sole named entry, so that as a source for studying the mobility of women and of the poor these directories prove disappointing.

From these sources, official, charity and commercial, the situation of women emerges as most definitely mobile, with some well-documented strands such as the preponderance of women among the city's homeless and beggars. However, the challenge is to procure hard facts, to be able to put names and addresses and dates on individual movements, and to build up some finer detail 'from the ground'. How often did women move, in what directions, over what distances, and for what reasons? And most importantly, what were the implications of such mobility for the social geography of the city?

CASE STUDY: RECORDS OF ST BRIGID'S ORPHANAGE, 1868–1875

The register entries of destitute children admitted to St Brigid's orphanage include many valuable references to the movements of mothers both immediately prior to their child's admission, and during the period the child was in the care of the institution. Founded in Dublin by Margaret Aylward in 1856, with its administrative office in 42 (later 46) Eccles Street from 1858, it developed a sophisticated network of closely-supervised foster families, to provide each child with 'a father's protection, a mother's love, and the endearments of a family circle' (*Second Annul Report*, 1858, p. 12). Only children who could not be cared for by their own relatives were admitted, and the restoration of children to surviving family members was actively pursued so that contact was maintained throughout the child's stay in the institution (Prunty, 1999, pp. 56–78). It is these forwarding addresses, and accompanying notes, which are an invaluable source for studying mobility among poor women.

Few of the children admitted were 'orphans' in the sense of being left totally alone, whether through the death, desertion or imprisonment of their parents. The vast majority, over 75 per cent, were in the care of women (married and unmarried) coping alone, most often due to the death of the child's father, but also as a result of desertion, or the illness or imprisonment of the fathers. About 14 per cent of all admissions were of non-marital children, and practically all these women can be classed as 'deserted'. Typical admission notes were 'newly widowed, young and good looking but extremely poor, could not earn anything with the child' (Mrs Masterson, Figure 25a) and 'seems decent but poor, not able to support the children' (Mrs Dalton, Figure 25a). With the youngest child or children, or perhaps the most sickly child, in care, the mother could 'get on her feet' again and in due course reclaim her child/children from the institution. Such was the aspiration of Mrs Margaret Delaney (Figure 25c) who on the admission of her children 'is now to be employed in a laundry at 7s'. The

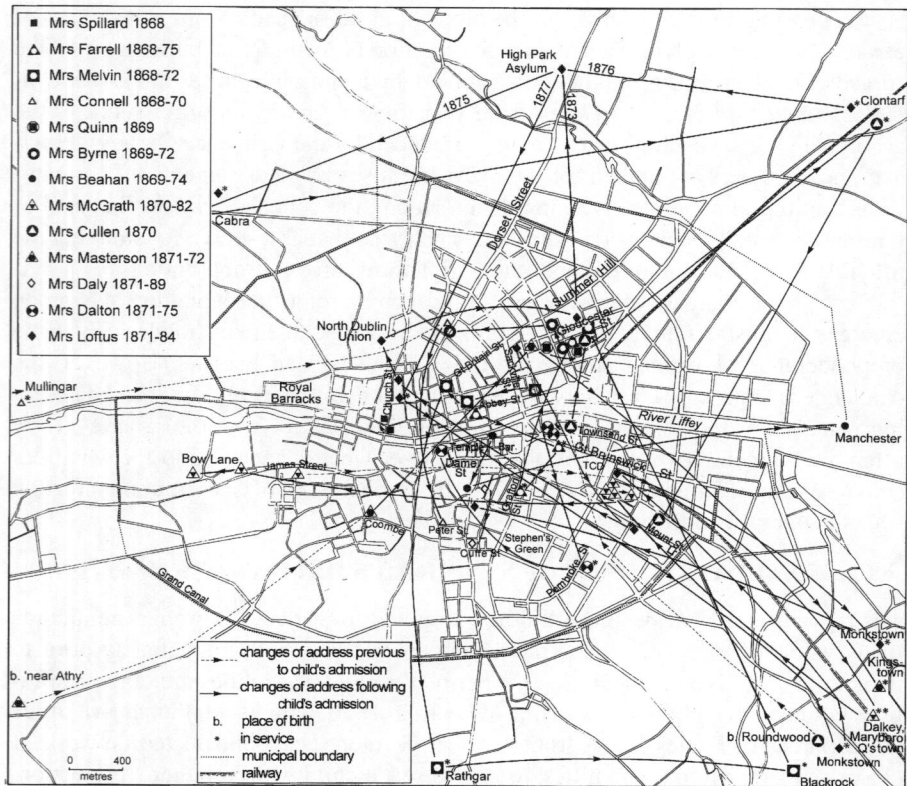

Figures 25a–d: Individual migration patterns of women whose childen were admitted to St Brigid's Orphanage, Dublin, 1868–75

length of time spent in the orphanage varied widely from one or two weeks, to the full span of childhood, although generally the orphanage provided what could be termed 'respite care' of some months. The termination of the child's sojourn in the institution also marks the end of the record of his/her mother's movements, with notes such as 'restored to his mother' (Mrs O'Toole, Figure 25c), 'with nurse till mother claims him' (Mrs Devine, Figure 25b), 'in service, under his mother's care' (Mrs Loftus, Figure 25a), generally marking the last contact.

The sample of 60 women dealt with in this study are self-selected: by definition they are women with responsibility for children, who are currently unable to care for them. The primary criterion for admission was that the child, already baptized as a Roman Catholic, should be in need both materially and spiritually, with a special case made for those 'in danger of loss of faith' i.e., those already subjected to the attentions of a proselytizing organization or in danger of being 'seduced' in the immediate future. While the vast majority of mothers were Roman Catholic, a number were or had been in interdenominational marriages, and a small number had

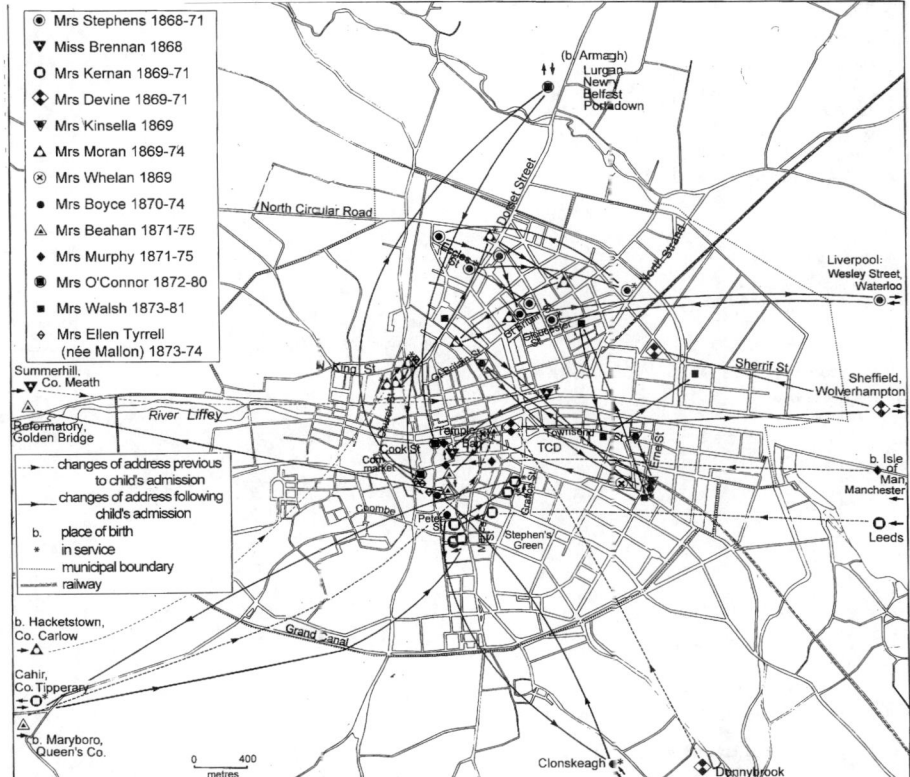

Figure 25b

changed denominations and were variously described as 'converts' or 'perverts'; Catholic children of such parentage were considered particularly vulnerable to the missionary zeal of other denominations, the most aggressive of which in Dublin were undoubtedly the Irish Church Missions and associated Smyly homes and schools.

In Figures 25a–d the individual changes of address of a random sample of 60 'Dublin' mothers whose children were admitted to the care of St Brigid's Orphanage during the period 1868–75, and whose changes of address were noted by the management, have been mapped. The years 1868–75 were chosen for particular analysis, as the institution was by then well established, admitting a total of 634 children during the period, for whom detailed register entries for 569 children, or 399 sets of siblings, are extant (Prunty, 1999, pp. 56–78). A 'Dublin' case has been determined as one in which a city address was given directly prior to the admission of the child. The mother's movements previous to the date of admission of her child are indicated by a dashed line; solid lines are used to denote all known movements of the mother during the period the child was in the care of St Brigid's. Where it is stated that the

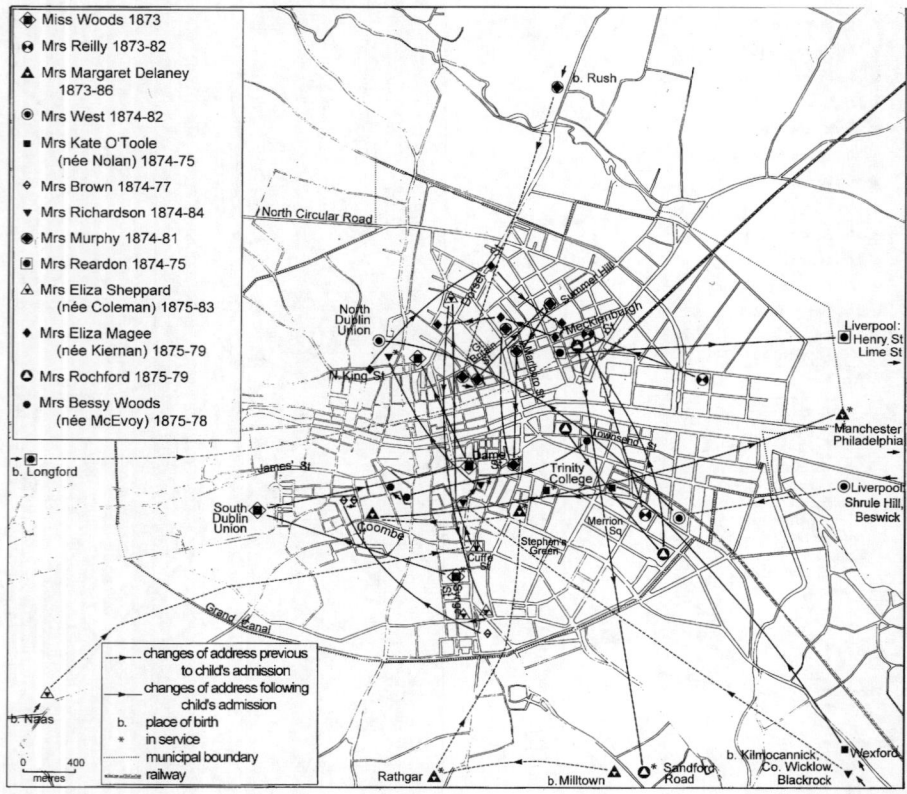

Figure 25c

woman is 'in service' an asterisk is added. The maps are illustrative rather than comprehensive; the varying length of time spent by each child or group of siblings in care means that the amount of detail available on their family movements is widely divergent. In a small number of instances women disappeared once their children have-been accepted, while in other cases 'lost' mothers turned up several years later to enquire about their children, or to reclaim them, with no record of their whereabouts in the intervening years.[22] Allowing for these limitations, Figures 25–26 do provide some very useful information, as they are based on the moves poorer women did in fact make, and the connections they forged between various parts of the city, its suburbs and further afield. As Richard Dennis in his discussion of nineteenth-century urban community and interaction says, 'anything which is based on what people actually did provides a helpful counterbalance to the preponderance of interpretations based on what a small number of contemporaries *thought*' (Dennis, 1984, p. 284).

22 For example SBO Register nos. 901 (2 August 1870), 1048–1049 (18 January 1873).

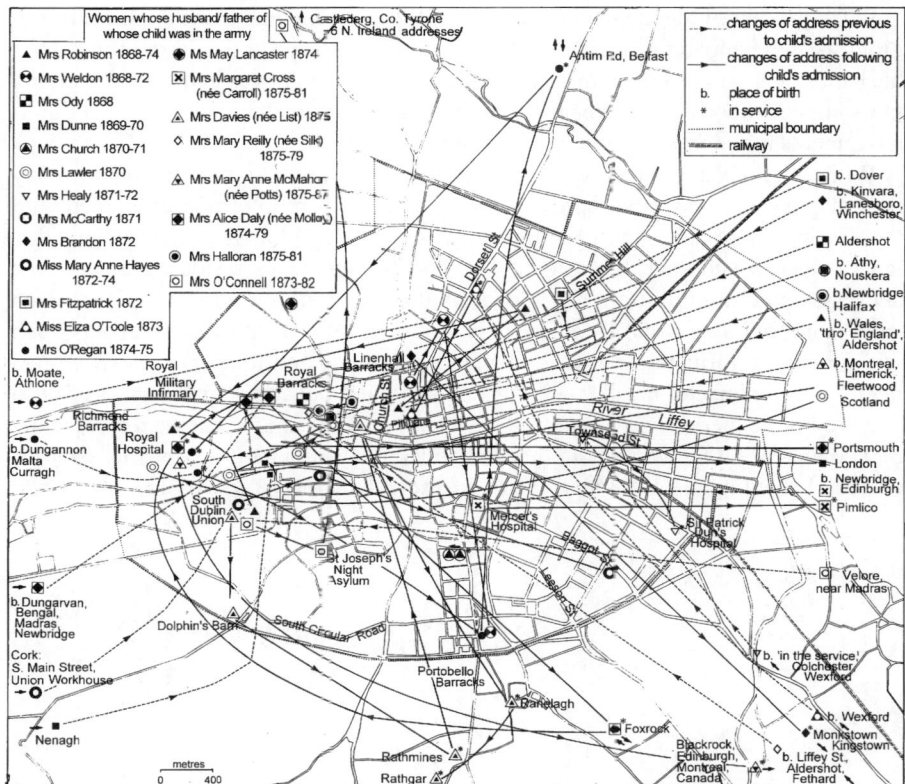

Figure 25d

Among the sample population of 60 women, 56 were married; maiden names are included where known.[23] Among the 56 married women, 41 were widowed, 6 were deserted, and a further 6 women were operating alone, without any indication of where their husbands were. In the three remaining cases the husband was unable to support the family, as he was incarcerated 'in lunatic asylum', in 'Arbour Hill prison' or simply 'sick'. Most women had one child admitted, but 17 women had two, and 9 women had three or more children accepted; in such cases the places of baptism of successive children provide valuable indicators of previous changes of address. Half of the mothers eventually reclaimed their child or children; in four instances they were restored to other relatives, three children died in the care of the institution, and in two cases there is no information on 'final destination'. The children who continued to live with their foster parents were eventually placed 'in service' or worked at home; most were adopted by the families that had reared them.

23 Unmarried: Miss Brennan 1868 (Figure 25b); Miss Woods 1873 (Figure 25c); Miss Mary Anne Hayes 1872–74, Miss Eliza O'Toole 1873 (Figure 25d); see also Ms May Lancaster 1874: 'she says she is married' (Figure 25d).

In the process of tracing the movements of these poor women, one distinctive subgroup became apparent, namely women who were widowed or deserted by soldier husbands, and unmarried mothers the father of whose child was in the army. Among the sample group of 60 women, 21 can be identified as 'army women' and their movements are plotted separately in Figure 25d.

While making no claims to comprehensive coverage, this random sample may nevertheless be considered representative of the large group of poorer women with the sole charge of children in late nineteenth-century Dublin. The direction and distances over which each woman moved, and the length of residence at any one address, reflect a multitude of personal choices, pressures, and perceptions. Each woman had her own circle of family, neighbours, employers and other contacts, each with its own information network, demands, supports and inadequacies. Each had her own experience of the city, with its opportunities and constraints. Places of birth and previous experiences of changing residence are also unique. However, when the movements of all 60 women are mapped collectively (Figure 26) recurring patterns emerge, providing insights into some of the more dynamic aspects of the city's social

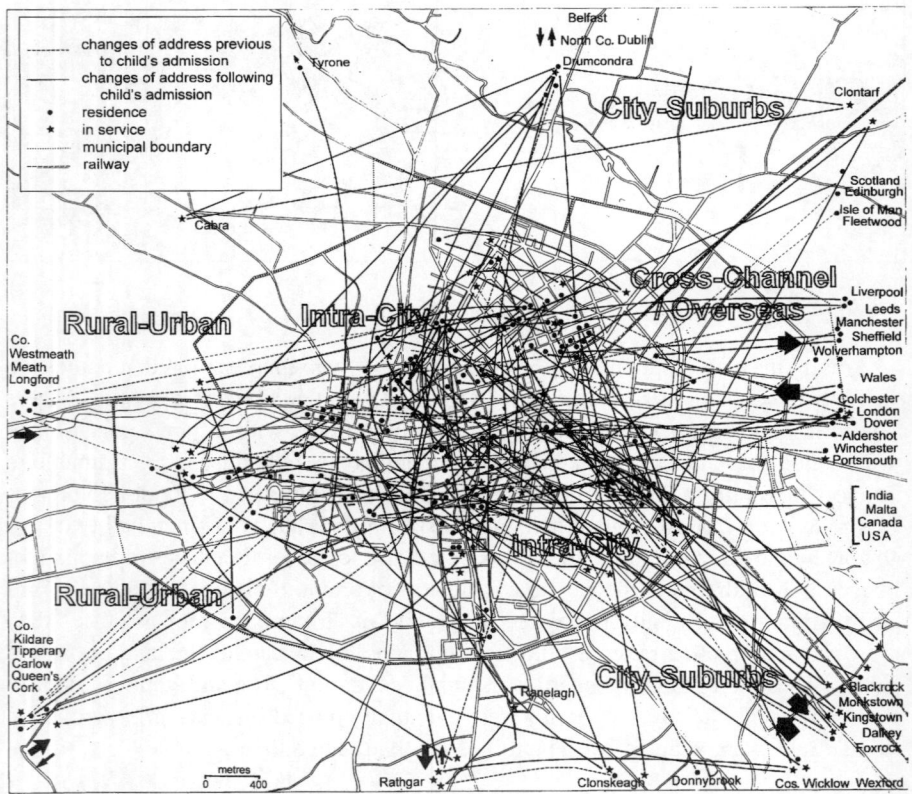

Figure 26: Migration patterns of women whose children were admitted to St Brigid's Orphanage, Dublin, 1868

geography, from the perspective of the very persons least likely to appear in 'official' records.

The principal elements of this mobility study, as introduced in Figure 25a, and developed in Figures 25b–25c, may be summarized as follows: migration into the city from elsewhere in Ireland; city-centre employment; a strong movement towards service employment in the 'respectable' suburbs, most especially to the south and south-east of the city; circular intra-city movements, both tightly localized and between certain poor areas; movements across the Irish Sea; and temporary moves to charity asylums and state workhouses in crisis situations. The movements of army women (Figure 25d) have a distinct geography, spanning military bases throughout the British Empire, and focusing on the immediate environs of the city barracks, the military hospitals and homes for servicemen.

i) Migration into the city from elsewhere in Ireland

Among the sample, places of birth outside Dublin are recorded for 21 women, a figure lower than the generalized picture found from analysis of the census tables in Figure 24. However, as the register fails to include the woman's place of birth in several instances, the real percentage of those born outside the city is probably higher. When the army women (Figure 25d) are excluded from the examination, the reason for migrating to Dublin is usually to enter domestic service, a move which in several instances was precipitated by widowhood.

Typical were the cases of Mrs Cullen and Mrs Masterson (Figure 25a), the former a 'wretchedly poor' widow whose moves included a brief spell at 21 Upper Mecklenburgh Street, on the margins of the red-light district, from where she got work in the highly respectable coastal suburb of Clontarf; the latter moved from service posts in Marlboro Street (north city) to the desirable south-side resort of Kingstown (Dún Laoghaire). Mrs Eliza Sheppard (née Coleman, Figure 25c), described as 'very decent looking' and 'strong and active', had kept a provision shop in Cuffe Street (Liberties district) but on her husband's death, left with no means 'but by selling her furniture', this Kildare woman 'intends going as thoro servant to some situation if she had her children settled', and like so many other women began a succession of moves both north and south of the Liffey in search of domestic work.

A few of the women who sought relief from this Dublin charity had known markedly better times before, such as Mrs Connell (Figure 25a), a native of Mullingar, Co. Westmeath, who once held a post as assistant matron in the workhouse hospital in the town.[24] On marrying a local man both moved to Dublin, living at 132 Dorset Street, a mixed north city street of provisions stores, licensed premises and tenements, where the husband worked as a baker in Brennans and Connollys. On the sudden death of her husband she was left with six children, 'could not get on with this young child', and on the infant's admission to the orphanage moved into service directly across the city at Mrs Hyland's, 31 Peter Street; as she then reclaimed her child no further moves are recorded.

24 SBO Register no. 728 (March 1868).

While a number of intervening moves between first arrival in Dublin and the place of residence at the time application was made to the orphanage are possible, the general pattern appears to be of migrants finding accommodation near the terminus of the highway along which they had travelled to the 'big city', a cause for little surprise. Thus among the north-city settlers are found women from north Co. Dublin (Rush), Co. Westmeath (Mullingar), Co. Meath (Summerhill), while the south city is home to women from south Co. Dublin (Milltown), Co. Kildare (Naas, Athy), Co. Wicklow (Roundwood, 'Kilmocannick'), Co. Laois (Maryboro) and Wexford. Exceptions to this pattern include the cases of a Carlow woman, Mrs Moran (Figure 25b), who crossed the Liffey direct to the north city district of Church Street, and Mrs O'Connor (Figure 25b), a native of Armagh, who bypassed the north side to move between the north of Ireland and the south city district.

Another characteristic of this movement into the city from elsewhere in Ireland is the lack of connection between Dublin and the north of Ireland. Movements to the north-east are recorded only for women who were born there, so that they mark a return to the home place in time of especial hardship rather than a flow of Dublin women in search of employment. The case of Mrs O'Connor or Connor (Figure 25b) exemplifies this situation. She was born in Market Hill, Armagh, married a stonecutter from Sandycove (south of Dublin city), and in 1872 was living at 14 Kennedy's Lane off Nicholas Street in the Liberties district, where she found her 12-year-old son unmanageable. She subsequently moved to Newry, Belfast and Portadown, all northern towns, before returning to 11 Lower Exchange Street in 1880. The movement northwards of two army widows, Mrs O'Regan and Mrs O'Connell (Figure 25d), can also be explained by their places of birth, Dungannon and Castlederg respectively.

ii) Circular intra-city movements, both tightly localized and between certain poorer areas

Following on the initial move to Dublin, numerous circular intra-city moves, both tightly localized and between certain poor areas, can be discerned, while some movements out of the home district can be viewed as temporary aberrations, until the dominant pattern reasserts itself.[25]

Among the multitude of women seeking to earn a living as servants and washerwomen, Mrs Kernan (Figure 25b) stands out as an exception, as she was evidently a skilled needleworker, and thus had more varied employment prospects. She was a convert to Catholicism of 16 years' standing, 'had considerable means before her

---

25 Mrs Moran (Figure 25b), provides a good example of multiple moves within a small radius. Born in Hacketstown, Co. Carlow, her two children were baptized in Dublin, in the adjoining north city parishes of St Michan's and St Mary's respectively. Between 1869 and 1871 she moved from a job in a bakery in 122 Upper Church Street into service with Mrs Maguire, 180 North King Street, and on to a Mrs Hughes, 22 Beresford Street, three addresses within less than 400 metres of each other; she then moved northwards into service at 5 Florinda Place off the Circular Road, then to a job in 4 Upper Rutland Street, and on to 15 Lower Dominick Street (off Great Britain Street), making at least six moves in three years. She is last known of at nearby 4 Johnson's Court.

marriage' to a Dublin-born coach builder, and both had lived in Leeds for at least 12 years, where their two children were baptized. On her husband's death Mrs Kernan was left penniless, and brought the children to Dublin, where they were taken in temporarily by St Brigid's, and the mother was 'lent a sewing machine for 6 months'.[26]

Mrs Murphy (1874–81, Figure 25c), who lived briefly with her child in the north county market-gardening centre of Rush, moved to the city, and then made several circular movements within a small compass.[27]

While the first address noted for Mrs Ellen Tyrrell (née Mallon, Figure 25b), entered as 'wretchedly poor', is at 111 North King Street, it is clearly a very temporary situation. The widow of a shoemaker, she herself 'used to bind cloth shoes'; on the admission of her two children she immediately crossed the Liffey to the heart of the shoemaking district, where the children had been baptized, taking up residence in 13 Nicholas Street. She moved a few yards from there to 'a back house' behind 4 Nicholas Street, and when re-married (as Mrs Bishop) moved around the corner to 3 Bride Street, and reclaimed her two children. The means through which her story came to the notice of the managers of St Brigid's Orphanage reveals something of the information networks operating in the city, which in turn greatly affected decisions concerning movement, and also the interdenominational rivalry which spurred on the development of the city's charities. Mrs Tyrrell is recorded as 'telling her poverty to a woman in a rag shop in Cooke Street' (*sic*); a Protestant lady who overheard the story gave her a note to the Irish Church Missions, D'Olier Street. However the recipient brought the note firstly to a neighbour Mrs Noble, 14 Back Lane, who called in the Catholic priest, and the family in need were directed with great haste to the Catholic charity.

If relocating several times within a defined area can be regarded as an indicator of community cohesiveness, certain areas emerge as particularly strong, while the linkages (or alternatively, the apparent lack of connections) between individual areas are also worth noting. On the north side, the Gloucester Street/Mecklenburgh Street area appears well connected internally, while its links extend both northwards to Dorset Street and southwards especially to the south docks sector of Townsend Street.[28] On the south side the South Cumberland Street/Townsend Street district was also the

26 SBO Register, no. 790, 791 (February 1869). Her subsequent movements are highly localized, centred on the commercial centre of Grafton Street, and the adjoining areas of over-priced low-status housing within yards of St Stephen's Green. From 4 Upper Mercer Street she moved to work in 82, and later 73 Grafton Street, followed by movements to 32 Peter Street and 5 Harry Street; a trial at domestic service in Cahir, Co. Tipperary is countered by a return to Redmond's Hill and Kevin Street where her older child lived with her.
27 Her progress of 30 Great Britain Street – 19 Denmark Street – 1 Huttons Lane off Summer Hill – 62 Marlboro Street was broken by a single short-lived movement south of the Liffey to take up employment in Mrs McEntyre's, 28 College Green (facing Trinity College). She then relocated to Johnson's Court off Great Britain Street, more familiar north city territory. Only one move is noted for another north city neighbour, Mrs Spillard (Figure 25a), but this is also strictly local: across the road from 4 Church Street to no. 160.
28 Mrs Byrne (Figure 25a) who is given a poor character reference ('drinks, was set up in business but failed, cannot be depended on') moved from 31 Lower Mecklenburgh Street to 13 Lower Gloucester

scene of return migration, most notably in the case of Mrs McGrath (Figure 25a), the widow of a railway worker for whom six local changes of address are known, interspersed with forays as far away as Queenstown (Cobh), County Cork.[29] A similar pattern is found in the case of Mrs Kinsella (Figure 25b) who returned repeatedly to this Townsend/Erne Street area.[30] Several persons have experience of both sides of the Liffey, connecting in particular the Gloucester Street and Townsend Street districts.

The movement westwards of Mrs Dalton (1871–75, Figure 25a) from Townsend Street to the Temple Bar district is one of several flows between these two south city districts, a move which is not surprising as part of Temple Bar was included in the Catholic parish of Westland Row (St Andrew's), and so shared schools as well as the services of clergy and charity workers. Canon Gregory Lynch, parish priest, wrote in 1861 of the squalid poverty in the lanes and courts of what was the richest parish in the city, exemplifed by Bass Place behind Merrion Square, Leeson Place behind St Stephen's Green, 'all the lanes off Townsend Street, Temple Bar, the streets between Townsend and the Quays, the lanes off the Quays'.[31]

In terms of self-sufficiency or lack of linkages with other areas, no single district emerges as strongly independent. While the Coombe/Liberties area, which includes the medieval core, appears least enmeshed in the cross-city flows, the number of entries from this sector is too small to allow conclusions to be drawn.

iii) Movement towards service employment in the 'respectable' suburbs, especially to the south of the city

The flow of women workers to the south is well-defined, and mirrors the expansion of the township of Rathmines and Rathgar (constituted 1847, extended in 1862), which stretched south of the Grand Canal to include Harold's Cross, Rathmines, Rathgar, Ranelagh, Sandford Road and Milltown. From among the sample of 60 women, the movement southwards was part of a more complex process of juggling the responsibilities of child care, the expectations of employers, and the affordability of suitable, or at least sufferable, accommodation. Women such as Mrs Melvin (Figure 25a), Mrs Margaret Delaney and Mrs Rochford (Figure 25c), and Mrs Davies (Figure 25d), all spent periods in domestic service in the terraced red-brick homes of this middle-class township. However, the more exclusive Pembroke township (constituted 1863), which extends the built-up area from the Grand Canal further to the south-east, was of less significance among this sample of poorer women,

---

Place, and on to 154 Upper Dorset Street, where the godmother of the child lived, now a widow 'and can support her'. Within one year Mrs Quinn (Figure 25a) whose husband 'ran away nearly three years ago to New York' moved from lodgings at 36 Mecklenburgh Street to share with her sister Jane Johnston at 17 Mabbot Street, another instance of close local ties.

29 Mrs McGrath: 27 South Cumberland Street; '3 or 11 South Cumberland Street'; Dalkey; Maryboro (Portlaoise, Co. Laois); Queenstown (Cobh, Co. Cork); 9 Hamilton Row; 20 Denzille Street; 11 South Cumberland Street; 12 Wentworth Place; 30 Bow Lane; 4 Bow Bridge. SBO Register no. 894 (25 June 1870).
30 SBO Register no. 840 (12 June 1869).
31 Canon Gregory Lynch to Dr Cullen, 23 May 1861, DDA: File 1, 340/1 no.78.

with only Donnybrook (Mrs Devine, Figure 25b) featured. Opportunities were found beyond the Pembroke township, following the line of the Dublin–Kingstown railway (opened 1834), in Blackrock, Monkstown, Kingstown [Dún Laoghaire] and Dalkey (Mrs Mary Anne McMahon, Mrs Brandon, Figure 25d; Mrs Loftus, Mrs Masterson, Mrs McGrath, Figure 25a), areas with both exclusive villa development and high-class terraced housing, as well as Foxrock (Mrs Alice Daly, Figure 25d), which is further inland but similarly high-status.

The pattern recorded for Mrs Melvin (Figure 25a), whose moves stretch from the north city to the southern suburbs and then back to the north inner city, is a typical example of intermixing short periods of suburban employment with efforts to operate from a city-centre base.

Indoor domestic service was perceived by the majority of these women as the only possible avenue of employment, despite the difficulties this created for child care. In the case of Mrs Boyce (Figure 25b), a Protestant neighbour Mrs Stewart, 9 Peter Street, very generously sheltered the woman and her five children after the death of their father, a wheelwright, and then petitioned St Brigid's to take care of one child, she herself taking charge of another without any expense to the mother. With her family responsibilities thus eased, Mrs Boyce succeeded in securing a situation with a Protestant gentleman in Clonskeagh. Within three years she was recorded as living once more in the transitional district between St Stephen's Green and the Liberties, this time at 50 Bride Street.

iv) **City-centre service employment**

The suburban townships provided service employment, but such work was also found within the city, both in high-class residential streets such as Eccles Street (Mrs Stephens, Figure 25b), in lesser residential streets such as Pleasant Street, North Strand, and Gloucester Street, and in commercial streets ranging from high-status Grafton Street, Wicklow Street and College Green, to more mixed streets such as Great Brunswick Street and Dorset Street. The search for work demanded frequent movement.

One woman who exhibited a great readiness to move in search of work was Mrs Margaret Delaney (Figure 25c). Born in Milltown, south Co. Dublin, she found employment in nearby Rathgar, before securing a situation in the Shelbourne Hotel near St Stephen's Green, followed by a brief movement to Ash Street off the Coombe, at which period her husband was dying of cancer in the Royal Hospital, Donnybrook. She returned to hotel work, but this time in the Dolphin Hotel, Manchester, followed by two further moves within Manchester (Fishmarket Gates, Shule Hill). From Manchester she crossed the Atlantic to Philadelphia, from where she requested that her child be restored to her, thus ending all record of any further moves. This example reflects a trend for some women to operate over an even wider field, in this case trans-Atlantic.

v) Cross-channel moves

The Irish Sea may be regarded as a highway to opportunities in Britain and further afield rather than as an obstacle to movement, judging from the fact that at least 25 of this sample of 60 women had some experience of life in Britain, although practically all were Irish-born. The migration field covered several major urban centres in England, most notably Liverpool, Manchester, Sheffield, Wolverhampton, Leeds and London, along with various garrison towns from Edinburgh to Dover. There is also evidence of several moves within Britain, which is to be expected following the high level of mobility exhibited in Dublin. While the nature of the source, dependant on the length of time each woman's child (or children) was in care, makes this a very incomplete record of movement, nevertheless there is evidence that cross-channel moves were an intrinsic part of contemporary migration patterns, with such moves often countered by return to the street from which the woman set forth. And behind such long-distance moves were very human situations: Mrs Stephens (Figure 25b), whose husband 'a great drunkard' had deserted to America, ventured just once to Liverpool after a succession of highly localized movements in the north city. Mrs Devine (Figure 25b, 'very badly off and in poor health') left her husband in the lunatic ward of the workhouse hospital and an intolerable brother with whom she was living ('who drinks and annoys her, out of her mind with affliction') before temporary moves to Sheffield and Wolverhampton. Mrs Reardon (Figure 25c), born into a 'respectable drapery establishment' in Longford, crossed the Irish Sea in the hope of meeting up with her husband who 'went away from Liverpool a short time ago, not known where'. Domestic crises intersected with economic factors in the crisscross of individual migration paths.

Cross-channel moves often meant downward social mobility. Mrs West (Figure 25c), whose children were born in Liverpool, seems to be a native of Dublin, as her mother Catherine Burdett had a very respectable address at 21 Claremont Road, Sandymount in 1881. While there is no indication whether Mrs West's first recorded address in Dublin (2 Emerald Terrace, Grand Canal Street) is that of her employer or her own residence, her later movement to 28 Ward, North Dublin Union workhouse, indicates worsening financial and/or health circumstances, and she fails to retrieve her children from St Brigid's.

Few changes of address while overseas are detailed, as moving outside Ireland often marked an interruption or end to contact with the orphanage. However, along with the changes within Liverpool recorded for Mrs Reardon (Figure 25c), there are three addresses within Manchester recorded for Mrs Beahan (Figure 25a). She had been put under considerable pressure by the local Catholic priest to disentangle herself from the 'soupers': 'she has now consented to give up three of her children and try to support herself and the other child by honest labour'. In pursuit of 'honest labour' she removed herself in time to Manchester; after a total period of five years she reclaimed the two surviving children.

vi) The use of Charity asylums and the state workhouse for temporary shelter

From the extent of contemporary public concern with the operation of the state's Poor Law system, and the coverage which charity asylums for homeless and destitute women and children received, it is instructive to consider the role of the state workhouse and church-run charity alternatives within the context of overall patterns of mobility, as evidenced in this examination of changes of address of 60 poor women.

The workhouse appears under three headings: as a place of birth for illegitimate children; as an unattractive place of refuge for destitute women with children; and as a last resort when ill or burdened with old age. Movements to and from the workhouses are relatively few, especially among non-army women (Figures 25a–c), underlining how the indoor relief available in the workhouse was shunned rather than exploited by the vast majority of these undoubtedly very poor women. The workhouse was the only option available to many unmarried women in the last weeks of pregnancy. Typical was the young mother of John Patrick Woods (Figure 25c) who had to leave her position in Pleasant Street (near Synge Street) and enter the South Dublin Union workhouse to have her child; she moved from the workhouse to lodgings in George's Place, before marrying and moving to 20 Coleraine Street.[32] Even where the workhouse is not recorded as the place of birth for non-marital infants, it was perceived as one of very few refuges open to such mothers and their children. Miss Brennan (Figure 25b) of Summerhill, Co. Meath, was working as a kitchenmaid in 'Scott's London Driving Rooms', Eden Quay, when she met a man by the name of Montgomery, 'labourer, 10 acres' by whom she had a child. The infant was baptized in the church of St Michael and John's, Exchange Street, at which time Miss Brennan gave her address as 51 Upper Exchange Street. With no means of support, and the infant 'almost dying', the young mother 'could not get it taken into the workhouse without herself' and used the standard threat of handing the child over to 'the Protestants' to ensure its admission to St Brigid's.

The circumstance of deserted or unmarried women with children was less than enviable. Under English law from 1844 a father could be compelled to pay maintenance money for the support of his illegitimate offspring, which in 1872 was fixed at five shillings per week, and could extend until the child reached 16 years of age. While this legislation had its inadequacies, it was better than that applying at the time in Ireland, where more restrictive legislation 'exonerated the reputed father from punishment or contribution'. The Poor Law guardians were left with the sole power to sue the father, and then only in respect of destitute and pauper children, whose maintenance would otherwise fall totally on the rates (Brooke 1873, p. 206). Although there are instances of women attempting to secure maintenance from the father of the child, through the law and otherwise, an unmarried woman with a child or children was in a particularly vulnerable position.[33]

Most of the details in St Brigid's Orphan Registers are of persons who are mak-

---

32 SBO Register no. 1108 (21 June 1873).
33 SBO Register no. 1121 (23 August 1873).

ing every effort to avoid the workhouse, for themselves but primarily for their children, so it is understandable that the state institution should appear in an almost exclusively bad light. Indoor workhouse relief was practically the only aid available under the Poor Law in Ireland. In 1861 94 per cent of those in receipt of statutory poor relief were workhouse residents, while the comparable figure for England was only 14 per cent. A particularly harsh anomaly between the Poor Law as it operated in both countries made it illegal in Ireland to grant outdoor relief to a widow unless she had two children, and even then it was at the discretion of the guardians, a discretion it was claimed was rarely exercised (Hancock, 1862 p. 223). Among applicants to St Brigid's, some simply 'would not go to the Poor House'[34] or bring the children there 'on any account'.[35] Others had been there, such as Mrs McGrath (Figure 25a), 38 Golden Lane, who had spent 12 months with her infant but 'could not think of remaining there, is young and well looking'.[36] Mary Anne Hayes (Figure 25d) from Cork was in the South Dublin Union with her child for six months and also refused to return.[37] 'Mother very poor, was in workhouse twelve months but could not think of remaining there',[38] 'would not bring the children in on any account',[39] 'was badly treated [in the North Union]'[40] are all typical references to the Poor Law system as perceived and experienced by some of the people it was intended to serve. The workhouse rule which insisted that all children must be accompanied by their parents made the indoor relief available there highly unattractive to most of the unmarried mothers applying for the admission of their children to St Brigid's, with the complaint, 'could not get it taken into the Work House without herself'.[41] The vigour of the statements, so often repeating the same sentiments, make it clear that the workhouse very successfully deterred rather than attracted persons in need, living up to its founding vision of being an unattractive place of last resort.

A positive perspective on the workhouse and allied institutions, however, is provided by those who found employment therein. Mrs Connell (Figure 25a) was, in better days, the matron in charge of the workhouse in Mullingar. Mrs Richardson (Figure 25c), a native of Kilmocannick, whose mother Mrs Brereton 'has lands and is well off', also moved in slightly higher employment circles than most of the women in this sample; after some time in service in Blackrock, she is recorded as living at 1 Aungier Street, followed by a situation in 'Refreshment Rooms', 31 South Great Georges' Street, at the very acceptable rate of '12s per week and diet'; she followed that by securing a position in 1877 in the Lunatic Asylum, Richmond (in the grounds of the North Dublin Union workhouse).

---

34 See SBO Register nos. 776 (9 January 1869), 883 (12 March 1870).
35 See SBO Register no. 1163 (14 February 1874).
36 SBO Register no. 1155 (24 January 1874).
37 SBO Register no. 1000 (8 June 1872).
38 SBO Register no. 1155 (24 January 1874).
39 SBO Register nos. 1163–1165 (14 February 1874).
40 GA: 0/DB/18A no. 70, 19 April 1875.
41 SBO Register no. 724 (18 April 1868).

The case of Mrs Loftus (Figure 25a) provides a rare glimpse into the range of institutional and private accommodation available to women in late nineteenth-century Dublin. State workhouse, magdalen asylums, tenement lodgings and indoor servant accommodation all featured in Mrs Loftus' pattern of mobility which is worth tracing in detail. She was first noted at 25 Upper Sackville Street [O'Connell Street], corner of Gregg's Lane, from where she moved to work as a wet nurse for Mrs Walker, 51 Lower Mount Street; from here she moved in with her mother, Mrs Francis, 33 Beresford Street (parallel to Church Street), before taking temporary refuge in the North Dublin Union workhouse. From here she entered the Female Penitents Retreat, Gloucester Street, in the heart of the red-light district, before moving to the much larger asylum operated by the same religious community at High Park, Drumcondra (1873). From this asylum she entered service in the northern suburbs: with a Miss Petits, 30 Cabra Parade (1875), followed by a position in Clontarf, 7 Victoria Terrace. She entered the High Park asylum again (1876), before returning to her mother's district (1877), moving in with the Howards, 52 Beresford Street. She then tried her fortunes in the southern suburbs, moving firstly to work with Messrs Bergin and Co, Drapers, Monkstown Avenue, then to lodgings in 129 South Cumberland Street (to the rear of Trinity College), returning briefly to Monkstown, before trying yet another part of the city, this time moving to 32 Lower Stephen's Street, at Mrs Hayden's. The register entry emphasizes that her use of the magdalen asylums had nothing to do with prostitution: 'mother was lawfully married but was sent to the above asylum by a priest for safety for a while'.

vii) Army women

Women whose husbands or the fathers of whose children were soldiers exhibit distinctive patterns of mobility and employment: Dublin was part of the circuit of garrison towns in which temporary residence was taken up during the tour of duty. Within Dublin, army women secured accommodation in the immediate environs of the barracks, and favoured institutional over domestic employment. The sample group of 21 cases mapped in Figure 25d may be taken as representative of a substantial group of army widows and deserted army wives, and a smaller number of unmarried women (in Figure 25d the cases of Mary Anne Hayes and Eliza O'Toole), all of whom had the primary care of young children whose fathers were soldiers.

When the changes of address for army women (Figure 25d) are compared with the patterns established by other poor women with similar child-care burdens (Figures 25a–c), the most striking feature is the extensive British Isles and overseas experience amassed by the army women. Evidence for this is largely based on their own places of birth and of marriage, and the places of baptism of successive children. The Curragh, Newbridge, Athlone, Athy, Nenagh, Roscrea, Longford, Limerick, Cork, Wexford and Dungannon all hosted military personnel, as did Edinburgh, Fleetwood, Colchester, Dover, Aldershot, Winchester and Portsmouth in Britain. Postings at the further reaches of the British Empire in Halifax and Montreal in Canada, and in Bengal, Velore, Madras and Nouskera in India were part of the circuit of army movements involving women and children as well as men. During the period

1868–75 there were 36 cases of soldiers' children (representing 51 individual children) admitted to St Brigid's Orphanage; of these only 10 had been baptized within the city boundary (5 in Francis Street and 2 in the South Dublin Union workhouse), one each in Rathmines and Kingstown, while the vast majority had been born in various military centres in Ireland, Britain, India and Canada, with one child born in Malta. Brothers and sisters were generally baptized in different places, such as John and Margaret Cleary, baptized in James' Street and India respectively, or Henry and John Reilly, baptized in Aldershot and Fethard, Co. Wexford respectively.[42] Many of the women for whom a Dublin address was recorded at the time of their child's admission clearly had little previous contact with the city. When allowance is made for the fact that places of birth of siblings not admitted to the orphanage are unknown, and that previous changes of address of the child/children admitted to St Brigid's are likewise unknown, it becomes clear that the picture presented in Figure 25d must be a gross underestimation of the extent and range of mobility among even this small sample of army women.

Within Dublin city a remarkable aspect of the army women's movements is the complete by-passing of two of the areas most important to the generalized group of poorer women: the Gloucester Street/Mecklenburgh Street district to the north of the Liffey and the Townsend Street district to the south. Instead, the army women were drawn to the west of the city, where the Royal Barracks (erected 1704), a massive complex with accommodation for eight regiments (McCullough, 1989), provided the principal focus of settlement (Park Gate Street, West Temple Street, Barrack Street, Queen Street, Tighe Street, Ellis's Quay) and also employment opportunities. This situation is mirrored south of the river by the presence of the Royal Hospital at Kilmainham, established exclusively for 'those who by reason of Age, Wounds or Infirmities, since their first coming into our Army, are grown unfit to be any longer continued in Our Service' (McParland n.d.). On a lesser scale but also exerting influence in this study, were Linenhall Barracks (north city) and Portobello and Richmond Barracks (south city). Familiarity with accommodation possibilities in the environs of the barracks, and the employment polices of the military institutions, led army women to gravitate towards these areas even after the death or desertion of their husbands. They also feature as hospital employees (Mercer's and Sir Patrick Dun's hospitals), and rely to a significant extent on indoor relief such as that provided by the state workhouse (South Dublin Union) and charitable night asylum (St Joseph's, Barrack Lane). The very distinct geography exhibited by army women in terms of overseas experience and preferences within Dublin is further complicated by the intermittent involvement of some in the large market for suburban domestic service, in Rathmines, Rathgar and Ranelagh, and in Foxrock, Monkstown and Kingstown.

Among the most-travelled of these women was Mary Anne Potts, who met her Limerick-born husband while he was with his regiment in Montreal, Canada, and followed him back to Limerick, on to Fleetwood (Lancashire) and then to Dublin

---

42 SBO Register nos. 913–914 (3 December 1870); nos. 1319–1320 (14 August 1875).

where he died in the Royal Hospital; Mrs Potts can be traced to a series of hospital and domestic posts in Ireland before moving on to Edinburgh, and thence to a 'shirt and collar manufactory' in her native Montreal.[43] Another well-travelled woman with Canadian interests was Mrs Robinson, a native of Wales, who married an Englishman and travelled through England with her husband's regiment, earning the substantial wages of 3s 6d per day by 'washing for the Regiment'. On his desertion from the 13th Hussars while in Canada, she was left in dire poverty but with a few hopeful connections ('child's grandmother Mrs Tuohy and husband John Tuohy is groom to Colonel Mackenzie).[44]

The extensive web of army connections is also well illustrated in the case of Mrs Fitzpatrick, born in Dover, where she had met her husband who was the 'army bandmaster for the Volunteers'.[45]

The admission of a child or children to the institution eased child-care responsibilities for a number of army women, at least temporarily, and allowed them to take up employment. Most combined periods of institutional work with shorter periods of domestic service, with occasional recourse to the workhouse, and an overall readiness to move outside the country if the opportunities should be perceived as more hopeful. There were also considerable efforts made to have sons admitted to the Royal Hibernian Military School, Phoenix Park, entry to which was restricted to boys between 7 and 12 years old, 'the orphan sons of soldiers, or the children of soldiers in foreign service' (Barrett, 1884). The movements of Mrs Alice Daly (née Molloy) could be considered typical. Born in Dungarvan, Co. Waterford, she married a Cork-born soldier (Royal Artillery, B Battery, 20th Brigade), and gave birth to three children in different military centres in India (entered as Gucla, Bengal; Madras; and simply 'India'), before following her husband's regiment to Newbridge. On his death she moved to Dublin to 53 Queen Street, adjoining the Royal Barracks. Once two of the children had been admitted to St Brigid's (October 1874) she went into service in Foxrock, Co. Dublin. A year later she returned to town to a situation with a Dr Carter, in the Royal Hospital, Kilmainham; from there (September 1878) she crossed the Liffey to 8 Park Gate Street, in the vicinity of the Royal Barracks, and in March 1879 she moved to Portsmouth to enter service with Surgeon-Major E. A. Gibbon, of Derby Road, Northend. Her experience also provides brief glimpses into the operation of the army's welfare network and its influence on the mobility of army widows: Colonel Herrick of her husband's brigade ('now in Horse Artillery, Newbridge') promised to get one son into the Hibernian School 'if he were the proper age and get the mother a situation'. Colonel Yarris (*sic*) of the Royal Artillery 'who sent her to Luke Street proselytising school saying it was a Catholic school' obviously took sufficient interest in the woman's case to direct her to the Irish Church Missions school adjoining the Linenhall Barracks, even if he was not aware of or concerned with the school's controversial practices. Her last known place of employment was with a high-ranking military family in Portsmouth, at which stage

43 SBO Register no. 1328 (9 October 1875).
44 SBO Register no. 732 (May 1868).
45 SBO Register no. 1040 (November 1872).

she had secured a place for her son in the Hibernian School, and had placed her two daughters in an indoor orphanage with the Presentation nuns, drawing most effectively on both military and church support networks.

The Royal Hospital Kilmainham (RHK) was a significant employer of army widows, with a preference for those 'whose husbands were killed in battle, or died while on foreign service'.[46] The register of St Brigid's notes only that certain women found employment in the RHK previous to or following on the admission of their child to the orphanage; the personnel records of the hospital allow the fortunes of some of these women to be followed through, as well as providing significant detail on recruitment procedures, conditions of employment, daily duties, and wage levels. The case of Mrs Margaret O'Regan can be reconstructed from data in both archives, tracing her movements as the wife of a hospital sergeant and apothecary from the Curragh to Malta, and later as an army widow moving between the Royal Hospital Kilmainham and posts in Belfast.[47]

According to a circular issued in the 1870s, applications would be considered from 'soldiers' widows of good character, from 23 to 45 years of age', who were able to read and write and 'do simple addition and subtraction to the satisfaction of the Civil Service Commissioners'.[48] Those working with the able-bodied pensioners were to be 'strong, active, cleanly housemaids', while nurses hired for the infirmary in addition had to have 'some experience as (or be likely to become) hospital nurses'.[49] Conditions of employment were good, with pay ranging from 1s to 1s 6d per day according to seniority, 'a room each partially furnished, with an allowance of coals and candles and a gown and petticoat annually, to be victualed according to the established rules of the House'.[50] It was a tightly structured situation, where for example no nurse could leave the premises before the evening meal or be off the premises after curfew.[51] No allowance was made for child-care duties, as in the case of a widow whose application was dismissed in 1869 with the note 'this woman appears a healthy proper person not much energy, has child which is objectionable'.[52] The admission of Margaret O'Regan's children to St Brigid's therefore was essential to her job prospects in this establishment. She was appointed to a permanent position on 2 January 1876 and by April had secured the Civil Service certificate. She was promoted through the ranks, with glowing references ('has fully maintained the good order, cleanliness and regularity of the rooms, is kindly disposed toward the old men, careful of everything in her charge, and attentive to her duties') to become head nurse

---

46 Royal Hospital Kilmainham, Minutes, 27 May 1886 [hereafter RHK].
47 SBO Register no. 1216 (1 August 1874).
48 RHK, printed circular, no date but enclosed with folder re. nurses duties, 1871. It was found difficult to attract women 'suitable in every respect for the duties to be performed, yet at the same time sufficiently educated to undergo the required examination' (W. Carte to Sir, 23 July 1874); of eight nurses employed in July 1874, only three had satisfied the Civil Service Commission examination (L. Fyers Banks, memo re. case of Margaret Murphy and Civil Service examination, 26 April 1889).
49 RHK, printed circular, no date but enclosed with folder re. nurses duties, 1871.
50 RHK circular 1871; Minutes, 27 May 1886.
51 RHK, Minutes, *Duties of the Matron, Nurses*, 26 April 1875.
52 RHK, Memo by William Carte, Surgeon, 19 April 1869.

in September 1883 at an annual salary of £36.10.0.[53] St Brigid's ended its responsibility for her older child in 1879, but she kept him with the same foster mother in Celbridge that the institution had employed, paying this woman directly herself.

While there is much overlap among the stories and migration patterns of each of the army women, significant personal details contribute to an understanding of what influenced decisions to move, and what sources of income were possible. Mrs Ody (husband in the 1st Royal Dragoons), a widow with four young children, 'none old enough for the Hibernian School', moved from Aldershot to 4 West Temple Street beside the Royal Barracks, but supported her family by doing washing for a 'Mrs Dr Walshe', 31 Lower Leeson Street. Also in the Royal Barracks district lived Mrs Halloran, a native of Newbridge who married a hospital sergeant (87th Regiment, born Cavan), and followed him to Halifax, Nova Scotia, where one child was born. Two years later she moved to Dublin where as a widow she lived at 28 Queen Street before a short move to 5 West Liffey Street, and was reliant on occasional remittances from 'an uncle in America'. Mrs McCarthy, born in Athy and who had travelled throughout India (widow of a Cork-born soldier, sergeant-major, 19th Regiment), lived around the corner at 2 Ellis Quay where she 'receives 5s over the rent' for her house, and also undertook needlework. Mrs Brandon (born Kinvara, Co. Galway), married a soldier whose birthplace was Lanesboro, Co. Longford), and gave birth to her first child in Lanesboro and her second child in Winchester. On arrival in Dublin she contacted a Protestant friend, Mrs Little, 'who kept the canteen, Linen Hall Barracks' and gave the mother and two children refuge. From this safe but temporary base the mother found suburban employment: 6 Longford Terrace, Monkstown, with Mr Bates, and later in 45 Clarinda Park East, Kingstown.

On the south side of the Liffey several similar stories emerge, mostly of women who moved temporarily to Dublin to be near relatives and friends at a time of crisis. In their application to St Brigid's Orphanage dangers to their Catholic faith within the Protestant army establishment are noted, with some army widows claiming pressure by proselytizing groups to part with their children.[54] Obstacles to the professional training of Catholic women as nurses are also detailed, with Mrs Healy 'obliged to pay £1 entrance money and board on account of not being a Protestant' to Sir Patrick Dun's hospital where she hoped to get a diploma as a midwife.[55] Flexibility and mobility were essential in the struggle to make an independent livelihood.

Several army widows are recorded as re-marrying, but they always chose partners from within army circles which further reinforced their distinctive patterns of mobility. Mrs Lawler, a widow who in 1875 was resident beside the Royal Barracks (24 Tighe Street), crossed the Liffey to the south-side military quarter (40 Watling Street, on to 39 Bow Lane), where she married a 'protestant pensioner'; after a brief interlude in Scotland she entered the South Dublin Union workhouse. Mary Reilly (née

53 RHK, Minutes, 27 September 1883, *Appointment of Head Nurse*.
54 Mrs Dunne: SBO Register no. 795 (March 1869); Mrs Church: SBO Register nos. 886 & 887 (January 1870).
55 Mrs Healy: SBO Register no. 920 (January 1871); Margaret Cross SBO Register no. 1294 (25 May 1875).

Silk), a native of Liffey Street in the north city barracks district, travelled with her husband (corporal, 56th Regiment), to Aldershot and on to Fethard, Co. Wexford, before settling in 3 West Temple Street when widowed, close to where she herself was born. Here she re-married, this time to a Protestant soldier named Herd, who however died within four years, at which stage she retrieved her children from St Brigid's and further moves are unknown.

Deserted or unmarried army women had recourse to the workhouse for the birth of their children, as was the case among the general population of poorer women (Figures 25a–c). And following the birth these mothers were, of dire necessity, amongst the most mobile of the women in this study. Mrs Mary Davies (née List), a deserted army wife who entered the South Dublin union workhouse to have her baby, had at least five changes of address over one year (Figure 25d).[56] Young Mary Anne Hayes, unmarried, of South Main Street, Cork, gave birth to her baby in the Cork Union workhouse before an unhappy six months in the South Dublin union workhouse; the father was incarcerated in Arbour Hill military prison so was obviously of little support.[57] In a similar predicament was Miss Eliza O'Toole, a native of Wexford, working as a servant near Dorset Street, whose spirited pursuit of the father came to naught: 'father deserted 4 months ago because the mother wrote to his commanding officer to claim support for the child'.[58] Each of these young women found domestic posts once their children were – temporarily – in the care of St Brigid's.

CONCLUSIONS

When the changes of address of the 60 women (including 21 army women) examined in this study are mapped collectively (Figure 26) there is conclusive evidence for considerable mobility over short periods of time, spanning rural-urban, intra-city, city-suburbs and cross-channel/overseas moves. Indeed, the general picture of high levels of mobility among women which is portrayed by summary census tables dealing with passenger traffic through Dublin port (Table 6), and the percentage of the population with non-Dublin birthplaces (Figure 24) is certainly borne out by the case study material. Women of different backgrounds and from very different districts gravitated in large numbers towards Dublin, drawn to the city for a variety of reasons: on its own merits as a major urban employment and relief centre, but also as a bridgehead to possibilities beyond Ireland, and the most important gateway for those returning to the country.

While public discussion focused on the controversial question of distressed persons and mendicants 'flooding' Dublin in search of assistance, this sample study creates a larger context within which such claims can be examined. The register entries substantiate the orphanage's claim that 'fully one half of those that resided in Dublin at the time of their admission had been driven a short time previously, by distress,

---

56 Mrs Mary Davies, SBO Register no. 1295 (5 June 1875).
57 Mary Anne Hayes, SBO Register no. 1000 (April 1872).
58 Eliza O'Toole, SBO Register no. 1121 (September 1873).

into the city from different counties of Ireland'.[59] A charity such as St Brigid's came to the rescue of some who, at least for a time, were unable to provide for the children in their care. Significant numbers of women in distress certainly perceived Dublin as a place of refuge and support, most critically in time of widowhood, but this is part of a larger picture involving the complex interweaving of job opportunities, domestic crises, child-rearing duties and previous moves by family and neighbours. Securing residential child care, whether for a temporary period or long term, immediately expanded the woman's range of options and with it the geography of both employment and residence.

The migration field of this sample of poorer 'Dublin' women in the period c.1868–80 (Figure 26) has some distinctive features: a marked extension to the southern and south-eastern suburbs in search of service employment, and across the Irish Sea to both industrial cities and military centres in Britain. The port of Liverpool appears closer to Dublin in many respects than Galway, Cork or Waterford. The absence of flows between northern Ireland and Dublin for all but three women whose place of birth was in the north, contrasts sharply with the steady flow of women between Britain and Ireland. There was greater first-hand familiarity among Dublin women with barrack life in India and North America than there was with life in the Ulster counties.

Against this background of cross-channel and overseas migration there remained a certain loyalty to discrete areas in Dublin, as exemplified by women returning repeatedly to the same district, even to the same street, despite the intervention of several years of extensive travelling. While the residential areas which feature in this study of mobility were notorious among health and housing officials for their squalid conditions, and (in several cases) for the low level of morals, this analysis of changes of address highlights other aspects of their dynamic social geography, notably the close kinship structures and shared provincial origins in individual districts, and the information networks which brought news of work opportunities. The policies and practices of relief agencies, notably the Poor Law Union and Church charities (both Protestant and Catholic), were also intimately known at the local level, as was the best stance to take with each; in the case of St Brigid's the threat of handing a child over 'to the Protestants' generally ensured an effective and speedy response. Overall there was a readiness among these women to move house or change situation at short notice, utilizing both sides of the Liffey, without the major uprooting that changes of residence imply in the late twentieth century. As the well-to-do relocated to the suburbs in large numbers, the downgrading of formerly fashionable residences proceeded apace; this in turn expanded the quantity of low-status (but still expensive) tenement accommodation, the very type of tenurial system which reinforced high levels of mobility. To the west of the city the continued functioning of the military barracks and the Royal Hospital ensured that the local 'army districts' retained their character, regardless of which regiments were currently stationed in the city, or at what strength the garrison was maintained.

59 *SBO Tenth Annual Report*, 1866, p. 5.

The emergence of army women (Figure 25d) as a definite sub-group with its own specific geography is an important and unexpected revelation about the social fabric of nineteenth-century Dublin. Most significant is the appearance of this group in the records of a 'mainstream', i.e., non-army, organization. In terms of choice of residence and institutional employment the army women are a distinct group; however, as they apply on an equal footing with other poor women to St Brigid's, and several enter regular domestic service in the suburbs, they also intersect with the larger population. Even from this small sample they are clearly the most-travelled females in the city, with experience in exotic places such as Madras, Montreal and Malta interspersed with postings in the more mundane centres of Newbridge and the Curragh. The bonds which existed among army women, whether unmarried, married, widowed or deserted by their men, were no doubt strengthened by their overseas experiences, while their integration into army employment structures fostered their separateness. The identification of the army women as a distinct subgroup is a reminder that the city's social fabric could best be described as a mosaic of subgroups, whose geography is determined by factors including kinship, origin and occupation as well as accommodation supply and demand, city contacts and flows of information. In the case of the military subgroup, the large number of soldiers barracked in the city throughout the nineteenth century, and the women and children attached to the regiments, both legitimately and illegitimately, along with their complex mobility patterns literally spanning the British Empire, ensure that this group makes a critical contribution to the complexity of the city's social geography.

This experiment in utilizing charity sources to map mobility among women has highlighted some areas which merit further exploration, such as the patterns of movement among army women. While the lack of household census data will continue to be an obstacle to the reconstruction of past migration patterns in Ireland, this analysis has demonstrated that the study of mobility needs to be over much shorter time scales than the 10-year intervals provided by census materials. It also needs to extend beyond county and even country borders. However, the painstaking reconstruction of patterns of movement is not an end in itself; the important questions that need to be answered cover perception, behaviour, decision-making and social relations, the kind of material that no census provides (Dennis, 1990, p. 288). It is also evident that the situation illustrated in Figures 25–26 is merely a glimpse of a much wider and more complex picture. Where links can be established, as for example between Dublin women and British military centres, the need for detailed cross-channel co-operative research is indisputable.

This study also highlights the distance which still has to be travelled before the inclusion of a gender perspective in geography becomes the norm. It may not be a matter of prejudice among geographers, but 'many are unsure how to incorporate information on women into their research. The result unfortunately is a historical landscape in which only half of the residents normally are visible' (Kay, 1991). In historical geography the problem is greatly compounded by the paucity and structure of source material, such as registers of electors and lists of property holders, ratepayers and household heads, all of which practically exclude women. There is also the matter of class and occupation, where men and women of insufficient standing are lost under generalized headings such as 'lodgers' or occupiers of tenements. Against such a background the use of charity sources becomes more urgent, to complement (and contradict) the 'official' record, so that the differing experiences of 'ordinary' women and men may be allowed to surface. The records of children's charities are particularly valuable in this respect, as they include personal and family detail which is rarely obtainable outside family papers and individual diaries. In the case of St Brigid's the great number of children for whom records were kept in unbroken succession from 1857 makes this source the equivalent of many such personal records.

The unearthing of new gender-specific sources has been greatly advanced in Ireland by the creation of a large computerized database by the Women's History Project (Irish Manuscripts Commission, directed by Maria Luddy), launched September 1999. The massive explosion in the range and quality of materials now accessible to the researcher will allow new questions to be explored, covering such issues as the repercussions of the suburban movement on community cohesion, employment possibilities, family structure, child care and daily travel patterns. It will help move research into the complex world of appraisal of lifestyles and livelihood of people (Lawton, 1987, p. 263). It will also function as a corrective against routinely writing as though the experiences and travel patterns of one set of persons (for example, skilled male workers of Irish birth) can be readily generalized to women and to other classes of men and women.

REFERENCES

AALEN, F. H. A. (1992), 'Health and housing in Dublin: past, present and future', In F. H. A. Aalen and Kevin Whelan (eds), *Dublin City and County: From Prehistory to Present*, Dublin, 279–304.

ANDERSON, MICHAEL (1982), 'Indicators of population change and stablility in nineteenth century cities: some sceptical comments', In James H. Johnson and Colin G. Pooley (eds), *The Structure of Nineteenth Century Cities*, London, 283–98.

BARRETT, ROSA (1884), *Guide to Dublin Charities*, Dublin.

BROOKE, W. G. (1873), 'Report on the differences in the law of England and Ireland as regards the *Journal of the Statistical and Social Inquiry Society of Ireland*, protection of women', Journal of the Statistical and Social Inquiry Society of Ireland, 1873, **6**, 43, pp. 206–7,

BURKE, HELEN (1987), *The People and the Poor Law in 19th Century Ireland*, Dublin.

BUSTEED, MERVYN and ROB HODGSON (1994), 'Irish migration and settlement in nineteenth century Manchester with special reference to the Angel Meadow district', *Irish Geography*, 27, 1, 1–13.

COWAN, P. C. (1918), *Report on Dublin Housing*, Dublin.

CULLEN, LOUIS M. (1992), 'The growth of Dublin 1600–1900: character and heritage', In F. H. A. Aalen and Kevin Whelan (eds), *Dublin City and County: From Prehistory to Present*, Dublin, 252–57.

DALY, MARY E. (1985), *Dublin, the Deposed Capital: A Social and Economic History, 1860–1914*, Cork.

DENNIS, RICHARD (1982), 'Stability and change in urban communities: a geographical perspective', In James H. Johnson and Colin G. Pooley (eds), *The Structure of Nineteenth Century Cities*, London.

DENNIS, RICHARD (1984), *English Industrial Cities of the Nineteenth Century: A Social Geography*, Cambridge.
FAHY, A. M. (1984), 'The spatial differentiation of commercial and residential functions in Cork City 1787–1863', *Irish Geography*, **17**, 14–26.
FINNEGAN, FRANCES (1982), *Poverty and Prejudice: A Study of Irish Immigrants in York 1840–1875*, Cork.
HANCOCK, W. NEILSON (1862), 'The difference between the English and Irish Poor Laws as to the treatment of women and unemployed workmen', *Journal of the Statistical and Social Inquiry Society of Ireland*, **3**, 217–35.
HEARN, MONA (1990), 'Life for domestic servants in Dublin, 1880–1920', In Maria Luddy and Cliona Murphy (eds), *Women Surviving: Studies in Irish Women's History in the Nineteenth and Twentieth Centuries*, Dublin, 148–79.
KAY, JEANNE (1991), 'Landscapes of women and men: rethinking the regional historical geography of the United States and Canada', *Journal of Historical Geography*, **17**, 4, 435.
KEARNS, KEVIN C. (1994), *Dublin Tenement Life: An Oral History*, Dublin.
LARGE, D. (1985), 'The Irish in Bristol in 1851: a census enumeration', In R. Swift and S. Gilley (eds), *The Irish in the Victorian City*, London, 37–58.
LAWTON, RICHARD (1979), 'Mobility in nineteenth century British cities', *Geographical Journal*, **145**, 206–24.
LAWTON, RICHARD (1982), 'Questions of scale in the study of population in nineteenth-century Britain', In R. H. Baker and Mark Billinge (eds), *Period and Place: Research Methods in Historical Geography*, Cambridge, 99–113.
LAWTON, RICHARD (1987), 'Peopling the past', *Transactions of the Institute of British Geographers*, New Series, **112**, 259–83.
LAWTON, RICHARD and COLIN G. POOLEY (1992), *Britain 1740–1950: An Historical Geography*, London.
LETFORD, LYNDA and COLIN G. POOLEY, (1995), 'Geographics of migration and religion: Irish women in mid-nineteenth century Liverpool', In Patrick O'Sullivan (ed.), *Irish Women and Irish Migration,* 89–112.
LUDDY, MARIA (1992), 'An agenda for women's history in Ireland, part II: 1800–1900', *Irish Historical Studies*, **28**, 109.
LUDDY, MARIA and CLIONA MURPHY (1990) (eds), *Women Surviving: Studies in Irish Women's History in the Nineteenth and Twentieth Centuries*, Dublin.
MacCURTAIN, MARGARET and DONNCHA O'CORRÁIN (1978), *Women in Irish Society: The Historical Dimension,* Dublin.
MacLARAN, ANDREW (1993), *Dublin: The Shaping of a Capital*, London.
MARTIN, JOHN H. (1988), 'The social geography of mid nineteenth century Dublin city', In William J. Smyth and Kevin Whelan (eds), *Common Ground: Essay on the Historical Geography of Ireland*, Cork, 173–88.
McCULLOUGH, NIALL (1989), *Dublin: An Urban History*, Dublin, 136.
McKAY, DONALD (1990), *Flight from Famine: The Coming of the Irish to Canada*, Toronto.
McLOUGHLIN, DYMPNA (1990), 'Workhouses and Irish female paupers, 1840–70', In Maria Luddy and Cliona Murphy (eds), *Women Surviving: Studies in Irish Women's History in the Nineteenth and Twentieth Centuries,* Dublin, 117–47.
McPARLAND, EDWARD (n.d.), *The Royal Hospital Kilmainham*, Co. Dublin [RHK archive].
MURNANE, BRIAN (1988), 'The recreation of the urban historical landscape: Mountjoy Ward, Dublin c. 1901', In William J. Smyth and Kevin Whelan (eds), *Common Ground: Essays on the Historical Geography of Ireland*, Cork, 189–207.
NICHOLLS, GEORGE (1838), *Second Report on the Poor Laws (Ireland)*, London.
O'BRIEN, JOSEPH V. (1982), *Dear Dirty Dublin: A City in Distress, 1899–1916,* Berkeley and Los Angeles.
O'SULLIVAN, P. (1992), *The Irish World Wide: History, Heritage, Identity, Vol. 1: Patterns of Migration,* Leicester.

O'SULLIVAN, P. (1995) (ed.), *Irish Women and Irish Migration,* London.
POOLEY, COLIN and RICHARD LAWTON (1988), 'The social geography of nineteenth century British cities: a review', In Dietrich Denecke and Gareth Shaw (eds), *Urban Historical Geography: Recent Progress in Britain and Germany*, Cambridge, 159–74.
PRESTON, MARGARET H. (1993), 'Lay women and philanthropy in Dublin, 1860–1880', *Eire-Ireland,* Winter, 74–85.
PRUNTY, JACINTA (1995a), 'Margaret Louisa Aylward, 1810–1889', In Maria Luddy and Mary Cullen (eds), *Women, Consciousness and Power in Nineteenth Century Ireland,* Dublin, 55–88.
PRUNTY, JACINTA (1995b), 'From city slums to city sprawl: Dublin 1800 to the present', In Howard Clarke (ed.), *Irish Cities,* Cork, 109–22.
PRUNTY, JACINTA (1998), *Dublin Slums 1800–1925, A Study in Urban Geography,* Dublin.
PRUNTY, JACINTA (1999), *Margaret Aylward 1810–1889, Lady of Charity, Sister of Faith,* Dublin.
ROBINS, JOSEPH (1987), *The Lost Children: A Study of Charity Children in Ireland, 1700–1900,* Dublin.
ROYLE, STEPHEN (1978), 'Irish manuscript census records: a neglected source of information', *Irish Geography,* **11**, 110–25.
ROYLE, STEPHEN (1991) 'The socio-spatial structure of Belfast in 1837: evidence from the first valuation', *Irish Geography,* **24**, 1, 1–9.
Shaw's Commercial Directory and Illustrated Guide to the City of Dublin, Dublin, 1850; facsimile edn Belfast, 1988.
SWIFT, R. and, S. GILLEY (eds) (1999), *The Irish in Victorian Britain, The Local Dimension,* Dublin.
Them Also: The Story of the Dublin Mission (1866), London.
Thom's Official Almanac and Street Directory, Dublin, 1850–1901.
WARD, MARGARET (1991), *The Missing Sex: Putting Women into Irish History,* Dublin.
WHITELAW, JAMES (1805), *An Essay on the Population of Dublin, being the Result of an Actual Survey taken in 1798, also Several Observations on the Present State of the Poorer Parts of the City of Dublin,* Dublin (facsimile reprint in *Slum Conditions in London and Dublin,* Farnborough).

Chapter 8

TRAMPING ARTISANS IN NINETEENTH-CENTURY VIENNA[1]

JOSEF EHMER

The geographical mobility of artisans in early modern central Europe has become an important theme of social history. Historical research has produced abundant evidence showing the extent of artisanal migratory movements and, in particular, the urban crafts' dependence upon immigration. The peculiar structures and functions as well as the cultural and institutional frameworks of artisan migration have been widely discussed among historians in the last few decades (Hochstadt, 1983; Jaritz and Müller, 1988). Migration of artisans in the nineteenth century, in contrast to that of the early modern period, has not received the same attention. This is probably due to a change in research perspectives as far as spatial mobility during the Industrial Revolution[2] and the ensuing period is concerned. The migrational movements associated with the processes of industrialization and urbanization in the nineteenth and twentieth centuries were subject matter for the emerging social sciences from their very inception, and they continue to occupy the central focus of attention of modern 'social historical migration research' (Bade, 1988). Of pre-eminent interest has been migration to the emerging industrial centres and large cities, migrational inter-relationships between large urban centres, as well as overseas emigration (Bade, 1987). With respect to time frame, we notice a strong concentration of research upon the period from about 1880 up to the First World War, which is well documented with source material derived from aggregated governmental statistics (cf Langewiesche, 1977). These sources convey a picture of a 'spectacular increase' in migration during the decades prior to the Great War (Langewiesche and Lenger, 1987, p. 91). At the same time, though, it seems to be 'very unlikely that decisive significance can be attributed to the rise of factory-based production alone as the cause which directly triggered large-scale mobility' (Lenger, 1986, p. 68). This certainly raises the question of the persistence of traditional forms of migration in industrializing societies and, in particular, of the role of the tramping artisan in the context of industrial and 'modern' modes of migration in central Europe.

Some recent studies of journeymen's migration in nineteenth-century central Europe point very clearly to the prevailing importance of this type of geographical mobility during the Industrial Revolution. This relates first and foremost to the sheer

---

1 I would like to thank Melvin Greenwald for his generous help with the translation of this chapter into English.
2 In central European economic history, the term 'Industrial Revolution' usually refers to the period of technological change and economic growth from the beginning of the nineteenth century to the 1870s.

volume of mobility. Analyses conducted by Bräuer for Chemnitz and Elkar for Bamberg show the huge dimensions of journeymen's migration in the middle of the nineteenth century. Over the course of several decades, an average of approximately 1,000 journeymen per year arrived in the small Bavarian town of Bamberg, most remaining only a short time (Elkar and Huthsteiner, 1991). In Chemnitz, one of the industrial centres of Saxony, from 1836 to 1861, an average of 2,500 immigrant 'crafts and factory journeymen' who found work for at least one day were registered each year (Bräuer, 1982).

The second striking fact is an enormous discrepancy between the number of tramping journeymen and that of permanently available jobs. According to guild records from Leipzig, an average of 1,900 journeymen were employed during the year 1834; 1,915 began new jobs, 1,714 left their jobs and 9,235 arrived and departed without having found work (Zwahr, 1978, p. 51). For Frankfurt in the 1840s, the number of transient journeymen passing through the city each year was estimated at about 10,000; for 1857, the number was put at approximately 21,600, of whom an estimated 80 per cent continued on their way without having found a job. Evidence for the middle decades of the nineteenth century suggests a 'sinking hiring rate accompanied by rising inbound migration' (Ahn, 1991, p. 81). During the year 1861, approximately 44,700 journeymen travelled to Hamburg where they were registered as seeking work; there they were confronted by a yearly annual average of about 8,700 jobs available in crafts and trades (Kocka, 1991, p. 616). These examples of central European towns could go on at great length. They illustrate the fact that nineteenth-century journeymen's migration was connected with a permanent turnover of the urban labour force and with highly fluctuating urban labour markets.

Thirdly, quantitative as well as qualitative sources such as guild statutes, travel diaries or autobiographies reveal a surprising persistency of institutional and cultural traditions within the artisanal tramping system. This refers to the social features of the tramping journeymen, who were young and unmarried and spent only a couple of years on the road before they tried to establish themselves as master artisans. Using a phrase which was created to describe the peculiar institution of 'service' in European history (cf Hajnal, 1982; Mitterauer, 1985), one might call them 'lifecycle tramps'. Tradition also included the existence of institutional frameworks and social networks which guided the tramping artisans and supplied them with contacts and support: lodging houses, travel allowances, employment regulations and the like. Finally, in nineteenth-century central Europe, migration and mobility remained part of the journeymen's culture and self-esteem. It was what it had been for centuries – the normal experience of the great majority of journeymen.

Because of all these reasons, traditional journeymen's migration in central Europe may be assumed to have retained major importance within the migrational movements of the Industrial Revolution. The aim of this chapter is to examine the spatial mobility of nineteenth-century artisans using the example of Vienna and, especially, to look at continuities and changes of traditional migration patterns. Vienna is very well suited as a field of research concerning these questions. During the nineteenth century, it experienced a rapid population growth from about 230,000 inhabitants in

1800 to a little more than two million in 1900. Vienna was not only the political and cultural, but also the economic, centre of the Habsburg Monarchy. Nevertheless, in the social and economic structures of the city, small-scale production maintained its dominance throughout the nineteenth century. The number of master artisans rose from 23,000 in 1837 to 118, 000 in 1910, an increase which more or less paralleled the general growth of population. (Ehmer, 1984). From the total of 306,000 'workers' counted in Vienna by the census of 1869, between 50 and 75 per cent were apprentices and journeymen in crafts and trades, while only about 16 per cent were employed in factories (Ehmer, 1994, p. 255).

As in the Austrian Empire in general, guilds remained important corporations. During the eighteenth century, a type of 'state guild organization' had developed in Austria, in which guilds were not only coerced and directed but also preserved and protected by the state. From the end of the eighteenth century and in particular in the first half of the nineteenth century, the influence of the guilds slowly receded though they were not completely abolished. The Commercial Law of 1859 formally dissolved the guild system but established compulsory 'trade associations' which preserved many tasks and organizational traditions of the guilds which were even strenghtened in the amendment of the law in 1883. The strong position and the long persistency of the guild system had the effect of producing extraordinarily rich source materials, such as apprentice enrolments, journeymen registers, listings of masters and workshops, minutes of guild meetings, ordinances and statutes, etc. This chapter presents initial findings of the quantitative analysis of guild records and tries to combine these with evidence from census listings and various qualitative sources.[3]

EXTENT AND SEASONAL RHYTHMS OF THE MIGRATION OF JOURNEYMEN

The combination of census listings and guild records provides quantitative evidence on various aspects of the tramping system. According to the journeymen's ordinances which were issued by the Viennese city council in the late eighteenth and early nineteenth centuries, every journeyman coming to Vienna 'shall make his way to the lodging house to put up there and at no other place' on the very day of his arrival or, at the latest, on the next day.[4] The administrative treatment of the tramping journeymen was subject to change in the period investigated, and was not uniform among the individual guilds either. As a rule, in the lodging house itself, in a

---

3   A further and more detailed analysis of guild records will be performed in the research project 'Mobility and stability in the Viennese craft guilds, 1740–1860', which is funded by the Austrian Research Council (P10807-Soz). I would like to thank the members of the research team, especially Annemarie Steidl who provided statistics from the tailors' journeymen register (1836–50) and Sigrid Wadauer who helped me with information concerning journeymen's autobiographies. On the Viennese guild system in the eighteenth century, see Ehmer (1996).
4   Cf 'Handwerksartikel für die Gesellen der Seiden- und Wollenstrumpfwirker' (1772), Wiener Stadt- und Landesarchiv (hereafter: WStLA), Innungen/Urkunden 76/6; 'Gesellen- und Zuschick-Ordnung für die Hutmacher-Innung' (1815), WStLA, Innungen/Urkunden 63/4.

guild office, or in the guild master's house, the travel documents of the journeymen were examined and the names and some other data of the tramps were entered into a registration book. The journeyman was given a place to sleep in the lodging house. If he was to stay in Vienna longer and wanted to work there, a regulated system of job placement took place. According to the statutes of the hatmakers' guild from 1815, each Sunday, Monday, Tuesday and Thursday between 2.00 and 4.00 p.m., masters in need of a hand and journeymen in need of a job were to meet in the lodging house. If a tramping journeyman did not want to work in Vienna or if there was no demand for workmen, he was normally supposed to leave the city again after a couple of days, once he had received a travel allowance and had his travel documents confirmed. In the late eighteenth century, three days was the usual period an unemployed journeymen was allowed to stay in Vienna, while ordinances from the early nineteenth century mention an eight-day period.[5]

Of course, all these regulations were not so easy to enforce, especially in the large trades where, on some peak days, more than one hundred journeymen arrived in Vienna. For instance, the journeyman baker Karl Ernst, who was apprenticed in a small town in the south-western German Black Forest and tramped to Vienna in 1878, describes in his autobiography that sometimes as many as 500 journeyman bakers gathered in front of the bakers' office in search of a job. Viennese master bakers used to send a letter to the office if they needed a journeyman (Ernst, 1911, pp. 180, 192). In spite of these problems, the impression is that most of the journeymen registration books were kept carefully and in fact did register more or less all the journeymen arriving in Vienna and/or starting to work in the city, if only for a day. These books were kept by guild officials until May 1860, when the guilds were formally dissolved. After the dissolution of the guilds, compulsory trade associations performed many of the tasks of the former guilds, among them the registration of journeymen. In some of the old guilds, for instance the bakers or the cabinet makers, the transition to trade associations did not visibly change bureaucratic traditions of registering journeymen: the same hands entered the same data into the same books.[6] Even if only a limited number of journeymen registration books have survived in the archives, they are excellent sources throughout the nineteenth century.

Firstly, they reveal striking information about the sheer volume of journeymen's migration. The 'Book of the in- and out-migrating journeymen put into jobs' ('Vormerkbuch über die ein- und ausgewanderten und in Arbeit eingebrachten Gesellen') of the clothmakers for the period of 10 October 1836 to 8 May 1850, for instance, registers 131,933 arriving journeymen in Vienna for this period.[7] If we compute this as an average for a year, this would mean 11,276 in-migrating journeymen per annum between 1837 and 1847. As a comparison, the survey of trades of 1837 mentions 1,502 master tailors and about the same number of journeymen.

5 Ibid.
6 Cf Archiv der Wiener Bäckerinnung, HS 21/12 (Gesellenprotokoll 1830–1863); Archiv des Museums für Angewandte Kunst – Archiv der Wiener Tischlerinnung (Gesellenzuschickbücher 1873–1906; Registerbände).
7 WStLA, Innungen/Bücher, 29/26 ff.

Table 7: Seasonal rhythm of migration of journeyman tailors

	Proportion of journeymen arriving each month (per cent of the annual total)		
	1837	1842	1847
January	4	4	4
February	3	2	2
March	9	9	10
April	18	16	15
May	15	18	17
June	8	8	7
July	6	3	3
August	6	2	2
September	3	4	6
October	15	20	17
November	9	10	13
December	4	4	4
Total (%)	100	100	100
Total (N)	9,547	11,028	11,978

Sources: Guild records: WStLA, Innungen/Bücher 29 (Vormerkbuch).

For each working place, there would consequently be about seven to eight immigrants looking for work. Of course, the tailors were one of the largest crafts in nineteenth-century Vienna. As a contrast, the guild of the bag makers registered 153 arriving journeymen from 1815 to 1829, which would mean ten arrivals per annum.[8] In this craft, during those 15 years about the same number of journeymen immigrated as in the tailors' craft in a single day.

The migration of the journeyman tailors to Vienna followed a pronounced seasonal rhythm (see Table 7). Very few journeymen arrived in the winter months from December to February and during summertime (July and August). Spring and autumn were the peak seasons of migration. About half of the annual total of tramping journeymen tailors registered in April, May and October, between two-thirds and three-quarters from March to May and from October to November. One of the busiest months in the pre-1848 period was May 1847, when 2,028 tramping journeyman tailors arrived in Vienna. This meant more than 500 each week and 75 each day. High migrational activities in spring and autumn can generally be observed in early modern artisanal mobility: they seem to reflect seasonal travelling conditions. The pronounced peaks in April, May and October at the same time are probably due to the specific annual business cycles in the tailoring trade.[9]

[8] Vormerkbuch über die ein- und ausgewanderten Gesellen vom Mittel der bürgerlichen Taschnermeister, WStLA, Innungen/Bücher, 54/7.
[9] On very similar seasonal rhythms among eighteenth-century German journeymen, see Reith et al. (1992), p. 39; Elkar (1987), p. 104; on French tailors at about 1780, see Sonenscher (1986), p. 81.

Table 8: Percentage of in-migrants among Viennese journeymen in particular suburbs and crafts, 1827–80

Suburb/ craft	Enumeration years	Percentage of in-migrants* in the sample (N)	Total number of journeymen
Gumpendorf	1827	75	72
Gumpendorf	1857	76	1,964
Schottenfeld	1857	74	307
Hernals	1880	76	433
Crafts in Schottenfeld	1857		
Cabinet makers		84	111
Shoemakers & tailors		83	99
Locksmiths		81	37
Bakers & butchers		76	33
Masons		52	21
Silk weavers		26	78
Ribbon weavers		14	79

* In-migrant: not born in Vienna or its suburbs.
Sources: Census listings (Vienna database on European family history).

At the current stage of research, one cannot say whether relations between tramping journeymen and permanent working places such as those of the tailors were also representative for other crafts, although some hints point in that direction. If the situation were typical for the Viennese crafts as a whole in the 1830s and 1840s, about 140,000–160,000 journeymen would have come to Vienna every year – not exactly a small number for a city which, suburbs included, had 356,000 inhabitants in 1840, even if one considers that the majority of the arrivals remained only a few days or weeks. In that case, all known data on mass migration in the late nineteenth century pale in comparison to the volume of migration attributable to craft journeymen alone (cf Ehmer, 1994, p. 106).

In spite of the huge artisanal mobility during the Industrial Revolution, the proportion of immigrants among Viennese journeymen shows strong continuities from the early modern period until the nineteenth century. Data on the regional origins of journeymen in different central European cities during the early modern period show uniformly that, as a rule, at least three-quarters of all journeymen were in-migrants, and in many cases nearly all were (Ehmer, 1994, p. 102). The data available for nineteenth-century Vienna confirm this picture (see Table 8).

As shown in Table 8, about three-quarters of all the Viennese journeymen were in-migrants throughout the nineteenth century. This average value, however, obscures big variations among the individual crafts and trades. In the textile trades, which were organized in a proto-industrial system of domestic production, or in the building trades, in which wage labour was dominant since medieval times, journeymen of local origin formed the majority. In these sectors, a local and self-reproducing working class had developed. In most of the crafts – for example, among the shoemakers, tailors, locksmiths, carpenters, bakers and butchers, to mention only the most important ones – journeymen whose birthplace was Vienna were very rare. According to the census of 1857, 16 per cent of the cabinet makers, 17 per cent of the tailors and shoemakers, and 19 per cent of the locksmiths were born in the city or in its suburbs, whereas about half of the bricklayers, three-quarters of the silk weavers and 86 per cent of the ribbon weavers were born in the city.

MIGRATION, FAMILY AND THE LIFE COURSE

These differences correlate to the journeymen's marital status and household position. In early modern Vienna, as in central Europe in general, the tramping system was part of a mode of life of 'small commodity production': journeymen were not only an extremely mobile group until well into the second half of the nineteenth century, they were also single and, while employed, they normally lived with their masters. Marrying, forming a household and settling down as a citizen were connected with the position of independent master artisan in these crafts, either as an employer or self-employed. Data for nineteenth-century Vienna show that this traditional pattern was still alive. For instance, according to an analysis of the samples of the census of 1857, no journeyman baker was to be found who was not single and living in the household of his master. A different pattern was shown by proto-industrial domestic silk weavers or ribbon weavers as well as masons or carpenters. As we have seen, many of them were not migrants but were born in Vienna. Also, many of them were married and lived in their own households, in contrast to their colleagues in small-scale production.

These differences are paralleled by the age structures. Most of the journeymen in the traditional crafts and trades were young men in their late teens or twenties who hoped to settle down as a master artisan at a later stage of their life. Being a workman in the textile trades and in the building crafts, on the other hand, was rather a lifelong fate. During the nineteenth century, the transitional zone between these two poles widened. The number of married journeymen in traditional crafts slowly started to grow, and in some crafts boarding and lodging became an important alternative to living in one's master's household. Nevertheless, the combination of mobility, living-in and bachelorhood prevailed to a surprising extent (see Tables 9 and 10).[10]

The example of the cabinet makers shows the persistence of traditional patterns as well as signs of change. Between the 1820s and the 1850s, only about 5 per cent of the journeymen were from Vienna and its suburbs, as had been the case during the eighteenth century (Zatschek, 1958). Correspondingly, in 1857, no more than 10 per

---

10 For a more detailed discussion of traditional artisanal modes of life, their persistence into the nineteenth century as ell as for a comparison between central European and English tramping patterns, see Ehmer (1991), especially pp. 179–82.

Table 9: Percentage of married journeymen, Vienna/Schottenfeld, 1857

Occupation	Proportion married (%)
Bakers	0
Butchers	6
Shoemakers	6
Tailors	9
Cabinet makers	9
Locksmiths	21
Weavers	35
Ribbon weavers	39
Silk weavers	46
Masons	71
All journeymen Total number (N) = 307	29

Source: Census listings (Vienna database on European family history).

Table 10: Household position of journeymen, Vienna/Schottenfeld, 1857

	Head	Son	Kin	Boarder/lodger	In master's household	Total number
	%	%	%	%	%	N
Bakers	0	0	0	0	100	12
Butchers	6	22	0	11	61	18
Shoemakers	7	7	0	4	82	70
Tailors	10	3	0	35	52	31
Cabinet makers	10	5	0	16	69	67
Locksmiths	21	7	0	21	51	14
Masons	71	10	0	19	0	21
All journeymen	17	9	1	20	53	307

Source: Census listings (Vienna database on European family history).

cent of the journeymen cabinet makers were married men and household heads. Only from the 1860s onwards did the proportion of journeymen born in Vienna begin to rise, although it never reached 20 per cent even in the first decade of the twentieth century (see Table 11).

The combination of being unmarried and living in lodging houses or in one's master's house enabled journeymen in a certain phase of their life to exist in a state of more or less permanent mobility. If a journeyman found work in Vienna, this would not

Table 11: Geographic origins of Viennese journeymen

	1820 %	Cabinet makers 1852–55 %	1873–79 %	1901–06 %	Bag makers 1815–29 %	Tailors 24 April 1837 %
Vienna*	4	6	13	22	6	7
Lower Austria	6	5			2	8
Alpine Austria	3	5	3	2	9	3
Czech Lands	17	55	58	60	11	56
Hungary	15	10	8	11	5	11
German Lands	43	13	11	1	65	15
Others	4	3	5	4	0	0
Unknown	8	3	2	0	2	0
Number (N)	2,659	395	421	625	153	131

* 1873–1906: Vienna including Lower Austria.

Sources: Guild records:
Cabinet makers: 1820: Zatschek (1958) (total number of all journeymen getting a job in Vienna); 1852–1906: Guild archive (sample of registration books).
Bag makers: total number of all journeymen getting a job in Vienna (WStLA, Innungen/Bücher 54/7).
Tailors: total number of journeymen arriving on 24 April 1837 (WStLA, Innungen/Bücher 29/36).

mean the end of his migration. Only if he managed to establish himself as a master would he be able to turn away permanently from the migratory life and to settle down. That was not totally impossible. Most of the Viennese master artisans were immigrants as well, although to a slightly lesser extent than the journeymen (Ehmer, 1994, p. 110). However, in absolute terms, the chances of a tramping journeyman attaining the position of master in Vienna were rather low. Let us return to the example of the tailors: Table 12 shows that, among the master artisans as well, only a small minority was born in Vienna, its suburbs and its rural surroundings – throughout the entire century about 13 or 14 per cent. An even smaller segment consisted of Viennese masters' sons. On the other hand, the 1,500 master artisans' workshops which were counted in 1837 were reproduced only very slowly. In 1836, a total of only 102 new trade licences were granted: 11 of those went to the sons of Viennese masters, and 10 more to journeymen born in Vienna. The large majority of the new trade licences were consequently given to immigrating journeymen: 81of 102 or, in other words, 80 per cent. At first glance, that seems to be considerable, but compared with the approximately 10,000 tramping journeymen who came to Vienna during the very same year, this figure was next to nothing. Fewer than one per cent of the tramping journeymen established themselves in Vienna as master tailors.

Table 12: Geographic origins of Viennese master tailors, 1825–59

	1825 %	1836 %	1845 %	1859 %
Vienna	13	20	14	14
Alpine Austria*	4	11	13	8
Czech Lands†	37	43	60	67
Hungary	11	11	6	8
German Lands	30	12	6	1
Others	0	2	1	0
Unknown	5	1	0	2
Number (N)‡	54	102	112	154
Percentage of Viennese masters' sons among the newly-licensed masters	7	11	4	3

* Including a small number from Lower Austria.
† Including a small number from other Habsburg Crown Lands.
‡ Total number of master tailors becoming members of the guild in the respective years.

Sources: Guild records (WStLA, Innungen/Bücher; Einverleibungsbuch der Kleidermacher vom Jahre 1825–1860).

This does not mean that migrating journeymen remained in their position all their lives.[11] If we look at the German language area then we can see that the chances of becoming an independent master artisan were quite good in the middle of the nineteenth century. In the first decades of the Industrial Revolution, the number of small commodity producers generally increased. In the territory of the German Empire, at least a third of the apprentices into the tailor's or shoemaker's craft reached the position of master in their trade even towards the end of the nineteenth century (Ehmer, 1991, pp. 203–13). Only a few of them, however, got the chance to establish themselves in one of the big cities through which they passed during their migration. The highest chances of settling down as a master artisan existed in the many small towns or villages in the rural areas – perhaps the very places where apprentices and journeymen originally came from.[12]

FLUCTUATIONS IN THE LABOUR MARKET

Permanent mobility is also expressed in the fluctuations within the Viennese labour

---

11 Elkar (1987), p. 100 calculated an average travelling period of 6.5 years, based on German guild records.
12 Where and in which social position the travelling period of journeymen ended has not yet been investigated systematically. Among those tramping journeymen who wrote travel diaries or autobiographies, a considerable number went back home to the places or regions where they were born or apprenticed to become master artisans there. See Ernst (1911), Wirth (1911), Dewald (1936) and Scholtz (1993).

market. A relationship of seven to eight tramping journeymen per master, as was the case with the tailors in the 1830s and 1840s, was high compared with other central European cities in the middle of the nineteenth century, but not extraordinarily high. As already mentioned, in much smaller and less attractive cities such as Frankfurt, Hamburg or Leipzig, there were about five in-migrating journeymen per working place per annum.[13] That means that only a small percentage of the tramping journeymen would find a job in any of the cities in which they arrived, and if they did find a job it was usually only for a short period of time.

Viennese guild records allow us to calculate the proportion of tramping journeymen entering a job and the average duration of jobs. In the 'Vormerkbuch' of the tailors of 1836–52 already mentioned, the guild administrator took note of the new and registered journeymen when they later left their first job. In the first eight days the registration book covers, from 10 to 17 October 1836, 243 journeymen were registered as having arrived in Vienna, of whom 142 (58 per cent) found a job. Compared with other central European cities at the same time, that proportion is rather high, which is probably due to the huge labour market of the capital city.[14] We can assume – even if the source is not unambiguous in that respect – that the other 101 journeymen travelled on without finding work in Vienna. As shown in Table 13, about a third of the in-migrants kept their first job less than three weeks, about two-thirds less than two months and only about eight per cent longer than half a year. There were, however, three who stayed longer than a year and one longer than two years. The average number of days each journeyman worked for a master was 76, while the median number was 35 days.

A larger sample from the registration books of cabinet makers confirms this picture on the whole. Of the 3,168 journeymen cabinet makers who found work between September and December 1851, 27 per cent stayed less than a month in their first job, 31 per cent between one and two months, 19 per cent between two and three months, and 23 per cent longer than three months. A very similar pattern is shown by the 10 journeyman bakers who arrived in Vienna in December 1830 and stayed there during the subsequent years, being employed by a total of 48 different master bakers. Twenty-three per cent of their jobs lasted less than one month, 22 per cent between one and two months, 41 per cent between three and six months, 10 per cent between a half and a full year, and only 4 per cent longer than one year.[15] The average number of days each journeyman baker worked for a master was higher than those of the tailors: 133 days as an average, 91 as a median (see Table 13).

Even if the average duration of jobs was low, the accumulation of a series of long-term and short-term jobs could bind journeymen to Vienna for a couple of years. One of the registration books of the bag makers' guild covers the period from 1801 to

---

13 Sonenscher (1986), p. 81 calculates for Rouen tailors in the late 1770s a ratio of 9.3 journeymen registering for work (new arrivals and natives) per master.
14 Cf Ahn (1991), p. 81; Pallach (1983), p. 382.
15 Archiv der Wiener Bäckerinnung; Archiv der Wiener Tischlerinnung (cf fn. 6).

Table 13: Duration of the first job taken in Vienna: journeyman tailors who arrived in Vienna from 10 to 17 October 1836

Number of days on the job	Number of journeymen*		
	N	%	% cum.
1–7	15	10.6	10.6
8–14	18	12.7	23.3
15–21	12	8.5	31.8
22–30	17	12.0	43.8
31–60	32	22.5	66.3
61–90	9	6.3	72.6
91–182	27	19.0	91.6
183–365	8	5.6	97.2
366+	4	2.8	100.0
Total	142		

Mean: 76 days
Median: 35 days

* Altogether from 10 to 17 October 1836, 243 journeyman tailors were registered as having arrived in Vienna; 101 of them travelled on without finding a job, while 142 (58 per cent) took at least one job.

Source: Guild records (WStLA, Innungen/Bücher 29/36, Vormerkbuch über die ein- und ausgewanderten und in Arbeit eingebrachten Gesellen, 10.10.1836–28.8.1837).

1817. It mentions many journeymen who only worked for a short period in Vienna, but also others with surprisingly long periods spent with one employer. For example, the journeyman Johann Friedrich Möglich from Leipzig (Saxony) was employed with only four masters from his arrival in Vienna on 1 June 1808 to his departure on 21 August 1816. First, he stayed for eight years until 5 October 1815 with the master Johann Nebe in the suburb of Braunhirschengrund; then three months, until 21 January 1816, with the master Johann Schäffle in the city; after that only one day, 5 February 1816, with master Beschauer in Neustift; and finally half a year, until 2 August 1816, with the master Stephan in Leopoldstadt – a drastic mixture of long-term stability and rapid changes.

The register of the journeyman bakers starts in 1830 and covers the period until 1863. Here too, stays in Vienna could last from no more than a few days to more than ten years. Table 14 presents the employment careers of two journeyman bakers who worked in Vienna for a relatively long time. Christoph Lang, born in 1795 in Bavaria, came to Vienna in July 1821 and worked there until his death in August 1841. Franz Seeling, born in 1833 in Bohemia, came to Vienna in February 1852 and continued to be recorded in the register until it was terminated in January 1863. Both of them were unmarried men. The employment carreers of both bakers were characterized by the alteration of long- and short-term jobs. Both of them worked in several parts of the city, from the inner city to distant suburbs to small towns situated

Table 14: Job histories of Viennese journeyman bakers, 1830–63

Christoph Lang, journeyman baker, born in 1795 in Bavaria, arriving in Vienna in July 1821

Location of bakery*	Date of entrance	Date of leaving	Number of days at work	Number of days out of work
1. VI-Josefstadt	1.12.1830	12.4.1831	103	214
2. VI-Josefstadt	13.11.1831	15.6.1834	952	72
3. VI-Wieden	27.8.1834	10.11.1834	74	153
4. VI-Margarethen	11.3.1835	24.4.1835	43	47
5. VI-Leopoldstadt	11.6.1835	3.7.1835	22	35
6. VI-Josefstadt	8.8.1835	28.8.1835	20	80
7. VI-Windmühle	16.11.1835	16.2.1836	92	

2.5.1836: ill, hospital
9–18.4.1838: ill, hospital

| 8. LA-Hainburg | | –4.10.1837 | | |
| 9. VO-Neulerchenfeld | 23.1.1838 | 5.11.1838 | 285 | |

17.11– 10.12.1838: ill, hospital

10. VO-Braunhirschen	31.12.1838	30.9.1839	275	82
11. VI-Erdberg	21.12.1839	24.4.1840	120	40
12. VI-Himmelpfort	4. 6.1840	4.10.1840	153	62
13. VO-Neustift	5.12.1840	24.5.1841	171	7
14. VI-Wieden	1.6.1841	30.6.1841	30	

13.8.1841: ill, hospital
26.8.1841: died in hospital (Allgemeines Krankenhaus)

Franz Seeling, journeyman baker, born in 1833 in Bohemia, arrived in Vienna on 9 February 1852

Location	entrance	leaving	days at work	days out of work
1. VI-Neubau	16.2.1852	1.6.1852	105	6
2. V-Center	8.6.1852	28.6.1852	21	4
3. VO-Braunhirschen	3.7.1852	30.7.1852	28	49
4. LA-Baden	17.9.1852	1.10.1852	14	31
5. VI-Landstrasse	2.11.1852	28.2.1855	837	9
6. VI-Landstrasse	9.3.1855	29.3.1855	14	32
7. VO-Sechshaus	21.4.1855	8.6.1857	768	30
8. VI-Himmelpfort	8.7.1857	8.7.1857	1	6
9. VO-Simmering	15.7.1857	13.8.1837	30	92
10. LA-Lanzendorf	12.11.1857	30.11.1857	19	20
11. LA-Mödling	20.12.1857	15.4.1860	838	96
12. VI-Alservorstadt	19.7.1860	19.7.1860	1	23
13. V-Center	11.8.1860	24.9.1860	45	35
14. VI-Wieden	30.10.1860	8.11.1860	9	22
15. VI-Neubau	1.12.1860	15.6.1861	159	1
16. VI-Margarethen	17.6.1861	27.12.1861	223	51
17. VI-Wieden	17. 2.1862	24.1.1863	345	22
18. VI-Mariahilf	15. 2.1863	15.1.1863	335	

(end of registration book)

* Locations:
V-Centre: Vienna centre (city centre);
VI: Vienna – inner suburbs (belonging to Vienna's taxation area since 1704)
VO: Vienna – outer suburbs (incorporated 1890)
LA: Lower Austrian towns nearby Vienna

Source: Guild records (Archiv der Wiener Bäckerinnung, Gesellenprotokoll, HS 21/12, L, S).

TRAMPING ARTISANS IN NINETEENTH-CENTURY VIENNA 177

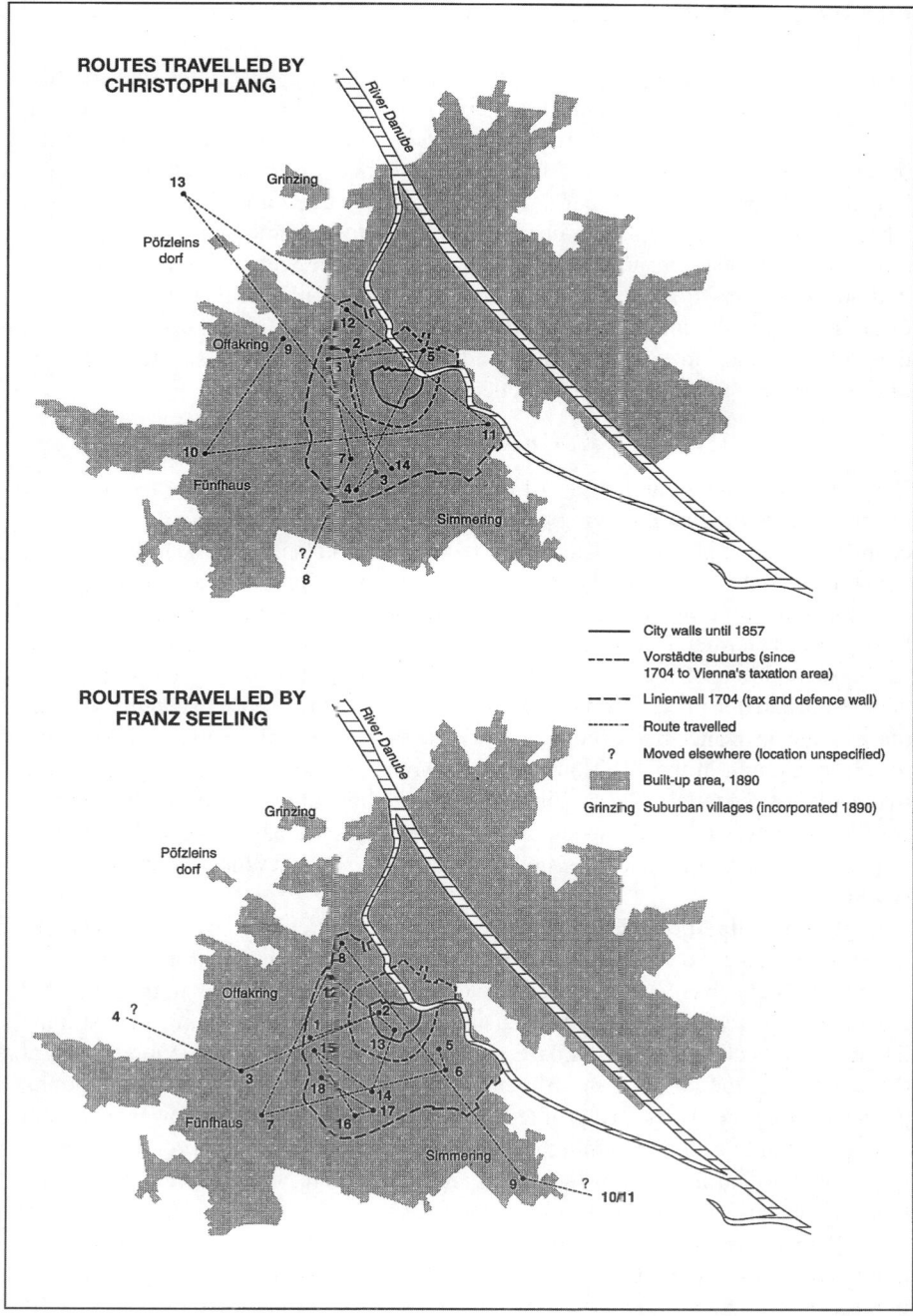

Figure 27: Routes travelled by Christoph Lang and Franz Seeling

nearby, such as Mödling, Baden or Hainburg (see Figure 27). A regional concentration in certain parts of the city is not to be observed. The whole city and its surroundings seem to have been a unified labour market for journeyman bakers. It is striking that between jobs, there were periods lasting from a few days to several weeks. Was it likely that these times out of work (or at least of unemployment in the bakers' trade) were spent undertaking unskilled work in one of the factories or casual jobs in road construction? What did the journeymen live on in these intervals and where did they stay? Did they wait for a new job in the lodging house of the guild or did they live as boarders and lodgers? Did they leave the area of the Viennese guild without being erased from the registration book, as should have been the rule? To these questions, the journeymen registration books provide no answers. Probably, these gaps indicate an existence outside artisanal traditions and outside the influence of the guild, and therefore were not reflected in guild records.

GEOGRAPHIC ORIGINS

In spite of the strong continuities of the tramping system as a whole, the places of origin of the journeymen moving to Vienna changed radically during the nineteenth century. The example of the journeymen cabinet makers (see Table 11) shows a shift which is basically valid for all the journeymen. Until the pre-1848 period, large proportions – in single years more than 40 per cent – of the Viennese journeymen came from various German states, especially from southern and south-western Germany. In the second half of the nineteenth century, the proportion of Germans gradually decreased, and disappeared almost totally at the turn of the twentieth century. In their place came migrants from the Czech lands, particularly Bohemia and Moravia, which, beginning in the 1860s, made up two-thirds of all journeymen. In the mass trades such as the tailors, the transition in the predominant regions of origin occurred earlier. In small and highly specialized crafts such as the bag makers, the German influence was strongest and persisted most strongly well into the second half of the century.

In general, a traditional long-distance migration was replaced by a new medium-range migration pattern (Ehmer and Fassmann, 1985). The causes for this development have not been entirely clarified. As a working hypothesis, one might guess that the increasing separation and internal integration of the developing big national labour markets alienated German artisans from their old destination, Vienna, and, at the same time, the crisis of the Bohemian proto-industries forced so many young people to emigrate. The social profile of the migrating journeymen, however, did not change within this shift: resembling their German ancestors of the pre-1848 period, the Bohemian journeymen of the 1850s and 1860s were young, single, lived with their masters and were permanently ready to move.

From many autobiographies of German as well as Bohemian journeymen, we know that for most of them, Vienna was not the final destination but only a stop during a wide-ranging tour. Particularly in the reports of German journeymen, specific routes show up, which went through the economically best developed regions in the German language area and included major cities. A northern German journeyman would, for example, travel through the Rhine valley to the south, stay for a time in Switzerland, and would turn to the east along the Alps to finally reach Vienna, perhaps on a boat or raft along the Danube. After his stay in Vienna, he would return home, travelling in a north-westerly direction through Bohemia and Saxony. A Bohemian journeyman would probably first visit Vienna and then turn west to Germany or east to Hungary (Vcsahlikova, 1994).

INSTITUTIONAL AND CULTURAL TRADITIONS IN THE TRAMPING SYSTEM

Since the very beginnings of the tramping system in the fourteenth century, and especially from the sixteenth to the eighteenth century, tramping journeymen moved within dense and widespread networks of social contact and support which were maintained by journeymen's associations and guilds. These networks included lodging houses or houses of call where arriving journeymen could stay overnight or a couple of days in order to seek a job or to meet resident colleagues or potential fellow travellers. They also included a sort of travel allowance or donation given to those journeymen who did not find a job and moved on. Its form varied: a certain amount of cash, food and drink, or accommodations for the night. When, during the course of his travels through villages or small towns, a journeyman chanced upon a master of his trade, he could expect an invitation to a proper meal or to spend the night, or to receive a few *Kreuzer* in cash. In larger cities, in which several workshops practising the same craft could be found or where a guild existed, a travelling journeyman did not try to make contact with an individual master but rather sought out the lodging house for his craft (Ehmer, 1997).

During the early modern period, systems of lodging houses and travel allowances developed in most of the crafts and trades, but there were differences among them as well. In small crafts featuring a very wide-ranging labour market, where a few journeymen circulated over large distances, travel allowances had assumed the status of a legal obligation (Reith, 1990, p. 443). In other crafts, they existed as a social custom. During the eighteenth century, governmental authorities in the Habsburg Monarchy as well as in the Holy Roman Empire in general sought to systematically regulate and to standardize the system of allowances and lodging houses. The 'General Handicrafts Act and Fundamental Patent' of November 1731. for instance, had decreed:

> that no journeyman [was permitted to receive or demand] more than 15 Kreuzer, or 20 Kreuzer at the very most, in cash or in the form of food and drink ... And each journeyman shall also seek his accommodations in his proper lodging house and refrain from all forms of begging, [and], if he has obtained no employment within three days, continue upon his way.[16]

It is doubtful that the authorities were ever successful in these efforts to standardize and to control a variety of practices. In a large city such as Vienna and especially in the mass trades, it was of course the extraordinarily large number of arriving and departing journeymen which made unification such a difficult task. Besides the legal

---

16 K.K. Theresianisches Gesetzbuch, Vol. I, Vienna 1789, p. 203.

forms of keeping lodging houses, receiving or giving allowances, or placing a journeyman into a job, there existed clandestine forms and practices as well. In all these matters, the dividing line between legality and illegality was anything but sharp. The Viennese cabinet makers' guild, for instance, mentioned in 1753 a proper lodging house 'in the inn named The Holy Trinity' as well as three additional lodging houses in various suburbs 'so that it is made easier for the numerous immigrating and emigrating journeymen to find accomodation and work'.[17] Twenty years later a complaint by the guild now labelled the lodging houses in the suburbs as 'doss houses' or hidden houses which the government was petitioned to remove. The 'true' lodging house was rarely frequented by the journeymen, whereas large numbers of them had taken up residence for extended periods in the doss houses.[18] In that period, between 1,200 and 2,400 journeymen cabinet makers would have passed through the town each year. This was an enormous mass compared with most of the other crafts and trades of this time, but it was not too much compared with the numbers we have already encountered in the nineteenth century. The growing numbers of tramping journeymen in the nineteenth century obviously widened the variety of practices and customs to secure one's living or to find social contact, financial support or a job.

Nevertheless, the traditional customs of travel allowance and lodging house display an astounding continuity in the nineteenth century. Autobiographies dating from early as well as from late in the nineteenth century indicate the existence of lodging houses and the custom of granting and receiving financial support in Vienna. The white tawer Johann Eberhard Dewald from the German Rhineland reached Vienna in September 1837 and spent 'a lazy three weeks' at the lodging house (Dewald, 1936, p. 113). The brass founder Josef Wirth, originating from Konstanz, arrived in Vienna in late 1850. He received from the brass founders' guild the sum of five Gulden which allowed him a pleasant stay and extensive sightseeing for about a fortnight (Wirth, 1911). The baker Karl Ernst describes the Viennese lodging house in 1878 (Ernst, 1911, p. 195).

These autobiographers found similar conditions in most places they came upon in the course of their tour. They received travel allowances quite frequently, either from guilds, individual masters or even communal authorities (cf Dewald, 1936, pp. 42, 43, 70, 83, 110, 120, etc.). They spent their nights in lodging houses, in other inns or with a master whom they had helped for one or two hours (cf Scholtz, 1993, pp. 171 ff; Vosahlikova, 1994). Beginning in the middle of the nineteenth century, lodging houses operated and travel allowances offered by guilds were supplemented by similar services provided by Catholic young men's associations and early trade unions. Journeymen looked for short-term jobs in order to have their laundry washed and repaired, and they lost their jobs and had to tramp on because of seasonal lack of work or due to a more serious economic crisis (Scholtz, 1993, pp. 65, 100, 104; Dewald, 1936, p. 86). Even the reciprocal character of allowance continues to be mentioned in autobiographical sources dating from the nineteenth century.

17 WStLA, Alte Registratur 58/1756 (A 1/97).
18 WStLA, Alte Registratur, Berichte 282/1774 (6.6.1774).

Traditionally, each journeyman who was granted a form of allowance, either from an individual master or at the lodging house, thereby pledged himself to accept work offered to him. Johann Eberhard Dewald describes in his travel diary how he, together with a fellow journeyman, in the 1830s presented himself to the guild in Budapest and requested an allowance, despite the fact that he actually did not wish to remain in the city.

> There was surely a sufficient number of German masters there who would not begrudge us our ancient guild right to an allowance. And indeed we did get more than a pittance and we were even referred to a Hungarian master who had a job opening. It wasn't particularly enticing to me and I wanted to pay a visit to my Hungarian cousin in Szegedin anyway. But since we had already laid claim to our guild rights, it would have been unfair simply to have tossed our duties to the wind. (Dewald, 1936, p. 120)

Scholtz, travelling at the same time from Prague to Vienna, was luckier when he refused to accept work in the Upper Austrian capital Linz in spite of dramatic complaints by a master: 'As we had not taken allowances, nobody could force us to work' (Scholtz, 1993, p. 44).

MIGRATION AND SOCIAL CONTROL

Beginning with the eighteenth century, political authorities strengthened their efforts to bring the growing number of tramping journeymen under observation and control. Guilds were among the very few institutions which were at all available to carry out police functions. Under the 'General Handicrafts Act and Fundamental Patent' of November 1731 for the Holy Roman Empire, itinerant journeymen were required to be in possession of certain travel documents (*Kundschaften*).[19] It was the duty of the guild chairman to have these documents printed in the legally prescribed manner, as well as to issue and to control them.

Over the course of the eighteenth century, the legal provisions regarding *Kundschaft* documents were enforced in actual practice. Numerous guild archives contain massive numbers of *Kundschaften* dating from the second half of the eighteenth and the early decades of the nineteenth centuries (Stopp, 1982). Aside from certain minor modifications, all of these documents appear essentially identical: a large format page printed on one side, bearing the stamp of the respective city and a form displaying the requested information. The physical description tended to become more comprehensive over time, including eye colour and the shape of the face and nose as well as 'particular distinguishing features' and the question of religion. In addition, the signatures of both the journeyman and the master for whom he had worked were required. In smaller cities, a municipal official also signed the *Kundschaft*.

To cite one example: the *Kundschaft* which 19-year-old journeyman locksmith Thomas Steiner submitted to the guild upon his arrival in Vienna in April 1825 had been issued by the 'Honorable Guild of *Bürgerlichen* Locksmiths of the Sovereign City of Retz', a town in northern Lower Austria, and was signed by Thomas himself,

---

19 K. K. Theresianisches Gesetzbuch, Vol. I, Vienna 1789, p. 216.

a municipal official and three masters: his employer, the guild chairman and vice-chairman. It shows a quite well-rendered view of the city of Retz and states that Thomas Steiner was born in the village of Willing in the Znaim district of the province of Moravia. He worked 'faithfully and peaceably' for 42 weeks in Retz. His appearance is described as follows: 'Stature: medium; Face: lean; Hair: blond Eyes: brown; Nose: pointed; Particular distinguishing features: both ears pierced'.[20] As this example shows, *Kundschaften* could be quite an effective instrument for the identification and control of journeymen. This was only possible, however, when each individual guild was precise and incorruptible in their issuance and abuses could be prevented – an assumption which could hardly be guaranteed in actual practice.

From the early nineteenth century on, numerous individual German states began to erect an even tighter network of police control over the movements of migrant journeymen. Bavaria in 1808 was the first to replace *Kundschaften* with *Wanderbücher*, log books which the journeyman had to have with him at all times, showing not only his last place of employment but also all places where he had previously worked and thus the entire route of his travels. The replacement of attestations occurred relatively late within the Habsburg Monarchy, where *Wanderbücher* were first instituted in 1829. Over the long term, the authorities actually seem to have been successful in achieving their objectives of tighter police control over migrant journeymen by combining the activities of guilds and police. Guilds were obliged to issue travel documents and to make sure of their credibility, while frontier guards or policemen at the city gates controlled the bearers of the document. Nineteenth-century autobiographies are full of episodes describing quarrels and conflicts between police and tramping journeymen.

Besides the travel documents, housing arrangements were important means to control tramping journeymen. This refers to lodging houses as mandatory arrival points for tramping journeymen, but also to masters' households where most journeymen resided in the shorter or longer periods of employment. In the first half of the nineteenth century, efforts to subordinate tramping journeymen to the authority and control of the master artisans were again revived by fear of revolutionary activities. In the pre-1848 period, some German states stipulated mandatory residence in the master's household (Ehmer, 1991, pp. 199–202). This was not the case in Vienna, but – as Table 10 shows – most journeymen in the trades with high mobility in fact lived with their masters.

A further expectation authorities associated with the tramping system was the hope to avoid accumulation of unemployed labour and, therefore, to reduce the danger of social unrest, especially in times of economic crisis. As already mentioned above, eighteenth- and early nineteenth-century journeymen's ordinances stipulated a maximum number of days an unemployed journeymen would be allowed to stay in the city. Even if the practical meaning of such regulations must not be overestimated, they did remain potential instruments of power in the hands of the authorities. When the Viennese silk weaving industry was hit by an economic crisis in 1791–92, the

---

20 Kundschaft Thomas Steiner (private collection, Josef Ehmer).

city administration's orders to the guild chairmen were 'to send away all journeymen who were not permanent residents of Vienna'. The government of Lower Austria specified that all unmarried journeymen who were unemployed for longer than three days had to leave the province (Gugitz, 1922, pp. 162–64).

CONCLUSION

In nineteenth-century central Europe, the migration of journeymen increased in volume and retained many of its traditional structures and functions. Obviously, the tramping system satisfied the needs of guild masters, political authorities and of journeymen themselves, as it had done a century before. In which way, however, was this traditional migration pattern compatible with the process of industrialization? Some concluding remarks should deal with that question.

In the early modern period, the economic logic or function of journeymen's migration may be seen as a key mechanism to regulate the artisanal labour market. Preindustrial small commodity production might be characterized by a generally limited and highly fluctuating demand for products and services. In central Europe, the way to cope with that economic structure was a split of the labour market into a stable segment of the labour force and a fluctuating and permanently mobile one. The stable part of the labour force consisted primarily of resident master artisans, the mobile part of tramping journeymen. In the economic transformations of the nineteenth century, this traditional dual labour market retained its economic function in many crafts and trades.

In the nineteenth century, industrialization was connected with the rapid expansion of the capitalist market economy in non- or pre-industrial commercial sectors. The backbone of this process was the transformation of small-scale handicraft production into outwork. At the very time when classic proto-industrial trades like textile manufacturing were absorbed or destroyed by the factories, the putting-out system spread into the footwear, garment, furnishing and other industries. Shoemakers, tailors, cabinet makers and the like shifted towards mass production to satisfy a growing demand for consumer goods in their respective urban communities as well as in new markets, even abroad or overseas. The growth of production and the widening of markets promoted the subordination of crafts and trades under merchant capitalists and local middlemen. Dependency on trans-regional markets and merchant capitalists caused instability of employment. Outwork in the crafts and trades in the middle of the nineteenth century can be described as a fragile economy of low wages and a 'syncopated rhythm' of work 'with its alternating periods of feverish activity broken by slack spells' (Laurie, 1978, p. 343).

These processes can be seen in various European regions and even in North America during the first half of the nineteenth century. In many Western European cities, this meant that traditional artisanal branches were on 'the full swing from a corporate, or guild mode of production to an industrial capitalist one' (Johnson, 1979, pp. 68–9). Joan Scott described in her essay on the Parisian tailors the social meaning of such a swing. Traditionally, 'the basic unit of production was not the family but a team of skilled male workers whose livelihood depended on their wages …

Proletarianization meant a move from the workshop of one's master to one's own household' (Scott, 1984, pp. 71–73). The peculiarities of central Europe can be seen in this fact that master artisans' workshops kept their dominant position as places and units of production (Ehmer, 1991, pp. 214–28). The circulation of single, in-living journeymen between and within the large cities such as Vienna created a highly flexible trans-regional labour market and served to maintain a balance between labour demand and labour supply, as it had done for centuries. As it seems, the old journeymen's tramping system fitted perfectly into the new economic environment.

REFERENCES

AHN, B.-J. (1991), *Handwerkstradition und Klassenbildung. Eine sozialgeschichtliche Studie zum Verhältnis von Handwerksmeistern und -gesellen in Frankfurt am Main 1815–1866*, Bielefeld.

BADE, K. (ed.) (1987), *Population, Labour and Migration in 19th and 20th Century Germany*, Leamington Spa.

BADE, K. (1988), 'Sozialhistorische Migrationsforschung', In E. Hinrichs and H. van Zon (eds), *Bevölkerungsgeschichte im Vergleich*, 63–74.

BRÄUER, H. (1982), *Gesellenmigration in der Zeit der Industriellen Revolution*, Karl-Marx-Stadt.

DEWALD, J. E. (1936), *Biedermeier auf Walze. Aufzeichnungen und Briefe des Handwerksburschen Johann Eberhard Dewald 1836–1838*, hg.v. G.M. Hofmann, Berlin.

EHMER, J. (1980), *Familienstruktur und Arbeitsorganisation im frühindustriellen Wien*, Vienna.

EHMER, J. (1984), 'Ökonomischer und sozialer Strukturwandel im Wiener Handwerk – von der industriellen Revolution zur Hochindustrialisierung', In U. Engelhardt (ed.), *Handwerker in der Industrialisierung. Lage, Kultur und Politik vom späten 18. bis ins frühe 20. Jahrhundert*, Stuttgart, 78–104.

EHMER, J. (1991), *Heiratsverhalten, Sozialstruktur, ökonomischer Wandel. England und Mitteleuropa in der Formationsperiode des Kapitalismus*, Göttingen.

EHMER, J. (1994), *Soziale Traditionen in Zeiten des Wandels. Arbeiter und Handwerker im 19. Jahrhundert*, Frankfurt.

EHMER, J. (1997), 'Worlds of mobility; migration patterns of Viennese artisans in the 18th century', In G. Crossick (ed.), *The Artisan and the European Town, 1500–1900*, Aldershot, 172–99.

EHMER, J. and H. FASSMANN (1985), 'Zur Sozialstruktur von Zuwanderern nach Wien im 19. Jahrhundert', In *Immigration et société urbaine en Europe occidentale, XVIe–XXe siècle*, Paris, 31–45.

ELKAR, R. S. (1987), 'Schola migrationis. Überlegungen und Thesen zu neuzeitlichen Geschichte der Gesellenwanderung aus der Perspektive quantitativer Untersuchungen', In K. Roth (ed.), *Handwerk in Mittel- und Südosteuropa*, Munich, 87–109.

ELKAR, R. S. and R. HUTHSTEINER (1991), 'An approach to formal statistical analysis of historical data based on the town of Bamberg', In H.-H. Bock and P. Ihm (eds), *Classification, Data Analysis and Knowledge Organisation*, Berlin, 311–17.

ERNST, K. (1911), *Aus dem Leben eines Handwerksburschen*, Neustadt/Schwarzwald.

GUGITZ, J. (1922), 'Der Aufstand der Zeugmachergesellen im Jahre 1792', In J. Gugitz und C. Blümml, *Von Leuten und Zeiten. Ansichten aus dem alten Wien*, Vienna, 155–89.

HAJNAL, J. (1982), 'Two kinds of preindustrial household formation system', *Population and Development Review*, **8**, 449–94.

HOCHSTADT, S. (1983), 'Migration in preindustrial Germany', *Central European History*, **16**, 195–224.

JARITZ, G. and A. MÜLLER (eds) (1988), *Migration in der Feudalgesellschaft*, Frankfurt.

JOHNSON, C. (1979), 'Patterns of proletarianization: Parisian tailors and Lodeve woolen workers', In J. Merriman (ed.), *Consciousness and Class Experience in Nineteenth Century Europe*, New York, 65–84.

KOCKA, J. (1991), *Arbeitsverhältnisse und Arbeiterexistenzen. Grundlagen der Klassenbildung im 19. Jahrhundert*, Bonn.

LANGEWIESCHE, D. (1977), 'Wanderungsbewegungen in der Hochindustrialisierungsperiode. Regionale, interstädtische und innerstädtische Mobilität in Deutschland, 1880–1914', *Vierteljahrschrift für Sozial- und Wirtschaftsgeschichte*, **64**, 1–40.

LANGEWIESCHE, D. and F. LENGER (1987), 'Internal migration: persistence and mobility', In K. Bade (ed.), *Population, Labour and Migration in 19th and 20th Century Germany*, Leamington Spa, 87–100.

LAURIE, B. (1978), 'Life styles of Philadelphia artisans', *Labour History*, **15**, 332–50.

LENGER, F. (1986), *Zwischen Kleinbürgertum und Proletariat. Studien zur Sozialgeschichte der Düsseldorfer Handwerker 1816–1878*, Göttingen 1986.

MITTERAUER, M. (1985), 'Gesindedienst und Jugendphase im europäischen Vergleich', *Geschichte und Gesellschaft*, **11**, 177–204.

PALLACH, U.-C. (1983), 'Fonctions de la mobilité artisanale at ouvriére – compagnons, ouvriérs et manufacturiers en France et aux Allemange (17e–19e siècles)', *Francia*, **11**, 365–406.

REITH, R. (1990), *Lexikon des alten Handwerks*, Munich.

REITH, R., A. GRIESSINGER and P. EGGERS (1992), *Streikbewegungen deutscher Handwerksgesellen im 18. Jahrhundert*, Göttingen.

SCHOLTZ, J. D. (1993), *Meine Reise 1805–1812. Die Aufzeichnungen des Tuchscherermeisters Johann David Scholtz aus seinen Wanderjahren, erstmals hg. von S. Scholtz Novak*, Bremen.

SCOTT, J. W. (1984), 'Men and women in the Parisian garment trades: discussion of family and work in the 1830s and 1840s', In P. Thane, G. Crossick and R. Floud (eds), *The Power of the Past: Essays for Eric Hobsbawm*, Cambridge, 67–96.

SONENSCHER, M. (1986), 'Journeymen's migration and workshop organization in eighteenth-century France', In S. L. Kaplan and C. J. Koepp, *Work in France: Representation, Meaning, Organization, and Practice*, Ithaca and London, 74–96.

STOPP, K. (1982), *Die Handwerkskundschaften mit Ortsansichten. Beschreibender Katalog der Arbeitsattestate wandernder Handwerksgesellen 1731–1830*, Vol. I, Stuttgart.

VOSAHLIKOVA, P. (ed.) (1994), *Auf der Walz. Erinnerungen böhmischer Handwerksgesellen*, Vienna.

WIRTH, J. (1911), *Konstanzer Licht- und Schattenbilder seit 1848. Bearbeitet nach den Schilderungen des Gürtlermeisters Josef Wirth in Konstanz von G. König, Bodensee-Chronik (Beilage zu den Konstanzer Nachrichten, September–November)*, Konstanz.

ZATSCHEK, H. (1958), *550 Jahre jung sein. Die Geschichte eines Handwerks*, Vienna.

ZWAHR, H. (1978), *Zur Konstituierung des Proletariats als Klasse. Strukturuntersuchung über das Leipziger Proletariat während der industriellen Revolution*, Berlin.

Chapter 9

MIGRATION AND URBANIZATION IN NORTH-WEST ENGLAND: A REASSESSMENT OF THE ROLE OF TOWNS IN THE MIGRATION PROCESS

COLIN G. POOLEY and JEAN TURNBULL

INTRODUCTION

This chapter aims to challenge traditional assumptions about the role of towns in the British migration system from the eighteenth to the twentieth centuries, using evidence from north-west England.

The conventional picture of nineteenth-century migration, painted by contemporaries (for instance Danson and Welton, 1859; Ravenstein, 1885, 1889; Redford, 1926) and frequently restated by a large number of later writers (for example Lawton, 1959; 1973; Friedlander and Roshier, 1966; Anderson, 1974; Pooley, 1983; Tucker, 1983; Mills, 1984; Withers, 1985; Baines, 1986; Nicholas and Shergold, 1987; Swift and Gilley, 1989; Withers and Western, 1991; Pooley and Whyte, 1991), is of a direct short-distance shift of population from the countryside to towns, or from small towns to larger towns up the urban hierarchy. Thus in 1859 Danson and Welton stated of migration to the industrial town of Preston in Lancashire:

> A stream of population constantly passes into Preston from the north. This we may reasonably suppose to consist, to a large extent, of persons born in the districts of Fylde, Garstang and Clitheroe, to whom such movement is not only obviously profitable, but also comparatively easy. (Danson and Welton, 1859, pp. 48–49).

The districts named as sending migrants to Preston were all predominantly rural.

More generally, Charles Dickens caught the flavour of contemporary opinion when he stated in *Dombey and Son:*

> Day after day, such travellers crept past, but always ... in one direction – always towards the town. Swallowed up in one phase or other of its immensity, towards which they seemed impelled by a desperate fascination, they never returned. (Dickens, 1982, pp. 404–05)

Although, cumulatively, large numbers of people were transferred from the countryside to towns in the nineteenth century, it is argued in this chapter that the process was less simple than such contemporary comment would suggest. Rather than a series of one-way moves up the urban hierarchy, it is suggested that many moves were complex and circulatory. Moves between villages and from one small town to another were common, and return migration from large towns to small towns and rural areas was quite frequent. Furthermore, reasons for migration were also complex, and it is suggested that for many migrants the attractions of an urban labour market were not the only or most important motives for moving. Figure 28 suggests some of the complex connection between migration, economy and society.

The fact that many studies of migration in the past are necessarily based on cross-sectional records (such as censuses) has distorted our view of the role of towns in the migration process. Census-based studies over-simplify the migration system because they tend to show an origin and destination which span a long period of time from place of birth to place of residence on census night. Thus intermediate moves which may be circulatory or which may encompass a wide range of settlements and experiences are omitted.

It can be argued that census-based studies both overstate and understate the role of towns in the migration process. Rural to urban moves are overstated because, although overall there was a shift of population from countryside to town, this was achieved through a complex series of intermediate moves that the origin and destination data of censuses cannot reveal. Conversely, frequent short-distance moves within towns are understated because cross-sectional sources miss frequent changes of residence.

A complete picture of the role of towns in the migration process can only be gained through the collection of longitudinal residential histories for individual migrants. Historical geographers have begun to use an increasingly wide range of sources to try to produce such longitudinal profiles. The linkage of censuses and other listings provides some limited information, but many intermediate moves are still lost (Pooley and Doherty, 1991). Other studies that have tried to provide detailed information on migration patterns and processes have used records relating to the migration of apprentices to urban areas (Lovett et al., 1985), the movement of skilled workers supported by their trade unions (Southall, 1991a), the movement of criminals apprehended by the law (Nicholas and Shergold, 1987; Pooley, 1994), and migration caused by the operation of the Poor Law (Parton, 1987; Taylor, 1989; Withers and Western, 1991).

However, such sources do not provide a full lifetime residential history, and are in effect organized according to the reasons why movement took place (for instance, all those removed from a parish by the Overseers of the Poor) and thus cannot provide a cross-section of migration decisions. Other studies have focused on individual diaries (Lawton and Pooley, 1975; Parton, 1980; see also Burnett, 1974; 1982; Burnett et al., 1984), letters (Erickson, 1972; Richards, 1991), accounts (Southall, 1991b; Pooley and D'Cruze, 1994) and oral testimonies (Jones, 1981; Bartholomew, 1991). Although most revealing about migration decisions, and in some cases providing full life histories, such sources can deal only with a very small number of respondents whose typicality it is very difficult to assess.

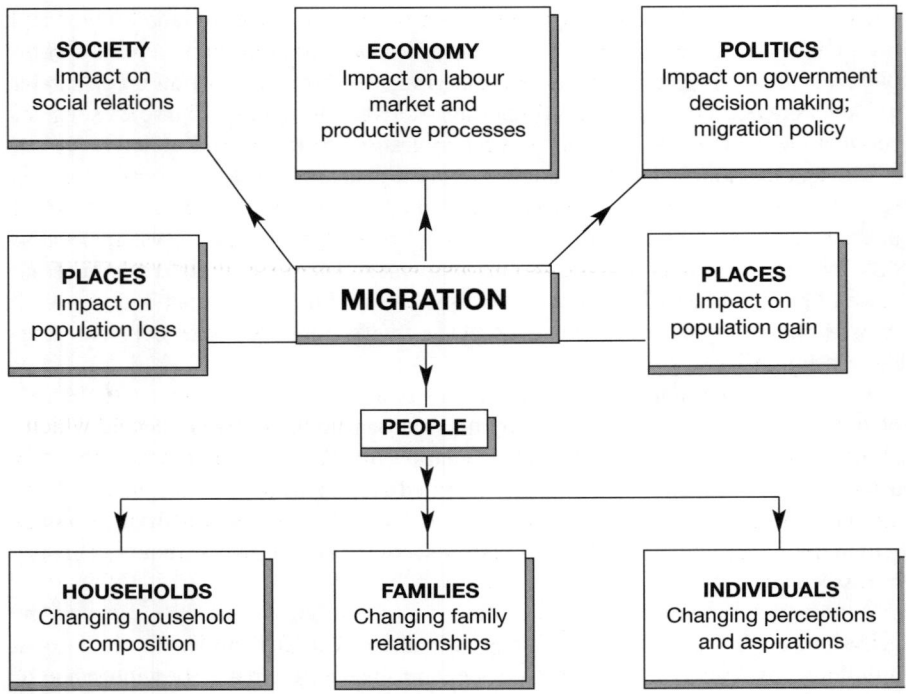

Figure 28: Suggested links between population migration and structural, spatial and individual processes of change in past economy and society

THE COLLECTION OF LONGITUDINAL MIGRATION PROFILES

Analysis in this chapter is based mainly on an unusually large and detailed collection of longitudinal residential histories collected from family historians. These data are backed up by one particularly detailed family history compiled in 1826.[1] The main data set consists of information on 2,251 individuals who made a total of 8,568 residential moves with an origin, destination, or both in Lancashire and Cheshire (using pre-1974 county boundaries). Individuals for whom information is available were born between 1750 and 1930, and for the purposes of analysis are divided into three cohorts: those born 1750 to 1830 (27.3 per cent of all moves), those born 1831 to 1890 (48.6 per cent), and those born 1891 to 1930 (24.1 per cent).[2]

---

1 'Family history of Benjamin Shaw' (Preston Record Office, DDX/1154/1 and DDX/1154/2). See also Crosby.
2 The data were collected as part of an ESRC-funded project on the longitudinal study of residential histories. Data have been compiled for all parts of Britain, but this chapter focuses on the analysis of information from individuals who at some time lived in Lancashire or Cheshire. Data were compiled using the following methodology. Members of Family History Societies throughout Britain were contacted through their newsletters or magazines and were asked for their cooperation in the research. Members of Family History and Genealogy Societies devote considerable amounts of time to research

There is clearly scope for considerable bias in data collected from family historians. First, it must be stressed that for the most part, family historians rely on standard historical sources with all their associated problems of bias and omissions. Although in some cases they will have access to diaries, personal documents and oral evidence, most information will be drawn from mainly cross-sectional sources such as the census enumerators' books, parish registers, vital registration certificates, wills and similar sources. Like other researchers, family historians may have made errors of record linkage, and sometimes they may have been tempted to infer reasons for migration which suited the story they wished to tell. However, in the vast majority of cases the degree of supporting detail given suggests that the evidence is meticulously researched and recorded with care. In many cases it is probably more accurate than similar evidence collected by academic researchers.

Second, there must also be some queries about the representativeness of data provided by a self-selected group of family historians, who themselves selected which individuals to provide information on. Data used in this analysis were compared with information in the population censuses of 1851 and 1891 to check their representativeness.[3] There are clear demographic biases related to the objectives of family historians and the nature of the sources they use. Because family historians tend to be more interested in following a name down the male line, and because of the relative invisibility of women in many sources, there is a strong bias towards males. Overall, only about one-third of the residential histories relate to females, with a slightly higher proportion of females in the later periods. Family historians are also more interested in ancestors who married and had children (and thus produced a family line). There is thus a bias in the lifetime histories towards those who eventually married and towards those who lived to old age (Table 15). The birthplace distribution of people in the data set is relatively close to that of the census (Table 16). The principal bias is an under-representation of the Irish-born, which could be due to their high mortality (family historians are less likely to have traced relatives who died young), their poverty and hence relative invisibility in some sources or, possibly, to a lack of family historians who have traced their ancestors from Ireland to England.[4]

---

about their ancestors and investigate available sources with a high degree of diligence and enthusiasm. Those who responded to the initial request for help with the research were sent detailed data entry forms requesting full information about the residential histories of people whose lives they had traced, including information on reasons for moves, companions during migration and job changes after migration. It was stressed that full residential histories were required including those who moved only a short distance or not at all. The final data set, covering the whole of Britain, consists of some 16,091 lifetime residential histories.The collection and computer-entry of data was begun in 1991 and 1992 with the aid of research grants from the Nuffield Foundation. The research continued with the support of the ESRC (grant R000234638).

3 Thus the characteristics of all people in the data set alive in 1851 and 1891 and living in Lancashire and Cheshire were compared with the relevant census population for Lancashire and Cheshire.

4 It is possible that we inadvertently reduced the response from those with Irish ancestors by saying that we were not recording movement in countries other than Great Britain, but we did stress our interest in movement to Britain.

Table 15: Comparison of sample populations with census populations by gender, marital status and age, 1851 and 1891

Population characteristics	1851 %	1891 %
males in sample population	70.5	64.3
males in census population	48.8	48.2
females in sample population	29.5	35.7
females in census population	51.2	51.8
single in sample population	31.5	33.7
single in census population	61.9	61.1
married in sample population	60.6	59.7
married in census population	32.9	33.3
widowed in sample population	7.9	6.6
widowed in census population	5.3	5.6
age <20 years in sample population	36.1	24.5
age <20 years in census population	45.7	45.6
age 20–39 years in sample population	32.6	33.4
age 20–39 years in census population	32.8	31.8
age 40–59 years in sample population	23.2	29.6
age 40–59 years in census population	16.1	16.9
age 60+ in sample population	8.1	12.5
age 60+ in census population	5.4	5.8
Total sample population	660	893

The sample populations consist of all those alive on the census nights of 1851 and 1891 and living in Lancashire or Cheshire, taken from the total sample of 2,251 individuals returned by family historians. The characteristics of the sample populations are compared with the population profile of Lancashire and Cheshire, taken from the Census of Great Britain (1851), and the Census of England and Wales (1891).

The sample population also over-represents those living in smaller settlements in 1851: 52.6 per cent of the population of Lancashire and Cheshire lived in towns of over 10,000 people but only 42 per cent of the sample population lived in such settlements. This may, in part, be due to the lack of Irish-born who would have been mainly urban dwellers, but it must also reflect the fact that it is easier for family historians to trace individuals in small settlements. This is potentially important for the analysis of movement through towns of different size, and should be borne in mind in subsequent interpretation. However, by 1891 the bias had almost disappeared as 64.4 per cent of the census population lived in towns of over 10,000 people then compared with 61.6 per cent of the sample population. Other biases include a small skew towards those from higher social groups, due mainly to difficulties in tracing the poor; and it is obvious from the range of sources used by family historians that some of the stated reasons for migration are deductions based on circumstantial evidence. It is also likely that some short-distance moves were not picked up in the

Table 16: Comparison of sample populations with census populations by region of birth, 1851 and 1891 (per cent)

Census region	1851 sample	1851 census	1891 sample	1891 census
London	0.8	0.7	0.9	0.8
South-East	0.8	0.3	0.9	0.5
South Midlands	0.8	0.2	1.7	0.7
Eastern	0.0	0.2	0.6	0.4
South-West	0.4	0.4	1.5	0.8
West Midlands	2.5	2.1	4.3	3.5
North Midlands	0.8	1.4	1.8	1.6
North-West	82.3	77.4	73.8	78.9
Yorkshire	5.5	3.4	4.8	3.1
Northern	3.2	1.3	3.1	1.2
Wales	0.8	1.9	2.4	1.8
Scotland	0.9	1.3	2.6	1.4
Irish	1.2	8.6	1.6	4.0
Total sample	660		893	

The sample populations consist of all those alive on the census nights of 1851 and 1891 and living in Lancashire and Cheshire, taken from the total sample of 2,251 individuals returned by family historians. The birthplace regions of the sample populations are compared with those of the population of Lancashire and Cheshire, taken from the Census of Great Britain (1851), and the Census of England and Wales (1891).

sources available, particularly in the earlier periods. Despite these caveats, the data provide a more detailed and accurate picture of migration in north-west England than any other available evidence.

THE ROLE OF TOWNS IN THE MIGRATION SYSTEM

Urban definition, and especially the criterion of population size, is always arbitrary (Carter, 1981). In this chapter, settlements are initially divided into eight arbitrary size classes, plus settlements which were effectively suburbs of other large towns (Table 17). As noted above, the data are analysed in three cohorts with town size determined according to the 1801 census for those born 1750 to 1830; the 1851 census for those born 1831 to 1890; and the 1951 census for those born 1891 to 1930. For some later analysis (Table 21), size classes are further simplified to remove small numbers in some categories. No assumptions are made about the extent to which settlements of a given size had attained urban functions (this clearly varied considerably over time and space), and these data could be re-analysed in many different ways, using towns of different sizes at various time periods. However, the analysis presented here does allow examination of the extent to which migration took place between settlements in a series of size bands, and enables the assumption that much migration moved people up the urban hierarchy to be specifically assessed.

Table 17: Distribution of origins and destinations by settlement size and birth cohort (per cent)

Settlement size	Cohort 1750–1830 origin	Cohort 1750–1830 destination	Cohort 1831–1890 origin	Cohort 1831–1890 destination	Cohort 1891–1930 origin	Cohort 1891–1930 destination
<5,000	62.4	60.6	46.6	47.1	24.2	25.4
5,000–9,999	6.5	6.4	7.0	7.5	3.7	3.6
10,000–19,999	12.7	15.4	4.5	3.9	6.4	8.0
20,000–39,999	0.4	0.3	7.8	7.9	14.9	14.9
40,000–59,999	0.3	0.0	3.0	3.3	8.7	9.0
60,000–79,999	17.0	17.1	7.6	7.8	3.0	3.1
80,000–99,999	0.4	0.0	3.1	2.9	4.9	4.8
100,000 +	0.3	0.2	15.4	14.2	26.7	24.4
Suburbs	0.0	0.0	5.0	5.4	7.5	6.8
Total origins/destinations	2,245		3,823		1,762	

Data calculated from 8,568 moves undertaken by 2,251 individuals returned by family historians. Only moves with an origin and destination in Britain included.
Suburbs are defined as settlements which, during the relevant period, became incorporated into larger towns.
The table should be read as follows: 62.4 per cent of all origins for migrants born 1750–1830 were in settlements with less than 5,000 population and 60.6 per cent of all destinations for migrants born 1750–1830 were in settlements with less than 5,000 population, etc.

In 1851, Britain was essentially urbanized, with 10 cities of more than 100,000 population, 17 with populations of 50,000 to 100,000, 42 with 20,000 to 50,000 inhabitants, and 61 with populations in the range 10,000 to 20,000 (Census, 1851). In 1851, 25 towns of over 10,000 population were located in Lancashire and Cheshire, the highly urbanized and industrialized region in which all the migrants in this sample lived at some point in their lives. By 1891, Lancashire and Cheshire contained 79 towns of over 10,000 people. The origins and destinations of recorded moves reflect the distribution of population. A total of 62.4 per cent of all moves for people born 1750 to 1830 started in places of under 5,000, declining to 46.6 per cent for those born 1831 to 1890 and 24.2 per cent for those born 1891 to 1930. In each time period, destinations and origins are approximately balanced (Table 17). It would seem that smaller places continued to play a significant role in the migration system of north-west England and that flows from small to large places were, at least in part, matched by those from large to small.

Migrant origins and destinations were very dispersed with very few individual towns represented in more than a small number of moves. Although most origins and destinations were within north-west England, there was some interchange between Lancashire/Cheshire and most other parts of Britain (Figs 29 and 30). Destinations which accounted for more than 2.0 per cent of all moves consisted entirely of towns in Lancashire or Cheshire (Table 18). Although London was the most popular individual destination outside the north-west, it accounted for less than one per cent of all destinations. Most moves were clearly short-distance within a mainly regional migration system, and moves with an origin and destination in the north-west accounted for 70.5 per cent of all moves. Most moves with an origin outside the region came from adjacent areas of Yorkshire, the West Midlands and northern England. The majority of moves from overseas originated in Ireland and Western Europe (although the Irish-born are under-represented in the sample). Most moves from the region had a destination in northern England or the West Midlands, whilst moves overseas mainly consisted of emigration to the USA.

Table 18: Settlements accounting for 2 per cent or more of all destinations by birth cohort

Cohort born 1750–1830 destination	no.	%	Cohort born 1831–90 destination	no.	%	Cohort born 1891–1930 destination	no.	%
Liverpool	276	11.8	Liverpool	463	11.1	Liverpool	201	9.7
Manchester	118	5.0	Manchester	224	5.4	Manchester	136	6.6
Preston	70	3.0	Preston	147	3.5	Chester	65	3.2
Salford	69	3.0	Accrington	120	2.9			
Bolton	67	2.9	Bolton	118	2.8			
Bury	66	2.8	Salford	109	2.6			
Accrington	60	2.6	Burnley	95	2.3			
Burnley	55	2.4	Blackburn	91	2.2			
Total destinations	2,340			4,165			2,063	

Data calculated from 8,568 moves undertaken by 2,251 individuals returned by family historians.
The table should be read as follows: 276 moves by migrants born 1750–1830 had Liverpool as a destination, and these accounted for 11.8 per cent of all moves undertaken by migrants in this birth cohort, etc.
Data for Liverpool and Manchester include the cities and their immediate suburbs.
For the birth cohort 1891–1930 only three destinations contributed 2 per cent or more of all destinations. The next most important destinations were Burnley (1.7 per cent), Birkenhead (1.7 per cent), Preston (1.7 per cent), Nelson (1.7 per cent), Blackpool (1.6 per cent) and Macclesfield (1.5 per cent).

Table 19: Intra-settlement moves by birth cohort and settlement size (per cent)

Settlement size	Cohort 1750–1830	Cohort 1831–90	Cohort 1891–1930
<5,000	37.4	41.3	30.7
5,000–9,999	63.7	65.8	31.4
10,000–19,999	56.6	68.3	58.0
20,000–39,999	0.0	51.1	61.2
40,000–59,000	0.0	75.0	55.8
60,000–79,000	68.4	68.1	68.0
80,000–99,999	0.0	51.4	73.3
100,000 +	0.0	51.2	50.0
All moves	47.4	50.7	45.4
Total intra-settlement moves	843	1,524	568

Data calculated from 8,568 moves undertaken by 2,251 individuals returned by family historians.
Suburbs are included with towns over 100,000 population. Zeros for the cohort 1750–1830 indicate that there were no recorded moves from towns of the relevant size.
The table should be read as follows: 37.4 per cent of all within-region moves with an origin in a settlement of less than 5,000 population had a destination in the same settlement.

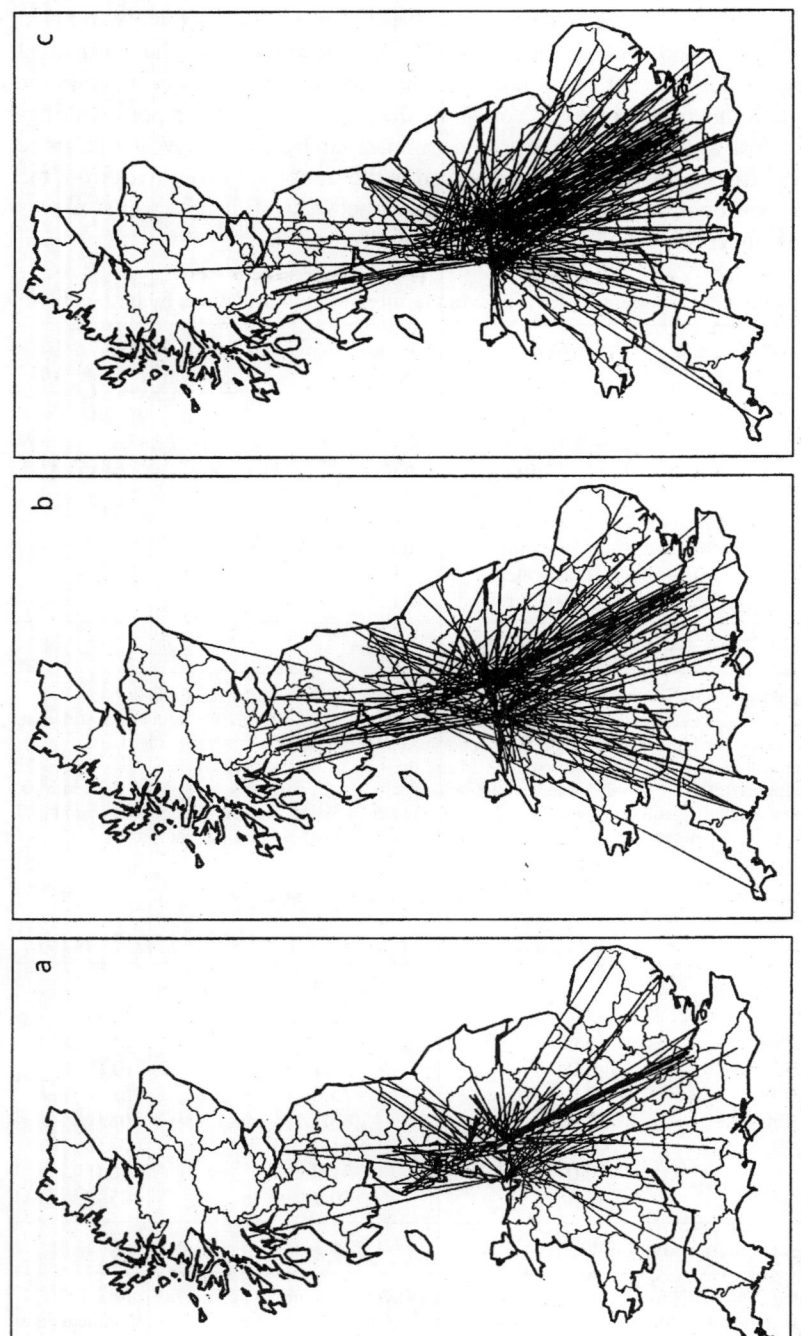

Figure 29: All moves with an origin in Lancashire or Cheshire and a destination elsewhere in Britain: (a) all migrants born 1750–1830; (b) all migrants born 1831–90; (c) all migrants born 1891–1930
Source: Calculated from 8,568 moves undertaken by 2,251 individuals returned by family historians.

MIGRATION AND URBANIZATION IN NORTH-WEST ENGLAND 195

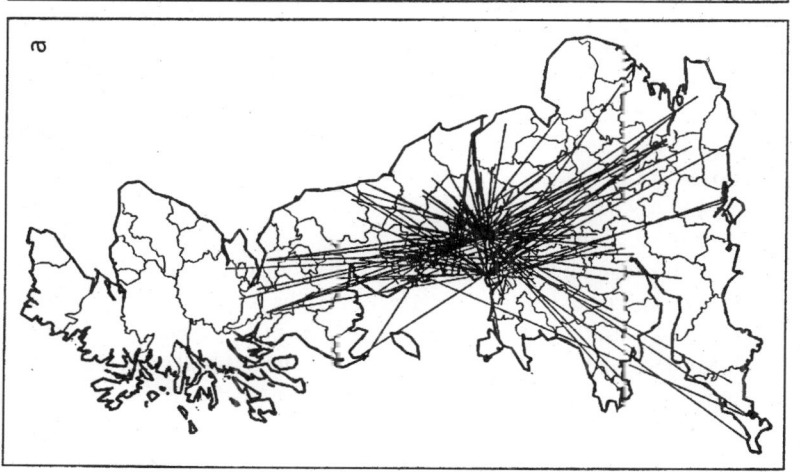

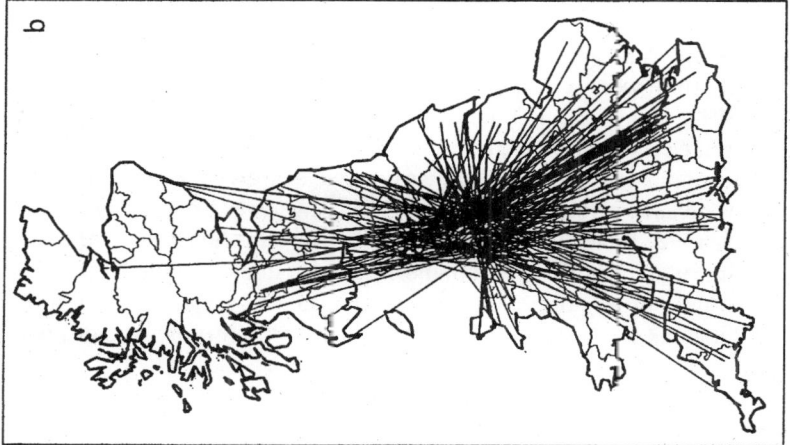

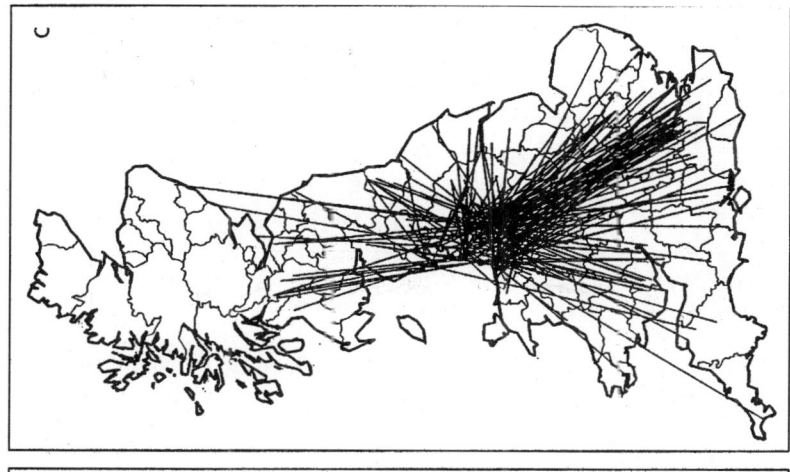

Figure 30: All moves with a destination in Lancashire or Cheshire and an origin elsewhere in Britain: (a) all migrants form 1750–1830; (b) all migrants born 1831–90; (c) all migrants born 1891–1930
Source: Calculated from 8,568 moves undertaken by 2,251 individuals returned by family historians.

Table 20: Mean distance moved (kilometres) by type of move and cohort

Type of move	Cohort born 1750–1830	Cohort born 1831–90	Cohort born 1891–1930	Total sample
All moves	33.0	42.8	71.0	47.8
Moves within region	8.6	9.1	10.4	9.3
Moves into region	126.9	158.7	181.1	157.6
Moves out of region	116.3	164.1	192.3	167.2

Data calculated from 8,568 moves undertaken by 2,251 individuals returned by family historians. The region of study is defined as the historic counties of Lancashire and Cheshire.

The importance of short-distance mobility is highlighted by the significance of intra-urban moves. In total, 48.6 per cent of moves within the region had both their origin and destination in the same community, a figure that was remarkably stable for all three cohorts. Not surprisingly, larger settlements had the highest proportion of intra-urban moves but, even in small communities, between 30 and 41 per cent of moves which had an origin and destination in a settlement of under 5,000 people in Lancashire or Cheshire were within the same settlement, with the lower proportion in the cohort 1891–1930 (Table 19). It is likely that frequent short-distance moves are under-represented in the data set, but it is clear that movement within the same community was a common experience for many people (see also Dennis, 1977; Pooley, 1979). These characteristics are reflected in the average distances moved by migrants in the sample (Table 20). Within-region moves were only around nine kilometres on average, with little change from the eighteenth to the twentieth centuries. Moves into and out of the region were over similar distances, ranging from approximately 120 kilometres for those born 1750–1830 to 190 kilometres for those born 1891–1930.

Such characteristics are consistent with the results of other migration studies (for example, Withers, 1985; Withers and Western, 1991; Pooley and Whyte, 1991), but the longitudinal data collected in this project also allow a much more detailed appraisal of the ways in which individuals moved through the urban system. Table 21 summarizes the extent to which migrants moved between settlements of different size in the three time periods under consideration. The most striking feature is the dominance of moves within and between small settlements of under 5,000 people. Overall, such moves accounted for 79.1 per cent of all moves for the cohort born 1750–1830, dropping to 46.8 per cent of moves for those born 1890–1930. The figure was lowest for moves into the region, but even in this case, the proportion of moves between small communities of under 5,000 remained above 40 per cent in each time period. For almost every town-size category, the majority of moves were between settlements of a similar size (with many of these moves consisting of intra-urban mobility). Most migrants had origins and destinations in small settlements and most of those with origins in larger towns either stayed within the same community or moved to another town of a similar size.

Table 21 also allows assessment of the extent to which movement up or down the

Table 21: Moves between settlements of different size by birth cohort (per cent)

Origin settlement size (thousands)	Destination settlement size					Total moves
	1	2	3	4	5	
All moves for cohort born 1750–1830						
1. <5,000	79.1	2.5	10.2	8.0	0.2	1,402
2. 5,000–9,999	29.0	53.8	9.7	6.8	0.7	145
3. 10,000–39,999	32.1	4.1	56.3	7.2	0.3	293
4. 40,000–99,999	27.8	4.5	7.5	59.9	0.3	399
5. 100,000 +	50.0	16.7	0.0	33.3	0.0	6
Total moves	1,360	144	351	384	6	2,245
All moves for cohort born 1831–90						
1. <5,000	71.2	4.1	8.3	7.4	9.0	1,780
2. 5,000–9,999	22.7	59.5	5.2	4.8	7.8	269
3. 10,000–39,999	26.9	5.5	46.7	6.4	14.5	469
4. 40,000–99,999	23.7	1.7	5.0	61.8	7.8	524
5. 100,000 +	28.3	2.4	5.5	5.0	58.8	781
Total moves	1,800	287	450	538	748	3,823
All moves for cohort born 1891–1930						
1. <5,000	46.8	5.4	16.0	11.0	20.8	425
2. 5,000–9,999	39.4	16.8	21.2	18.1	4.5	66
3. 10,000–39,999	18.4	3.8	54.1	10.9	12.8	375
4. 40,000–99,999	17.1	4.1	15.0	48.1	15.7	293
5. 100,000 +	17.3	0.7	12.4	9.0	60.6	603
Total moves	448	64	404	295	551	1,762

Data calculated from 8,568 moves undertaken by 2,251 individuals returned by family historians. Only moves with an origin and destination in Britain are included.

The table should be read as follows: 79.1 per cent of migrants born 1750–1830 with an origin in a settlement of less than 5,000 people had a destination in a settlement of the same size; 2.5 per cent of those born 1750–1830 with an origin in a settlement of less than 5,000 people had a destination in a settlement with 5,000–9,999 population, etc.

urban hierarchy occurred. For the cohort born 1750–1830 only 21 per cent of moves from an origin settlement of less than 5,000 people went to a larger place (the remainder were to settlements in the same size category), and almost half of those that moved from a place with fewer than 5,000 people to a larger settlement moved directly to a town of 10,000–19,999, and most of the remainder to towns of 60,000–79,999 population. Similarly, in later periods, the majority of those who moved from small settlements went not to the next largest town-size, but disproportionately to larger towns. Thus for the cohort 1891–1930 towns 20,000–39,999 and cities of over 100,000 population attracted the most moves directly from small places under 5,000 population. Although numbers are smaller, similar trends are shown when the data are broken down by moves into, within and out of the region, the tendency to move directly to larger settlements being particularly noticeable for moves into the region. Thus, although most moves which originated in a small place had a destination in a settlement of similar size, those who did move up the urban hierarchy tended to go directly to quite large towns. This challenges the observation of Ravenstein that most movement was step-wise up the urban hierarchy (Ravenstein, 1885, 1889; Grigg, 1977).

The assumption that most moves were up the urban hierarchy, from smaller to larger settlements, is also challenged by an analysis of moves from towns of other sizes. Whilst moves from small places of under 5,000 were, by definition, either to places of a similar size or to larger places, moves from other towns could be either up or down the urban hierarchy. Focusing on all moves together, with the exception of moves from towns 5,000–39,999 for the cohort born 1891–1930, in every instance more moves went to places smaller than the origin than to towns larger than the origin settlement. Thus for the cohort born 1831–90, of the 269 moves from towns of 5,000–9,999 population, 22.7 per cent were to smaller settlements, 59.5 per cent were to towns within the same size range (including moves within the same settlement), and only 17.8 per cent were to larger settlements. Likewise, of the 781 moves originating in a large town of over 100,000 people (Liverpool or Manchester and their contiguous suburbs), 58.8 per cent remained within one of these cities but 41.2 per cent moved to smaller settlements. It should be stressed that these were not just moves to adjacent suburbs which were effectively part of the built-up area, as migration to suburbs in large towns has been identified separately (amounting to 12.5 per cent of moves from Liverpool and Manchester and recorded as intra-urban movement in Table 20). The average distance moved from a city of over 100,000 people to a small settlement of under 5,000 ranged from 13.3 kilometres for the cohort born 1750–1830 to 18.9 kilometres for those born 1881–1930. Although remaining in the same region, and part of a broader process of suburbanization and counter-urbanization, these were clearly moves to discrete settlements physically distant from the origin city. A typical pattern was movement from Liverpool to Southport or from Manchester to Macclesfield (Fig. 31). Although numbers are smaller, similar trends are shown when the data are analysed according to whether moves were within, into or out of the region.

Clearly the pattern of movement between towns of a particular size is related to the distribution of urban settlements within town-size classes within a region. However, the data indicate that, taking all moves together, movement within or between settlements of a similar size, or from larger to smaller settlements, was a more common experience than movement from small to large places. This is further confirmed if the sequential pattern of moves for individuals is examined (Table 22). For the cohorts born 1750–1830 and 1831–90, there is evidence that the first move undertaken by an individual living in a settlement of under 5,000 people was disproportionately to a larger place (thus 70.4 per cent of people born 1750–1830 originated in a place of under 5,000 people but only 56.2 per cent had a destination in a

MIGRATION AND URBANIZATION IN NORTH-WEST ENGLAND 199

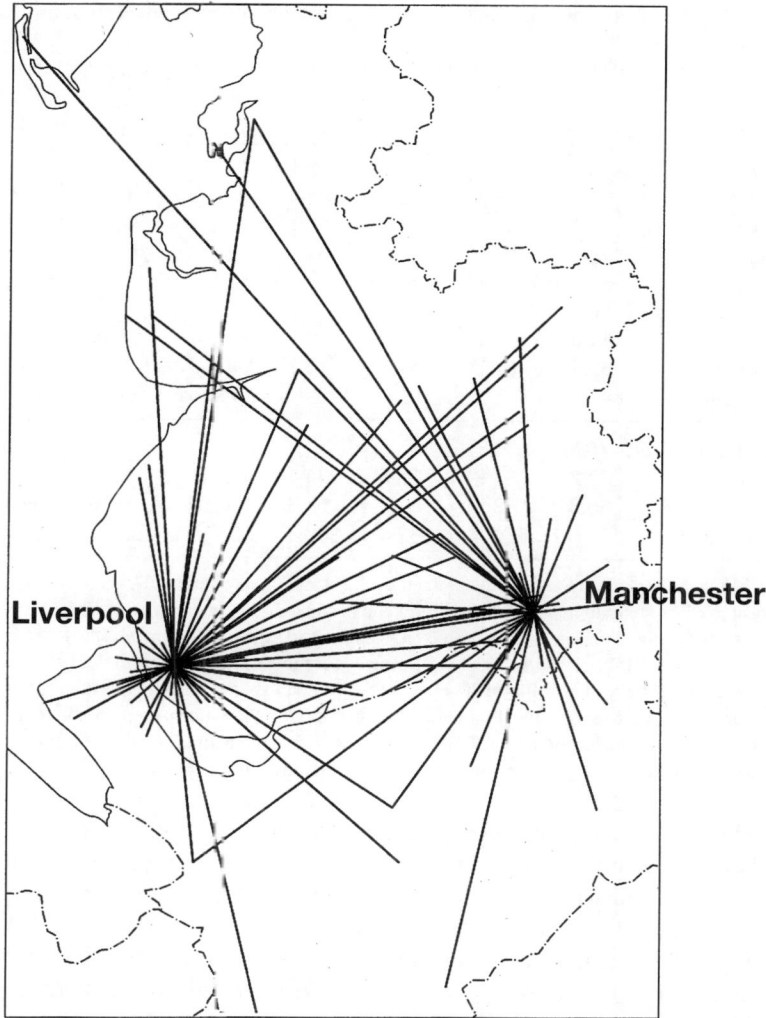

Figure 31: All moves from Liverpool and Manchester to destinations elsewhere in Lancashire or Cheshire
Source: Calculated from 8,568 moves undertaken by 2,251 individuals returned by family historians.

settlement of this size). However, thereafter, the proportion remaining in settlements of the same size category was quite constant. For those born 1891–1930, there was even less change with some evidence of counter-urbanization as smaller places gained relative to larger ones.

Table 22: Sequential within-region moves by settlement size and birth cohort of migrant (per cent)

Settlement size	Origin	Destinations						
		1	2	3	4	5	6	>6
Cohort born 1750–1830								
<5,000	70.4	56.2	50.6	42.9	45.3	45.5	44.9	41.2
>5,000	29.6	43.8	49.4	57.1	54.7	54.5	55.1	58.8
Total migrants	584	584	504	392	296	200	127	211
Cohort born 1831–90								
<5,000	45.0	35.9	33.5	29.2	31.6	30.0	29.7	31.8
>5,000	55.0	64.1	66.5	70.8	68.4	70.0	70.3	68.2
Total migrants	845	845	802	709	550	404	283	503
Cohort born 1891–1930								
<5,000	33.2	37.7	38.6	36.7	37.1	43.6	35.6	39.7
>5,000	66.8	62.3	61.4	63.3	62.9	56.4	64.4	60.3
Total migrants	334	334	332	308	251	202	160	469

Data calculated from 8,568 moves undertaken by 2,251 individuals returned by family historians. Data in this table refer only to moves with an origin and destination in Lancashire and Cheshire.
Town sizes for moves before 1831 were taken from the 1801 census, for moves 1831–70 from the 1851 census, for moves 1871–1930 from the 1891 census, for moves after 1930 from the 1951 census.
The table should be read as follows: 70.4 per cent of migrants born 1750–1830 originated in a settlement of under 5,000 people. Following their first move 56.2 per cent were in a settlement of under 5,000, following their second move 50.6 per cent were in a settlement of under 5,000 people, etc.
Destination >6 is an amalgamation of all moves after an individual's sixth move.

What this means in terms of migration experience is that, although at some time in their lives many people did move from a smaller to a larger settlement, this was only part of a much more complex and continuing migration experience. In any lifetime, the majority of moves were likely to be within one settlement or between settlements of the same size and, overall, any individual was at least as likely to move down the urban hierarchy as to move up it. Demographically, this process did shift population from the countryside to the town, emphasized by the fact that moves early in an individual's lifetime migration history were marginally more likely to be from countryside to town. Thus whereas 20.3 per cent of all moves were by people under 20 years old, and 50.4 per cent were by migrants aged 20–39, the figures for migrants from small settlements of under 5,000 people to towns of over 10,000 population were 23.1 per cent and 54.6 per cent respectively. This process could in turn raise urban fertility rates and create an ageing rural population with significant long-term effects for rural communities (Saville, 1957; Lawton, 1968; 1973; Woods, 1992), but in terms of overall lifetime migration experiences, movement from countryside to town was just one piece in a much more complex migration process.

Most people moved many times in their lives. Of, say, five residential moves, one may have been from the countryside to the town whilst others may have been between similar settlements or down the urban hierarchy back to a rural origin area. However, it is the rural-to-urban moves that have attracted most contemporary and later attention, particularly the many census-based studies that rely on static origin and destination data (Smith, 1951; Friedlander and Roshier, 1966). The much more common and complex milling about of people moving through a range of small settlements, usually within one locality, has received less attention, although some local history studies have drawn attention to this phenomenon (Holderness, 1970; Escott, 1988). The fact that urban populations are slightly under-represented in the sample does not invalidate these conclusions, as the number of people who moved between small settlements, or from large to smaller places, remains substantial.

In summary, this brief analysis of the role of different towns within the migration system of north-west England reveals some interesting trends and challenges some assumptions. Large towns did not dominate the migration system and the majority of all moves were within and between smaller settlements. Contrary to much popular perception, but confirming Ravenstein's (1885, 1889) observations on migration flows and counterflows, movement from small settlements to large was at least matched by migration from large towns to small settlements. Thus, rather than migrants being sucked into large urban areas, never to return, most movement was focused on small and medium-sized settlements, many moved between places of a similar size, and there is some evidence of circulatory and return migration. People thus often moved within an area that was well known to them, rather than being sucked into an alien urban environment.

WHY PEOPLE MOVED

Explanation of the spatial patterns of mobility outlined above must be related to the reasons why people moved. These are dealt with only briefly in this chapter, focusing on the extent to which known reasons for movement can explain the spatial pattern of moves outlined above. Taking all the data together, stated reasons for migration were dominated by employment-related objectives, followed by marriage, housing and family reasons (Table 23). Work was the dominant migration motive for both men and women, but a higher proportion of women moved on marriage (to their future husband's home) and women were also more likely to move for family reasons, probably reflecting greater female responsibility for caring within the family network (see, for instance, McDowell and Massey, 1984; D'Cruze, 1994). It can be suggested that such factors may have placed severe constraints on the ability of some women to achieve their lifetime migration aspirations as they subordinated their own preferences to the decisions and needs of others (Morokvasic, 1983; Grundy, 1989). Shorter-distance moves within the region were less likely to be stimulated by employment motives and were more likely to be due to marriage or housing reasons. Moves into or out of the region were particularly dominated by work-related reasons (Table 23).

Table 23: Reason for migration by birth cohort, gender and type of move (per cent)

	Work	Marriage	Housing	Family	Armed forces	Retirement	Other/ combined	Total moves
Cohort born 1750–1830								
All males	52.3	14.0	9.8	3.7	0.6	3.5	16.1	1,159
All females	38.6	27.4	7.6	5.7	1.4	1.4	17.9	368
Moves:								
within region	43.3	20.4	13.0	4.2	0.0	3.0	16.1	1,089
into region	66.5	12.4	0.0	4.0	2.8	2.4	11.9	251
out of region	58.3	5.3	0.5	4.3	2.7	3.2	25.7	187
All migrants	49.0	17.2	9.3	4.2	0.8	3.9	16.6	1,527
Cohort born 1831–90								
All males	41.4	15.4	15.5	3.6	3.4	2.2	18.5	1,946
All females	32.0	20.7	17.0	5.6	0.5	3.2	21.0	1,148
Moves:								
within region	30.7	22.5	23.5	4.2	0.4	3.0	15.7	2,075
into region	62.0	7.8	0.6	4.7	3.6	1.3	20.0	529
out of region	42.7	5.9	1.0	4.5	9.2	2.2	34.5	490
All migrants	37.9	17.4	16.0	4.3	2.4	2.6	19.4	3,094
Cohort born 1891–1930								
All males	36.0	9.6	19.2	2.2	9.3	2.3	21.4	1,117
All females	32.9	13.5	23.4	7.2	1.3	2.6	19.1	796
Moves:								
within region	21.7	15.7	34.4	4.2	1.3	2.0	20.7	1,122
into region	64.8	4.4	1.4	4.1	4.1	2.2	19.0	364
out of region	43.1	5.4	2.3	4.5	19.7	4.0	21.0	427
All migrants	34.7	11.2	21.0	4.2	6.0	2.5	20.4	1,913

Data calculated from 8,568 moves undertaken by 2,251 individuals returned by family historians.
The table should be read as follows: 52.3 per cent of males born 1750–1830 migrated primarily due to work reasons.

Interpretation of changes in the reasons for migration over time must be undertaken with caution, both because of the relatively small sample of information for the eighteenth century and the differences in sources available. The data suggest that, although work was the dominant reason for moving in each time period, this became relatively less important from the mid-nineteenth century as a wider range of non-work-related moves developed. Movement on marriage was especially important in the eighteenth century, but declined thereafter, and movement for housing, family reasons and on retirement became particularly important in the twentieth century. Work-related moves were especially dominant during the period of rapid urbanization and industrialization in the first half of the nineteenth century. Emigration in the second half of the nineteenth century and military service for men in the twentieth century were also increasingly important reasons for migration.

The relative importance of movement on marriage in the eighteenth century could reflect a heavy dependence on marriage records in the collection of family histories, thus missing moves for other reasons, but it is notable that the relative significance of marriage as a reason for moving declined sharply in the first half of the nineteenth century when the range of sources is only marginally better. Although data availability may be part of the explanation, it also seems clear that in the late nineteenth and twentieth centuries people were moving for a wider range of reasons, reflecting factors such as an increased range of housing which encouraged movement to match housing space with family and financial circumstances, reducing family size, increasing aspirations and a more spatially scattered family which led to more migration in order to be close to relatives.

The substantial minority of moves in all periods that were for non-work reasons go some way towards explaining the spatial pattern of migration outlined above. It might be suggested that movement to larger towns would be stimulated mainly by economic motives, with migrants seeking wider opportunities in a large urban labour market. The fact that many moves were for family, housing and other reasons provides some explanation of the relatively low profile that large towns had within the migration system. Many people moved with family or to be near family within a familiar area. They stayed within small towns or rural districts and never experienced life in large urban areas. Closeness to family also provided support systems during and after migration, and some moved from large towns to small settlements to be near their family in times of crisis.

INDIVIDUAL EXPERIENCES

The aggregate trends outlined above can be illustrated through individual case studies drawn both from the longitudinal records collected from family historians, and from other sources. Six brief examples from the 2,251 cases collected from family historians are given here.

Charles W. was born in Manchester in 1808 and his life history illustrates the relatively frequent movement within and around one conurbation which was common in the nineteenth century (Fig. 32a). By 1812, Charles had moved from Manchester with his parents and two siblings to live in the small town of Macclesfield (8,743 population in 1801) some 29 kilometres to the south of Manchester. This was a move from a large city to a smaller town, and the probable reason for the move was related to his father's trade as a cabinet maker. Charles remained in Macclesfield until he was 29, by which time he was married with four children. In 1837 he moved to Salford, part of the Manchester conurbation, with his wife, children and sister. He was employed as a letter-press printer and his move was to secure better work. Between 1841 and his death in 1872 he moved eight times in the Manchester and Salford area. These moves were stimulated, first, by the need for a larger house and, second, by the desire to move to a house with a shop for his sister (who was still living with him). Charles continued to work as a printer and, in 1845, left his sister in the shop

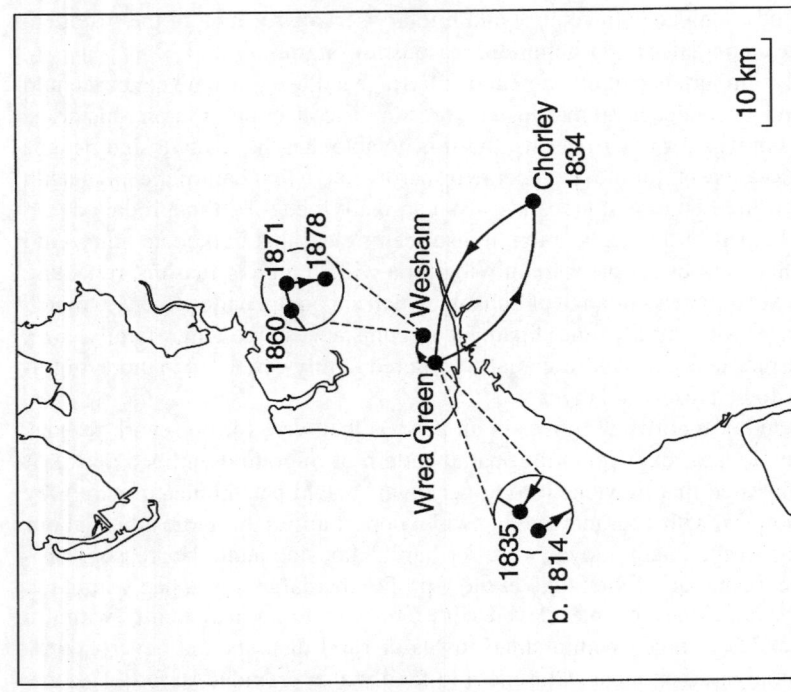
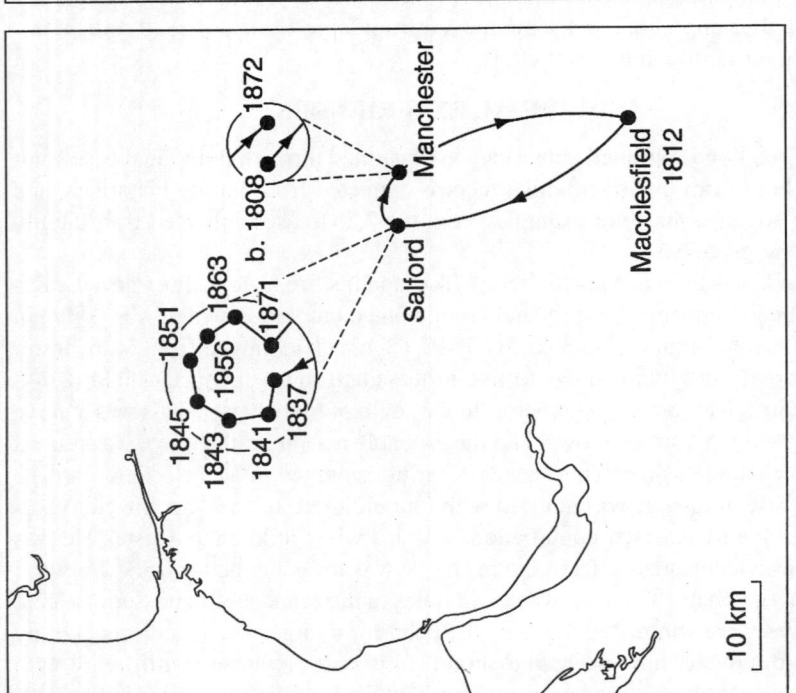

Figure 32: The migration paths of (a) Charles W. (1808–72) and (b) John A. (1814–85)
Source: Selected from 8,568 moves undertaken by 2,251 individuals returned by family historians.

and moved to a new house in the Ordsall area of Salford. Subsequent moves were housing-related until in 1871 (after his wife's death) he moved to live with his daughter in Salford and, the following year, moved again to live with a different daughter in Levenshulme, Manchester. This example illustrates frequent short-distance and circulatory mobility within a single conurbation, has one instance of a move down the urban hierarchy, and emphasizes the importance of family and housing reasons in motivating such movement.

Whereas Charles W. spent most of his life in a large urban area, John A., born a few years later in 1814, illustrates moves between villages and small towns within a clearly-defined area of central Lancashire (Fig. 32b). John was born in Wrea Green, a village on the Fylde some 13 kilometres from Preston. At the age of 20 he moved to the small Lancashire town of Chorley (population 12,684 in 1851), just to the south of Preston, probably to seek work as a weaver. However, a year later in 1835, he moved back to the village of Wrea Green following his marriage to a local girl, taking employment as an agricultural labourer. He remained in the same village until 1860 when, with his wife and eight children, he moved just three kilometres to the village of Wesham, on the outskirts of the small Fylde settlement of Kirkham (population 2,799 in 1851). He moved twice more over very short distances within Wesham before his death in 1885. Whilst in Wesham he was variously described as a labourer or mill labourer and, it is supposed, moved for a combination of housing and employment reasons. The life history of John A. typifies the many people whom, despite the rapid urbanization of the nineteenth century, lived all their lives in villages and small towns, and moved within a confined and no doubt familiar area.

A third example illustrates similar themes, but shows the way in which longer-distance migration was forced on some families (Fig. 33a). Thomas B. was born in 1844 in the industrial village of Heap, just outside Bury (Lancashire), the son of a cloth cutter. In the late 1850s, following the death of his father, he moved with his mother some eight kilometres to the town of Middleton (population 9,472 in 1871) on the outskirts of Manchester, to live with his maternal grandmother. Here Thomas was apprenticed as a clogger (clogmaker). Around 1865 Thomas married and moved to the hamlet of Birtle, situated on the edge of the moors some five kilometres from Bury. He was now working as a clogger and had effectively moved back to the locality in which he had been born. Around 1870 Thomas and his family moved in Birtle and at this time he also changed his employment from clogger to woollen dresser. However, this move was clearly not successful and in 1876 he and his family moved some 140 kilometres to the small Lancashire (now Cumbria) town of Dalton-in-Furness (population 9,310 in 1871). The motive for the move was clearly work as he began a new career as an iron miner in nearby Ulverston. Again, a complex pattern of family migration is apparent, stimulated by a combination of family crises, work and the support of relatives. Thomas and his family moved easily between small towns and mainly industrial villages in Lancashire but, until forced to move further for work, had a strong attachment to the locality of Bury where he had been born. Despite his obvious need for work, he never moved to one of the larger industrial towns of Lancashire.

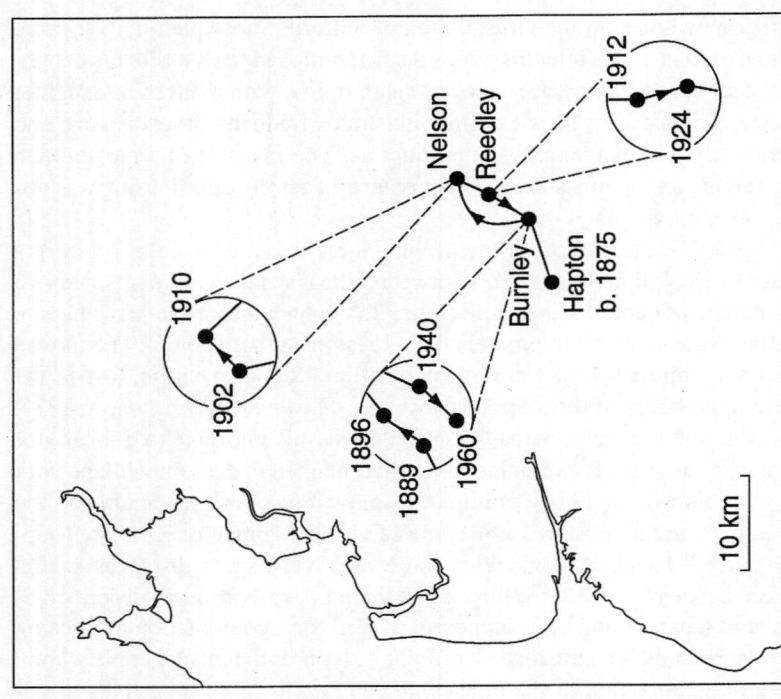
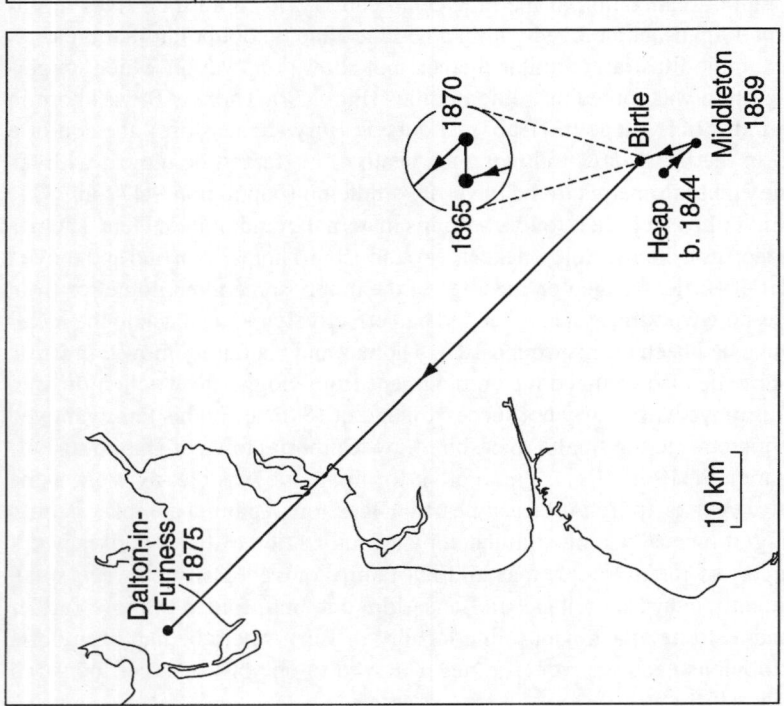

Figure 33: The migration paths of (a) Thomas B. (1844–90) and (b) Mary W. (1875–1962)
Source: Selected from 8,568 moves undertaken by 2,251 individuals returned by family historians.

The migration history of Mary W. also illustrates the way in which people often moved between nearby towns and villages in a circulatory fashion, and for a variety of reasons (Fig. 33b). Mary was born in 1875 in the village of Hapton, some five kilometres from the Lancashire town of Burnley. Her father was manager at Hapton Valley Colliery. In 1889, at the age of 14, she moved with her mother, four brothers and two sisters into the industrial town of Burnley (population 87,016 in 1891). The immediate reason was the fact that her father had been killed in an accident and the family had to leave the house which went with his job. Mary did not change her work as a dressmaker in Burnley following this move, and removal to the urban area of Burnley would have shortened her journey to work. At the age of 21 she married and moved with her husband to a new address in Burnley. Significantly, she continued to work as a dressmaker, but now worked from home rather than being employed in a workshop in Burnley. In 1902 she and her husband moved about seven kilometres to the adjacent small town of Nelson (population 32,816 in 1901), the move being precipitated by a change in her husband's work. During the next 22 years, Mary moved three more times in the same area due both to changes in her husband's work and the desire for a bigger house. In 1912 this entailed moving from the town of Nelson to the adjacent village of Reedley. In 1940, at the age of 65, Mary and her husband moved from Reedley back into Burnley, both to be nearer their eldest daughter and to acquire a smaller house after the children had left home. Twenty years later, and following her husband's death, Mary moved again in Burnley to live with her daughter. As with the other examples, Mary moved through an area with which she was familiar, her moves were stimulated for family, housing and employment reasons, and her history includes moves from large towns to nearby smaller settlements.

The movements of Olivia S., born in Altrincham (Cheshire) in 1884, illustrate the increasing importance of suburbs, and small settlements on the edge of large towns, in the late nineteenth and twentieth centuries, and the continued importance of family ties in migration decisions (Fig. 34a). By the 1880s, Altrincham (population 11,250 in 1881) was a free-standing commuter settlement some 12 kilometres from Manchester, although Olivia's parents were employed in Altrincham as shopkeepers. In 1890 she moved with her parents to larger premises within Altrincham, but on her marriage in 1913 she left home for the first time and moved with her husband to the Liverpool suburb of Wavertree. Whilst in Altrincham she had worked in her father's shop, but following marriage she had no further employment. Despite her marriage, ties to her parents remained strong and, in 1920, she moved with her husband and daughter to the village of Hale. This is adjacent to her home town of Altrincham and the reason for moving was the desire to be close to her parents following the death of their only son (her brother). However, she remained here for only two years before her husband's work took them to Fulwood, a residential suburb to the north of Preston (Lancashire). They remained here for 10 years, but in 1932 moved back to Hale to care for her sick parents. Olivia remained in Hale until her death in 1940.

The importance of caring responsibilities and family ties for women is also illustrated in the example of Ada B. who, like many others, moved within and between

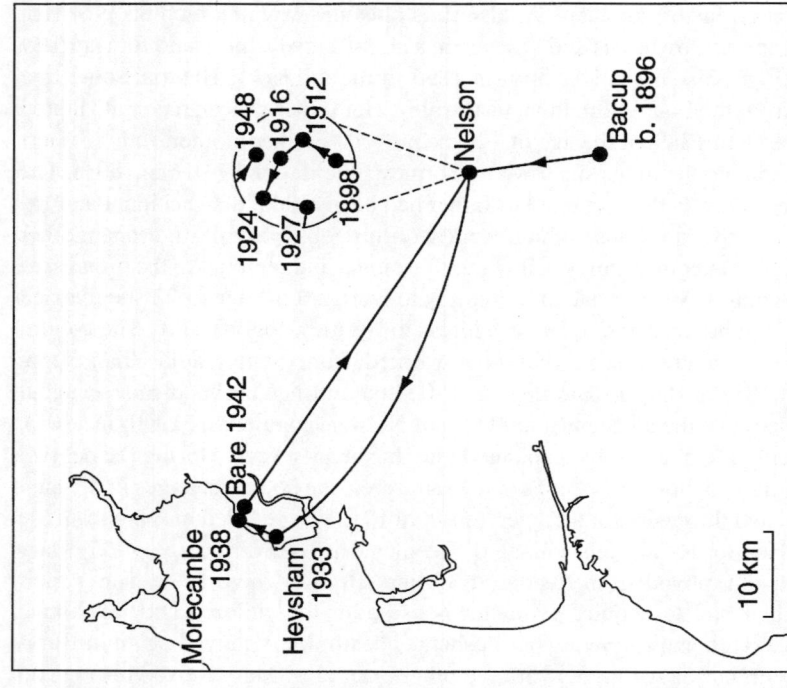
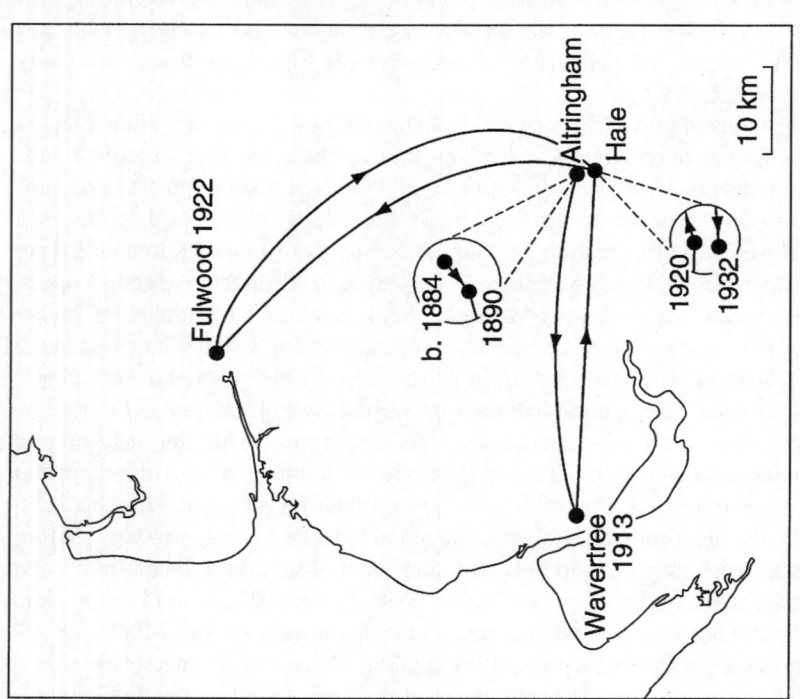

Figure 34: The migration paths of (a) Olivia S. (1884–1940) and (b) Ada B. (1896–1976)
Source: Selected from 8,568 moves undertaken by 2,251 individuals returned by family historians.

small Lancashire towns in the late nineteenth and twentieth centuries (Fig. 34b). Ada was born in Bacup (population 23,498 in 1891), east Lancashire, in 1896 where her father was an insurance agent. Two years later she moved with her parents and five siblings the 19 kilometres to the adjacent town of Nelson (population 32,816 in 1901). The main reason for this move was that Nelson offered better employment opportunities for her elder brothers and sisters who were seeking work in the cotton mills. In 1912, at the age of 16, she moved with her mother to a smaller house in Nelson, as her siblings had left home and her father had emigrated alone. The effects of the First World War led to the next move as an extended family of mother, daughter, sister, niece and nephew were forced together due to war-time conditions, and a larger house in Nelson was needed. In 1924 a similar extended family group moved again in Nelson to a more convenient house. All this time Ada worked as a cotton weaver. In 1927 she and her elderly mother moved again within Nelson as Ada gave up her employment in the cotton mill and went as housekeeper to live with her widowed brother. This lasted for six years, but in 1933 her brother re-married and Ada was forced to move and seek new employment. Rather than returning to the mills, she went as housekeeper to a family in the small town of Heysham (population 7,294 in 1931), on the Lancashire coast. In 1938 the family moved away and she was forced to move again. Ada stayed in the same locality and took the position of housekeeper and carer for an invalid lady in the adjacent town of Morecambe (population 17,248 in 1931). Four years later the lady died and she gained a similar position in the Morecambe suburb of Bare. In 1948 this second invalid lady also died, and at the age of 52 Ada moved back to the same house in Nelson that she had lived in 20 years previously to act as housekeeper for her ageing sisters. Ada remained at this house until her death in 1976. This example not only demonstrates movement between and within small towns, but also emphasizes the extent to which single women often took on caring responsibilities for their families.

These experiences, drawn from the life histories provided by family historians, are backed up by other documentary sources, including a detailed family history of the Shaw family, compiled in the 1820s. This source has been fully analysed elsewhere (Pooley and D'Cruze, 1994), but it clearly illustrates the way in which migration took place within and between small settlements in north-west England before the family eventually arrived in a larger labour market. The movement of Joseph Shaw, born in the remote Pennine village of Garsdale in 1748, illustrates these points well (Fig. 35). As a boy he was employed in the domestic woollen industry and, at the age of nine, was apprenticed to a weaver who worked in various unspecified locations in Westmorland (now Cumbria). By 1767 he had served his apprenticeship and returned to Garsdale to work as a weaver. In 1771 he married and moved to a hamlet about one kilometre from the nearby village of Dent.

During the next few years Joseph Shaw and his family moved frequently, most moves being stimulated by a desire to improve both housing and employment prospects. In 1773 he moved some 25 kilometres to the small market and industrial town of Kendal (population 6,892 in 1801) to seek better trade as a weaver, but his wife (Isabella) did not settle in the town; she missed the village of her birth, and the

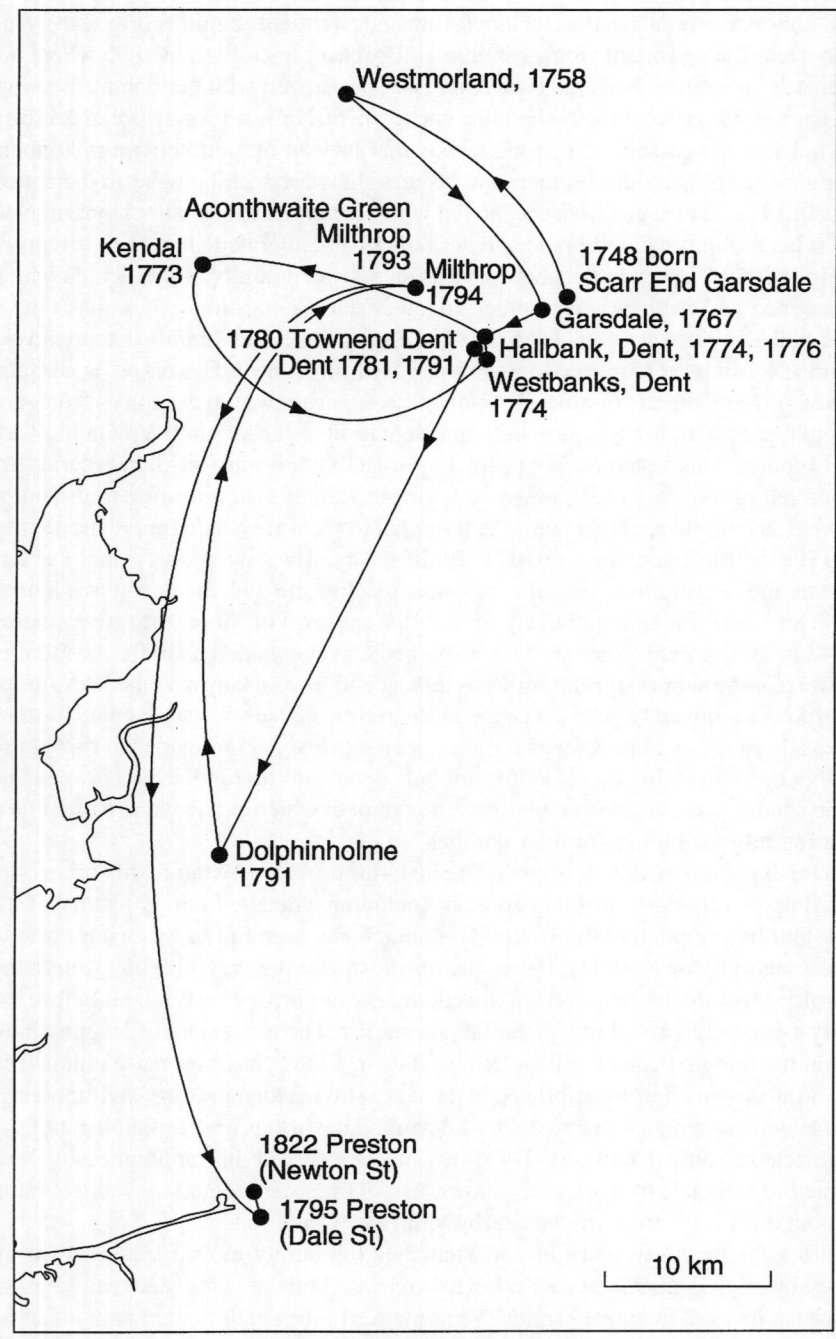

Figure 35: The migration path of Joseph Shaw (1748–1823)
Source: Family history of Benjamin Shaw (Preston Record Office, DDX/1154/1 and DDX/1154/2).

following year they returned to another hamlet just outside Dent. Over the following years they moved several times within the district.

By 1791 the Shaw household consisted of seven children, all living at home and ranging in ages from 19 to 2 years. Poor trade in the Dent area stimulated a longer-distance move of some 52 kilometres to the rural factory community of Dolphinholme (near Lancaster). The main attraction was a new mill that provided employment for the children, and the move was stimulated by the attempts of the mill owner to recruit labour around Dent. Initially, Shaw found it difficult to settle to factory work. He argued with the mill owner and temporarily left his employment, but after a few weeks he settled to the routine of the factory.

The Shaws lived together as a family in Dolphinholme for less than two years before the mill owners began laying off hands. Within the family, only the eldest son was not made redundant because of his apprenticeship, and Joseph Shaw was forced to move in search of work. Not only had migration to Dolphinholme failed to bring the expected benefits in terms of better-paid and more secure work, but during this period there had also been much illness: most of the family were sick at some time and no fewer than three of Joseph's children died within a few months of each other in 1792/93. It is thus not surprising that in 1793, what was left of the family left Lancashire and returned north, as Joseph again took up weaving. They settled in the hamlet of Aconthwaite Green, Milthrop (Cumbria), only a few kilometres from Garsdale and Dent.

The following year the family moved into Milthrop village, but in 1795 Joseph, Isabella and their daughter Hannah moved south to the industrial town of Preston, Lancashire (population 11,887 in 1801). Although the expanding labour market in Preston may have been part of the attraction, the main reason for moving was clearly to be near their son Benjamin who was now married and living there. In 1822 Joseph (who was now living alone) was taken ill and moved in with his daughter Hannah; four months later, in February 1823, he died in Preston at the age of 75.

The lifetime migration of Joseph Shaw thus confirms that much migration was not a simple one-way movement from countryside to town, but that there were complex (often circulatory) flows, which could involve return migration and movement between rural areas and industrial villages. Moreover, the reasons why Shaw migrated were very diverse, including the desire for economic improvement, responses to particular crises and the desire to be close to relatives. Although the industrial town of Preston undoubtedly did offer a wider range of employment opportunities than more rural areas, this was not Shaw's main reason for moving to Preston. His initial motivation was based on the desire to move near to relatives.

CONCLUSION

Although in total the population did shift from the countryside to the towns from the late eighteenth century, the use of longitudinal records and family histories emphasizes that this was not a simple one-way process. Much movement took place within rural areas or between small towns, not all moves were stimulated by economic motives, and some moved down the urban hierarchy from large towns to smaller settlements. Even detailed family histories leave many unanswered questions about migration decisions and motives, and we will never know how alternative destinations were appraised and evaluated by migrants in the past. However, it is suggested that by focusing attention on longitudinal migration biographies it is possible to construct a much more detailed profile of where and why people moved and assess the impact of migration on people and places. It is also possible to connect these moves much more clearly to the social and economic changes that were affecting British society in the past, and explore the links between migration and such processes (see Fig. 28).

The dominance of moves within and between the same types of settlement, many of them over very short distances, suggests that for most people migration was not an especially traumatic or alien experience. Migrants often moved with, or close to, their families in a region with which they were quite familiar. Even longer-distance moves often passed through familiar territory, or entailed the use of family contacts to aid migration. It was not unusual for people to move from large settlements to small, often returning to an area in which they had previously lived. None of these trends are particularly surprising if they are compared with known patterns and processes of migration in both the developed and less-developed parts of the world today (for example Appleyard, 1989; Champion and Fielding, 1992; Castles and Miller, 1993). As today, migration patterns were complex, and the act of migration was stimulated for a variety of reasons. However, whereas most sources only allow glimpses of these patterns and processes in the past, analysis of a large number of residential life histories within a specific regional context does enable a much fuller picture of migration in the past to be constructed.

REFERENCES

ANDERSON, M. (1974), 'Urban migration in nineteenth-century Lancashire: some insights into two competing hypotheses', In M. Drake (ed.), *Historical Demography: Problems and Projects*, Milton Keynes.

APPLEYARD, R. T. (ed.) (1989), *The Impact of International Migration on Developing Countries*, Paris.

BAINES, D. (1986), *Migration in a Mature Economy*, Cambridge.

BARTHOLOMEW, K. (1991), 'Women migrants in mind: leaving Wales in the nineteenth and twentieth centuries', In C. Pooley and I. Whyte (eds), *Migrants, Emigrants and Immigrants: A Social History of Migration*, London and New York, 174–90.

BURNETT, J. (ed.) (1974), *Useful Toil*, London.

BURNETT, J. (ed.) (1982), *Destiny Obscure*, London.

BURNETT, J., D. VINCENT and D. MAYALL (eds) (1984, 1987), *The Autobiography of the Working Class: An Annotated and Critical Bibliography*, Brighton.

CARTER, H. (1981), *The Study of Urban Geography* (3rd edition), London.

CASTLES, S. and M. MILLER (1993), *The Age of Migration*, London.

CHAMPION, A. and A. FIELDING (eds) (1992), *Migration Processes and Patterns*, London.

CROSBY, A. (ed.) (1991), *The Family Records of Benjamin Shaw*, The Record Society of Lancashire and Cheshire, vol. 130.

DANSON, J. T. and T. W. WELTON (1859), 'On the population of Lancashire and Cheshire and its local distribution during the fifty years 1801–51', *Transactions of the Historic Society of Lancashire and Cheshire*, **11**, 35–74.

D'CRUZE, S. (1994), 'Care, diligence and "usefull pride": gender industrialization and the domestic economy, 1770–1840', *Women's History Review*, **33**, 315–46
DENNIS, R. (1977), 'Inter-censal mobility in a Victorian city', *Transactions of the Institute of British Geographers*, New Series, 349–63.
DICKENS, C. (1982 edition), *Dombey and Son*, Oxford.
ERICKSON, C. (1972), *Invisible Immigrants: The Adaptation of English and Scottish Immigrants in Nineteenth-Century America*, London.
ESCOTT, M. (1988), 'Residential mobility in a late-eighteenth century rural parish: Binfield, 1779–1801', *Local Population Studies*, **40**, 20–35.
FRIEDLANDER, D. and R. ROSHIER (1966), 'A study of internal migration in England and Wales', *Population Studies*, **19**, 239–79.
GRIGG, D. B. (1977), 'E. G. Ravenstein and the laws of migration', *Journal of Historical Geography*, **3**, 41–54.
GRUNDY, E. (1989), *Women's Migration: Marriage, Fertility and Divorce*, London.
HOLDERNESS, R. A. (1970), 'Personal mobility in some rural parishes of Yorkshire, 1777–1822', *Yorkshire Archaeological Journal*, **42**, 444–54.
JONES, R. M. (1981), 'Welsh immigrants in the cities of north-west England, 1890–1930: some oral testimony', *Oral History*, **9**, 33–41.
LAWTON, R. (1959), 'Irish migration to England and Wales in the mid-nineteenth century', *Irish Geography*, **4**, 35–54.
LAWTON, R. (1968), 'Population changes in England and Wales in the later nineteenth century', *Transactions of the Institute of British Geographers*, **44**, 55–75.
LAWTON, R. (1973), 'Rural depopulation in nineteenth-century England', In D. R. Mills (ed.), *English Rural Communities*, London.
LAWTON, R. and C. G. POOLEY (1975), 'David Brindley's Liverpool: an aspect of urban society in the 1880s', *Transactions of the Historic Society of Lancashire and Cheshire*, **126**, 149–68.
LOVETT, A., I. D. WHYTE and K. WHYTE (1985), 'Poisson regression analysis and migration fields: the example of the apprenticeship records of Edinburgh in the seventeenth and eighteenth centuries', *Transactions of the Institute of British Geographers*, New Series, **10**, 317–32.
McDOWELL, L. and D. MASSEY (1984), 'A woman's place?', In D. Massey and J. Allen (eds), *Geography Matters!*, Cambridge, 128–47.
MILLS, D. (ed.) (1984), *Victorians on the Move*, Thornborough.
MOROKVASIC, M. (1983), 'Women in migration: beyond the reductionist outlook', In A. Phizacklea (ed.), *One Way Ticket*, London.
NICHOLAS, S. and P. SHERGOLD (1987), 'Internal migration in England, 1818–39', *Journal of Historical Geography*, **13**, 155–68.
PARTON, A. G. (1980), 'The travels of Joseph Smith, well sinker 1877–1897: a study in personal migration for work', *North Staffordshire Journal of Field Studies*, **20**, 33–40.
PARTON, A. G. (1987), 'Poor Law settlement certificates and migration to and from Birmingham, 1726–57', *Local Population Studies*, **38**, 23–29.
POOLEY, C. G. (1979), 'Residential mobility in the Victorian city', *Transactions of the Institute of British Geographers*, New Series, **2**, 349–63.
POOLEY, C. G. (1983), 'Welsh migration to England in the mid-nineteenth century', *Journal of Historical Geography*, **9**, 287–305.
POOLEY, C. G. (1994), 'The mobility of criminals in north-west England, c1880–1910', *Local Population Studies*, **53**, 15–28.
POOLEY, C. G. and S. D'CRUZE (1994), 'Migration and urbanization in north-west England, c1760–1830', *Social History*, **19**, 339–58.
POOLEY, C. G. and J. DOHERTY (1991), 'The longitudinal study of migration: Welsh migration to English towns in the nineteenth century', In C. G. Pooley and I. D. Whyte (eds), *Migrants, Emigrants and Immigrants: A Social History of Migration*, London and New York, 143–74.
POOLEY, C. G. and I. D. WHYTE (eds) (1991), *Migrants, Emigrants and Immigrants: A Social History of Migration*, London and New York.

RAVENSTEIN, E. G. (1885, 1889), 'The laws of migration', *Journal of the Royal Statistical Society*, **48**, 167–227, and **52**, 214–301.
REDFORD, A. (1926), *Labour Migration in England, 1800–1850*, Manchester.
RICHARDS, E. (1991), 'Voices of British and Irish migrants in nineteenth-century Australia', In C. G. Pooley and I. D. Whyte (eds), *Migrants, Emigrants and Immigrants: A Social History of Migration*, London and New York, 19–41.
SAVILLE, J. (1957), *Rural Depopulation in England and Wales, 1851–1951*, London.
SMITH, C. T. (1951), 'The movement of population in England and Wales in 1851 and 1861', *Geographical Journal*, **107**, 200–10.
SOUTHALL, H. (1991a), 'The tramping artisan revisits: labour mobility and economic distress in early Victorian England', *Economic History Review*, **44**, 272–91.
SOUTHALL, H. (1991b), 'Mobility, the artisan community and popular politics in early nineteenth-century England', In G. Kearns and C. Withers (eds), *Urbanising Britain*, Cambridge, 103–130.
SWIFT, R. and S. GILLEY (eds) (1989), *The Irish in Britain, 1815–1939*, London.
TAYLOR, J. S. (1989), *Poverty, Migration and Settlement in the Industrial Revolution: Sojourners Narratives*, Palo Alto, CA.
TUCKER, W. (1983), 'Patterns of migration of textile workers into Accrington in the early nineteenth century', *Local Population Studies*, **30**, 28–34.
WITHERS, C. (1985), 'Highland migration to Dundee, Perth and Stirling, 1753–1891', *Journal of Historical Geography*, **11**, 395–418.
WITHERS, C. and A. WESTERN (1991), 'Stepwise migration and Highland migration to Glasgow, 1852–1898', *Journal of Historical Geography*, **17**, 35–55.
WOODS, R. A. (1992), *The Population of Britain in the Nineteenth Century*, London.

ACKNOWLEDGEMENTS

Thanks to all the family historians who provided data for the project and who thus made this research possible, to the Nuffield Foundation and the ESRC for financial support, to participants in a conference at Liverpool for constructive comments when an early version of this chapter was presented, to Barry Rowlingson for assistance with GIS, and to Nicola Higgitt and Matthew Ball for cartography.

INDEX

Note: 'n' after a page reference indicates a note number on that page. Numbers in bold type refer to Figures or Tables on that page.

Accrington, Britain 193
Albert, Jean 65
Aldershot, Britain 153
alehouses 78
Allerton, Britain 108
Alpine migration 47–66
   and an emergent urban proletariat 48, 49
   climatic instability, effects of 48, 50
   crisis out-migration 48, 49, 50, 53, 65, 66
   disparagement of migrants 48–9
   economic migration 65
   entrepreneurial activity and 57–8, 60–6
   and fertility regulation 47
   migrants' remittances 54, 57
   seasonal migration 47, 48, 59, 64
   taxation, effects of 50
Alpine regions
   debt bonding alliances 58, 61, 62, 65
   economic expansion 57
   inheritance systems 58
   inter-generational advancement 59
   kin relationships 58, 59, 61, 62, 63, 66
   land, property and capital transfers 58
   marriage strategies 58, 61
   population increase 57
   pre-industrial economies 51
   regional and micro–regional specialization 59–60
   social and economic stratification 58
   subsistence crises 48, 58
   trading activity 57, 59, 60–6
   see also Savoy
Altcar, Britain 99
Altrincham, Britain 207
Anabaptists 110n
Apprenticeship Books 113

apprenticeships 99
   female apprentices 114, 121
   indentured migrants 102
   Liverpool apprenticeship records 91
army women 153–8
   accommodation possibilities 153, 154
   admission of children to institutions 144, 155
   bonds between 160
   British and overseas experience 153
   deserted women 158
   in Dublin 144, 153–8, 160
   employment opportunities 153, 154, 155, 156–7
   hospital employees 154
   mobility patterns 155, 157–8, 160
   overseas experience 160
   unmarried mothers 153, 158
   widows 146, 155, 156, 157–8
artisans
   geographic mobility 164
   master artisans 172, 173, 182
   in Vienna 164–84
   see also journeymen; tramping artisans
Ashton, Britain 76
Association for the Relief of Distressed Protestants 136
Athlone, Ireland 153
Athy, Ireland 146, 153
Austria
   guilds 166
   trade associations 166
   see also Vienna
Auvergne, France 58, 60
Avignon, France 64
Aylward, Margaret 136, 139

bachelors 41, 120

Bacup, Britain 209
bag makers, Viennese 168, 174–5, 178
bakers, Viennese 167, 174, **176**
   job histories 175–8, **176**
Ballyhurrow, Ireland 37, 38–9
Ballyknockane, Ireland 36, 37
Ballyporeen, Ireland 35–6
Bamberg, Bavaria
   journeymen migrants 165
banking systems 61, 62
baptisms
   Lancashire colliery children 72, 73n, 74n, 81, 81n
Barcelonette, France 57
Basque Pyrenees 59
Bavaria 59, 182
Béarn, France 59
Beaucaire, France 64
beggars 122, 135, 139
Bérard, Jacques 62
Biella, Italy 60
Birtle, Britain 205
Bishop's Stortford, Britain 113
Blackburn, Britain 193
Blackrock, Ireland 149, 152
Blavier, Marie–Anne 121–2
Bohemia 178
Bolton, Britain 193
bonded hiring 80, 80n
book trade 62–3, 64
Boolakennedy, Ireland 39, 40
Boudaille family 124–5
Boudaille, Suzanne 127
Bouvard, Alexis 60
Briançon, France 60
'bright lights' syndrome 3–4
Bristol, Britain 131
Britain
   Irish migrant destination 159
   role of north-west towns in migration system 186–212
   urban populations 192
Bruyant, Gérarde 127–8
Bruyant, Henriette 128
Bruyen, Jean-Baptiste 125, 126
Budapest, Hungary 181
building trades 169–70
Burnley, Britain 193, 207

Bury, Britain 193

cabinet makers, Viennese 167, 170–1, 174, 178, 180
cannell collieries 74n
career migration 4, 7, 111, 112–13
   Liverpool 112–13
   north-west England 201, 202
census-based studies of migration 2, 3, 187
Chablais, France 60
chain migration 4, 111
   Liverpool 113
charity asylums 151–3, 154
   see also workhouses
Chemnitz, Germany
   journeymen migrants 165
Cheshire, Britain 188
   intra-urban moves **193**, 196–8, **197**, 201
   migrant origins and destinations 192–3, **193**, **194–5**
   movement along the urban hierarchy 198, 200
   urban populations 190, 192
   within-region moves 198, **200**
Chester, Britain 193
children
   colliers' children's baptisms 72, **72**, 73n, 81n
colliery workers 76, 77
   economic cost 123
illegitimacy 121, 122, 127, 129, 151
   urban infant mortality 123, 125, 128–9
Chorley, Britain 205
circular migration 4, 7, 111, 112, 205, 207, 211
   Dublin 146–8
   Liverpool 99, 112, 113–14
   north-west England 186, 211
Clavans 65
clergy, migration by 113
Clieveland, John 103–4
Clieveland, Richard 103, 104, 112
Clogheen-Burncourt, Ireland 10, 11–45
   acquisitiveness of the larger farming class 21, 29
   brides marrying within and outside the parish 32, **33**, 34
   brides moving into and within **42**

INDEX

changes in names of families occupying holdings 19, 20, **20**
changing number and size of farms 15, **16**
distribution of farm-holdings (pre-Famine) 13–15, **14**
distribution of farm-holdings (post-Famine) 16–18, **17**
distribution of farm-holdings (c. 1970) 18–19, **18**
extinct families 27
farm amalgamation and consolidation 17–18, 21, 45
farmer proprietorship era 13
fragmented land ownership patterns 19
global migration field (1900–68) 12, **12**
kin-based continuity 19–20, 22–9
land transfers (1851–1900) 21–3
land transfers (post-1900) 27–8
landlord era 13
males in non-paternal farms 30, **34**, 35, 45
marriage patterns 32, 35
migrants' destinations within Ireland **12**
population 13
range of land values 11, 13
Shanbally Estate **14**, 19
small-farm family erosion 20
social structure 13, 18
three-generation households 25
townlands 13
Clonskeagh, Ireland 149
Clontarf, Ireland 145
coal industry *see* Lancashire coalfields
Colchester, Britain 153
colliers
  average age at death 73n
  average age at marriage 81
  colliers' children's baptisms 72, **72**, 73n
  deaths and injuries 75, 75n
  drunkenness and absenteeism 78
  ewomen and children 75, 76, 77
  female and child workers 75, 76, 77
  generational succession 79, 81, 82
  hewers 73, 73n, 74, 77, 78, 78n, 80
  kinship networks 76–7, 81, 84
  lifetime persistence 79, 81
  marriage patterns 72–3, 79n, 81
  migration patterns 83–6, **85**
  occasional workers 75

occupational rigidity 86
part-time workers 75–6
recruitment selection criteria 76
Roman Catholic colliers 73n, 76, 82
short-distance migration 80–3, 86
spatial mobility 80–3
stranger workers 86
wage systems 74, 77–80
community stability 132
Contamines, Savoy 60
Cork, Ireland 153
Cornette, Marie-Anne 123–4
cottier/small-holding class 9, 14, 18, 21
counter-urbanization 199
County Clare, Ireland 10, 23
County Tipperary, Ireland 10, 11, 24
  see also Clogheen-Burncourt, Ireland
County Wexford, Ireland 134–5
County Wicklow, Ireland 134, 135
Cowan, P.C. 136
credit and loan arrangements 6, 61, 62, 65, 66
criminals 187
crisis migration
  Alpine regions 65, 66
cross-channel migration 133, 136
  Dublin 158
  women 150
Croxteth Colliery, Britain 86
Curragh, Ireland 153

Dalkey, Ireland 149
Dalton-in-Furness, Britain 205
Daly, Alice 155–6
Danvers, Daniel 103, 112
Dauphiné, France 51
death
  adult sex ratio at burial (Liverpool) 114
  Lancashire colliers' average age at death 73n
  urban infant mortality 123, 125
debt bonding 6, 58, 61, 62, 65, 66
Dent, Britain 209, 211
Dickens, Charles 186
Dissenters 105, 110n
distance migrants 103, 104, 113
dock labouring 132
Dolphinholme, Britain 211

Dover, Britain 153
dowry system 31–2, 123
   capital sums 123
   dowried spinsters 119, 120
   goods in kind 123
   Ireland 31–2
   Rheims 119–20
   working to accumulate a portion 119–20, 121
dowry system (Savoy)
   aristocratic dowries 54
   capital sums 52
   goods in kind 52, 54–5
   and migrants' remittances 54
   peasant dowries 54–5
   registers 52
dressmakers 127–8, 207
Dublin, Ireland
   absence of flows between northern Ireland and 159
   army districts 154, 159
   army women in 144, 153–8, 160
   birthplaces of Dublin's population 133–5, **134**, 158
   city-centre service employment 149
   city–suburbs migration 148–9, 158
   cross-channel migration 133, 136, 158
   emigrant tables 132–3, **133**
   female night refuges 137–8
   female occupations 138
   gender breakdown 134, 135
   homelessness 137–8
   in-migration from elsewhere in Ireland 136, 145–6
   interdenominational rivalry 147, 157
   intra-city migration 146–8, 158
   loyalty to discrete areas 159
   mendicant classes 135
   military personnel 135
   overseas migration 149, 158
   rural-urban migration 158
   St Brigid's Orphanage 139–58, 161
   service employment 148–9
   social subgroups 160
   suburban development 138, 148–9
   tenement dwellings 137, 139, 159
   turnover of dwelling occupancy 137
   women's mobility in 131–61
   workhouses 151–3
Dungannon, Ireland 153

economic migration 65
   see also career migration
Edict of Nantes (1598) 62, 63
Edinburgh, Britain 153
Enlightenment 123, 127
Entwistle, Bertil 104
Ernst, Karl 167, 180

family historians 189–91
family reconstitution 7
   Liverpool 94n, 95–9
farm ownership in Ireland 9–45
   agrarian combinations 43–4
   bachelor-spinster farms 41
   eldest son's obligations 24
   expansionist territorial policy 45
   failure to maintain viable economic holdings 43
   family case histories 35–40
   farm consolidation 17–18, 21, 44, 45
   farmer proprietorship 13
   inheritance patterns 10, 22–9
   inheritance preference system 23–4
   kinship network and land transfers 22–9, 44–5
   kinsman's preferential purchase rights 45
   'landfast' families 35
   landlordism 9, 13, 43, 44
   leaseholding tenantry 13, 44
   loss of status on selling a farm 28
   males in non-paternal farms 30, **34**, 35, 45
   marriage and 10
   piecemeal changes in farm and field boundaries 28
   pre-Famine Ireland 9
   and sibling settlement 24, 44, 45
   see also Clogheen–Burncourt
Faverges, France 60
   marriages and dowries in 52–3, **53**, 54, **54**, 55, **55**
   peasant probate inventories 56
Fleetwood, Britain 153
Foxrock, Ireland 149
Frankfurt, Germany
   journeymen 165, 174

INDEX

French Revolution 2, 128
Fulwood, Britain 207

Garsdale, Britain 209
gemeinschaft society 6
Geneva, Switzerland 60
Geveva, Switzerland 61
Giraud family 61–2
Gonnet, Pierre 65
Grand Cadastration (1728–30) 50
Grasset, François 63
Great Famine (1845–51) 9, 16–17
Griffith's Valuation Surveys 13, 16
Grisons, Switzerland 60
guild records 166n, 174
guild statutes 165
guilds 7, 167, 168, 179, 181
   Austria 166
   issue of travel documents 182
   police functions 181
   transition to trade associations 166, 167

haberdashers 64
Haigh Colliery, Britain 76
Hale, Britain 207
Hamburg, Germany
   journeymen 165, 174
Hapton, Britain 207
harvest migration 113
hatmakers 167
Haute Giffre 60
Heap, Britain 205
Hearth Tax 1673 103
Heysham, Britain 209
Holme, William 95, 98–9, 112, 115
Hôtels-Dieu 126, 129

illegitimate children 127, 129, 151
   infant mortality 127, 129
   institutional abandonment 122
   Irish farming community 30
   maintenance money 151
   tracing the father 122
indentured migrants 102
Industrial Revolution 164, 165
industrialization 1, 3
   expansion of capitalist market economy 183

migrational movements 164, 165
population growth 74n
putting-out system 183
regulation of artisanal labour market 183
small commodity production 173, 183
infant mortality 123, 125, 128–9
inheritance patterns 6
   Alpine regions 58
   inheritance by an only daughter 26
   inheritance by nephews and nieces 26
   Ireland 10, 22–9
   matriarchal inheritance 25
   peasant probate inventories (Savoy) 55–6
inter-generational loan and deed bonding arrangements 59
'intervening opportunities' concept 3, 41
Ireland 9–45
   absence of flows between Dublin and 159
   attitudes towards family land 10
   emigration 9, 131, 132–3
   Great Famine (1845–51) 9, 16–17
   household census material 131, 131n, 160
   inheritance patterns 10, 22–9
   landlordism 9, 13
   marriage patterns 24–6, 29–35, 40–1
   migration to Britain 159
   Poor Law 17, 135, 151, 152
   population (1800) 9
   State Land Commission 19
   structure of farm households (1901 and 1974) 27
   see also farm ownership in Ireland
Irish Church Missions 137, 141, 147, 155
Italy 59

journeymen
   age structures 170
   authority of master artisans over 182
   autobiographies and travel diaries 165, 180, 181, 182
   contacts and support 165
   duration of jobs 174–5, **175**
   falling hiring rate 165
   geographic origins of Viennese journeymen 171, **172**, **173**, 178–9
   guilds *see* guilds
   household position **171**
   lodging houses 166–7, 179, 180

marital status 170, **171**
master artisan opportunities 172, 173
period of stay for unemployed
  journeymen 167, 182–3
registration books 167, 178
residence in master's household 170, 182
social profile 170, 178
trade licences 172
unemployment 178
journeymen's migration behaviour 164–5
  in Germany 165
  long-distance migration 178–9
  nineteenth century 165
  percentage of in-migrants in Vienna 169, **169**
  seasonal migration 168, **168**
  volume of migration 167–8
  see also tramping artisans

Kendal, Britain 209
Kilcaroon, Ireland 35
Kiltankin, Ireland 36, 37
Kingstown (Dún Laoghaire), Ireland 145, 149
kinship networks
  Alpine regions 58, 59, 61, 62, 63, 66
  chain movements 7, 113
  Lancashire colliers 76–7, 81, 84
  and land transfers in Ireland 19–20, 22–9, 44–5
  and match-making in Ireland 31
  matrilineal kinship links 77n
Kirkless Colliery, Britain 76–7
Kundschaften (travel documents) 181–2

La Grave, France 57, 61
Ladies' Association of Charity of St Vincent de Paul 136
Lake Como, Switzerland 60
Lancashire, Britain 70–87, 188
  intra-urban moves 193, 196–8, **197**, 201
  migrant origins and destinations 192–3, **193**, **194–5**
  movement along the urban hierarchy 198, 200
  urban populations 190, 192
  within-region moves 198, **200**
Lancashire coalfields 70–87, **71**

alehouses 78
annual outputs of individual pits 74, 75n
annual outputs of south–west coalfield (1720–99) **70**
attractions of mining work 79, 80
cannell collieries 74n
colliery lifespan 74
colliery workforce estimates 72–3
differing conditions 76n
estimated manpower requirements 73, **73**
median number of hewers per pit 74
reckoning systems 74–5
see also colliers
land ownership
  Alpine regions 58
  see also farm ownership in Ireland
landlordism 9, 13, 43, 44
Lang, Christoph 175, 176, 177
law of removal 136
Leeds, Britain 150
  law of removal 136
Leeds and Liverpool Canal 70
Leipzig, Germany
  journeymen 165, 174
lifecycles, mobility through 4, 5, 6, 111
Lightbody, William 105, 113
Limerick, Ireland 153
Limousin, France 60
Linz, Austria 181
Lisfuncheon, Ireland 36, 37
literacy
  functional literacy 59, 60, 62
  rise of 2
Little Ice Age 48, 49
Liverpool, Britain 74, 90–116, 131, 150, 159, 193, 198
  apprenticeship records 91
  career migration 112–13
  chain migration 113
  circular migration 113–14
  economic growth 92
  female employment 92, 114
  information sources 92–4, **93**
  local migration 112
  male-orientated employment structure 92
  maritime migrants 113–14
  migration from 198, **199**
  origins of migrants 91, 112

INDEX 221

parish registers **86–7**, 94, 95, 101n, 105n
population growth 74, 90–1
rate assessment (1708) 94–5
seasonal migration 113–14
trading connections 91–2
trans-atlantic commerce 91, 115
women's mobility 114–15
workhouse inmates 136
local migration 4, 7, 111, 112
  Liverpool 112
lodging houses 166–7, 179, 180, 182
London, Britain 150
  migrant destination 192–3
  population 1
Longford, Ireland 153
longitudinal migration profiles 187, 188–91, 212
Lyons, France 61, 62

Macclesfield, Britain 198, 203
magdalen asylums 153
Maghull, Britain 99
Magland, Savoy 56n, 60
Manchester, Britain 109, 131, 149, 150, 193, 198
  individual migration experiences 203, 204, 205
  migration from 198, **199**
maritime migrants 113–14, 115
Marlette, Anne 125–6
marriage patterns
  Alpine regions 58, 61
  colliers 72–3, 79n, 81
  movement on marriage 201, 202, 203
  see also dowry system; marriage patterns (Ireland)
marriage patterns (Ireland) 24–6, 29–35, 40–1
  absence of pre-marital sexual intimacy 30
  cross-cousin marriages 26, 45
  'intervening bridal opportunities' 40–1
  match-making process 30–2
  parental selection of incoming partner 25
  parents as stumbling block to marriage 25
  in small-farm cultures 25
Maryboro, Ireland 146
Massif Central, France 59
match-making process 30–2

courtship 30
importance of family name 32
kin controls 31
partner's matrimonial history 31
see also dowry system
Melling, Britain 95, 99
mendicancy 122, 135
  in Dublin 135
  female beggars 135, 139
merchants 60, 62, 63
  migrant backgrounds 61
  and village economies 62, 64, 65
Middleton, Britain 205
migration
  bureaucratic control of 2
  links with economy and society **188**
  in medieval and Renaissance Europe 1
  'missing persons' 115
  models and theories of 2–3
  modernizing period 1–2
  pre-industrial period 90, 102
  Ravenstein's 'laws' of migration 3
  role of towns in migration process 186–212
military service, and migration 202, 203
Milltown, Ireland 146
Milthrop, Britain 211
mining families 6–7
  see also colliers
mobility 4, 5
  culture of mobility 6
  indicator of community stability 132
  Lancashire colliers 80–3
  and migration 5
  mobility patterns 5
  purposive 5
  residential mobility 131–2
  through lifecycles 4, 5, 6
  using charity sources to map 160–1
  women in Dublin 131–61
  women in Irish farming communities 45
modernization 1–2, 3
Monkstown, Ireland 149
Moone, Robert 101, 102
Moravia 178
Morecambe, Britain 209
motives for migration 4, 92, 111, 187, 201–3, **202**

employment-related objectives 201, 202
family reasons 201, 202, 203
housing 201, 202, 203
marriage 201, 202, 203
military service 202, 203
non-work reasons 201, 202, 203
on retirement 202
Mullingar, Ireland 145, 146, 152
multiple source record linkage 90, 94, 110

Naas, Ireland 146
Nancy-sur-Cluses, Savoy 61
Nelson, Britain 207, 209
Nenagh, Ireland 153
Newbridge, Ireland 153
Nicholson, Dorothy 108, 110
Nicholson, John 115
Nicholson, Matthew 105–10, 113, 115
Nicholson, Samuel 105, 108, 109, 110, 113
night refuges, female 137–8
Nonconformism 105n, 108, 109
Nottingham, Britain 113

O'Regan, Margaret 156–7
Orrell, Britain 73
overseas migration
    from Dublin 149, 158
    from Liverpool 115
Overseers of the Poor 187

Paisley, Britain 110
parish registers
    Lancashire 72, 72n, 74n, 79n
    Liverpool **86–7**, 94, 95, 101n, 105n
Parr, Britain
    poor law migrants 84
passports and border controls 2
Patten, Hugh 101, 102, 112–13
pedlars 60, 63, 64–5
Pembroke, Ireland 138
persistence, and community stability 132
policing
    by guilds 181
    development 2
Poor Law 80n, 81n, 151
    indoor relief 151, 152, 154

in Ireland 135, 151, 152
outdoor relief 152
poor law migrants 81, 84, 135–6, 187
public perception of 152
and the rationalization of Irish farm structures 17
residency requirement 135
see also workhouses
Poor Law removal orders 115n
population growth
    England and Wales 74n
    industrializing countries 74n
    Lancashire 73–4, 74n
    Liverpool 74, 90–1
    urban populations 1–2
    Vienna 165–6
Portsmouth, Britain 153
Potts, Mary Anne 154–5
Presbyterians 110n
Prescot, Britain 70, 76
    alehouses 78
    baptisms 74n
    coal mining 70
    marriage registers 79n
    parishes and townships **71**
Preston, Britain 186, 193, 211
prostitution 122, 153
Pyrenees 59

Quakers 110n

Rathgar, Ireland 138, 148, 149
Rathmines, Ireland 138, 148
Ravenstein, E. G. 2–3
Reedley, Britain 207
Regnault, Elizabeth 126–7
religious denominations
    charitable relief 128, 136, 137–8, 139–58, 159
    interdenominational rivalry 147, 157
    reception and support mechanisms 113
remittances, migrants' 54, 57
return migration 60, 148, 187
Retz, Austria 181, 182
Rheims, France 119–29
    textile industry 120
    unbalanced adult sex ratio 119, 128
    women textile workers 119–29

INDEX

Roman Catholics
  charitable organisations 136, 137–8, 139–58
  Lancashire colliers 73n, 76, 76n, 82
  young men's associations 180
Roscrea, Ireland 153
Roundwood, Ireland 146
Royal Hibernian Military School, Ireland 155, 156
Royal Hospital Kilmainham, Ireland 156–7
rural-to-urban migration 3
  Dublin 158
  north-west England 187, 200, 201
Rush, Ireland 146, 147

St Brigid's Orphanage, Dublin 139–58, 161
  admission criteria 140
  admission notes 139
  foster families 139, 143
  length of time spent in 140
  migration patterns of children's mothers **140–3**, 141–58, **144**
  non-marital children 139
  restoration of children to family 139, 143
  soldiers' children admitted 144, 154
St Helens, Britain 80
  baptisms of colliers' children 81n
  burial registers 79n
  collier dynasties 79, 82
  colliers' average age at marriage 81
  Welsh colliers 86
St Joseph's Night Asylum, Dublin 138, 154
Saint Sigismond 60
Salford, Britain 193, 203, 205
Sallanches, France 60
Savoy
  capital wealth 51–6
  dowry and probate records 51–6
seasonal migration
  Alpine regions 47, 48, 59, 64
  harvest migration 113
  Liverpool 113–14
  maritime migration 113–14
  supportive visits 114
  Viennese journeymen 168, **168**
Seeling, Franz 175, 176, 177
Sefton, Britain 99
sessional migrants 104, 114

Shaw, Joseph 209–11
Sheffield, Britain 150
short-distance migration 3n
  Lancashire colliers 80–3, 86
  north-west England 187, 193, 196, 201, 205
silk weaving industry 182–3
Skelmersdale Colliery, Britain 75, 77, 78, 80
skilled labour, organized mobility of 7, 182, 183, 184
Smyly, Ellen 137
social solidarity 7, 78, 113
Southport, Britain 198
Southwark, Britain 109
Spain 59
spinsters
  dowried spinsters 119, 120
  independent households 127–8
  older spinsters 127–8
  undowried spinsters 119–22
Standish Colliery, Britain 75, 76, 78
Stouffer, S. A. 3
Strasbourg, France 61
subsistence migrants 115
sugar baking industry 103–4
Summerhill, Ireland 146
Sutton, Britain
  poor law migrants 84
Switzerland 59

tailors, Viennese 167, 168, **168**, 172, **173**, 174, **175**, 178, 183
Tarbock, Britain 99
Tarleton, Ann 99–102
Tarleton, Dorothy 115
Tarleton, Edward 99
Tarleton, John 101, 113
taxation 2, 48, 49, 50
tenement dwellings 137, 139, 159
Tessin, Switzerland 60
textile industry 183
  domestic industry 120
  economic crisis 128
  female workers 119–29
  piece-work 120
  Rheims 119–29
  Vienna 169
Thomas, Ursula 125

Thônes, Savoy 52
Tithe Applotment books 13, 15
Town Books (Liverpool) 94
townlands 13
trade
  Alpine regions 57, 59, 60–1
  early modern period 1
  Liverpool 91–2
trade associations 167
  Austria 166
trade unions 180, 187
tramping artisans 7, 165, 166–84
  administrative control of 166–7, 179–80, 181–2
  housing arrangements 182
  institutional and cultural traditions 165, 179–81
  Kundschaften (travel documents) 181–2
  lodging houses 166–7, 179, 180, 182
  medium-range migration pattern 178
  period of stay in a city 167
  police control 182
  regulation of labour market 182, 183, 184
  seasonal rhythm 168, **168**
  travel allowances/donations 167, 179, 180–1
  Wanderbücher (log books) 182
trans-Atlantic commerce 91, 115
trans-Atlantic migration
  from Dublin 149, 158
  from Liverpool 115
  women 149
Turin, Italy 60

unmarried mothers 121, 122, 127, 151
  army women 153, 158
  Irish farming community 30
  in the workhouse 151, 152, 158
urban definition 191
urban fertility rates 200
urban hierarchy, movement along 3, 7, 198, 200
urban populations 48, 49, 190, 192
urban-to-rural migration 101, 102
urbanization 6
  Dublin suburban development 138, 148–9

migrational movements 164

vagrant migrants 115, 122
Vienna, Austria 164–84
  artisans 164–84
  in-migrants among journeymen 169, **169**
  journeymen *see* journeymen
  labour market fluctuations 173–8
  local self-producing workforce 170
  number of artisans 166
  population growth 165–6
  textile trades 169
  worker population 166

wage systems
  day-wage earnings 78, 78–9n, 80
  Lancashire collieries 74, 77–80, 80n
  piece rates 74, 80
Wanderbücher (log books) 182
Warrington, Britain 101, 108
Wesham, Britain 205
wet nurses 121, 122, 123, 128, 129
Wexford, Ireland 153
widowers 120
widows
  army widows 146, 155, 156, 157–8
  with children 124–6
  colliers' widows 81n
  dependent children 119
  entrepreneurs 124, 125
  mobility 114–15
  older widows 125–6
  port populations 101, 114–15
  poverty 126, 128
  re-marriage 124, 157–8
  without children 119, 124, 125
  young widows 124–5
Wigan, Britain 70, 80
  baptisms 74n
  coal mining 70
  parishes and townships **71**
Williamson, Samuel 101, 113
wills
  gender bias (Liverpool) 94
  peasant probate inventories (Savoy) 55–6
  and sibling settlement (Ireland) 24
Winchester, Britain 153
Winstanley Colliery, Britain 77

INDEX

Wolpert, J. 4
Wolverhampton, Britain 150
women
  army women 144, 153–8
  artisans' wives 123–4
  beggars 135, 139
  caring responsibilities 114, 132, 207, 209
  cross-channel migration 133, 150
  downward social mobility 150
  in Dublin 131–61
  female night refuges 137–8
  homelessness 138, 139
  housewives 119, 122–4
  in Liverpool 114–15
  longevity 120
  marriage and mobility 102n, 114
  maternal values 123
  migration for family reasons 201, 207, 209
  migration on marriage 201
  mitigation of migration behaviour of others 115
  motives for migration 114, 201, **202**
  seasonal migration (supportive visits) 114
  short-distance migration 3n
  trans-Atlantic migration 149
  unmarried mothers 30, 121, 122, 127, 151, 152, 153, 158
  see also army women; marriage patterns; spinsters; widowhood
women's employment
  agency employment 121
  apprentices 114, 121
  army women 153, 154, 155, 156–7
  colliery workers 75, 75n, 76
  domestic service 120–1, 127, 132, 138, 145, 148–9
  dressmakers 127–8
  hospital employees 154, 156–7
  in Liverpool 92, 114
  shop assistants 120
  textile workers 119–29
workhouses 151–3
  army women 154, 158
  destitute women 151
  Dublin 151–3
  the elderly 151
  illegitimate children 151
  Liverpool 136
  public perception of 152
  unmarried mothers 151, 152, 158
Wrea Green, Britain 205

York, Britain 131

Zelinsky, W. 3